'THE SPIRIT LIVETH ON'

- ST. ANNE'S
- MISSION /SETTLEMENT
- YOUTH & PELLA CLUB
- VAUXHALL

[handwritten inscription and signature, dated 16-5-16]

Joe. P. Plant

Other titles from Joe P. Plant

Up to Their Necks - the Story of a National Serviceman
ISBN 978-1-78222-054-1

Cornwall's First Town in the Frontline: Torpoint's War Diary 1939 to 1946
ISBN 978-1-90761-103-2

Kindle editions:
THE ADVENTURES OF A SOLDIERS WIFE – PART I IRELAND / ENGLAND 1915-1928.
THE ADVENTURES OF A SOLDIERS WIFE – PART II THE MEMSAHIB'S INDIAN
EXPERIENCE 1928-1933
THE ADVENTURES OF A SOLDIERS WIFE – CLIMATIC CHANGES BLIGHTY 1933-1974

Published by Joe Plant
First published 2015

ISBN 978-1-78222-400-6

Book design, layout and production management by Into Print
www.intoprint.net
+44 (0)1604 832149

Printed and bound in UK and USA by Lightning Source

The following Compendium of St. Anne's History has been Compiled by
Joe. P. Plant.
From Photographs provided by
The Sisters of St. Anne's.
Family Albums
Six of St. Anne's Photo Albums & Autograph book
also
St. Anne's War-time Annals Magazine's
Including other Memoirs Submitted by
Club Members
Names and notations as remembered.
'Some Authors unknown'

And to quote Bishop Brown's own words

**"It is a story worth telling as showing accordingly to the old
saying that one thing leads to another."**

OVERVIEW OF THE ORIGINS OF ST. ANNE'S SETTLEMENT - YOUTH & PELLA CLUB

In 2009 by accident, whilst I was writing the story of my days as a National Serviceman. I required photos of my football days, playing for St. Anne's Youth Club team in Vauxhall. All I wanted was a photo of the football teams, I played with as a young member of the 'B' team then with the senior 'A' team, through 1949 to 1955. Initially I contacted the Priest at St. Anne's who advised me to contact Josie Spanswick, holder of some documentation. I did contact Josie, who informed me she had in her possession, three of the Club's photo albums ranging from 1945 onwards and that I should contact Olive Wood who was in the process, of collating some old Youth and Pella Club member's thoughts on their time at the Club, who might also have some photos. Upon speaking with Olive she did not have any of the Club's photo's, instead co-ersed me into compiling a story of the Club's history. I agreed to take on the task and she sent me all the documents she had collected. I must admit were quite limited and rather repetitive in their scope. Josie also sent me the three Photo Albums, which contained some very interesting and priceless photos of those exciting times we all enjoyed in St. Anne's Youth Club. Therefore those three Photo Albums became the basis of my research into the History of St. Anne's Youth and Pella Club in the Parish of St. Anne's Vauxhall, located in the South West London Borough of Lambeth,

I began the research, at the time in1948 when as a young football crazy scallywag was introduced to joining St. Anne's Youth Club, by my brother Michael (a member since 1945). Upon joining, it became a revelation to me, on the aspects of the different classes one could get involved in. I do remember quite vividly, those heady and engaging times and the friendliness of the young people I was to meet. The photos in the Albums were those of Club outings, holidays abroad, dances and visits by various Artistes. The only problem was that the photos did not contain any recorded information of the characters, dates or indeed, locations where taken, nevertheless resurrected memories and gave credence to the incidents and events, that I had become involved in all those years before. Thus was able to put pen to paper to produce a somewhat Draft compendium of photos accompanied by some text descriptions with a lot of questions. This Draft was circulated to the older members in an attempt to identify the names portrayed in those photos with some success. In the meantime Olive sent me some old copies of St. Anne's Magazine (THE ANNALS). These magazines were produced by the Girl Members during the years of the war onwards. I was totally unaware that they ever existed and laid them aside, waiting for further information to come forth. However, it was not until early 2014 when I began perusing through the copies of the Annals and discovered the significance of the information they held, to reveal the true history in chronological order of the Clubs survival during those dark days. I had also purchased a copy of the book "Through Windows of Memory" written by Bishop Brown that also revealed, when the origins of the establishment of a Mission began in the early 1890's. The idea and dream of a certain Scottish Priest by the name of Father William Francis Brown, a convert to Catholicism, later to be Consecrated as the Bishop of Pella, forcing me to take a different approach, in compiling the Manuscript in its present format.

However the origins of St. Anne's Club began in 1935, when Bishop Brown included within the established St. Anne's Catholic Settlement. A Youth Club for the Boys and Girls of St. Anne's School, located at the rear of the Church in Kennington Lane, along with those that had left the school, the young teenagers of that period. All were encouraged to become members, subsequently they became the nucleus of the newly opened Youth Club, widely known as 'The Club'. The following story provides the long history of the original Mission through to the present day; nevertheless my own memories of living in Vauxhall were quite vivid of the post-war era that we lived through.

In the Smokey and smog laden atmosphere of post war London. During the smog's the only thing that could be heard in the swirling yellow smog was the moaning of the tugs hooters on the river Thames, mixed by the varying changes of winds were the unforgettable smells of:- washed milk bottles from the United Dairies Bottling Plant, the local Marmite Factory and possibly the smell (dependant on the wind) of Coke fumes, from the North Thames Gas Board, located at the foot of Vauxhall Bridge South side. Whilst in the background, was the noise of the overhead Southern railway, the hubbub of buses, cars, lorries and clanking of trams, that were dampened during the winter's sulphur laden pea-soup smog's. In the morning, you did not need an alarm clock! Precisely at twenty-five past seven the Battersea Power Station Hooter would sound, followed five minutes later by a further long blast. 'It was time to get up! These would be the sounds and smells, readily identified by whoever lived in the vicinity of Vauxhall and maybe was a member of St. Anne's Club. His Grace the 'Bish' as we knew him made a profound statement in his "Parish History"

Quote:

'It is a story worth telling, as showing accordingly to the old saying that one thing leads to another."

Unquote

Therefore, I trust the following passages of the History of Saint Anne's. Does in many ways meet with His Lordship approval.

Joe. P. Plant

THE LOCATION OF ST. ANNE'S MISSION

William Francis Brown was a convert to Catholicism, who was later to be ordained as the Bishop of Pella. He was born in Park Place House Dundee, on the 3rd. May 1862. He was educated at Trinity College Glenalmond, and when in 1879 his family moved to London, he became a pupil at the University College Gower Street. He was undecided as to what his future would be. In 1873 a decision by his mother, his two sisters and brother, decided to convert to the Catholic Faith, subsequently their action was to shape his future quest in life.

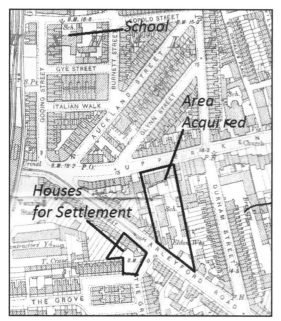

In 1879 he decided to seek instructions from a Priest at the Carmelite Church in Kensington and in July 1880. He was converted into the Catholic faith. From then on he became very interested in the Catholic faith and took an active part in its teaching, attending the Catholic University in Cromwell Road. In 1882 during Lent he attended a Retreat that finally made his mind up to that of becoming a Priest. In March 1886 he was ordained as a Priest in the St. Georges Cathedral by the Bishop of Southwark. John Butt.

He was sent as second assistant to Canon McGrath at the Church of the Sacred Heart in Camberwell. He was given charge of the local branch of the League of the Cross, and a year later was voted onto its Council. After his stay at Camberwell, in March 1892 he was appointed by Bishop John Butt, to take charge of a new area within the Diocese, that extended between Lambeth Bridge, Battersea, Clapham and Camberwell. The area known as Vauxhall where they (St. Georges Cathedral) had acquired a suitable site in Kennington Lane. Consisting of four houses including a piece of land that extended through to the Harleyford Road leading to the Oval Cricket Ground. As there was no Catholic Church or school in that vicinity, their intention and purpose was to set up and establish a Catholic Mission.

In the early 1890's when Father William Brown arrived in Vauxhall, it was an area in Lambeth of great poverty, illness and death, together with lack of work, where families with a unemployed father or no father to earn a living. To support their meagre needs, the mother and their siblings would be placed in the local workhouses: at Renfrew Street Kennington, the Workhouse in Black Prince Road or the Elder Road Institute in Norwood. There was no Roman Catholic Church in the Vauxhall area but, there was the St. Peter's National School C. of. E., located in Leopold Street next to the Lambeth School of Arts, where some of its students provided decorative artwork for the Royal Doulton Pottery Factory located on the shores of the Lambeth Embankment that extended into Black Prince Road, where there was another Institute. The Beaufoy Institute known as the Ragged School that did take in waif's and strays of the locality.

The purpose of Father William Francis Brown's relocation was to try and improve the welfare of his parishioners, by establishing a place where they could be taught, cared for and have a place of worship with a new Catholic Church'. One of the four Houses "Eldon House" in Upper Kennington Lane became the Priest House, and was occupied by him, a Curate by the name of Bovinzer and a Housekeeper.

Within a short period of time in 1892, there was a small school in Vauxhall Walk that from about 1860 was run by Priest's from the Westminster Diocese. The then present Priest was Fr. Peter Haythanthwaite. However Father Brown took advantage of that situation and no doubt Father Peter, retuned back to Westminster Cathedral. Within the little school in Vauxhall Walk, on Sundays Fr. Brown utilised it as a place to hold Mass and on the weekdays in Eldon House (The Clergy House) it was basically the beginning of a Mission. As the adjoining land was leased to a local Builder, part of it was the area where the new school was being built, that was completed in 1893, therefore on Sundays providing better accommodation to hold Mass to an ever increasing congregation. Fr. William Brown's next venture was to build upon the site adjoining the House, a purpose made Church. Originally the fascia was planned to be on the Harleyford Roadside of the site, but certain aspects dictated it to be built with its facia in Upper Kennington Lane, (as is known today). However, with the cost involved in purchasing the site, the building of the school and the dept. owed, with only payments from the tenants of the three Houses and the Builders repayments that went some way to reduce the incurred dept., the possibility of building a New Church was many years ahead, but by good fortune, a large bequest made to Bishop Butt by Miss Emily King of Norwood, was sufficient to pay in full the outstanding dept. of the school, thus provided a window to start the planning of the future St. Anne's Church.

However with still an outstanding high mortgage not more could be done to build his church. In 1899 the lease to the Builder on the site was renewed with an increase in rates provided the incentive to look positively at drawing up plans for the new Church. The three adjoining houses were demolished to make way for the new church. Fr. Brown acquired the service of a Mr. Fredrick Walters to draw up the plans and design the Church of St. Anne's. Once again due to lack of funds, progress came to a halt until further donations came forth. so by the end of 1900 on November the 3rd. the foundations were laid, and the foundation stone was put in place by Cardinal Francis Bourne the Bishop of Southwark. Work progressed up to the sanctuary wall, but again due to lack of funds progress came to a halt. But good fortune shines on those in need, and it came about by an unexpected but truly welcome source, that of a mutual friend the youngest daughter of a Mrs. Allanson who Fr. Brown had regularly attended too throughout her illness prior to her death. After her demise her eldest daughter Annie fell ill and died the following year in 1897. Upon the death of their father, both the daughters had been left a considerable amount of money and obviously after her sister's death, the youngest daughter Mary, inherited a good deal of the inheritance. Mary made a visit to the incomplete Church building and after a discussion with Fr. Brown, decided to provide the outstanding monies to finish off the building of the Church, with the exception of the mortuary chapel, the parish hall and the tower. Part funded by the Diocese of Southwark and by the generosity of other Lords and Ladies together with his parishioners, who supported his plans and ideas, to improve the severe conditions amongst his parishioners. It was approximately 10 years from the day, when Fr. Brown arrived in Vauxhall with the intention of building a school and a Church, he had achieved his goal. In January 1903 the Church was opened and soon attracted a large congregation.

With Fr. Brown's connections of not only Dukes, Lords and Ladies, Members of Parliament, Artiste and Authors amongst to whom he was introduced by Winston Churchill's Mother, was the American author Mrs. Pearl Craigie (died 1907) who wrote under the name of "John Oliver Hobbs." [Their unlikely liaison was described in a book written by Bishop Brown's niece, Margaret Brown under the title of - "The Priest and the Playwright. "] Over the next five years generous donations were made, that provided four alters with reredos, a pulpit Communion rails and several windows by Westlake and a further acquisition of an organ, that was exhibited at the Bradford Exhibition of 1905. By 1907 the outstanding features of the mortuary chapel, parish hall and tower were finally built and due to the outstanding mortgage depts. left to pay for his church, it could not be consecrated. Nevertheless an opportunity came about, when his solicitor's, informed Fr. Brown to purchase a piece of land which formed part of the garden of a house in Harleyford road, a possible valuable transaction. He decided to take it on. Furthermore it was in 1908 that another acquisition was to come about that was a Hall in the same garden. It was the headquarters of the Surrey Volunteer Regiment who also owned a Drill Ground in Kennington Lane. Both came together as a purchase price of £7,000. The Hall would provide a very good purchase for further parochial meetings and other functions. He decided to proceed and raised the required 10% and borrowed the sum of £6,250 from a friend and so in December 1908, he signed the deeds. Two years later together with their outstanding mortgage depts., and the cost of the rates on the Hall and Drill ground it was found necessary to sell that purchase for £9,000. In the process and after paying back the money owed to his friend, made a profit of £2,000.

Fr. Brown's next goal was to get his Church consecrated. He set his mind on a future date of March 1911, the twenty–fifth anniversary of his ordination into the Priesthood. With further funds becoming available and the Builders payments of the lease on the land, things progressed and the Church of St. Anne's was officially consecrated in March 1911.

However, the story does not end there; Fr. Brown was on the London School Board of Governors and was attending a meeting in Hoxton East London, where a Miss Honor Morton a local social worker, knew of Fr. Brown's quest and dreams to help the poor of his parish in Vauxhall. She introduced him to a certain Mrs Grace Gordon Smith. A person who had trained in midwifery and child nursing. Their's was a meeting that sparked of a future and long lasting working relationship. During their discussions Fr. Brown realised, this young beautiful small woman's potential had the same dreams and ambitions of helping the poor and needy as himself, albeit of a slightly different plight, that of sickness and ailments of the poor and needy, nevertheless, both having the same determination and outlook in their individual quests. Fr. Brown identifying Grace's ambitions suggested to her to visit Vauxhall, to see for herself the need for someone of her calibre and

fortitude that could indeed help the poor of his parish.

Grace Gordon Smith like Fr. William Brown was a convert to the Catholic faith, and by chance at the time of their meeting, she had been received into the Catholic Church at St. Augustine's Tunbridge Wells by Canon Keatings, in the same month of March as the Consecration of St. Anne's Church. Taking heed of Fr. Browns invitation, Grace, being a person not to let the grass grow under her feet took the suggestion to heart and did visit Vauxhall and there saw for herself the potential to start a small clinic. Grace immediately set about renting a small shop that so happened to be almost opposite St. Anne's Church. Once all the rent had been sorted out etc. On her own Grace started to clean up the premises ready to receive her potential clients. Cleaning and scrubbing the floors, applying a coat of whitewash to the walls, cleaned the windows and then when ready put a notice in the window

"WELCOME IF ANYONE HAS A SICK CHILD BRING IT HERE"

Then waited to begin her work. This is where Fr. Brown comes back into the story. He was out on one of his many missions of mercy, when he noticed the shop on the opposite side of the road had an unusual sign in the window. Very intrigued by what this notice stated, he crossed over and entered the shop. In one corner there was a statue of Our Lady, and sat at a desk was the very same young lady he had recently met in Hoxton. Fr. Brown obviously intrigued by the most unusual notice. Questioned what the notice meant and was informed by Grace, that she was running a clinic in rented premises.

Photo of shop front taken in May 2014 : Directly opposite St. Anne's

This unexpected second meeting of two persons with the same ideas, struck up a lasting relationship that was to develop over the years cumulating into the opening of later the St. Anne's Youth Club for Boys and Girls in the very same Hall that had been years before purchased by Fr. Brown.

The Settlement Hall was used to serve free meals to St. Anne's School children and the poor. It doubled up as the Clinic where all went to see the Doctor: as the three existing photos taken inside the Settlement Hall, circa 1912 / 1913. Illustrate the purpose of the Settlement was meeting its intended purpose.

Free Meals for children in the Hall

Waiting to see the Doctor

Seeing the Doctor

The following passages are an extract from Bishop Browns own comment on the establishment of St. Anne's.

PARISH HISTORY TAKEN FROM A MANUSCRIPT LEFT BY BISHOP BROWN

The Mission of St. Anne's Vauxhall, now the parish, was established on 24 March 1892. When the Rev. William. F. Brown was sent there by Bishop John Butt of Southwark. This territory was all formerly the St. George's Cathedral District that comprised quite a large area. This, in turn, was considerably reduced when, in 1903, a new Mission was opened in 1903 called Saint Francis Larkhall Lane. SW4. Another portion abutting on Brixton Road and Camberwell New Road was taking over by the (new?) Parish of the Sacred Heart. Camberwell, a few years later.

Vauxhall as a small Catholic Centre dates back to the early 1860's, when a retired teacher opened a small school in a disused shop in Vauxhall Walk near the Wesleyan Chapel. Not long afterwards, the order of Notre Dame of Namur, established at St. George's Road, near the Cathedral, built a school for girls and infants also in Vauxhall Walk, opposite what is now the Guinness Trust Buildings. The money for this was provided by Sister Mary Frances, Hon. Mrs. Petry, who became a nun when she was widowed and was a great benefactor to the institute of Notre Dame. In 1871 a small single storey school was built by St. George's Cathedral, for boys, the site being the portion of (a) the playground of the girls and infants. It was all very cramped, but school accommodation of any kind was very scarce in those days. The girls and infants building still stands, it is part of the premises of a metal merchants. The property was sold in 1894.

In 1891 the Diocese acquired a fine site for a church and school in Upper Kennington lane, now Kennington Lane. Its area was almost an acre in extent and it had a frontage also in Harleyford Road near the Kennington Oval, a very important consideration. On it, on the Kennington Lane side, there were four houses, the rest of the land being used as a builder's yard. The cost was £7,000 a small price for what was really a valuable site in a built up area. One or two factors helped to keep costs down. Although there were two frontages, the width was not enough under the London Building Act for a new street with Houses are both sides. Also it was not long after the notorious Jabez Balfour, and the Liberator Society, in which many Building Societies lost large sums of money, with the result that there was little money for speculative purchases. One house became the Clergy House; the builder rented another, together with a large yard, while the remaining two houses were let to tenants. Providentially, number 173 was vacant and it was possible for the Clergy to occupy it without delay. As there was no separate building for a church. Mass was said on Sundays in the Boy's school and on weekdays in the Priest's House. Confessions were heard there and Baptisms administered. In May the new school site became available and a fine three - storey building for Infants, Boys and Girls really three schools, was begun, the Diocese racing and the money £4,250 as in the site purchase, by loan. The interest on the large dept. was almost entirely met by the rents of the houses and the builder's yard. The school was finished in time for use as a church just before Christmas 1892. This was a great relief as a much larger building in a main road was now available next to the Clergy House. There were certain drawbacks, it is true. The first floor had to be used and the Blessed Sacrament had still to be reserved in the Clergy House. Marriages could only take place on Saturday's or Sunday and during the holidays, and the same applied to funerals, which however, do not take place in London on Sundays.

Early in January 1893. The new school in Harleyford Roadways opened, and soon had a large Roll. The school buildings In Vauxhall Walk were sold but not for much, and the proceeds helped to reduce the dept. on the Mission. The congregation increased after the move to the new school, was still small, and the income quite inadequate, particularly as Bishop Butt had decided that there should be two priests. For two years the Diocese made a grant of £100 a year, which was a great help. People kept asking when we could expect to have a church, but unfortunately that was a long way off. When the builder who rented the house next to the Clergy House as well as the larger the yard, gave up part of the land for the school, he was granted a lease of 21 years with breaks after seven years, as it was not expected, with all its burdens, Vauxhall could hope for a church for many years. It was hard, or otherwise St. Anne's Mission could never have been started, as the site was essential to any plans for the future. But it meant, in the event, waiting till 1903 for a church. It was a long and trying period of waiting but, in the end, patience and perseverance won the day, as we shall see.

In 1896 something happened which was a great encouragement. Miss Emily King of Norwood died leaving a very considerable sum to the Bishop of Southwark, to be used for providing schools in all parts of South London. Her executors were advised not to prove the will on account of vagueness, so the case had to go to court. The Bishop asked that the money should be applied to paying of the new schools at Walworth and Vauxhall; and the balance to be used for a new school at Upper Norwood, where the lady had lived for some considerable time. The Judge was Mr. Justice Eve and he apparently doubted whether it was right (that) any of the money should be used to pay debts on existing buildings, as against building other new schools. Eventually, however, and he made it an order allowing the application. But it certainly was a very near thing, for the late Mr. E. Fooks the Bishop's solicitor, told me that the Counsel for the Bishop had walked away from the Law Courts with the Judge, who said, he did not think he should have granted the order, and if he had to decide again he would not do it. The reduction of the large dept., on Vauxhall by £4,300 was really the turning point in a hard struggle for the provision of a church for the New Mission. Till then, any prospect of a church for many years to come was out of the question, because of the existing heavy capital debt. The loans amounting to over £7,000 and interest had to be found every year, to say nothing of reduction of capital. The income from the property was precarious, as two of the houses on it were old and might be condemned as unfit, unless much money was spent on them. The number attending Mass at school was small and the offerings barely enough to maintain two priests. Even had it been possible to get the church site for building was obviously out of the question to incur further liabilities with such heavy burdens on the mission.

In 1892 the Diocese granted Mr. W. Smith, builder, a lease for 21 years of 171 Upper Kennington Lane, and a large yard with buildings on it. At lease provided for a break at the end of the seventh year, with six month's notice, should the land be required for a church, and at the end of any other year with two years' notice. The rental was low and the builder had really got an excellent bargain. There was just time, after Miss King's will had been proved, to serve notice on the builder. But it did not follow that, in order to build a church, the entire site would be needed, and it became necessary to negotiate with Mr. Smith about his retaining the surplus land after giving up sufficient for a church. As the property had frontage both in Harleyford Road and in Upper Kennington Lane, it became necessary to decide on which to build the church. Harleyford Road had certain advantages of access, but its frontage was askew making it very difficult to plan a very satisfactory building without waste of ground. The other frontage could have a building at right angles to the street and was chosen without hesitation.

This suited Mr. Smith, as he could retain nearly all the yard, only giving up number 171, where he lived. So he took a new lease on an increased rent, and, even so, got it all on very favourable terms. The debt. Stood at about £7.000, the interest on it been met by the yard rent.

Things had moved forward and it became possible to publish the fact that there was a fine church site available. The three houses were pulled down and the site was ready for use, if only the financial arrangements would admit of making a beginning with a church. A benefactor who was interested in the Mission offered to pay for complete foundations of a church. Mr. Fredrick A. Walters was engaged as architect and he produced plans for a commodious church in red brick. It was decided to have a foundation stone laid, and this was done by Cardinal Bourne, then Bishop of Southwark. The foundations and heating chamber cost £1,200 which was paid by the anonymous benefactor. But there it stopped and people began to criticise saying the whole scheme was too ambitious and that in any case, it would have been better to have put in the foundations for a part of the church only, as there could be little prospect of building it all at once. I felt the force of these remarks, but was buoyed up with the hope of building a fine church for Vauxhall somehow or other.

A chance remark had made a great impression on me, and giving me a new outlook. I was a member of the London School Board from 1897 till 1904 when its work was transferred to the London County Council. One day during a board meeting, when some members were in the smoking room. Lord Morpeth said that Brown was going to build a church. At once, Sir Ernest Flower. MP asked how much I expected it to cost. I said about £5,000. He said why don't you go in for one that will cost £15.000; you will get the money much more easily. He added that people liked to be associated with a big scheme rather than something small. That settled it for me and a large lofty church was designed by Mr. F. A. Walters and in the end, was built without any reduction in size or height. But how to get money first remained a problem. The interest on the £ 7,000 debt. was met by the rent paid by the tenant but it could not remain unreduced indefinitely. Reductions was not easy, in fact remained a problem till it was all cleared off in 1911. But before sanction to begin the church could be asked for by the Mission, some scheme for debt reduction had to be put forward. Great efforts were made and, after substantial repayment had been made, work on the church was allowed to begin. Tenders had been obtained from several builders, including Mr. Smith, and the lowest was accepted. The firm being Goddard and Son of Farnham and Dorking. The tenders were for three sections viz., the first the Nave, second the Sanctuary, side Chapels and Sacristy, and last of the entire Tower with Mortuary Chapel and a hall above it. The total cost without Architects' fees, was £13,500, something beyond our dreams it seems. However, money did come in and it was decided to sign a contract for the Nave. This took quite a long time to build, and when it was finished, a doorway, one very large arch, and three smaller ones were open to the weather. Obviously they could not be left so it was proposed to close them with temporary brick walls, a very expensive undertaking, and most wasteful, as one day the walls in the arches would have to be taken down brick by brick. Then a remarkable thing happened. A friend of mine Mrs. Mary Allanson of Clapham, a wealthy and charitable woman, came to see the new church. She admired its size and height but was surprised to see the open arches at the East End. She asked what we were going to do about it, and I replied we should have to wall them up, as we must use the church as soon as possible. She remarked that it was a great pity as it would mean much trouble and expense for nothing. I agreed but said we would have to do it or not use the new building at all. Then she asked what it would cost to finish the Sanctuary, etc., of the church, and I told her £2,400, the amount of Goddard's tender. At once she said I will give you that let the work go on as soon as possible. Goddard was asked to agree to consolidate the two contracts and gladly consented, all the more so because a good deal of his plant was still on the job. I had, much against my will, to borrow some money, as there was not enough in hand for the two contracts, but fortunately not for long, as money came in well once there was a building on the site, and I had considerable longer time for the completion of the instalments. The four arches on the North side of the Nave were boarded up and remained so till the Mortuary Chapel was built some years later.

On the 31st of January, 1903, we were able to use the new church after it had been blessed. We had no solemn celebration of the event, as it was decided to have this later in the year. The was no permanent alter in the Sanctuary, so the small wooden altar which had been so long in the two schools was now brought in for another spell of temporary services. We were able to provide the benches and confessionals but it was our policy not to have permanent alters a Pulpit, Communion Rails, Font, etc., unless the money was given for them. As will be seen this policy was amply justified. The late Mr. William Sandford, a parishioner, who had been faithful to the Mission in its days of hard struggle, undertook to provide a High Alter if it did not cost too much for his means. A really fine design for Alter and rerendos was prepared by Mr. Walters. At first only a portion was erected but it gave the church a permanent if incomplete, alter and made it possible to have a dignified opening in September1903. Bishop Bourne afterwards Cardinal Bourne Archbishop of Westminster, had been transferred from Southwark, so that Diocese was vacant. As he had laid the foundation stone of St. Anne's, I asked him, with the consent of the Provost Moore, the Vicar Capitular, to perform the formal opening ceremony in September 1904. Among those present were Mrs. Pearl Craigie, the writer, and her friend Lady Randolph Churchill, mother of Winston Churchill. A large and fine organ had been ordered from a well-known builder J. W. Walker & Sons the firm asked if it might be lent to the Bradford Exhibition, from May till October 1905, this suited us as it gave more time for collecting the cost, £2,000 and was an excellent advertisement. The work of erecting began later that year, and was finished early in 1906. A beautiful case designed by Mr. F. A. Walters our architect. The Organ is well known to musicians and many distinguished organist have played on it.

The next important event was the full completion of the plan of the church by the addition of the Mortuary Chapel, the Hall above it, and a large saddleback tower, whose weathercock is about 90 feet above ground. The tower is not merely a landmark; it is visible from the railway and Kennington Oval and appears in one Test Match picture. It provides space for a heating chamber, part of a chapel and of the Hall, as well as the singer's room, and a belfry, which contains a bell made by Mears and Steinbank weighing eleven hundredweight. This was given in 1923 by the late Mrs. Ada Watney, and was consecrated by Bishop William Keating's, the Army Bishop. When the church Nave was built, a small tenor bell, two and a quarter hundredweight, by Carr of Smethwick, was hung in the bell tower above the sanctuary arch. The large bell is rung at the Consecration on Sundays, and at Benediction, Sundays and weekdays. The small bell, blessed by Bishop Bourne is used occasionally, but its sound does not travel far in the noise of the main Road and railway traffic.

The High Alter was consecrated on 6th. November 1906 by Bishop Patrick Fenton, Auxiliary of Westminster, and the pulpit and communion rails were given about the same time. But the

Mission was still in debt, partly for the site, and partly for the church. If the church was to be consecrated the debt. must be paid off, it was, therefore necessary to work vigorously and persistently to raise the money. However, it was accomplished by various means in time for the Silver Jubilee of Priesthood of Monsignor Brown on the 20th of March 1911. When a Church is consecrated part of the ceremony is the consecration of an alter usually the High Alter. As ours was already consecrated, it was necessary to have another, so the fine Lady Alter with its rerendos, was provided, the gift of a generous benefactor. Bishop Amigo gave his consent and graciously allowed the ceremony to be performed by Rt. Rev. George Ambrose Burton, Bishop of Clifton, a great friend of the Parish Priest. Everything went off splendidly and it was a beautiful spring day. High Mass was sung by Monsignor Brown, Bishop Amigo being on the throne. It was a proud day for St. Anne's Vauxhall.

In November the well-known Redemptorists. Fr. John Bennett and Fr. John Burke, gave the first full Mission in the Parish. It was attended by large congregations and was blessed in many ways.

In 1911 St Anne's Settlement was founded by Miss Grace Gordon -Smith in a very small way in a hired house in Kennington Lane. In 1912 a fine property was acquired in Harleyford Road, consisting of two houses with a large back garden. A hall was built and in 1921 two more houses were added to the property, and connected internally. Thus residential quarters for a Warden and a hostel for young women were provided. Miss Grace Gordon-Smith in 1927 founded the Sisters of Saint Anne, who later established foundations at Plymouth and Rotherhithe. The little Convent in Union Road Rotherhithe was destroyed by bombing, but a new foundation was opened after some time in South Bermondsey, near St. Gertrude's Church. After, the Sisters of St. Anne's began to attract subjects, it was evident that the Harleyford Road buildings were not suitable for a Convent and a Novitiate in various ways and it was decided that with the consent of the Bishop of Southwark and the Jesuit Fathers, to leave Vauxhall and make a foundation at Wimbledon. A fine House with large grounds was bought and a hospital was opened in the enlarged building. The Order has been fortunate in getting subjects and is doing important work for the sick. Their departure was a loss to Vauxhall, but it in any case, it would have had to take place when a bomb fell in a small garden and destroyed three of the four houses. The Parish of St Anne's, Vauxhall, owes a great debt of gratitude to Mother Mary Agnes, as subject to certain conditions, she handed over the property a large endowment to the Parish (subject to certain) conditions of continuity of work being fulfilled. All the property was bought by her, except a plot of land forming part of the garden of 46 Harleyford Road with a frontage to a side street, Vauxhall Grove. This was bought by Monsignor Brown some years before in 1911. It is a story worth telling as showing accordingly to the old saying that one thing leads to another. When a street, now called Vauxhall Grove, leading from Harleyford Road, was opened, there must have (been) an exchange of land with the owner of 46 Harleyford Road, by which an irregular plot was added to the back garden. The tenants of number 46 were allowed the use of the land for a nominal rent as long as their tenancy might last. They were a family of two brothers and two sisters and they supplied Messrs Burnett, the Distillers on Albert Embankment with certain articles used in the refining process made in a small shed next to number 46. There was an obligation on them on giving up the house, to erect the fence to separate the plot not owned by the freeholders of number 46 from the garden of that house. Some of the Dart's family died and the survivors left, but were not made to put up the stipulated fence. I was told by the rate-collector Mr. J. W. Henly, that the plot could be bought for £ 400 from whom I was now told. He pointed out it held a key position, as the houses in Harleyford Road, with deep gardens formed an important business site if only access would be obtained from the Vauxhall Grove return frontage of number 46. He urged that we might need some of the houses for social work, for which they were suited and most buildings could be put up on the site. It seemed a rather risky transaction, but had possibilities which turned out to be very important. However, it was a long time before anything came of it, but fortunately an undertaker rented it for stacking and seasoning elm planks for coffins. A very sketchy fence was put up to mark the irregular boundary line between the properties. It was a long wait but in the end Henly's prediction came true. Three of the Dart's family died and the last survivor gave up the lease. That set free number 46, the corner house of the property, which comprised a row of houses in Harleyford Road. It was obvious that the property was suitable for Residential Settlement and it was decided to buy some of the houses if possible. But it was held by lawyer trustees who refused all of proposals to buy and it seemed as if the plot had been bought to no purpose. Then, quite accidentally Henly found out that the trustees held the property on behalf of Mrs. Catherine Boise, who lived near Barnstaple. A letter to her asking if two houses could be bought for charitable purposes secured her consent and the Settlement secured permanent quarters. Monsignor Brown made a present of the back plot to the Settlement and part of its hall was built on it, the rest being added to the garden of 46. One large room was adapted for a Chapel and a small Sacristy was built adjoining. It was now possible to have a number of people engaged in the activities of the Settlement, which can be described as corporal and spiritual works of mercy. It was a great help to the Parish in many ways. After 40 and

The Right Rev. William Francis Brown
BISHOP OF PELLA

On the 12th March 1924 Father William Francis Brown was Consecrated Bishop of Pella.

42 had been bought a hostel for girls was opened and did excellent work in many ways. When the Convent of the Sisters of St. Anne was established in 1927, the hostel had to be given up as all the accommodation was needed for Novices and Sisters. The Sisters of St. Anne left Vauxhall in 1936 and made a new foundation at the Down's Wimbledon.

In 1937 notably alterations were made in the main hall and a small hall and a billiard room were added. The Settlement raised a loan of £3,000 and the Parish guaranteed interest and repayment. It took rather a long time but the use of Settlement buildings for St. Anne's Catholic Club and other parochial purposes justified expenditure. When the bomb damage is made good, it is hoped to improve the accommodation for social work considerably.

As has been mentioned St. Anne's School Harleyford Road adjoining the church was built in 1892. It had been crowded for a long time and in 1936 it was decided to erect a new Infants School which provided three classrooms and a Head teacher's room. This set free three rooms on the ground floor of the main building. But it was not sufficient and a second infants building was put up in 1932 and the whole of the original building became available for children over 7. But in order to make this addition it was necessary to acquire two houses adjoining the Clergy House which had long back gardens at a cost of £2,000. Part of the gardens formed a site for the new building. The Infant School now consists of two buildings between them providing 5 classrooms a cloakroom and lavatories of modern design. The L.C.C. have installed hot and cold water services to both. The cost of these important modern additions, including the purchases of houses, amounting to over £8,000. The rent from one of them is a slight off-set against the expenditure. The other house is rent free to Dames of St. Joan for a hostel of unmarried mothers. Much effort was needed to raise his large sum of money but in various ways it was done and the whole of the building belonging to St. Anne's Vauxhall are free of dept.

[Authors Note:] The list of the Settlement committee members was found in one of the archived documents. In 1918 on the 23rd. February: Members of the St Anne's Settlement to oversee the management and progress of the establishment were:

Fr. William Francis Brown

Miss Grace Gordon Smith.
Miss Elizabeth Thompson
Mrs. Ada Verte
Mrs May Gossage
Mrs Florence May Fry.
Gerald Knight Sprogdon
Rev John Sheen Bishop of Southwark.

Existing Photos of No. 40 Harleyford Road-

View looking through to Harleyford Road

The Chapel (Oratory)

Garden at the rear

Fr. Madden Bishop Brown. Fr. Koch Conducting
Mass in St. Anne's

Authors note: the following was provided into the response for memoirs of St. Anne's to be submitted]

Mrs. Joan Mills. Reflects: dated 2010.

My father, Frank Chaddock, was born in 1889 in Stockwell South London and with his siblings attended St. Anne's R.C School in Vauxhall where he met Father Brown.

I was born in 1928 in Vauxhall and aged four went to St. Anne's School to join my sister, brother and some cousins already there.

The enclosed photograph is of me in the infant Class taken about 1933. When Bishop Brown was at the school and saw me, he always asked how my father was.

After I married my husband and I with our four children lived in Stockwell and all the children went to St. Anne's with some of my cousin's children. This made three Generations who attended St. Anne's.

I also worked at the School when my children were there, first as dinner lady (as it was called then) and later as Secretary. My Mother also worked as a dinner lady at the school.

Some of my cousins and me joined the youth Club and had many happy times there. My maiden name was Chaddock and my cousin's names were the Ager's.

The Bishop would often bring into the playground a blown up balloon and would reward with a penny piece any child who would sit on it and burst it.

Bishop Brown often visited the pupils in the playground.

Miss McArthur is the teacher left hand side of photo.

1935

THE INSTIGATOR & FOUNDER OF

St. ANNE'S

SETTLEMENT YOUTH & PELLA CLUB

Bishop William Francis Brown Bishop of Pella.
Affectionately known as

'The BISH'

THE SETTLEMENT

Vauxhall was the area where our Grandmother Mary Cunningham moved to, circa 1933 to a small House in Wheatsheaf Lane, it was in that vicinity that her daughters with spouse's and their families also established their roots, all attending the services and Masses at St. Anne's, with their siblings attending St Anne's School, for instance the McDermott's who lived in Langley Lane, whose father Peter was the schools Caretaker. Granny and my Aunts association with the Settlement began when it was first opened in 1935. Tommy Wilberham who was born on New Year's Eve 1934 and first child to be Christened in St Anne's Church by Fr. Adolf Koch, in 1935. Within a month he had developed Whooping cough, the Doctor in the Settlement said it wasn't and stated it was just a bad cough. However his mother Francis went to her mother's and repeated what the doctor had said, she was told to go back to the Doctor and tell the Doctor that she (Granny Cunningham) said she had bourn twenty siblings and she knew it was Whooping Cough. Francis returned and told the nurse (Nurse Bullock) what her mother had said, the Doctor was informed and he confirmed Tommy did suffer from Whooping cough, so Tommy was accordingly treated by the Doctor.

My cousin, Pat Thomas (Grandson) remembers Granny Cunningham and her pal the 'Bish' would visit her in her House in Wheatsheaf Lane. As the pair of them were deaf, they would hollow and shout as they conversed with each other, so the whole street would be able to hear their conversation. It must have been an eye opener for anyone passing bye to become part of their conversation.

There were other things that one tried to avoid with a meeting with the 'Bish' in his confession box; Pat Thomas remembers when he was 13 he went to Confession, at that time the Confessional booths were on both sides of the church. One side was always full of waiting people, whilst the other, it being 'The Bishops Territory,' was void of confessors, not wanting to enter his domain? Pat seeing the opportunity and eager to get his confession over and done with, headed for the empty side and had an audience with the 'Bish.' Who would loudly ask questions of one's doings? Whether you had been on a farm doing things you should not have done?? Upon completion the confessor was provided with a big penance, in Pat's case he crawled out very red faced to face the opposition, of grinning faces. *I think this has happened to quite a few of us.*

I too remember my Granny Cunningham, Instructing me and my sister Margaret to take our rosary beads with us to confession I always wondered why? I dreaded going to Bishop Brown, as he always gave me for my penance the decades of the Rosary to recite in Church, my knees were raw. I don't think I deserved all that; I really was a good boy? J.P.

If the inevitable happened and you were forced into a visit to the 'Bish' The trick was to leave your rosary behind, so that if he asked.

'Have you got your rosary?' You could truthfully say.

'No, My Lord.' Otherwise you would get the whole novena as a penance.

ooOoo

As time progressed with interruptions throughout the years of the war, into the late forties and fifties, The Cunningham Clan was not the only family that enjoyed a long and memorable association with St. Anne's that became known as 'The Club.' Through its transference in 1935 to include a Youth Club, open to all young Catholic Youths from far and wide. This passage of history is not just about ONE families association with St. Anne's, as briefly referred to above, but that of the MacMonagale's, McAvoys, Agers, Bremer's, Healey's and countless others families who all in turn became members of 'THE CLUB.'

This is a photo of just one family of many others that attended St. Anne's Settlement when it was opened in 1936.

The Cunningham Tribe (Circa possibly 1937.) Then Present attendees of the Settlement
Bridie Dalton - Julia Cunningham - Sarah Plant- Francis Wilberham
Bridget Mc Dermott- Granny Mary Cunningham- Peg Fox.
and two young Settlement attendees and future Club members
Patricia Macdermott - Tommy Wilberham.

THE CLUB'S LOCATION.

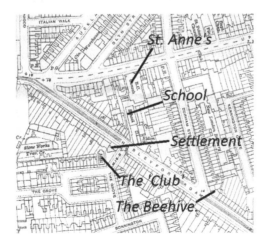

THE CLUB ENTRANCE.

VIA THE GROVE – VAUXHALL

On the Vauxhall Grove roadway outside the main entrance, was the meeting place of the chosen team players either football, netball, cycle rides etc., and would meet at a specified time prior to making their way to the nominated location by tram, bus or other forms of London transport. Inevitable one person would always be late; when they did arrive the Captain would berate them, specifically if it was the match ball carrier. Nevertheless, he was always the first person to arrive and the ball would be removed from the safety of its net dropped to the floor and proceeded to be passed backwards and forwards between other team members. However enthusiasm always got the better of some (Buddy Higgins) who would belt the ball against the opposite wall of the Household, much to the dislike of the occupants. I am sure that the culprits did nothing to stop this behaviour until the full team arrived, not so with the girls they all being to demure and proper. Nevertheless when the cyclist turned up on their bicycles of different types and colours some purposely borrowed for the occasion would spread themselves across the roadway, blocking of any through access and there was always two enthusiastic riders who continued to circle around the rest possibly to keep their leg muscles warm? Before they all set off in pairs down the Harleyford Road towards the Oval following the routes of the tram-lined roads of Camberwell, Peckham, New Cross, Blackheath etc. to their intended venue somewhere in Kent.

Then during the Summer months the Grove became the parking place for six Orange coach's as a pick up point for the Club's occupants to fill them up before whisking them away for a day at the seaside. They would return later that day and the occupants would fall out all red rosy and burnt from a day's exposure to the rays of sun. To go home and get changed for the dance that evening.

ooOoo

A WALK THROUGH THE ESTABLISHMENT

Photos taken February 2014

Through the outer door you enter into a small vestibule. Located on the right the Girls toilet, (*Doorway now bricked up*) A little further on, the door to the Kitchen, (now entrance door to the <u>Gents</u> Toilets).

Directly in front the double door providing access to the Dance hall. On the left hand side the door the Boys Cloakroom, turning right into a wide corridor affixed to the wall was a large Notice board where a list of the Committee Members? The team names of players chosen for either Football or Netball fixtures and details of notices were pinned up along with other events advising all of the events and other happening of the week and future dates on the Notice Board.

Entering the Dance Hall. At the top end on your left was a dart Board then another door to the Boys Cloakroom where the collapsible Table Tennis was stored stacked up along the back were fold up seats. At the other end of the Hall was a wide stage with access steps.

A large door on the left led though into a covered in passage way where the Gym equipment was stored plus another door into a large room used as a changing room for Panto's etc. and used solely by the Girls as a cloakroom. (That has now gone) Also at the far end on the opposite side was another door leading back into the corridor on your left was a pair of doors that led through a covered in Passageway leading through to the main House in Harleyford Road, just before you go up the steps into the House, another doorway led through to a large hut where a full sized Snooker Table was placed. Later in one of the rooms at the rear of the House a television was installed Black & White of course.

The following series of photos taken in February 2014 illustrate some changes that have taken place over the pre-ceding years.

Bricked-up entrance

Vestibule

Doorway

Corridor

Dance hall

Dance Hall - stage in background

Side door

Piano

Noticeboard

However:

LET US BEGIN THE CLUB'S HISTORY FROM 1935

"THE CLUB LEADER"
1935-1945
Fr. Adolf. P. Koch.

1935/6

Not much can be referred to regarding the Clubs history in its early years as there appears to be little or no records that can be referred too, with the exception of the Settlements diaries that record the Annual General Meetings Chaired by Bishop Brown that record the affairs of the Settlement with only brief references to the Club. Old photographs albums hold photographs of Club outings that sometimes identify where an event took place. So therefore these will be used as a record of its gradual development. Until 1941 when the Club's ANNALS were published and recorded the times and progress throughout the war and beyond.

3 Photos of The C.O.M. trip to Herne Bay Kent

2 Photos of the C.O.M. trip to Croydon

First Hike

Rambling @ Leatherhead 1937

1937

3 Photos of The C.O.M. trip to Leatherhead

1938

[Authors note] On July 7th. 1938 A certain Club member named P. Murray. Being of an adventurous nature, decided to make a cycle trip from Vauxhall all the way to Rome. He must have prepared well for his forthcoming trip, with maps of each country en-route, his tent, cooking equipment and a meagre supply of rations, and of course currency money. His account of his travels eventually appeared in the 1941 Christmas issue of the Clubs Annals. However being this is the only plausible record during 1938 I decided to enter his account at this point. It also illustrates the type of articles submitted showing the artist illustrations as they appeared in the Annals and it reads as follows:

CYCLING TO ROME
by P. MURRAY

On July 7th, 1938 I sat out on a run that was to take me six weeks and was to be an adventure. Equipped with a bicycle, camping kit. A fair knowledge of English, a smattering of German, no French and no Italian, my destination was Rome.

Embarking at Dover and landing in Calais, I mounted my steed of steel. Steering South my

Saint Christopher

route being through Beauvais to Paris. Paris was at the best for the visit of the King and Queen. I spent two days in company with a French cyclist admiring the decorations and visiting the places of interest.

We left for Versailles together where we visited the famous Château and booked accommodation at the Youth Hostel close by. Next morning we parted company but not before we had promised to write to each other. He returned to Paris, I resumed my journey. I pitched my camp on the bank of the riverYonne. I had a restless night on account of the constant passing of the express trains on the other side of the river. I lay and resolved never to pitch my tent near the railway track again!

When dawn broke through, I rose and continued on to Semur. I stopped to visit the Grotto d'Arcy, a number of large caves which extend about a mile. I was astonished at the wonders of floodlighting; waterfalls lit up like rainbows; dark corners suddenly lighted up to reveal the most amazing shapes and colours.

Coming out of this fairyland, I found it was raining so I went to the hostel in Semur and had a nice hot bath. A middle-aged lady who was mine hostess spoke little English and when I told her I was bound for Rome, nothing was too good for me.

Next morning was fine, so I set off for Dijon. Dijon is a fair sized city and as one cannot camp in a city, I made for the Youth Hostel where I met a tandem couple returning from a trip in Switzerland. They spoke perfect English and we spent a jolly evening together swapping yarns. They left early the next morning. Imagine my surprise when, whilst making some minor adjustments to my handlebars, they simply came asunder in my hands! I hastily hunted round for a cycle shop. I found many but they were all closed and I was beginning to wonder when Frenchmen started their day's work, when it dawned on me that it was July 14th. Fete Nationale when very few Frenchmen work. I was about to give up all hope when a Good Samaritan took me along to a man who builds cycles. With the aid of my phrasebook, we came to an understanding. The cycle was to be ready on the morrow, so in the meantime I joined in the festivities and celebrated my first week on the road.

Looking back I consider that I had not done too badly. I had two days in Paris and half a day in Semur which meant I had done for the half day cycling.

Next morning I called for my old faithful. I promise myself that I would sleep in Switzerland that night, so I wasted no time in heading for Pontarlier. As I approached the town I saw heavy clouds ahead; a thunderstorm had passed over and was travelling in front of me and the streets were still wet but the sun was shining brightly. I congratulated myself did a spot of clapping and set off for the foothills that lead to the frontier and Switzerland. I approached the customs and passed without even opening the panniers, and took it easy down to Lausanne. The scenery was beautiful and the right delightful to Lausanne, that quaint old town, where high above the rooftops the beautiful cathedral of Notre Dame shows its Gothic towers.

With the day fast fading, I continued along by the lakeside and arrived at Vevey where I pitched my tent. Later I was joined by two Swiss lads who pitched their tent near mine. They had some of my tea and I had some of their sausage in our communal supper. Conversation progress slowly because I had only a smattering of German.

Waking early I was on the road again before 8 o'clock. My friends were still sleeping and I did not waken them. Taking the road that skirted the lake, I was soon in Montreau. Leaving the lake, behind me, I pushed along a deep valley towards Martigny. Numerous cyclists passed me in the opposite direction, in twos and threes and sometimes in larger parties. It reminded me of home and the Club. Here I was joined by a Swiss cyclist who was going my way, we stopped near Vernayza where a river cataracts through a deep chasm. For a small charge we walked along a narrow platform and looked down at the white foamy waters, an awe-inspiring sight. We resumed our journey and kept company till we reached Martigny. Then he made for the Grimsal Pass and I for the grand St Bernard Pass. I had a good tuck in just to be sure I should not get the hunger knock, and I packed some cheese and rolls into my bag.

Feeling refreshed and fit for anything I set off at 2:30 p.m. in the sweltering heat and slight following breeze that helped considerably. I pedalled away at ease in low gear and, not aware of what was to come, thought I should reach the summit before 7 p.m. As I plodded along I admired the marvellous scenery, the river Rhône was keeping me company now on the right side of the road and now on the left. I felt grateful for its presence for its foaming progress against massive boulders, both cooled the air and pleased the ear. The road climbs through small mountain villages practically hanging on the mountainside. As I climbed cultivated fields gave place to grim visitas of unyielding mountainside. Desolate, barren and colossal in extent, it made you feel dwarfed by the gigantic proportions of it and in awe at its brooding loneliness. In those surroundings I halted to prepare my tea. I soon had my primus stove going and got some crystal-clear water from the stream. While waiting for it to boil I heard the noise of the postal bus. I lingered over my tea then looking at my watch saw that it was gone six so I hastily gathered my goods and chattels and resume my climb. I found I could still ride although I was forced to dismount more frequently. The sun was fading fast and the mist rising, making the air cold and clammy. I steadily plodded along in the half-light to the road. It was now past eight and was pushing, heaving and dragging my heavily laden by along for riding was out of the question. Visibility was reduced to a hundred yards and through the gaps of the swishing, eddying mists I caught sight of snow covered mountain tops wild and uncomforting, enough to freeze the stoutest heart. I paused to light a cigarette wondering if there were any policeman about for I had no light and there was no blackout in those days. Continuing doggedly I could just about lift the bike when I reached the hospice. I was greeted by the guest Brother who put a bottle of wine and bread and cheese before me.

In spite of my fatigue of the night before I was up with the lark next morning and after attending mass in the small chapel and taking breakfast I prepared for the ascent to Asti. I bade the guest Brother farewell and walked to the frontier. The second stage of my pilgrimage accomplished.

I was soon on my way down the other side into Italy. That descent required caution and discretion at the sharp bends covered with loose and treacherous gravel. A slight miscalculation and one is sent to one's doom many hundreds of feet below.

I was soon in Asti. I looked back at those snowcapped peaks. What a picture they presented and what a contrast to the almost unbearable heat of this, the sunny side, of that night barrier.

Asti is a small and ancient town, and I amused myself till the bank opened by exploring its narrow winding streets. After obtaining some Italian currency I entered a restaurant and ordered what was going. Spaghetti, spaghetti and spaghetti. I watched some locals out of the corner of my eye eating spaghetti with the ease and grace of the artist. Try as I might to imitate them I could not manage it and in discuss I ordered something else and finished up with a glass of wine. Refreshed and feeling fine I remounted and hit the trail for Chatillon. It was a delightful run downhill. I then pitched my tent by the river, made a cup of tea and turned in, feeling very pleased with my first day in Italy.

I was awake at dawn for it was my intention to travel early and rest at midday when the heat was full on, and then to carry on till dusk. However my plans were interfered with by the attention of a mosquito. I found I had been bitten and why I was swollen to enormous proportions, so I had breakfast and struck camp.

My next destination was Turin where I arrived about 6 p.m. and my eye was almost normal again by this time. I made my way to the cathedral only to find it closed but as I was about to wander away, a middle-aged man approached me and addressed me in English. This was a pleasant surprise indeed and we went to a nearby cafe and had dinner together. During the meal he told me that he had recently returned from Dublin after spending 14 years there, so we were on common ground and we talked of dear old Dublin. He took me to his home and next morning showed me round his city, taking me to church of St John Bosco and the Salesian Centre. I was indeed sorry to take leave my friend, but I thanked him and promised to write to him and climbed out of Turin.

I set off to live reached Novi a small village where I turned in. I was on the road again at 4:30 a.m but I was not alone for I met numerous peasants on the road, for this seemed to be the only time the heat permitted them to do anything in comfort.

My next stop was Genoa where I prowled round various churches, also the house of Christopher Columbus, a small hole ivy-covered building. After lunch I made for a shady spot for my usual "forty winks." So I continued, day after day up early, rest at midday finish at dusk. My road took me to La Spezia and on to Pisa. As I entered Pisa the first thing I saw was the famous leaning Tower. For a small charge I was allowed to climb to the top. It is reputed to be 16 feet out of line.

Leaving Pisa and and keeping as close to the sea as the road would allow I passed through the small town of Grosseto and stopped at a village to have a dip and some lunch. Then I was on the road again I shall always remember the village of Civita- Vecchia. I was riding along at walking pace when I was surprised to see everyone running in all directions making for doorways and entering houses. I wondered what was happening when around the bend of the road came a great bullock and he was charging full at me. It was too late to dodge into a doorway so I jumped onto a wall holding my bike by its back wheel ready to throw it at the brute if he came too close. Fortunately for me, he continued his stampede down the road.

At length I came to Paolo with the road turns inland for Rome. I looked at my map and saw that I was only 25 miles from Rome.

The road now climbs up and I find the gradients are a bit stiff and I passed what I took to be wine carts, a peculiar hood protecting the drivers head from the sun. I still push along, stopping here and there to buy fruit. Eventually arrive at the top of the hill and in the distance I caught a glimpse of the dome of St Peter's.

ooOoo

Other Photos of outings possibly by the C.O.M.

A Trip to Headley

A trip to Dorking

A trip to West Wickham

Nativity Play performed in the Settlement Hall by the infants of St. Anne's school Christmas 1938.

ooOoo

1939

Several trips were made during 1939: Fr. Koch went to Beaumont College near Windsor and visited Windsor Great Park.

Windsor Great Park

Windsor Great Park   *Taken at Beaumont.*

ooOoo

Some Club members also made trip to Ascot and Hampton Court where they enjoyed having fun on the 'CHILDREN's Swings 'Hey Ho' girls never grow up!'

HAMPTON COURT

ASCOT

A game of Tennis

STUDLEY ROAD.

Further outings took members to Oxted Surrey - Oxshot Surrey -Wernish near Guildford Surrey - and Frensham Ponds Farnham.

OXTED

OXSHOT

WERNISH

FENSHAM PONDS SURREY

3ᴿᴰ SEPTEMBER

THE BEGINNING OF THE

SECOND WORLD WAR

1939-1945

In 1939 during the Evacuation of London's schoolchildren. Granny. Mary Cunningham, accompanied her two Grandchildren, Margaret Plant & Tommy Wilberham, to join the party of St. Anne's School children. That were being evacuated to Reading.. More detailed stories of the evacuees are included below.

St. Anne's School was evacuated to
Reading in Berkshire
The children (some as young as four years old) were billeted with local families.
The Infant School was based in a large old House in Tilehurst.
Bishop Brown was a frequent visitor, and is seen in the photograph above with the local Canon
(Of the English Martyrs Parish) together with the pupils and Teachers of St. Anne's Infant
school
Miss Gardiner,- Miss Butcher, - Miss Baker & Mrs Bricknell (all from London)

ooOoo

Maria Martinelli (nee Caluori). Who joined the Club after the war, submitted her memoirs and her interesting story stems back to her school days in "St. Josephs" Pitman Street RC School Camberwell. Where other familiar names appear throughout the story. Later all members of the 'Club'. Relates her recollections, and her words, portray a good record of what evacuees endured.

Mrs Caluori with Marie and her sister taken in their back garden #17 County Grove. The church in the background is The Sacred Heart Camberwell New Road 1939.

[Authors note] The Clarity of some Photos within the Manuscript, are much to be desired, due to their age and possibly taken on a Kodak Box Camera, also some have been damaged by water? That was unable to be rectified. Nevertheless I have attempted to modify most, to create sharpness and exposure. Also those type scripted memoirs, submitted by Old Members, in many cases, have within them, covered several sections of Club Activities. Those paragraphs I have separated and replaced them in the appropriate headed section. Also changed the style of font for each individual, as illustrated by the following memoir:

Maria Martinelli Reflects:

I was 10 years and six months on the last Friday of August 1939 when the children of St. Joseph's school Pitman street Camberwell. Amongst our pupils were the Marconi's, Marcantonio the Bremers, Healys, Connolly's Pettifor's and Martinelli 's: in my class was Maria Marcantonio, Maria Bremer, a Healy and Connelly girl.

We did not know the boys as we never mixed with them. We were taken by coach with a gas masks to Victoria station. The driver was on the platform with a sealed envelope in his hand with our destination. It was Maria Bremer's birthday party that evening-I was miffed at missing it. My Mother went with us and became the person to move children from one Billet to another.

We arrived at Brighton station and were moved on to the Hove and taken to a hall where we were paraded around for the locals to pick who they would like to look after. People with boarding houses and no holiday guest would take several children. These children would have to do all the housework. I was with the local gravedigger. Two days later on Sunday we were coming out of mass when the sirens went off that was a signal for war. From then on no real lessons instead spent days in the hall all singing 'Sea Shanties' we must have learnt all of them!!! Went blackberry picking at Devils Dike. Us girls used to go for a walk to the Brighton pier every Sunday after mass.

In May and June of 1940 it was the evacuation of Dunkirk and the doors of the halls in Brighton and Hove were all wide open. Inside on the floors lay the soldiers in uniform-they exhausted and asleep. The fact that the weather was warm enabled more small boats across the channel to the rescue I can still picture those men.

Now we have to be moved as we are going to be invaded. It was August/September 1940. This time we know where we are going- Engelfield Green in Surrey. At this point I was 11 years and 6 months old. But I got billeted down the hill in Egham with a Salvation Army family. The bombing in London was now on-going and in Egham we had the same sirens as London, and they the family, would not leave me 'home alone' so about two or three times they took me to their services. This was found out through the confessional and I was moved within hours and re-billeted in Englefield Green with a lovely family with one spoilt daughter and they were spoiling me as well. I had the same pocket money as Wendy etc. Her Father was an inventor at Weybridge Aircraft Works so he had petrol all through the war and on Saturdays we would go shopping in the local towns Windsor etc., see a show and have tea. When the bombing in London was heavy Wendy and nine would sleep in the cupboard under the stairs, a bomb did fall in Egham killing someone. It was in one of the Colleges in Englefield Green that the Statue of 'Eros' was stored during the war.

I am now getting on for 12 years so should not be in the primary school. How do children evacuated from one Borough in London get moved to another school from another London borough. It was not simple it had to be arranged. So I was transferred to St. Bernard's from the Commercial road area of London. This was in the heart of Engelfield Green in a large private house with a very large garden, this is where I met the Daly's Kathleen, Pat and Margaret. I was put in Margaret's class. I think of that I was the only one moved at that time. In 1942 two boys joined our school, Peter and John Elliot. Mother brought them down from London to live with her brother who owned a Public House. Peter was in our class and John was two years younger in another class. Another famous visitor to Englefield Green was the Prime minister of the Polish Government in Exile. Wladyslaw Sikorsky who stayed at a rich bankers house on Middle Hill. He would walk all alone resplendent in his Ceremonial Uniform, a very colourful Cape and cap.

So we lived in safety in this tranquil village-cycling all over and in Windsor Park, which was near our school whilst the bombing went on. The news was not good. The days weeks, months went by. One morning I arrived at school and the headmaster said. 'We have invaded - take the day off.' The sky was full of planes roaring south over our school. I think from the old London Airport built in the ancient Village of Heath Row, since adapted for troop carrying. Large open trucks full of soldiers were endlessly going up again and it will cost an village and engineer water on the road to Portsmouth non- stop all whistling and waving as they went past.

We had great fun and school it was so relaxed as we were starting to push the Germans back and London became more safe. So lots of the evacuees started to return home their parents had missed them and sometimes we did not know if they were here or there We have now got our own youth Club in the church hall in - Harvest Road.. We had some other locals as well and we enjoyed it very much. I stayed in my Billet but later on had to move two children and found that the owners were moving away so rented the Cottage and I moved in some time later. That was how I managed to stay in Englefield Green until after the war. We kept the Cottage until 1947. As for some of the evacuee children returning home after D-Day such as Margaret Daly's family. They were in London when the pilotless planes and Rockets were bombing London. Some of the children were once agin evacuated.

I seem to have skimmed or over the years 1940 to 1944. Yes we did have lots of sirens and gunfire etc. After a foothold in Europe and elsewhere lots of evacuees and Teachers were returned back home to get the best jobs. We were now learning nothing we had only one third teachers in the school and 12 pupils in our class. I left school half term October 1944 age 15 years three months and went to work of the British American the Tobacco Company (BAT) they had been evacuated from Millbank London. My sole job was in the typing pool in in a very nice place behind Holloway College, tabulating all the information of sales etc, of all their different Brands of cigarettes worldwide. All this information was sent to Reykjavik. So I had the prospects of a job when I did return London but did not return for some years. After some time a cheeky boy joined BAT –it was John Elliot, and he used to march through the typing pool throwing sweets into the typewriters, especially mine because he knew me. The following Xmas I was shopping with a local friend at Staines Market when along came John, he enquired. 'What are you doing?'- 'Christmas Shopping.' said I. He insisted on buying me a pair of earrings. Several years later I learnt he had become a Priest, and furthermore later I heard he had become the Secretary to the Archbishop.

We celebrated Victory in Europe the 8th. April at 'The Lookout' next to where the Air Force Memorial is today, overlooking London in the distance with bonfires everywhere. Then in August the Atom Bombs were dropped on Japan and they surrendered on the 15th. Victory over Japan, so more celebrations and the big one the following year that we went to that as well.

I was just thinking of returning to London and heard that a London Youth Club was coming to visit our Youth Club on the Sunday. Guess Who?? Yes ; ST. ANNE'S VAUXHALL.

ooOoo

An extract from the 1945 Diary records the following:
JUL. 15.
The Guild of St. Agnes go off to Engelfield Green for the day. Judging by the balls, bats, swimming gear and colossal packets of food and sweets they intended to enjoy themselves in a big way - and did.

When I did return to London and joined St. Anne's. Paddy Healy said to me he would never forget my Mother. When he was a very young boy She was so kind and held my hand when he had to change his Billet. My friendship with Margaret Daly was also rekindled. After the war we went on a weeks holiday to the New Billy Butlins Camp. And thoroughly enjoyed ourselves.

Marie – Margaret

Marie – Margaret training for the Derby

ooOoo

Eileen McMonagle Reflects:

I had attended St. Anne's school from childhood until 11+, under the headships of Sister Marie (Infants) and Sister Cecilia (Juniors/Seniors). I was fortunate to have been given a place after an interview with Sister Mary Gregory of the Daughters of the Cross, Head teacher of the Brompton Oratory Girls School in South Kensington and had attended it for a year 1938-39. Before the outbreak of the war, the government had decided that all children should be sent to a place of safety and security. So my young brother and I were duly registered, labelled and sent to Reading via Vauxhall Station with St Anne's School. I rejoined the Oratory in February 1940 at Clacton-on-Sea. At the fall of Dunkirk, and threats of invasion, the two schools, both boys and girls were transferred in one day from the East Coast to the Rhondda Valley in South Wales. The journey took all day and we were obviously diverted many times until we finally steamed up the valley stopping at many small stations. The most interesting thing for all us children was leaving two of our teachers adrift on the platform as we merrily continued to the next station. We remained in Tonypandy for about three years and the people were very kind to us. We returned to London in early 1943 and became co-educational. Not in our own school (it had been requisitioned by the military) but in another nearby.

ooOoo

Harry Spanswick Reflects:

I commenced school in 1935 with Mrs. Gardiner infant teacher and the Headmistress was Sister Marie, Sister of Notre Dame de Namur.

In 1939, aged eight, I recall marching with the whole school along Harleyford Road to Vauxhall Station, brown label on my collar, a big bar of chocolate in my hand and happily singing along with all the other pupils. I was thoroughly enjoying the expedition to Reading, which was allocated as our evacuation town, until nightfall when I kept asking my older sister Marie when we were all going home? It was to be in five years time! The school was divided into three sections: the infants, under Sister Marie, were based at Tilehurst Road close to English Martyrs Church, the junior Girls were settled into Lancaster Lodge under the Headmistress Sister Cecelia SDN and the Boys and the seniors were with Mr. Sewell at St. James RC School in Forbury Gardens.

My Mother came to school as a school escort and took on the post of unpaid school keeper in residence at Lancaster Lodge (my brother was born there in 1940)

The Lodge was a large and beautiful Georgian House with a huge walled garden and it took a lot of hard work and energy to maintain it but it remained our home throughout the war years and was well used by the pupils there. In 1945 brought about the end of the war and also the end of my school years as well as our return to London I was fourteen when I left school and it was Bishop Brown who helped me find a seven year apprentice placement in the building trade as a solid and fibrous plasterer, a much needed skill with so much bomb damage to repair.

ooOoo

Josie Spanswick (nee Course) reflects.

From the age of four, my younger brother and I were often at the Settlement with our mother, to visit the health works for check-ups inoculations, medications (orange juice, malt and cod liver oil. supplements) and also to accompany her in keep fit sessions and sewing Classes.

In 1939 we were evacuated with the school to Reading in Berkshire and our teachers from the infant school came along too. Sister Marie (Sisters of Notre Dame) was the Head mistress and our teachers were Mrs. Gardiner, Miss Butcher, Miss Bricknell, Miss McCarthy and Miss Baker. We were placed with local families and, as infants attuned lessons at a large House in Tilehurst. The House had a big garden and we were taught how to plant and grow seeds and each Class had their own plot.. Bishop Brown would often travel from Vauxhall to check-ups on how we all were and usually brought along some sort of treat for us...

As Junior pupils, we attended half day sessions at St. James ' school; and spent the rest of the day at a local hall (Waverley) being taught country dancing and other physical activities, Sister Cecilia (Sister of Notre Dame) was the Head mistress and several of the teachers (Mr. Sewell, Miss Attwood) were also from the Vauxhall School.

St. Anne's at Vauxhall continued to open throughout the war and served those families who did not evacuate. I returned to London for several long periods of time and attended St. Anne's. we had to go home each lunch time as no food was served at school and often had to dive into a shelter should an air raid siren sound. Many of the windows the church and school were blown in and much damage were inflicted on our homes and shops in the area.

We rook the 11+ examination and with the help of the parish Priest and teachers I was fortunate to gain a place at Notre Dame School in Southwark (which is another tale of lifelong affiliation and education)

ooOoo

1940

The beginning of 1940. Was not a very good or pleasant time for anyone? Due to the issue of I.D. Cards, ration books and the start of rationing. Conscription was inevitable for many of the young Club Members, when they reached the required age. This would also apply to the young female members, who wanted to volunteer for service in the: ATS, WAAFS, WRENS or, Land Army. Later as you read through the editions of the St. Anne's Clubs Annals, there are many entries that refer to the Girls and Boys leaving the Club, to begin their service life, or returning home on leave, and in some instances, the fate of individuals demise or, becoming a P.O.W. In some far off land.

There are also stories submitted by serving Club members, of their life in a foreign country. Unfortunately, there are no written records of what took place in the Club, during the year of 1940. However the Evacuation of Dunkirk in May and June changed the course of the War that quickly led in September to the London Blitz by the German Luftwaffe. Those where the grim and dark days that were to last for many months. Yet the Club was still open and still carried on with the normal activities, including many outings as seen by the following photographs. Taken at

Virginia Waters during Easter 1940.

1941

APRIL 29TH. 1941. EASTER

Followed then into the events of 1941 when the Settlement and Club was hit by a bomb for the first occasion as illustrated by the below photographs, (found during research) as a positive record of the Clubs survival after the bombing incident.

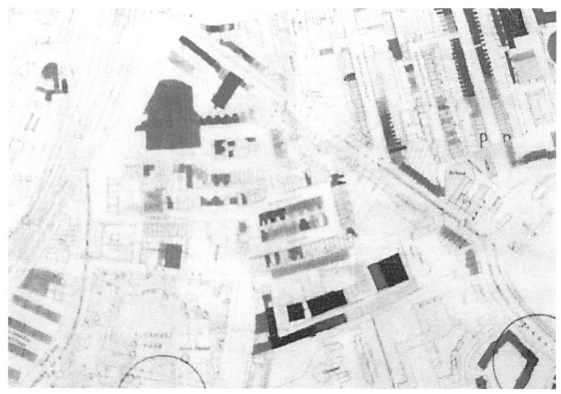

Map showing bomb damage in the locality of Vauxhall Grove and Harleyford Road
Bt Kind permission of the Lambeth Archives

PHOTOGRAPHS OF THE SETTLEMENT AND CLUB DAMAGED BY A HIGH EXPLOSIVE BOMB

The bombed Settlement Nos. 46- demolished 44 and 42 ruins as seen from Harleyford Road. And view as seen from Vauxhall Grove.

Nevertheless, although the bombing continued throughout the London Blitz. After the CLUB members cleaned up. The CLUB carried on with its usual routine. On occasions when the night bombing was at its heaviest. Members stayed and slept in the Club.

During a bombing raid, Father Madden whilst crossing Vauxhall Bridge saw a bomb hurtling down towards him. In his moment of anxiety, the only prayers he could think of saying was 'Prayers before Grace.'

"Our Father for what we are about to receive make us truly thankful."

Obviously God heard his plea and the bomb missed him.

ooOoo

A RAMBLE TO GUILDFORD TOOK PLACE ON WHIT MONDAY

Another outing arranged was one to Guildford

The below photo was submitted by Marie Macdermott (nee Stogdon), was taken, sometime during the Summer of 1941 The inscription on the back refers to 3rd. from left Josie Stogden.(long blonde hair)/ Doris Shepherd. Next but one is Fr. Koch (End of top line Rosemary Martyn)Monica Chance (2nd from right) & Maureen Stogden (sitting wearing a tie)' Date July 41.

N:B This might also have been at Guildford?

There was another trip to Chigwell in Essex. Several group photos were taken. (in Album) as shown below It was obvious that the threat of the German Bombers, did not deter or stop the Clubs Outings or, the games they played Cricket – Races & Rounder's

JULY 1941
THE BEGINNING OF THE PUBLISHING OF
St. ANNE'S ANNALS - MAGAZINE.

A word about these Annals, created in 1941 and published twice a year, copies of these have been given to me by Olive Woods and are in themselves, records of the "Clubs" history and its activities, during the period of the war years and post war. Totally published by the Club members with many articles submitted by other members for inclusion, these include Club Diaries, Short Stories, Reports on outings, Poems, Quizzes, Jokes etc. The production of these throughout the War years was an achievement in itself. With the on-going shortage of paper, time engaged to stencil type them up. Produce multiple copies and collate together. Yes, they were all hand produced, using a stencil cutting - machine and printed (not sure how) onto A5 sized paper, then collated into book form, centre fold hand stitched to secure the pages together. They were produced in quantities, number off unknown. It is a puzzle as to how these Annals were actually produced. However, there is an article that appeared in the 2nd. Issue of the September ANNAL 1941, that possibly provides a clue as to how these Annals were produced Text as follows:-

A Letter of Thanks

We want to thank all those who worked so hard to make our first magazine a success. Of course they won't like it, but we feel that their readers should know who did what and why and how, to have our first a copy ready for the feast of Saint Anne. So here we go—

The cover design and the drawings that adorned the pages we owe to Francis Desmond. We cannot help wondering how much midnight oil she burned over them.

How many of you office girls get tired of typing long letters? Mary Blessington quite cheerfully cut 23 stencils for us. A skilful job, and done in no time.

Then Eileen Blessington rolled up her sleeves and rolled 'em off on the duplicator. And how many contributes nearly died of brain fever for your entertainment

We thank those industrious members who gave up their Saturday afternoon fun (somewhat noisily) to sort out and put together and sew the copies (more or less correctly).

And we will end his letter, hoping you will continue to patronise the old firm for many more mags to come.

Thanks so much.
Mary Chance and Rosemary Martyn

PS. We take it in turns to pat each other on the back.

ooOoo

Possibly, that will clear up part of the problem, as to the fact that it appears to have been all done In-House, rather than with an Outside Printers. A very excellent and worthy achievement. They represent the workings and coordination of various Club members, in producing such an important document. I doubt very much if there is anybody still alive that can provide information of how these documents were produced, nevertheless, they were produced in their numbers and sent overseas to those Club members fighting in foreign lands.

The publication of these ANNALS has now become an important part in the History of THE CLUB. Each Annals will be transcribed chronologically year by year, including the scanning of the Headings and artistic sketches as they appeared. In the originals, due to the lay-out, some stories were cut and continued onto another page. This has been corrected to ensure the flow of text, furthermore, to differentiate from the then normal stencil cutting size of script, of either 6 or **8 font.** And to avoid straining anyone's eyesight. 12 Font Text had been used for the introductions - and 10 font size Garamond has been used throughout the ANNALS which is the modern equivalent to the old typed version which was 6 and 8 font size. Beginning in most cases with the heading "Editors Entry."

Therefore the entries in the Annals and transcribed within the following pages. Will be inserted under the below: "Subject headings". None of the Photos in the Clubs Albums were notated with any names, dates or location. If a photo has been identified, to fit a report or, occasion as written, it has been inserted within the text. The thumbnail sketches are copies of the orignals and are as sharp as possible given the requirements of modern digital printing. Apologies if not applicable? J.P.

a)   Editors entry.
b)   Appropriate Letters
c)   Clubs Diary
d   Other Reports
f)   Short Stories
g)   Articles of Activities
h)   Lyrics
i)   Poems
j)   Quizzes
k)   Jokes
j)   Last Page

One final point: It is with thanks to Olive Wood (nee O'Sullivan) and also to Eileen Healy (Nee McMonagle). Who fortunately kept copies of these valuable Annals?

ooOoo

CONTENTS

BREAKING the ICE

By Fr. Koch

Breaking the ice may be pleasant for swimmers who lack both sense and feeling. For me, here and now, it is a doleful task. It foreshadows the breaking of hearts heads pockets and worst of all, the Club crockery. Launching a magazine is like launching a battleship; it signifies trouble. Sad that so innocent a thing should cause so much strife. 'History proves it's inevitable. The simple faith of the editorial sanctum is truly refreshing. One trades in the future with its disillusionment. Would that this land of Make-believe could endure for ever. Yet youth is irrepressible. The appearance of this magazine denotes the line of least resistance the part of age. Wisdom once said no, but the need of a quiet life prevailed. Nelson one said: "England expects....." somebody else said "England is a nation of shopkeepers." The cry then became "The customers expect......" and customers are always right. Thus was a great democracy born. The voice of the people now demands a magazine.

"The Club Annals" is produced by members for members. In a small way it can be of service to them all, sharing their sorrows and joys at home and in exile. If they in their turn will share their adventures with us, the Annals could form a link between past and present near and far, in its informal pages. The happy family that was, is now scattered. If each one will send a greeting,and perhaps an anecdote, what pleasure awaits all friends?

We wish Godspeed to this venture. May its pages enhance a good name and foster a good Club spirit. Let every word and be in good taste. Dull is the jester when the jokes unkind. Nay, more. There's no wound deeper than the pen can give. Its dangers being remembered will thereby vanish, so let no one be afraid to "Come off his perch." What he may lose in dignity will be more than gained in affection. A little nonsense now and again is relished by the wisest men.

"Man! Thou pendulum between a smile and a tear, forget thy grief whene'er thou readest here.

ST ANNE By Mary Chance

Who shall find a valiant women?   Far
and from the uttermost coasts is the
price of her. She has looked well to
the paths of her house and hath not
eaten her bread idle.   Her children
rose up and called her blessed.
(Book of Proverbs, chap. 13.)

History tells us that for St Anne this great St who was from mother of our Blessed Lady. According to tradition, Anne and her husband Joachim lived in Sephoris about 3 miles north of Bethlehem, and they probably spent most of their years at Nazareth.

Anne was of the priestly tribe of Aaron, and Joachim a descendant of the Royal house of David. They live in an ordinarily Hill side house, and lived on the proceeds of their small property, a bit of land which yielded grain and fruits. There was much work to be done. Anne shared the toil with her husband, in due season using the sickle. Then there was the daily duty of bringing water from the one well in the town. It was an open place surrounded with cactus and olive trees. All the women and maids gathered here with their pitchers just before sunset, and midst of these beautiful women, Anne must have been outstanding, because later, she was to give the world the loveliest of all the daughters of Eve.

Often in the evenings when prayers were said, Anne and Joachim would bewail the fact that religion was declining amongst their race and spoke of their longing for the coming of the predicted Messias.

After many years and many prayers a daughter was given to them. They called her Mary.

God intended that the mother of his divine son should be perfect, therefore, it was only natural that he chose a good saintly woman to be the mother of the second Eve. In St Anne we have an example of a good ordinary life. She was simple, just a woman of the people, occupying her only tiny sphere in the hills. Looking after her husband and baby and going about her work in an unobtrusive way she resembled any other peasant woman. But in her heart she may have known that Mary was to be the mother of the promised redeemer. Perhaps that is why she consecrated her to the temple to be brought up in the shadow of the altar.

When Mary was 12 years old, Joachim died. There followed days of mourning when Anne and Mary fasted and prayed for the soul of the deceased but soon God willed that Anne should join her spouse and when she became ill unto death, she prayed for Mary and commended her to him who is the father of orphans.

Mary went down from the temple to visit her mother for the last time. St Anne with her failing strength raised herself on her couch and gave her daughter and her last blessing, then lay back on her pillow and slept the sleep of the blessed.

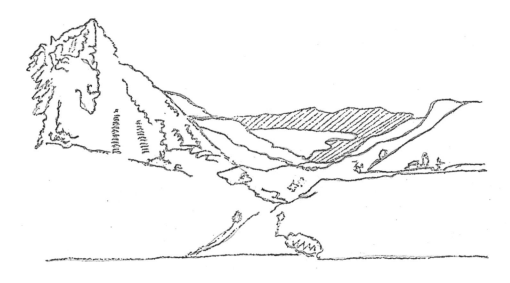

ooOoo

Club News

Keep-Fit

Have you joined the keep fit class yet, ladies? If not why not? Come and learn <u>to</u> do a handstand, somersault, and to balance on your left ear on the corner of the mantelpiece.

Singing

Some of you have a voice tucked away somewhere inside you, but are too modest to own up. We will find it for you, whether it be high or low-a tired tenor or nut- brown bass. So do come along to the singing class. We promise to have your voice trained and not "strained".

Discussion Circle

What do you know, and how much? Do you know why the Chinese are yellow? Why the Negro has thick lips? If shrimps make good mothers? Whether Empires are of any use to the world? What we should have done without Shakespeare? Do join this discussion group, even if you don't know anything, you need not talk, then no-one will know how much you don't know.

Dramatics

There's room for you in the mixed dramatics. "Mystery at Greenfingers." By J.B. Priestley, went off very well, and we are looking forward to some new productions soon. Evelyn Collins and Pamela Moore are to take part in the Stuart

Headlam contest, and we are all hoping for good results. Anyway, we wish them all the best of luck.

Dancing .

Saturday evening dances are in full swing again. Dancing to the radiogram and general frivolity takes place in the hall every night after nine.

ooOoo

MORE CLUB NEWS

Billiards

What goes on in the billiard room, is rather a mystery. But we have heard from time to time that there are some very good players in there, including Father Ryan and E. Brewster. Any chap who cares to take on a match with any of these experienced gentlemen, can apply to E. Brewster who will give them a cue.

Darts

There is a dart board on the wall in the corner facing the door in the small hall.

Whist

The Sunday evening whist drives are becoming very popular. Enjoyable, in fact. You can come and win a prize or just come for the entertainment. It is nice to see the earnest expressions on dad's face, and to watch mother trumping her partner tricks!

Boys' Night

Are you one of those boys who believe that when you've seen one girl, you've seen a lot? Don't let it worry you. Just come to the Club on Tuesday night, and I promise you there will not be one single solitary woman in the place. Though you may regret the absence of the fair sex when the tea bell rings!

Rambling

Miss Hilda Smith is arranging a ramble for August Monday, watch this notice board for details.

Books

Choose a book as you would choose a friend, and please treat it as you would treat a friend and return it to the library as soon as you have read it.

Tennis

There is soon to be a bit of a tussle on the tennis courts. When everything is settled, a list will be put on the board.

ooOoo

There was another Hike by the C.O.M. to Wernish at Whitsun - It appears that after the hike up the hill. The toil took the energy out of the Girls. So it was a lay down for a sleep.

4

It was about 7:30 p.m. when I arrived, and much as I was looking forward to joining the Club, I must confess I was feeling rather scared.

You see, I wasn't used to mixing with people, and as soon as I open the door, I seemed to be surrounded by them it was an ordeal!

As I had come alone, I was put in charge of somebody who was to show me round. It was quite an enjoyable tour of inspection. I was surprised at the number of rooms attached to the Club, there was the old library with plenty of books and a fine grand piano then I saw that the dearest little kitchen and another room that was known as the "green room" of course, being a mere female! I was not allowed in the billiards room.

The two rooms that were mostly used, were the two halls. One was used as a dance hall, and the other as a "quiet room" though I must say it was not very quiet when we went in.

Then I was taken round and introduced to all Clubites. I wondered how I should ever remember their names, but they looked such a jolly crowd and I began to feel that I had known them ages. A bell rang. There was a rush to the canteen for tea and cakes and lemonade and ices. As I sat with my tea, the last bit of shyness left me and I told some of my new friends about myself and listened to their accounts of themselves.

Time seemed to fly. A game of cards, a dance in the hall to the radiogram, a game of table tennis and then 10 o'clock and come and the time bell told us to go home to bed like good Christians.

We stopped for a little gossip of course, in spite of the time. "Will you join the singing?" Asked somebody. Before I could reply, someone else wanted to know if I can come to Keep Fit and another invited me to attend the Mixed Dramatics and Study Circle.

Some of my new friends walked part of the way home with me and we partied with "night, bless you, see you tomorrow!"

I felt so happy as I realise that I belong to a jolly good Club and would undoubtedly make friends that would last long after our Club days were over.

ooOoo

An evening at the GASWORKS

by Frank O'Sullivan

A debate was held at the Club on July 3rd. on the motion. "Money is the root of all evil."

It was very well attended and Mr Hay, leader of the Current Events Circle, was in the chair.

The debate was opened by Miss Josephine Taylor who emphasised that the chief reason that money was the root of all evil lay in the fact that money represented power and some people wouldn't commit almost any crime, the matter how dastardly, to obtain money. Miss Evelyn Collins also supported the motion, stating that the majority of the wars in history were caused indirectly by the jealousy of certain countries for those countries better off financially than themselves.

Mr Terry Bates (as the motion, his main argument being that money in itself was not an evil, but that it was the uses to which man put money that caused the evil.

Mr Frank O'Sullivan followed and argued that after examining the many meanings of the word evil, it would be seen that no money was the root of some evils, it definitely was not the root of all evils

The subject was then open for debate, after which the chairman summed up the proceedings and asked those present to vote on the issue.

A vote was accordingly taken and resulted in the defeat of the motion.

ooOoo

LITTLE COCK SPARROW
by Rosemary Martyn

"Of course," said Lydia Marchant decidedly, "the evacuees must go."

Donald Hilton slowly put down his teacup and there was a troubled look in his eyes as he turned them to towards his fiancee.

"But," he replied in a soft tone that somehow seem to match his delicate looking face, "I couldn't part with them Lydia."

Although his voice was gentle, the girl knew he meant every word, and she realised that he would have to tax her charms to the last degree in order to make him change his mind. Lydia had a game of her own to play, and she wanted the children out of the house.

"You see, dear," Explained Donald. "This is a big place for one man to live in and I thought it would be ideal for kiddies."

"But there are plenty of billets around here." Lydia point out.

"I know. But I am a cripple and can't do any active service in this war, so I'm just minding a few poor kids until they can safely return to London

"But they are not nice children. Did you have to have children Yom Whitechapel? And that little horror with the long black pigtails" -----.

The ghost of a smile hovered around the corners A the young man's mouth.

"You mean the Cock Sparrow."

"Cock Sparrow's right. She's the cheekiest little devil I've ever met."

"Yes she certainly is saucy. Just like one of those perky little sparrows you find on the London curbs. Those with the big bright eyes and little heads that jerk from side to side."

"And what about the other five?" Demanded Lydia. "Are they as delightful as your Cock Sparrow?"

"I doubt there is another child like her." replied Donald thoughtfully as he gazed through the French windows and across the expanse of lawn to where small figures could be seen playing by the lake.

"And what about the house?" Asked the girl. "Are you going to tell me that six slum children improve it?"

Donald picked up his cup and finished his tea before he answered.

"Dear old girl. He said soothingly, "the brats have their own part of the house and Mrs Green manages them and beautifully. They are no trouble at all, and I assure you they will make very little noise."

"Well I hope they won't spoil my few days of rest," she said," it is so peaceful here after London."

"Yes it is peaceful." Agreed, Donald he was relieved to think she had changed the subject.

Unfortunately, however, the peace was suddenly broken and the air became full of shrieks and howls of anguish.

"Gosh!" Donald hurriedly got to his feet and limped through the doorway and across the lawn to wear a little mob of evacuees were in a lively conflict.

"Here." He shouted above the din, "Haven't you been told before that you are not to fight?"

Nobody heard him; nobody saw him, therefore nobody heeded him, so he pushed himself into the middle of the fray. It was not a private fight; the six of them were all in it and that six of them were in real earnest. The air was full of red faces and waving arms and shouts of agony as fists found targets.

Donald saw all this for a brief moment, then when he bent down to part two of the combatants, a hand went astray and caught him a smack in his eye, momentarily blotting the whole scene from his vision. A stunned silence followed until Donald opened his good eye and blinked it severely at them.

"She done it." Volunteered a small boy with a large nose, pointing to the Cock Sparrow.

"You shut yer row, Ikey Mo." Warned a skinny boy with a face that reminded Donald of a Codfish.

"Now for heaven's own sake, don't begin again." Begged the young man. "Who started this set to and why?"

"She did----ow !!!" Began and finished Ikey Mo as Codfish tweaked his ear.

"You kids had Better going to tea." Donald told them sternly. "No not you" ----as the Cock Sparrow made a move with the others. "I want to have a little chat with you Miss."

Whitechapel made towards the house in a great hurry. Donald seated himself on the grass. The Cock Sparrow stood in front of him, hands clenched by her sides, chin on chest a picture of misery and remorse. One glossy plait slung over her shoulder, the other dangling in front.

"Sit down kidlet," invited her host. "I know you did not swipe me for the purpose!"

The chin was lifted off the chest, a faint smile flitted across the piquant little face she set herself so close to him that her head rested on his ribs.

"Why have you been such a naughty girl these last two days?"

She did not answer. He looked down at the glossy crown of her head.

"I'm waiting child."

The Cock Sparrow still remained silent. In Whitechapel a young lady of ten didn't mind being merely naughty. She clasped her hands in front of her knees and gazed towards the place where the Willows met the water of the lake.

Quite suddenly she broke the silence.

"Is that fancy Lady your sweet 'eart? "She demanded.

"Yes," he replied half amused—half mystified.

"Well." Said the child as she rose abruptly to the feet. "She don't like us and we don't like 'er. An I betcher we love yer more'n she do!"

"You're jealous," he told her. Then a thought crossed his mind. "Did you start that fight because somebody told you you were jealous of Miss Marchant?"

"Nope! Ikey Mo says to me, he says, yor yeller now this dame's rabbi on us. Yor ferit in case yer boyfriend falls for 'er! So I sloshed 'im an, with 'e sloshed me. Then Codfish sloshed 'im an' Winkle sloshed Codfish so Elfie sloshed Winkle an' then Gertie sloshed Elfie"----

"And you sloshed me," said Donald wearily. "Oh go and get your tea!"

When she reached the house, however, the Cock Sparrow did not join Codfish and Co. In the playroom where they generally took tea period she quietly ascended the wide stairs leading to the part of the house that was forbidden to Whitechapel. On the first landing she paused and looked carefully round her, but cautious though she had been, somebody had heard her stealthy footsteps. Before she could dive into an alcove, Lydia's voice came from the landing above.

"What are you doing, you impudent little monkey? You have no business to be here at all! What are you up to in this part of the house?"

"Oh I'm just pickin' a bunch o' bluebells!" replied the Cock Sparrow.

"The noise you little beast made just now has given me a shocking headache!" The second flight of stairs was between them. They glared at each other across the banisters.

"Bloomin' good job too!" Said the Cock Sparrow.

"What?"

"You 'eard!"

"Go at once to the housekeeper and get me something for my head!"

"Would a brick do?"

"That's enough of your cheek. Go and get some aspirin or something."

"Garn' the wheels fallen off the pram!"

Then an audacious plan came to the child. Without another word she turned and hurried to her own quarters.

"Greeny. She panted, flinging a thin arm round the housekeeper's wide waist. "The glamour girl upstairs 'as part of a 'nedache. She wants you to give 'er something to make 'er sleep."

"So've I got a 'eadache but they won't let me sleep!"

"Do give her something, Greeny dear."

"All right. I'll send one of the maids up with it!"

The Cock sparrow, satisfied with that part of her plan, once again made her way to the first landing that was out of bounds to her. This time she was unchallenged in and she tiptoed along to the end of all in the corridor and peeped through the keyhole. Seeing that the room was unoccupied, she opened the door and walk in. It was Donald's study, a beautiful room and tastefully furnished. But the Cock Sparrow did not look round her, she made for the mantelpiece and stored herself in front of the photograph of a lovely lady.

"Dear lady," said the child to the picture. "I've come to see you again. You can hear me, can't yer? That's good. Mr Donald said you was his ma, when I asked him this morning. Doncher think it was mean of yer to die 'an leave 'im all alone with a hoppy foot? But maybe you 'ad to die and it wasn't your fault, still, don't you worry, I'll look ar'ter' im for yer. I won't let that woman muck 'im about. She on'y wants that pearl necklace you've got on now, she don't want Mister Don. Tell yer 'ow I know. She arst 'im to show it to 'er last night 'an I was lookin' through the key'ole 'an eyesore the greedy grabbing' look in 'er eyes." The Cock Sparrow brushed two tears from her cheeks. She was so carried away by her emotions, she failed to hear limping footsteps along the corridor. Donald stood in the doorway and frowned at the Cock Sparrow.

"I was talking to your ma."

"You'd no business to come in here. Have you seen Miss Marchant?"

"Yes she's gorn out for a long walk." Lied the child.

"I suppose the noise you all made has made her head bad. If I hear a sound from you again today, I'm going to put you across my knee spank you hard!"

"I bet you wouldn't!"

"Oh yes I will, and I'll hit you hard."

"Well don't forget."

She ran back to the playroom. Ikey Mo' was having an all in wrestling match with Codfish. Winkle and Gertie had helped themselves to the cook's cosmetics and were painting their faces. Elfie was making paper pellets and flicking them at the cat.

"Anyone in on a lark? " Asks the Cock Sparrow.

"You Betcher!"

"Well all git a wooden spoon and saucepan lid and meet me outside Mr Don's study. I'm goin' up ter see if Lady 'air oil' as got off to sleep yet!"

The little rascal again entered the forbidden part of the house. She crept to Miss Marchant's room, and the door had not been properly closed, she pushed it open wider and peeped in. Lydia was in a deep sleep. For a brief minute, the Cock Sparrow wondered if she would waken. As a precautionary measure, the Cock Sparrow tiptoed up to the bed and pulled the clothes over the sleepers ears. Then she joined Whitechapel outside the study door. Next moment, the band began to play in more than one. Donald heard the voices above the din of the 'band.'

"When banana Skins are Bl-hooming I'll come slidin' back to you."

"I'll teach them." Donald was cross, in fact he was furious. One thought was in his mind and one thought only. These young brats must be chastised as soon as possible. The sooner the better. He grabbed a stick to help him along then flung open the door.

Whitechapel stopped the band. Five of them rushed downstairs at the Cock Sparrow stood out of his range and put her tongue out at him.

"Come and get me." She invited him as she stood on the bottom stair of the second flight, "come and keep your promise."

Then red in the face, and too angry for words, Donald moved quickly towards her and she gave a squeal of fright as he nearly caught her. She dashed up the stairs like a streak of lightning Donald followed closely. But as she neared Lydia's door, she was very careful to make no noise. It was with relief and joy she saw her enemy lying as soundly asleep as ever when she darted into the room.

"Come out after room, you little hussy." Shouted Donald I know where you're hiding I found you. Come out.

Puffing and panting, the Cock Sparrow pulled the silk bedspread over the face of the sleeping Lydia and fastened it so it would not slip. She just managed to hide herself under the bed when the door opened and Donald stormed into the room.

"Ha! "He said as he made for the bed, brandishing the stick like an African warrior waving a Club. He tried to pull the bedspread off, but it was too securely fastened. Whack. The receiver, after the swipe squirmed like an eel.

"You hussy you-you-you."

Whack- whack- whack!!!

"Ow-wow-wow!!!"

"I've found you out you hussy! I'll teach you to make a fool of me!"

Whack. It was the last swipe but not by any means the least. He put such energy into it and felt rather exhausted as he walked to the door. In the doorway, he called to say sharply.

"And get out of here as quickly as you know how!"

The door slammed behind Donald, and Lydia, after a deal of fumbling with the bedclothes, sat up in the daze.

"Oh dear," she said, " he found out! Whoever could have told him?"

She slowly packed her bag. When at length she carried it downstairs, she came face to face with Donald. He was to surprise to speak.

"Yes I'm going," she starred at him. "It was the necklace I was after, but as you were thrown in with it, I much prefer to go without."

Donald was still too amazed for words. She opened the door and it slammed behind her.

He stood in the hall like a statue, until at last the meaning of her last words sunk into his brain. On his way up to the study, Donald wondered why his heart was not broken. He was feeling very relieved and wonderfully happy. He took out his pipe and sat in an easy chair. The door slowly opened and six heads peeped in at him.

"Mr Donald!"

"You kids again? "But he was smiling this time. "Come in and I'll tell you a story. Cock Sparrow you sit on my knee."—

"She done it---" Began Ikey Mo.'

"Bash 'im." Implored the Cock Sparrow.

ooOoo

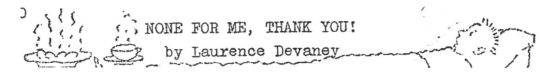

NONE FOR ME, THANK YOU!
by Laurence Devaney

Though I could not see it, I knew the doorknob was turning. Slowly it turned to the right, then back again to its normal position. Then again to the right......

It may have been my mother or my father, but I had awakened in a cold sweat and knew it was neither of them.

Luckily I am blessed with a mind that plans ahead and even now I was thinking out a plan of action. I looked around the room for a weapon but could see none, and in any case I was powerless to move.

Slowly the door opened and it came into view it was a colossal shape, filling the doorway. Higher than a man and leaning forward with hanging arms like a gorilla. It seemed to wear a suit of clothes, yet they did not stand out from it like clothes, but appeared to be moulded into its full. It was black, yet not a deep kind of black, and seemed to merge into the surrounding darkness.....The white top of the washstand stood out like a flame....

It began to shamble towards me, but I had found myself and casting off the bedclothes, I knelt upright on the bed awaiting it.

It reached the foot of the bed and gripped the rail the thing had no face! Then I flung myself at it. As my hands closed around its throat, I felt its arms round me like a vice... Its breath on my face, like an open grave made me feel sick. It lifted me from the bed as though I were a puny child, and I turned my head down with all my power pushed it into the blank substance of its face.

The struggle seemed to go on for hours in deathly silence and I knew it could not go on much longer. Slowly it bore me against the bedrail and began to bend me back.... I felt my eyeballs starting from their sockets and an iron bar came across my chest... My grip began to weaken.

Soon my spine would snap and they would find me in the morning—a horrible sight.

Then I prayed! God! How I prayed! Slowly its grip relax and I found a foothold against the bed and began to force back its head... Suddenly it flung me from itself with a ghastly cry and leapt from the room.

I collapsed onto the bed I did not faint... I had not even the relief of tears... I could not thank God for his deliverance.

The next morning I decided to cut out eating suppers!!!

ooOoo

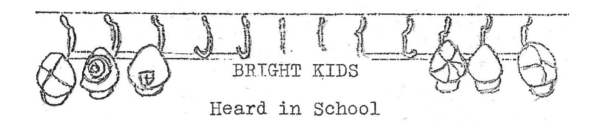

BRIGHT KIDS

Heard in School

A circle is two semicircles join together.

Cicero wrote most of his books in Latin

M. D. = Mother's darling.

A. D. = Means after dark.

A sinister woman is a woman who is not married.

They gave William the IVth. A lovely funeral. It took six men to carry the beer.

The liver is an infernal organ,

Matrimony is one of the United States.

General Wolfe was killed in his very last battle.

The population of London is very dense.

Bassanio sang a beautiful song called " Tell me where is fancy bread."

Some cows are very dangerous such as bulls.

ooOoo

EPITAPH
by R. Martyn

Here lies a poor woman who always was tired,
She lived in a house where help was not hired,
Her last word on earth were: "Dear friends I'm goin.'
Where washin' ain't done nor cleanin' or sewing.
Everything there is express to me wishes,
For where they don't eat there's no washing dishes.
I'll be where bright anthems will always be singin'
So 'aving no voice I'll be clear of the singin',
So don't mourn for me now, don't mourn for me never-
I'm going' to do nothin' for ever and ever.

Two greedy young gluttons from Streatham.
Bought 36 doughnuts and ate 'em.
The coroner said no wonder their dead.
Their mother ought not to have let 'em.

ooOoo

RENDERING an ACCOUNT
by "Charlie"

An artist was called into an old church in to repair a painting. When he presented the bill, the authorities refused to pay it until the details was specified. So the items were presented as follows.

	F.	C.
Correcting the ten Commandments	5	12
Embellishing Pontius Pilate and putting new ribbon on his hat	3	09
Putting new tale on rooster of St Peter and mending coat	2	20
Replacing left-wing of guardian angel	5	15
Washing servant of high priest	5	20
Renewing heaven. Adjusting stars and cleaning floor	7	16
Touching up Purgatory and restoring lost souls	3	06
Brightening up the hellfire and some odd jobs for the damned	7	16
Re-bordering Herod's robe and replacing his wig	4	15
Taking spots off Tobias	2	01
Enlarging head of Goliath and extending Saul's leg	6	20
Decorating Noah's Ark and putting new head on Sheba	4	12
Mending shirt of the prodigal son and washing his ears	3	13

ooOoo

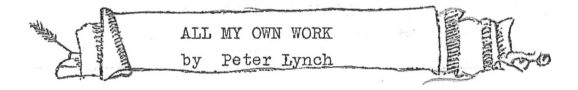

ALL MY OWN WORK
by Peter Lynch

The Editoress came up to me and asked me if I try and see if I could write a poem for a Mag. I said I tried to pull my thoughts out inverse if I could I'm glad it's not my livelihood, For those words come out all the time-I can't find words that really rhyme- and then the lines don't seem to scan - Shakespeare was a clever man - to write the things he used to write and make the last words of rhyme. A sight more clever then I'll ever be. I am not cut out for poetry. I wish I hadn't said I'd try, 'cos now I feel I'm going to cry! My disappointment is so great -- I can't write verse. I s'pose its fate!

ooOoo

THE LIGHT

From out the darkness of Wills despair,
The light appears as, some new made,
Soothing as it comes, the lines of care.
Chasing worried frowns until they fade.
Whence comes this light, is harbinger of cheer?
To whom shall we give thanks for what we've seen?
It is doubtful if these thanks are wanted here,
Provided that you buy this magazine.

ooOoo

COUGHDROP CORNER
Directed by Mary Anthony Chance

The Poem that tells of the boy on the burning deck is called;
(A) "The Wreck of the Hesperus." (B) "Casablanca." (C) "The Boy Stood On The Burning Deck."
(D) "The Flight Of Youth."
And is it by?
(A) Felicia Hemans (B) Charles Kingsley (C)Lord Tennyson.
Is an Igloo:
(A) A nickname for an Italian singer (B) A Eskimo's Hut (C) A Native of Venice.
The Monarch of England who was named Bluff was:
(A) Queen Elizabeth (B) Henry VIII (C) Charles 1ˢᵗ. (D) Charles II.
A Ciborium is:
(A) a canopy resting on column above the high alter. (B) Another name for a Tabernacle (C) The Pyx in which the blessing sacrament is kept.
And the plural of Ciborium is:
(a) Ciborium (b) Ciboriums (c) Cibori.
Answers on last page.

Waiter: "These are the best eggs we have had for years."
Customer: "Then bring me some you haven't had so long."

Teacher asked her class what Quakers were?
"People who live near a volcano miss." Called out a youth promptly.

Kind old gentleman to weeping child: Now be a good boy and stop crying."
"I can't." howled the child.
"Why not?"
"Because I'm a girl."

Uncle Mac and uncle Robert took their young nephew to the pictures. The attendant warned them that if the child made a noise they would have to take him out and get their money back.

Halfway through the film. Mac, said to Robert.

"What do you think of it?"

"Rotten." Replied Robert.

"Same here." said Mac, "Pinch the kid!"

Poor man: "Oh Doctor, my poor throat!"

Doctor: "What is it?"

Poor man: "Cigarettes. "

Doctor: "Smoking too many?"

Poor man: "No. Asking for'em."

There was an old man from Vauxhall

Who went to a fancy dress ball,

He went just for fun,

Dressed up as a bun,

And a dog ate him up in the hall.

Woman Speaker: "Generally speaking, women are"-

Nasty Man: "Yes they are!"

Woman Speaker: "Are what?"

Nasty Man: "Generally speaking."

ooOoo

POEM X WORD

Some people have tons of money

Whilst others have lots of fun

But to have the two together.

Is seldom done

Some people have heaps of trouble,

While others are always gay,

But you find if you hide your trouble,

CLUES

T' will be much better that way.

1ST. Line .....Animal Doctor

2nd. Line..... Possessive

3rd. Line..... Dress (slang)

4th. Line..... A Spanish title

5th. Line..... Not Hard

6th. Line .... True

7th. Line..... A fishes organ

8th. Line .... Wager

Answers on the last page

ooOoo

MONA'S CORNER
By
Auntie Mona

Dear fellow Club members.

In the very best of establishments, things go wrong from time to time. In the finest of Clubs, too, grouses occur now and again. Some people prefer to nurse a grievance and it spoils the friendly spirit of the Club. This is not fair. So if at any time things go wrong or you think you could improve any activity of the Club or any other matters relating to the Club, just say or write to Auntie Mona c/o of the editors.

Of course, This is not an invitation to have a smack at anybody, And do not mention names or give any personal descriptions.

Lots of love,
Auntie Mona.

ooOoo

Here are the answers
COUGHDROP CORNER
1.   Casablanca
2.   Eskimo Hut
3.   1a Felice Hemens
4.   Henry VIII
5.   All three
6.   Cibora
POEM X WORD
1.   = Vet
2.   = Hers
3.   = Tog
4.   = Don
5.   = Soft
6.   = Real
7.   = Fin
8.   = Bet

ooOoo

THE LAST WORD....

This is your own magazine. We want to hear from you. Send in your contributions, complaints and criticisms. Don't leave it to the others to do their bit, you jolly well turn to and see what you can do. That means you, and you and you in the armchair and you fiddling about with the radio. By the way. Have you paid your subs??

ooOoo

ST. ANNE'S ANNALS

CONTRI BUTIONS

Travels	in China
Of Beauty	and Love
Mona's	Corner
~ The	Ramble
Whither	etc., ~

SEPTEMBER 1941

A Letter of Thanks

We want to thank all those who worked so hard to make our first magazine a success. Of course they won't like it, but we feel that our readers should know who did what and why and how, to have our first copy ready for the feast of St Anne. So here we go --

The cover design and the drawings that adorned the pages we are to Margaret Desmond. We cannot help wondering how much midnight oil she burnt over the stop

How many of you office girls get tired of typing long letters? Mary Blessington quite cheerfully twenty three stencils for us. A skilful job, and done in no time period

Then Eileen Blessington rolled up her sleeves and rolled and rolled them off on the duplicator. And how many contributors nearly died of brain fever for your entertainment?

We thank those industrious members who gave up their Saturday afternoon fun (somewhat noisily)y to sort out and put together and sew the copies, (more or less correctly).

And we will end this letter, hoping he will continue to patronise the old firm for many many mags to come. Thanks so much.

Mary Chance and Rosemary Martin

PS. we take it in turns to pat each other on the back.

ooOoo

Our rambles have shown how badly we can stray without signpost compass or Maps.

The same is true of other journeys. Surely a Club magazine should occasionally study the path we are all taken together. Otherwise we may be straying badly.

Photos of The August Ramble.   *Fr. Koch Serving Tea*

Has the Club a purpose? It is just somewhere to "hang around". In the bad old days we mostly hung around but not for worlds would be go back to that now. The unpopularity of the "off" nights shows that the Club must be "up and doing". Doing what? Is it sufficient to aim at displays of this or that? Admittedly, they have their value, but mere physical effort is short lived. Comes the time when something more is needed... something more permanent. The church has always encouraged Guilds. They were common grounds for those of similar vocations where that mutual help and friendship could be found which is of such help when trouble comes. Activities there must be but their background is so much more important. Many times when we have seen a member's home life collapse, we have realised what Club life can mean. That is why nothing is too good for our Club. Gone is the view that the Club is just somewhere for the youngsters to be kept off the streets. To fill the Club with non- descripts would be easy. To do more harm than good will be easy too. Street corners are good enough for wasters who want nothing better. Those who join our Club must show that they are worth having. Even those we esteemed and trusted, sometimes show and our ways must part. It is a forced friendship to look the other way too often. If we hope to keep friends we must show that we put others before self. As each new side of our character is seen, true and deep friendships should ripen and stand the test of time. Then, when the years have passed away, we shall look back and perhaps to say, "I bless the day on which I joined the Club. I bless the friends I made there."

Time has again the adage proved. Old friends are best, the tried the true, God grant them their reward.

ooOoo

GETTING TOGETHER

Parish Priests in the Borough of Lambeth were invited to send representatives to meeting on Saturday, September 6TH. At St Anne's Club. Its purpose was to elect a boy and a girl to represent Catholic Clubs at a Youth meeting at Lambeth Town Hall the following week. Eric Burgess of Norbury and Josie Taylor of Vauxhall were chosen.

They then formed themselves into a Committee and called themselves the Lambeth Catholic Youth Committee. An interesting discussion about Committee elected from and by the members, But and adult in the background is desirable. All agreed that Catholic Clubs should co-operate and that Catholics generally should show more interest in Youth Movements.

The representatives from Streatham Hill would like fixtures for Football and Table Tennis.

The next meeting of the Lambeth Catholic Youth Committee is on Saturday, 11th of October, after which, meetings will be held quarterly.

The committee hope that in time Clubs will be started in other parishes in Lambeth and that there will be more co-operation between them all.

A. Bremer.

A BOROUGH DEVELOPMENT

As this is a magazine run for young people by young people, I hope an account of a meeting at the Lambeth Town Hall last Saturday will interest readers.

On September 13th. Two delegates from every Youth organisation in Lambeth,between the ages of fourteen and twenty,were present, for the purpose of expressing their views, on improvements that could be made for youth now and after the war. These young people are to be formed into a Committee to be known as Lambeth Youth Advisory Committee, until a more appealing name is found.

It was brought into being by the Lambeth Youth Committee which has been in existence for some time.

The government, for the first time in history, is to spend money on young people having reached school leaving age. This money is to be used for improving Clubs already in existence and for starting new ones.

We hope to keep you informed in these pages of the outcome of all meetings.

ooOoo

KEEP-FIT DISPLAY

The keep fit girls gave a display of drill and classical dancing. The instructress, Mrs Gibbs, assisted at the piano by Mrs Stanley and the girls themselves, made it a very successful display. The display commenced with physical jerks to music and was followed by what was billed as "Torture", but if one could judge what the merry expressions on the faces of the "tortured ones," they were enjoying it as much as the audience:

Everybody liked the "stunts" and were quite taken aback at some of the clever performances. Running somersaults backwards as well as forward, hand stands over Mrs Gibb's back and over backs. Some of our girls clearing four backs:

His Lordship the Bishop of Pella sitting near the front took a lively interest in the proceedings and in an early part of the programme rose and made a short speech of appreciation. He congratulated Mrs Gibbs on a splendid work, the outcome of which was plain for all to see.

After the interval, the performers went Greek. They wore pretty costumes of different colours trimmed with flowers leaving plenty of bare arm and bare leg. Colourful scene after the navy and white of the evening. We must congratulate them on the Greek dancing, but what happened to the country dancing? Is a fair question? Anyway it gave the show a bit of comedy as a few false steps mattered little.

A collection was made during the evening which raised 25/- for the Red Cross fund.

All you young ladies who have not as yet joined the keep fit classes, remember, a healthy body makes a healthy mind, and a good kick a day (or week) will keep the doctor away!

ooOoo

BOY'S NIGHT by Frank O'Sullivan

Of late the girls of the Club have come to think that young boys, coming to the Club for the first time are overwhelmed by the bevy of beauty arrayed before the young eyes.

They think that these young innocents in consequence become shy, and do not like to come again.

With this assumption right or wrong, in mind they asked for Tuesday night to be set aside for the exclusive use of the boys, The idea being to encourage new male members.

We started about eight weeks ago and had a large gathering on the first night. The boys seemed to enjoy it without the disturbing influence created in their young minds by the presence of the fair sex.

They played among other things: Billiards Table Tennis and Handball. Handball presented several amusing incidents. The boys main object being to see how many times they could sit on one another.

They came again the next week and for that matter every week since.

Perhaps this article may serve as a reminder to the girls, that even boys sometimes "want to be alone."

(Good thing too: Ed.)

ooOoo

QUELLE BONNE IDEE?

What a good idea it would be to have a Club Photo Album.

Mr E. Smith has offered an album to the Cause, and already a good many photos of hikes and rambles had been collected.

If anyone else has similar articles please lend us the negatives for copying (or better still present the Club with one or two crisp, clean snaps) together with place and if possible the date of the hike. Miss Joan Noakes will do the artistic touches. When a reasonable amount of snaps are in the album it will be on view at the Club, so we can proudly show new members what we do and how we do it.

And while we are on the subject of photos, no doubt you have all heard of the proposed "Photo Club" anyone interested can put their names on the list on the noticeboard.

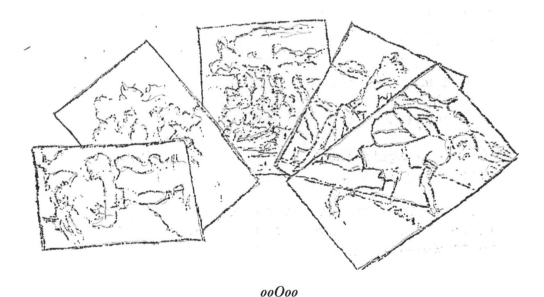

ooOoo

A QUESTION TO YOU

Can you tell a story without speaking? I was asked one day. It puzzled me very much. I thought about it for a long time before I gave my answer.

I started to imagine all sorts of things. Supposing I had a story to tell and I could not speak (what would you do "chums") I must write it. No. I was challenged again. Can you tell a story without speaking, singing, writing or acting? I was given 24 hours to submit my answer. I left the room without a word. The question seemed to engulf me. Is it possible to tell a story without speaking? I did not speak again that night.

The following day I gave my answer. Yes. I could tell a story without speaking, singing, writing or acting. This man is a marvel, I can hear you say. No, I'm not even clever or possessor of any special or supernatural gifts. My answer wasa decided <u>YES</u>. I could tell the story without speaking, singing, writing or acting. Have you found the answer yet? put your answer here no cheating. Write your answer in the square before you read on.

The answer is simple. Of course you can tell a story without speaking, etc. I am half inclined to make you wait for the answer until the next issue. But perhaps that is too long. Yes. I can tell a story with a photograph.

if you want to tell stories with your camera join The Camera Club and we will help you. Give your name to the secretary, Monica Vanstone. Become a member and put life into your photos. I'll see you in the dark room. After reading my story I hope you won't condemn me to tell all by future stories with pictures.

Click Click.

F. B. McManus.

ooOoo

OBITUARY

It was with great sorrow and regret that we learned the sudden and tragic death of our comrade Sgt Peter Lynch R.A.F. Who crashed on the morning of Tuesday, July 22nd., and was killed with the rest of the crew.

For one night he laid in St Anne's Church - St. Anne's that he knew so well, his great happiness six weeks before.---- His Requiem was said by Father Koch who afterwards officiated at his graveside on July 26th.

Our sincere sympathy goes out to Monica his widow. We admire the courageous way she is feeling her loss. In our prayers we shall remember all those Peter held dear, when he left them and step forth alone .....

IN MEMORIAM

ON PARTING
by Anthony Lynch

Weep not my friends I leave on those below.
Weep not for me. Pray for my soul,
But not with thoughts of woe.
And sympathy.
For while you mourn my earthly empty shell.
So shall my spirit sorrow for your plight Rather then, let your praises swell.
Rejoice with me that I have found The Light.
Our span below is but an interlude.
Where we prepare.
And though completion causes solitude.
Do not despair.
The fuller understanding shall soon be.
The mystery of life and death explained,
Untimely partings, grief and misery.
So done and finished, happiness regained.
R.I.P.

ooOoo

The Ramble

A Ramble took place on August Monday.
We started about 10:30 from Waterloo for Guildford.

Then we started hoofing it. After about three miles walking, someone suggested dinner and the proposal met with universal acceptance. The dinner I'm afraid developed into war on a minor scale, ammunition being in the form of pine cones. After hostilities had ceased we recommenced our walk, journeying another four or five miles to Wonersh Seminary.

Upon arrival a few of the visitors immediately commenced to investigate the temperature of the swimming pool. The rest proceeded to prepare the tea. Tea disposed of we toured the seminary and we were afterwards entertained by Father Carhill who greatly pleased us with his fine repertoire of amusing songs and his renderings on the Seminary's magnificent organ.

After thanking the priests and nuns for a lovely afternoon we started for home around 7:30. We arrived home at 9:30 having (apart from a little rain) A very pleasant day.

By Frank O' Sullivan

ooOoo

Yet another Outing to Chigwell in Essex

WHAT ABOUT A GAME

Of Cricket Rounder's / or... Just racing

ooOoo

"OF BEAUTY AND LOVE"

By P.A. Moore

All was in loveliness and beauty to Maria and Otto. The distance hills, the gleaming rays of sunshine. Flickering through the whispering trees, a gentle flowing stream wended its way through the many boulders, down to the little village of Santa Gertrude. Flowers, hundreds of them of sweet fragrance and glorious blended hues, and keeping in tune with all this loveliness, the birds singing their sweetly sounding notes to the Maker of beauty.

Hark, what is that they hear?

Childish laughter.

Yes, here they come, a golden haired boy and girl, hand-in-hand round the bend of the stream and out of sight with only the echo of their laughter left.

"Maria," Otto gently said. "Do you remember how we wandered through those woods?"

"Yes." Murmured Maria not wishing to disturb the wonderful atmosphere. A golden pause whilst each pursued their own thoughts.

"Sitting here now," went on Otto, "it seems but a short while ago. You are my fairy princess and this was first, our castle of childish fancies, and then, loves nest."

"And then," Maria took up the story, but smiling at some inward thoughts. "How sad was I when you went to Vienna to learn all there was to learn about music. I would come up here and weep, for I missed you so, and as the sun sank behind the hills, in memory of my love and his much loved violin, I would sadly sing out our Ave Maria."

"Ah, my dear old violin. It was on my sixteenth birthday Monseigneur Vanez gave it to me. How proud I was in Vienna, that very same violin would stop me from leading a life of corruption, for in it I could see Maria singing by this very stream and waiting ever so patiently for my return."

Maria smiled again.

"Then after those long years I was determined to come back to Santa Gertrude. I had passed my examinations, had great thoughts of fame, but there was one thought dominating all others, and that was to make you my wife."

"How thrilled and happy I was Otto.

"But a demure and shy little maiden it was me I led out of the church, her face all blushes!"

"Then came breakfast on the village green." Maria's face now was a alight with a pleasant recollection of wonderful day. "And dancing! How we danced until we had not any breath left."

"Poor old Pierre disgraced us by getting drunk!" Laughed Otto.

"And Dame Thessoly falls in the stream with all the best linen on!"

"Then we both quietly stole away to this our little haven of peace of love, of beauty. How I loved to dwell on you, so pure and free from ugliness of mind, not taken up with the world and its insincerities.

"My dear Otto, you make me blush." Broke in Maria. "Remember I am the almost an old woman now!"

"But still my very own wife and true love." he replied. "Then came that wonderful offer to play in the opera house at Budapest."

"Yes once more I was left with only the spirit of Otto but the years passes fairly quickly, what with looking after the cottage and the dairy and making myself generally useful in the village. It was not often we were together in those years when your reputation was steadily growing. I was shy of my husband when he told me how famous he was becoming, and I just simple peasant girl. "Then I was blessed with that gurgling piece of humanity named Paul Otto Linheimer.".

"I was nearly mad with joy. I am a father.

I shouted everywhere, I have a son, a son and then after eight years you consented to come and live in Budapest to give our son an education fit for a king, I drank a bottle of wine in one go!"

"I am afraid though, that little Paul did not want h to leave to go to school. He had a very easy time with our dear friend Monseigneur Venez spoiled him. Nevertheless, yet he had to live up to the reputation his famous father, a peasant's life was not for him."

They relapsed into silence once more.

"How strange life is," said Otto, "Here we are back again in this little love nest, taking over the cottage once more. With one small difference Otto. There are many friends buried beneath these tombstones down there in the cemetery. Such dear friends, one of whom was Monseigneur Vinez." Otto whispered, "Without whose advice so strong and impressing, I may have fallen into the corruption of the world. I pray that Paul will keep to all the paths of wisdom and beauty." Finished Otto.

"Paul Otto Linheimer." Breathed Maria. "Composer. Violinist, a leader of music, with such a fine voice, my son. We must thank the good God, my dear Otto, for his great blessings. Our hopes and ambitions are fulfilled."

The birds were singing softer their praise, the trees were whispering louder, and the sun was beginning to set behind the hills, casting a rosy light everywhere. When those two souls, no not two, but really one walked down the gentle slope of the hill round the bend of the stream and out of sight.

But let us stay a little longer end imagine Maria and Otto wending their way to the little church. Where filled with memories of youth, love and great, comradeship they kneel together while the rose rosy light shines all-round. They had contributed their best to life and unconscious to the fact that they taught others of beauty and love.

ooOoo

OLD PETER

by Rosemary Martyn

The night was bitterly cold and old Peter shivered and drew his tattered coat close about his thin body. In the sickly light of the streetlamp his face showed up. Stark a pinched against the surrounding darkness. His frozen hands were hidden in the shadows below. In one of them he held a tin containing eleven boxes of matches and in the other, he clutched a penny. It was all he had in the world. A policeman bloomed up behind the old man.

"Hi." he said to Peter, "You can't loiter 'ere. You get a move on dad! "

Old Peter moved on. For a moment the Constable hesitated then he fumbled in one of his many pockets, and found the shilling. "Hi." He shouted again, and when Peter turned round he threw the shilling into the tin of matches. "There is a coffee stall up the road, git yourself something ot!" He said gruffly.

The old man shuffled towards the coffee stall with eagerness. When the lights blinked cheerily at him, through the dimness, he caught a glimpse of a woman crouching against the wall. There was an air of misery and despair about her.

Peter did not hesitate; he threw his shilling and his penny into her lap, he told a gruffly. "You can't sit there, there's a coffee stall over the road, git yerself some think OT!"

.... to travel hopefully is better than to arrive."
R. L. Stevenson.

By Arthur Hay
For three years I lived in a beautiful valley set amid the Hakka Hill South China.

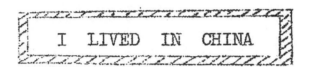

I LIVED IN CHINA

Wu- King -Fu is the postal name given to the five tiny hamlets which cluster together on the banks of a winding river. And the only way to cross this river is by a series of twenty-four single rickety planks, chinned together to prevent them floating down the river in high water. The port of Swatow is seventy miles away. There are about 6000 people living by farming. In character they are very similar to the Scottish "Crofters" especially by their eagerness for education and in their ambition to make a name and fortune for themselves.

Here in this valley, which surpasses in beauty even the English Lake District, we were untroubled by buses and tubes; the nearest railway, which was only thirty miles long, was sixty miles away from us; and the nearest road was twenty-five miles in either direction.

There is a choice of three of travelling to and from this place, by foot, as we usually did - at our own pace; by sedan chair - at the speed of our bearers; and by river - at the whim of the river which is tidal low down and which is subject to varying depths of water according to the season of the year.

When travelling on foot we had literally to "watch our step." The roads are only narrow earth parts which wind through the paddy fields, and if we were tempted to admire the scenery, we were liable to a free mud bath in one of the rice field so path runs straight for more than ten yards (probably due to a desire to complicate the activities of evil spirits, which in popular superstition haunt every sport to entrap the unwary traveller) and viewed from the hills the field in the valley have the appearance of pieces in a gigantic jigsaw puzzle. Different times of the year further complicate walking in two ways. The crops when they were grown tall altered the whole aspect of the countryside, and we were often in danger of taking wrong paths and at best adding considerably to the distance we travelled; while in the rainy season the parts were flooded and streams grew into rivers which had to be waded as best we could.

We never travel by river unless we had a lot of baggage because it was much slower. It was pretty however, and the samping on the boat was great fun. The boats were like large punts, over the centre of which were bamboo and banana leaf awnings as protection against the sun or rain. They were worked by two men, one at each end of the boat, punted, rowed or pushed and pulled according to the depth of the water. On embarking it was customary to take off our shoes so that we should not dirty the freshly washed floorboards of the boat. Then we settle down to a pleasant leisurely journey on the river. Our meals were cooked under the boards at the stern, and at sunset when the boatman tied up for the night under a bank, we made up our beds and struggled to fix the mosquito net under the awning. All day we watched the hills and the clumps of bamboo reflected in the water, buffaloes splashing, women pounding the clothes with stones at the water's edge, and cormorant fishing on bamboo rafts. At night we listen for a while to the gossip of the boatman of our own and other boats moored in the same place, and fall asleep to the croaking of the innumerable frogs in the neighbouring fields. There were but three drawbacks in travelling by boat. The river for all its beauty, was used indiscriminately as sewer and water supply; we were pestered by mosquitoes as soon as the sun set and they always seemed just to have finished a long fast; during the whole day we provided a free feast of myriad's of hungry eye flies. These have been described as "coal black demons the size of a large pin head which swing into eyes and ears with sudden maddening buzz and settle on any part of the body which is exposed." No matter how many we managed to kill, yet, since one by itself can make existence misery, although always to survive to ensure the continuance of torment.

We only travelled by sedan chair in exceptional circumstances. The chair, similar to a small deckchair and canopied with some and rain (?) Resisting cloth, is fixed on two long stout bamboo poles, and is carried on the shoulders of two or three men (the number of bearers depends upon the weight of the passenger). The men usually travel at three and half miles an hour and during the night journey I have known them to go for three hours at this pace without rest. They are jovial and talkative, and rarely seem in the least discomfort even after the longest journey. Our last journey in this way was exceptional in more respects than one. The week previous had been one of the of torrential typhoon rains and unseasonable thunderstorms. As a result the roads were in a terrible condition.

Our adventures began when a chair pole break, a thing which had not happened in the last twenty years, and my wife and baby came somewhat suddenly to earth, but without hurt. The men tried to borrow new poles, but no one seemed inclined to take pity on our plight, so my wife with the baby sat in my chair and I walked to Phi(three and a half miles)to another village where the men managed to get a pair of poles and remake the chair. Next we came to a stream which looked rather like a river. There was originally a three span stone bridge across, but the rains had eroded the farther bank and one of the spans had collapsed. My wife's chairman waded across until the front man was up to the waist and in difficulties, and then my two went to the rescue and got her safely to the other side. I crawled over the broken bridge leaving the chair to go empty. Then we got to patches of the path which were underwater, about 9 inches. We reached the village of Phak-Thap at noon and had lunch. There we were told that we could not possibly get through to the city of Kit- Yang. However, the men tried and they were most helpful throughout. We got on another half hour's journey, but in some of the places the men were waist deep in water and had to be guided by local people who walked ahead to show them where the path was. Sitting in the chairs us sitting in the water whenever the men were more than knee deep! The baggage was remarkably lucky, for in the worst parts a home-made raft got it through dry. The surrounding country was completely flooded and quite impassively, so we had to abandon the chairs and then take to the boat. After four hours on this boat, nvery hungry, we eventually arrived at the West Gate of Kit - Yang just before dark, to find that we could not get under the bridge to the North Gate, so we had to tramp through the city with the baby and all our belongings and it was quite dark before we reached the American Mission Compound Where we stayed and had a very comfortable night. A memorable last journey in South China.

ooOoo

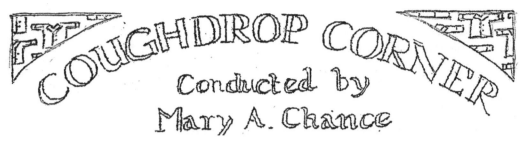

COUGHDROP CORNER
Conducted by Mary A. Chance

Is your grey matter active?

1. Quadrille is a: (a) kind of dance performed by eight people; (b) a square; (c) an instrument used by astrologist.

2. Robin Hood's best chum was called "Little John" because: (a) he was huge in build ; (b) his surname was little; (c) he was slightly "daft"; (d) he was very tiny.

3. If you were a Abacist you would be: (a) a person who studied the customs of African tribes; (b) good at figures; (c) a man who collected mosaic patterns.

4. If someone gave you some "Ceyenne" you would: (a) give it to the police as it is dangerous; (b) use it in cooking; (c)give it to the baby on a biscuit.

5. A persons who suffer from hypochondria will be well advised to: (a) try and forget it;(b) see an eye specialist.
Answers on back page.

ooOoo

"Who is that man over there snapping his fingers?"
"That is a deaf-mute with the hiccups!"
"The first alcohol ever distilled, they say, was Arabian.
"That explains those nights!"

CALLER: "I found something very absorbing on your desk.
POET: "One of my poems, I expect."
CALLER: "No. A piece of blotting paper"!

ooOoo

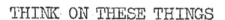

```
THINK ON THESE THINGS

    by  Rosemary Martyn
```

The sorrowing heart that gaily sings,
The bird that soars on injured wings,
The soul that to its ideal clings ----
Think of these things.

Are they not beautiful enough?
When hills be steep and way be rough,
And yet the heart of courage seems,
Think on these things.

Of beauty and of good report,
Is that domain the spirit's fort.
Where peace is king and love holds court,
Have these in mind.
To evil sounds death be your ears,
Blind be your eyes when there appears,
The ugly sight of cringing fears,
Be deaf and blind.

ooOoo

How to make a Club Succeed

1. The best way is to ignore it completely.
2. Never attend general meetings or open discussions on Club policy. Whispering campaigns are more effective.
3. If any misguided members sacrifice themselves for Committee work, insist that the Club is run by a clique and Only favourites get a fair chance. If you haven't been elected, the votes have obviously been wangled.
4. Never cooperate with those on duty. Your penny. Entitles you to be waited on hand and foot.
5. Whatever the committee does, don't forget that it is always wrong.
6. Never pay subs until cornered, but grumble if the best of everything is not provided.
7. Chewing gum, cigarette burns, et cetera., should be use with skill and ingenuity.
8. Remember that gramophone records break nicely and that table tennis-balls fit neatly into your pocket.
9. Always refuse when asked to do anything. You can then pose as a martyr when you are left out of things.
10. Make sure that newcomers are that newcomers are ignored if not made thoroughly unwelcome. Then complain if the Club makes no headway.
11. Don't forget that horseplay and hooliganism help. Furniture cost nothing.
12. Take an important part in a play. You can walk out the night before it should come off.
13. Remember that once you have done the Club a good turn, you can henceforth, completely disregard all rules.

ooOoo

Dear fellow Club members

In our last issue you were asked to air any grievances, well here is one from two people namely that the Club is unsociable.

I wonder if these people have really tried to get to know the rest of the Club members, had they joined any of the classes for instance. Have you got a voice, If so Let's hear it, or perhaps Dramatics is more in your line. Even if these do not appeal to you, Come along to the Keep-Fit, you do not have to do anything too strenuous and it's good fun. These classes starting again shortly, come along and give them a trial.

Now for a word to you who have been in the Club sometime I am sorry to say that we really are rather unsociable at times. I have seen strangers come in to the Club and no one has attempted to go speak to them. So please in future when you see any new members, do try to make them welcome. Tell them the different activities of the Club and ask them to join in whatever you are doing. As for the boys it's up to you to ask them to dance, they can't very well ask you can they? It is up to all Club members to see that newcomers are not frightened away, we need them so that when those who have had to join the Forces come back, the Club will be bigger and better than ever.

Lots of love.

Auntie Mona.

WANTED

Articles on the following subjects ......

Peace and Youth's opportunity.

Youth Organisation; Its purpose and form The Serious side of Club Life.

The Ideal Club.

Youth and the Spiritual Life.

Shelter life; Its opportunities and dangers. Things that need improvement.

ooOoo

The Answers To Coughdrop Corner

A quadrille is a dance performed by eight people.

Robin Hood's best Chum was called "Little John" because he was huge in build and his name was "Little".

An Abacist is a person good at figures.

Cayenne is a pepper used in cooking.

A person who suffers from Hypochondria should be well advised to forget it

ooOoo

ST.ANNES ANNALS

19 41

NOËL

A Letter from Reading

It was a great pleasure to receive a copy of "St. Anne's Annals" and thus, though in exile, to imbibe a breath of fresh air from dear old Vauxhall. It came between two very heavy and trying days, but the effect of reading it, turned the tragedies of the day before and the possible ones of the days to come, (do you know anything about billet troubles?") Into comedies. It was really most uplifting. All who have had anything to do with the production of this bright breezy little magazine, and with the Club where there exists the splendid spirit that makes it a possibility, are to be congratulated. A very special tribute should be paid to Father Koch, who from his first moment in Vauxhall, has thrown himself heart and soul into drawing together the young people of the parish - into making the Club something, on which, looking back in years to come, you can say, in your own words of the September issue - "I bless the day I joined the Club, I bless the friends I made there." The fact that your Club is officially part of the great National Youth Movement, gives it a stability, and to us, "the adults in the background" an assurance that St. Anne's will be well in the running when after the war, "we endeavour to restore all things in Christ" in a peaceful England.

It gave me great pleasure to be asked to write something for the Christmas Number. while doing so, a thought came which I pass on to you, as a tentative suggestion. What about leasing a page to the pens of your future members - the boys and girls away here "somewhere in England?" It would be a hold on them and would make them very interested (in a far off, awestruck way) in you all. Thus your magazine will become a net to catch souls. The children will be thrilled and you would sometimes. Have items of real interest and occasionally a few laughs. It would link us all up. Anyway it is worth considering.

As this is the Christmas Number, I will conclude by wishing all, compilers and readers of the Annals, a very happy peaceful Christmas.

"May the little hand of Christ bless your year?"
"May the great heart of Christ hold you dear. "
Sister Cecilia. S. N. D.

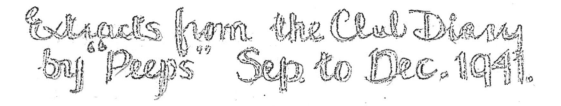

The writer may have overlooked various items of interest and also ne of old acquaintances. Should anyone have such information she will be pleased if they will bring it to her notice.

September 27. We were reminded of the old Handcrafts class and the Legion, when Myrtle Newson called to see us. We were pleased to see her and look forward to the days when she will be with us again. Natta Pye also looked in. She has been in the Land Army just six weeks and has already acquired a country bloom. We wonder if she will like it so much in the winter. Let us know will you Natta ?

October 4. Bert Nicholls, now in the army, and Johnny Gurnham, is in the Navy both on leave, came to the dance, both looking well. J.G. Has grown much taller. Their presence reminded us of Tom Cape. As anyone heard from him lately?

October 6. Steve Cain wins the boys Table Tennis Tournament – as usual.

October 11. Again at the dance – (our dances seem to be a popular feature with the boys on leave, so will members present please make them feel at home again) - we saw Jack Watson in Naval uniform. Life on the Ocean Wave suits our lads. How are our other boys from St George's? We shall be pleased to see any of you when you are on leave.

To be Cont. /-

(Two entries for the same day writer unknown)

International Youth Rally

On October 11th. I was asked to represent St Anne's at the Royal Albert Hall, for the International Rally.

The Hall was crowded with Youth from many countries and a great welcome was extended to many foreign diplomats but the greatest was given to N. Maisky!

The rally was opened by the announcer who read messages from high personages wishing the rally every success. All listened next to the Minister of Labour, the Rt. Hon. Ernest Bevin who spoke of the great tasks which lie ahead of the Youth of today and how they should fulfil them. After this we were entertained by the singing of the Polish, French and Canadian Army choirs.Young people (some with bald heads)from Austria, Greece, Hungry, Yugoslavia, Czechoslovakia, Spain, China and Russia, each demonstrated then national folk dances and songs and read messages from the Youths of their country.

The finale was a grand Tableau by the young workers of Britain, together with the representatives of the countries mentioned above and each of our men's and women's forces. Then the whole audience, including all the Allied countries and even Italy and Germany took this pledge:

To work, save, pray and fight for VICTORY.

ooOoo

MORE NEWS OF THE L. C. Y. C.

10 members of the Lambeth Catholic Youth Committee met for the second time on Saturday, 11th October at St. Anne's Club.

Eric Burgess of Norbury has been called up since our last meeting and F. O'Sullivan was chosen to replace Eric as delicate to the Lambeth Youth Advisory Committee.

We gathered round the electric fire and threw ourselves wholeheartedly into an interesting discussion of the position of Catholic Youth Organisations generally. We were all struck by the serious lack of organised Catholic Youth activity and decided that we must do something to extend the scope of existing Clubs first of all and then establish new Clubs later on.

We are keeping each other posted with activities in the various parishes in this Borough so that we can pool resources.

The committee is starting in a very small way on a gigantic task, but with your loyal support and bright ideas we may be able to give all young people in Lambeth the chance to join a Catholic Club.

J. E. Lillestone.(Hon. Sec.)

ooOoo

Diary Cont. /-

October 13. The much talked of Junior "Girls Club" was successfully launched. Every Monday at 6:30 one sees Father Madden, Estelle and Delphine and the other girls having a most enjoyable time. Estelle seems to know all the jolly games in existence. There is no need for youngsters to be lonely these days, so if anyone knows of any shy ones please bring them along. Now is the time for them to make good friends in healthy surroundings, as we know from my own experience.

Eileen Smith heard from Mary Maroon. She sends her best wishes to all and says her heart is still at St Anne's. How we wish we could still see her skipping on Father's precious floor again.

October 17. How many times do we each find that we cannot clearly put into words some doctrine of our religion? Let Father Madden help you on Friday's at 8:30. If you cannot come every week, ask him to deal with your particular difficulty one night.

October 18. Ernie Cameron appears at the Dance looking fit. We have learned that since seeing Jim Mason on this night, he has gone overseas. May God keep him and all the other lads, who have gone out there, safe always?

Danny Birkett Now out East sends many letters home, in which he sends his regards to all his friends. He says that when he comes home he intends to have a holiday in the heart of the English Country, far from sand and sea.

Johnny Colfer has practically recovered from his injuries. He sent his best regards to all his friends. He would like to have the Club, just as it is, trans-planted to Scotland.

October 20. Our boys play St Thomas's Club at table tennis. Altogether an enjoyable evening ending with a win for St Anne's.

October 26. Return T.T. Match played and lost by our boys at St Thomas's.

October 26 Midnight-

Police find Club door open. Enter cautiously. Suspicious noise! But it was only Benedict. Nothing missing - very mysterious.

October 27. Table Tennis matches again. This time between St Thomas's girls at home. Win for St Anne's looking forward to our return girls at home.

November 1. After only one practice game out Netball team against the Palace Own. We lost The more there are of you the more likely you are to get a game. Two teams have already been entered in the league. We want a third.

November 2. Another Nuptial Mass for Club members. This time it was for Cpl Arthur Blessington and Peggy Casey. We wish them every happiness. Arthur is expecting to go overseas. Recently Fred Parsons was happily posted near London so we have seen him quite a lot - he is looking very fit. He has received a long letter from Ron Pawson who is now serving with the RAF in Canada. It isn't necessary to join the Navy to see the world these days.

Mr Bryan, R.A.F. graced the whist drive with his cheerful presence.

November 3. A ballroom Dancing Class has commenced and it looks as though it will be very popular. What a pity the time clashes with our singing class. Many of the singers would like to join it but enjoyed the singing too much to leave it.

November 9. Mr Barr A.R.C.M. Gave us our second talk on the appreciation of music. It was very enjoyable and even those who don't understand a note of music, and had thought it would be above us, found it most interesting. The hour flew all too quickly for we wished to hear more of Mr Barr's rendering of examples. That he had pointed out to us. Don't be put off by the title of this class. Come along and judge for yourself. Needless to say, the added comfort of the library and the new radiogram made it more enjoyable.

By the way, have you heard the ghost in the library? During singing we thought we could hear the siren until we found it was the vibration of our voices in the grand piano.

November 10. Monica Lynch (nee Chance) joined the WAAFS to-day. We all wish her the best and hope she'll make good friends.

Joan Noakes is still at Pinewood but her spirit pervades the Club always. There is news of her every week, four she regularly writes to many of the girls. She's keeping a snapshot album of Club events. If you have any snaps of rambles, etc., tucked away please bring them along to be included.

November 14. Talk of the - - Joan Noakes is back again - for good. Look out for trouble some of you who haven't returned your library books - and it serve you jolly well right.

We have all missed Paddy O'Brien of late and were surprise to hear that she has been in hospital. We shall not be seeing her again as she is going to York. Everybody wishes you better Paddy.

So you see we are still keeping the Club active. All old members are welcome, we do not forget you. Come along and see us when you're on leave. New members are also welcome. Don't be shy, join one of the classes and get to know everybody.

To you all, far and near, we wish

A happy and Holy Christmas.

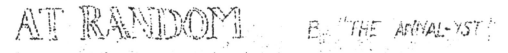

Beginning on December 10th. a Club will be started for children over 11 on Tuesdays and Fridays from after-school hours until just before Black-out. The hours will be adjusted as the evenings get longer so that each session will be about 2 hours. Games and hobbies will be held in winter, and outdoor games will be played in the summer. When the 11 - 14 age group is called up for War work the younger ones will be allowed in.

Over 50 Tate Library books are missing, apart from our own books, the Club will be heavily fined if they are not returned. We earnestly ask all borrowers to search their shelves for these books just in case one has been overlooked. The "honour" system has worked for five years, when this scheme was first started. Don't say it is breaking down now.

Steve Cain and William Boganzzi. Were elected Captain and Secretary respectively, at the football meeting recently. Best of luck in the forthcoming matches

A few more netball Matches are wanted. The league is quite small this year. We have two teams, Pella and Howard, so we can play anybody, anytime, anywhere.

Bring your friends to the three plays at the Club on Friday 12th of December, by the Dramatics Group. Admission free. Collection for the Club debt. You are sure to enjoy them.

Best wishes to St. Helen's Club just started at Stockwell. It has already proved a formidable rival!

We welcome the newcomers to the magazine staff, i.e. H Smith and R. Birkett; diarists, E Brewster; cartoonist, C

Ruffoni; Special reporter, and a batch of some 14 pavement artist. Our difficulties are increasing so just in case there is not another issue, we'd like to say how we've enjoyed helping and how willingly all have pulled together. Thank God such a spirit flourishes between all members, old and new.

An ultra-safe shelter is being built in the garden to take 30 bunks. So even if Jerry does come while you're at the Club you needn't worry.

ooOoo

St. ANNE'S THRIFT CLUB.

The share out in connection with the above Club will take place on Sunday, December 14, after the 11 o'clock Mass. For those who did not avail themselves of this service last year we are sorry but wish them better luck next year.

We shall be running the Club again for 1942. Remember the date Sunday, December 28th. and thereafter every Sunday after 11 and 12 o'clock Mass.

St. ANNE'S WAR SAVING GROUP

If you are not interested in the Thrift Club perhaps the War Savings Group will fill your requirements. You can buy a 6d stamp or a 15/- Certificate during Club times.

An agent to collect from the Club members during the week is urgently needed.

ooOoo

AIMS

S* Columba.

The provisions of the Catholic Atmosphere for leisure time activities of Catholic Youth.

To organise such use that they may appreciate the central principle of Catholic activity: UNITY

To train them, by means of a suitable program, to be capable of taking their place in the public life of the community and thus bring Catholic principles into effect in social and economic affairs.

To prepare them for organised activity in the Knights of St Columba.

Here, then are the answers to the prayers of the Catholic parents and youths. A comfortable Club with all that the youth could wish for in the way of game and amusements or more serious activities, their own meetings one on a democratic basis by their own elected leaders, a chaplain to guide them, Catholic men to help them. Parents of boys, are you going to let this chance slip? No? Well turn up any Tuesday evening at 6:15 until 8:30 for boys up to 14, and until 10 pm for those up to 21.

Remember- Catholic boys and youths only. Ask for an application form and join this nation-wide organisation.

ON KINDNESS
by Joan Irenery

ooOoo

When I was very young and still at school, kindness in my opinion always brought to mind an elderly relative of mine now unfortunately, dead. I say unfortunately, because I would have liked so much to have repaid him for the happy moment he gave me this uncle of mine had capacious pockets in his suits, into which he would put countless little packets of sweets and it was an un- ending source of amusement to him and ecstasy to me, to delve into his pockets. He was, I think, the kindest person I have ever encountered. He seemed to exclude benevolence. That is one form of kindness.

As I grew up I realise that being kind is not only giving. It hurts nobody to be civil to people they don't like. That is another way of being kind. The parable, "The Good Samaritan" bears this out.

We should, like St Francis of Assisi be kind to "all things little and poor" and this is an opportunity to mention kindness to animals. Although some people are absolute paragons of virtue and lead lives above reproach and are in general God-fearing enough, yet they treat animals with contempt and indifference and even with cruelty. The R.S.P.C.A. Is an excellent society because it must consist of people are really kind.

I do not consider philanthropist is very kind because the majority of these people are simply craving for publicity and the rest of it to evade income tax.

Sympathy, another name for kindness is a gift, a great gift and is kind naturally without being condescending or patronising is a blessing.

Why people always think of old men with white whiskers distributing gifts in connection with kindness I don't know. It usually is the poor or, people who have suffered considerably who are the generous ones and are always willing to part up with their last penny to aid somebody in trouble.

Kind people may not have their reward in this world; always remember the words of our Lord:
"Blessed are the merciful for they shall obtain mercy."

ooOoo

YOUTH AFTER THE WAR

Have you ever sat by a cheerful-looking fire in a very cosy armchair, with perhaps a little music, and dreamed dreams? If so, perhaps you have thought how fruitless war is and how little it profits us.

Considering this myself, I have concluded that the Youths of the World should have a far greater knowledge of each other. My idea is not really a new one. I think that after the war the Government should grant far greater facilities to the Youth of this country to travel abroad, and also receive young people from other countries here. I know this has been done to a certain extent, but not enough.

Don't you agree that it would be far better to see things for oneself than to listen to wireless propaganda or read tales in the paper?

There should be a great swapping of ideas and much could be learned. If it is true that so much hatred exist on the continent against us, is it not up to us to prove that this has no foundation in fact, but that it stirred up for political reasons?

Youth of today, it is up to us to build the New World! Let us make a grand job of it.

"Philanthropist"

SOUNDS in the Night by an Airman

This is a small R.A.F. Unit on the outskirts of the very much blitzed South Coast town. We do two hour night guards which sometimes seem very much longer. One night, when doing 12 to 2 period, I began to take note of the various sounds one hears, and the number is astonishing. There are quite a lot of what one can call natural sounds; the plaintiff wild cries of the colony of gulls who always come to rest on the mudflats of a nearby creek. Then the rustling of the trees as the wind sweeps through the branches. Quite near us there are greyhound kennels and the weird howling of the dogs always draws comments from the newcomers to the unit, but one soon get used to it. I have several times heard the hoot of the owl and the jarring note of the nightjar and for many successive nights in the springtime, the notes of the cuckoo. In a nearby meadow, horses are kept, and one can hear an occasional "whinny" from that direction. When the tide is in, one can hear the gentle lapping of the water against the wharves on the banks of the creek, and when the wind is right, the surge of the waves on the seashore. Then last, but no means least, of the natural sound, the fitful cries of a baby from one of the cottages.

Other sounds I have noticed are motors on the road which runs along the top the range of hills on the further side of the creek (a distance of about 3 miles. The unmistakable "swish" of trolleybuses running on a road about half a mile behind us. The foot beats and the occasional "Challenge" of the sentry at the entrance to the Naval Gunnery school, and also the night watchman doing his rounds and perhaps the sound of the car of our own Duty Officer coming up the lane.(It does not pay to miss this)

Bombers on an Aerodrome, either departing or returning after paying Herr Hitler a visit, and this Aerodrome is quite 4 miles away.

When a high wind is blowing, that particular "twang" of the telegraph wires; the chug-chug of the motor launch coming up the creek. If a raid warning comes, one sometimes mistakes this for a "Jerry" bomber. Occasionally "clanging" sound made by workman at a large works. The shriek and rumble of a train going to London, just makes one think of home and friends. And then to remind one that there is a war on, the sound sometimes the flashes of heavy gunfire out at sea.

This may sound a little "daft" but one has to occupy one's mind with something to keep awake on a warm night.

In the winter it is different, one has to keep moving to keep warm then, so there is little chance of falling to sleep!

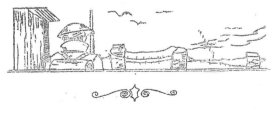

The Bodger by Lawrence Devany

. As I entered the shop, he was fiddling with a wireless set. He had on the counter, all sorts of shrieks and howls were issuing from it. The anxious owner was leaning forward across the counter, rather like a parent whose child was being examined. At intervals, that deep guttural voice come from the set, rattling off in German.

"You see," said the Bodger. "It gets foreigners but it won't hold them." He tapped the set which immediately went off into weird whistles and shrieks.

"It's not good like that." said the owner.

"No." Said the Bodger. "Best leave it till Monday."

"What time Monday?" Asked the owner. "Morning, afternoon or evening?"

"Hm-hmm - cogitated the Bodger. "Make it Monday evening."

"All right." Replied the owner. "Monday evening---Good night." He added as he walked out.

"Cheerio mate." Said the Bodger as he walked around the counter to where I stood with my bike.

"These D... baloney sets," he growled, "There're all the same. It's those D... jack switches. I've spent hours on trying this and that trying that, but now I go to the jack switch and it's that every time ! What's wrong? He asked.

"Oh." I said. "I've busted my brake cable and I'd like you to mend if you can. You see, is a cantilever and it may mean a new cable stop."

I had intended leaving the cycle and calling for it later, T but now I was hoping he would refuse the job. An intense dislike for the Bodger had come over me and the atmosphere of the shop almost choked me.

He bent down and examined the brake; he could hardly see out of his red-rimmed eyes. Then he began to unscrew the centre of the cable and gave myself up as loss.

People passed happily by outside in the sunshine. But in the shop it was practically dark. I cursed my folly in stopping here. However, I decided to stand by the bike to the end and not leave it in his precarious charge.

He managed to secure an end to the cable and screwed on it a solderless nipple. He broke the head of the screw in doing it and then I discovered he had left the collar off the cable which held it against the lever. The nipple wouldn't fit the socket which wasn't designed for it, so he started the file and then to saw it. Then he discovered that the saw blade was backward in its frame?

By this time I felt as miserable as a peasant in the Russian drama and when he finally hammered the cable home, I hurriedly paid him and left the shop without stopping to adjust the brake.

They say one lives and learns, but what agony one lives through it in order to learn.

ooOoo

ON EATING

My Very Dear Fellow Club Members.

As it is the festive season (more or less. More for some and less for others. I think it quite appropriate to give you a little skilful advice on the fine art of eating.

Some of you, I regret to say, treat eating as a frivolous pastime instead of remembering that it is a delicate art. There have been tears in my eyes when I have heard you tell each other "to go and eat coke". Coke, as you know is not an article that lends itself to mastication and it can only be swallowed at all by turning it into a vegetable. This is done by giving an 'earth choke with each mouthful.

Great experts on gastronomy have told us to chew our food well. How many of you have I seen with a jam tart? You bung the whole thing into your mouth, wag your lower jaw three times and it has gone. You should count 100 while you are chewing jam tart, and it should prove very economical and save you buying another three.

Never have more than three helpings of dinner, if you do, your friends will speak of you as a greedy hog. Unless you are a fat man with a big white waistcoat. Then you are known as a gourmet. But whether you be a greedy hog or a gourmet the result is the same. You step onto a weighing machine and the thing swears at you and throws your penny back at you.

Many of you "chew the rag" and this is not good for you and when you "chew the rag" about yourself, you afterwards "chew" at somebody else and it is bad for the soul.

One can never ascertain whether or not the Americans on this whole have good digestions. They use their jaws very much which is good exercise, and they "chew the fat", which I think is known as central 'eating.

Christmas to even good Catholics sometimes means nothing more and many trots from the sideboard to the table and this is not the true Christmas spirit you know. Do enjoy your peanut, your spot of pudding, a glass of milk, but remember all the other homes that celebrated Christmas all over the world three years ago. Then and now. They need our prayers. But nothing can ever change that true spirit of Christmas.

The Editress

ooOoo

COUGHDROP CORNER
by M. Chance

If you are handed a Winchester you would:(a) Drink it?(b) Eat it?(c) Put water or some other fluid into it?
What relation was Cupid to Psyche: (a)Husband (b)Kid brother? (c) Twin?

Is the Kremlin: (a) A river in central Moscow?
(b) The Wall Street of Moscow?
(c) The central part of Moscow?
Answers of back page.

OVERHEARD
AT THE DISCUSSION CLASS.
Instructor: Who is known as the Queen of the Nile?
Saucy young maiden: Dorothy Lamour?
Instructor: The father of history was?
Wise Guy: Adam
IN THE QUIET ROOM
1st, Girl: So you're going in the WAAF next week. Where are you going?
2nd. Girl: Well, first to X.....(mustn't tell)to train and then I shall be Waafted to a station.

IN THE SACRISTY
Alter Server: (hitting a similar article over the head with his hymn book) My that was a fine cosh I hope it didn't madden you.

ooOoo

hitlerism in the club
Leaves we might take out of Hitler's book!

1. Efficient Organisation and Staff work.
2. Real "Go to it" effort, all else ....
3. A grand purge troublesome elements.
4. Gestapo to collect the subs.
5. "Beating Up" Those who stick chewing gum under chairs.
6. Shooting actors who won't learn their parts.
7. Protection of those who revoke at whist drives.
8. A new order for those who "jitterbug" at dances.
9. A concentration camp for those who wander from the main party on rambles.
10. An iron cross for those who write for the magazine.
11. A Blitzkrieg against those who don't buy one.

ooOoo

1942

ST. ANNE'S ANNALS

EASTER 1942

SERVICE

In spite of the war, the Club is trying to hold its own. The National Association of Girls Club s has listed it as a Club for students to visit. The London Federation of Boys Club s sent an application form "in case we would like to use it" which we did. The Lambeth Youth Committee has placed it on their list of approved Club s for a recommendation to the 16 -17 Call-ups. The Board of Education Inspector expressed satisfaction when he called and the LCC District Organizer shows great interest and is always very kind to us. We take this opportunity of thanking Mrs. Diplock for the invaluable help. When we want an instructor she takes great pains to send us the very best. Old friends and new are loyal and generous. The spirit amongst our members was never better. Those who have gone will feel gratified to know that the foundation's they laid were sound. The new members are following proudly in their footsteps. And well they might. Reports trickle back of great things being done in all parts of the world by are older members. Some have laid down the lives and must not be forgotten in our prayers. Others are prisoners of war and need are prayers in their sufferings. Others again make our hair stand on end when they come home and relate their experiences. The Girls, too, are doing a fine job. We now have Girls in every possible branch of the Services. Many of the younger members are in the Home Guard, A.T.C or A.R.P. We have now formed a C.O.M Service Squad and the Squires Service Squad.

Cynics say it takes a World War to knock the selfishness out of us but we know it isn't just because of the War. Ever since Our Lord called his first Apostles, generous young soles have dedicated their lives to "service" in many religious and lay orders. Catholic youth should be of service because the way to enjoy life is to use every minute of it properly. Work hard, pray hard, play hard. The War is just one job to do. When that's over we'll tackle the next in the same spirit, using all the powers, God has given us to do the job He wants us to do in the way He wants it done, for Him or same things for those He loves, our neighbours- that's "Service".

A. P. KOCH.

ooOoo

EASTER 1942

Easter means much to some people and nothing to others. Some music Easter as an excuse for new clothes or to get married. Others look upon it as the herald of spring (if it doesn't arrive too early) and a few neither use it or regard it at all.

It was Eastertide when our Club was blitzed last April and much of what we hold dear lay in ruins. Remember standing and looking at what was left of the Club? The question of that moment was, do we carry on as best we can all close up?" You know the answer. Six and eleven silk stockings were rolled down, fashionable sleeves were rolled up. Girls with pails and flannels got down on the floor, Boys got up onto the roof.

Everyone did their job and worked with a will. By teatime we all resembled a gang of Negro all-in wrestlers. Did we enjoy our tea that day! There we sat round the Table surrounded by daffodils, bread and jam and grime and blast and every grubby face happy and contented. We hardly dared to breathe because the walls were "out" and we didn't want them to fall.

Forgive me for mixing the Resurrection of the Club with the Resurrection of Our Lord, but just as His Resurrection should make us better Christians, so should the rising of Our Club make us better Clubites. If the cap doesn't fit do not pull it on. Is too much limelight spoiling you it? Well, this Easter, ket each one of us really try to make ourselves worthy members of the Club that means so much to us.

Wishing you all a happy Easter.

BY THE EDITRESS

ooOoo

Extracts from the Club Diary

Since the last issue Frank.O'Sullivan has joined the RAF and Monica Vanstone the WAAF we wish them the best of luck.

November 30.1941.

Tom Stock home on leave. Looking fit

December 7.

Behold our Christmas number. We hope you all enjoyed reading it as much as we enjoyed preparing it. Jack Greer writes sending the best wishes. Thanks Jack. We hope these Mags will keep you in touch with us.

December 12.

After weeks of hard work Dramatics Class presented three plays. The first one, a skit on modern youth, was well done, but the girls did not seem to enjoy playing their parts. The next was very funny. Now we know how to make Mulligatawny without coupons. The third of the BISHOPS CANDLESTICKS was grand. It was fine to see the Boys doing so well. More please.

December 29.

The Club's a beehive. Costumes for the fancy dress, plans, excitement: Reason New Year's Party!

December 31.

It at last what a party food? Each had to bring sufficient for own consumption? GEE! They must eat a lot. Party went well. Costumes were the simple and effective especially. "No Coupons Left" Just a few shabby clothes. Easy? The large numbers made hard work of the games.

January 1. 1942.

Happy New Year to all, far and near.

January 4.

The C.O.M Reunion party was a great success. Mr. Hyde was a guest and the Boys vary considerably did the work for us and afterwards helped to get the greatest fun out of the games. This was a smaller party held in a small hall, compact and more enjoyable. When we came to the game of the QUEEN OF SHEBA (censored – Ed.)

January 10.

Usual routine again. Bitterly cold, but attendance was good. By the way Francis Desmond! It is most irregular to bring snow into the Club. And surely you weren't rolled in it.

January 24.

Netballers have only lost one match so far. In future, no interval during dances. Teas on sale from 8.30 to 9.30 and owing to rationing these are limited. First come, first served. This applies to every night.

January 28.

Barbara Abram announces that at five 'o' clock and a wee baby boy he was born to Daphne and Ernie Smith. A chip off the old block we hope.

January 29.

A crowd of us went to the Strand Theatre to see Donald Wolfit in HAMLET. Maybe we could arrange more parties – any suggestions?

February 1.

Grand to see so many G.S.A. Girls at 9.30 Mass this morning. Father Madden, Estelle and Delfina are doing a great job.

February 4.

Boys play Westminster Catholic Club at a Table Tennis. Win 18 - 7

February 12.

No coupons left? Join the needlework Class. Mrs. Stuff is the magician. She will help you to turn your old clothes into new. Tonight she showed us how to make a long coat into a skirt and bolero.

February 14.

Why is Father Koch looking so gay? I hear he has a secret which we have been trying to get out of him all the day.

February 15.

At Music Appreciation the secret came out. Father Madden says that the great Solomon is to come and play for us. What excitement! We can hardly contain ourselves.

[Authors Note: Solomon was a Concert pianist of great notability born in the East End of London in 1902 a child prodigy without any formal tuition his talent was recognised when he was seven. He gave his first concert in 1912 at the age of ten a great virtuoso of Beethoven broadcasting the full 32 sonatas for the BBC.]

February 19.

The Boys played the Table Tennis return With Westminster Catholic Club at home and beat them 22 – 9 five un-played.

February 22.

Another Club couple were married today Paul Palumbo and Maisie Wheal. We wish them every happiness in future. This afternoon at Squires played Worcester Park at Table Tennis and won. 18 – 7.

February 25.

The Keep- Fit Class gave a display of their work and Dances. All praise to Mrs. Gibbs and Mrs. Stanley who has played the piano since the Club was first formed in 1935.

February 27.

We were terribly sorry to hear that Jim Mason was taken prisoner in Singapore. Prayers Please.

March 1.

Solomon came and played Beethoven's Sonata "Waldstein", one of Chopin's nocturnes and his Polonaise. – It was absolutely grand. We still can't believe it was true.

March 2.

The Class are preparing a passion play for Friday March 27. The Choir are to sing some of their beautiful motets and chorales. The C.O.M. and G.S.A., held a joint meeting to form a Service Squad. In future we are to undertake any jobs that Father Koch and Father Madden want doing. Volunteers are wanted. There are lots of jobs, remember many hands make light work.

March 3.

Grand piano disappears from Library. Its space was badly needed. A smaller one was given by Mr. Wadley will take its place.

March 5.

Squires form Service Squad.

March 7.

Miss Allen called. Paddy O'Brien is going into hospital for a long time. She is up North and will be glad if her old friends will write. H, Smith has her address. Please remember her in your prayers. Miss Allen's Brother Donald last week was killed in an air crash.

R. I. P.

March 9.

List of jobs is up - many have volunteered but more are wanted. So don't be shy.

ooOoo

In the 1941 Christmas issue of St. Anne's Annals - Sister Cecilia sent a Letter of thanks and a suggestion that the evacuees of St. Anne's could write articles for the Magazine if a page could be provided.---therefore

THE FOLLOWING TWO ARTICLES SUBMITTED- EMPHASISES THE IMPORTANCE OF WHAT THE CLUB MEANT TO SO MANY OF IT'S YOUTH MEMBERS EVEN THOUGH EVACUATED. From 1939 to 1944.

SOME ACTIVITIES of ST ANNES on READING

CONCERT. We gave four performances of A.A. Milne's "Princess and the Woodcutter" Everyone who saw it expressed great pleasure, and so we were we played for our hours of preparation. Maria Spanswick was the Princess, her three Prince-Suiters were, Ada Bosworth, Betty Elligott, and Maria Richie, but the lucky bridegroom was the Woodcutter, Pauline Brackstone. (Maureen Bedding 12)

CHURCH SINGING. Midnight Mass was at 4.00 PM Christmas eve we sang Mass II in a very crowded church, at the offertory, the Adeste was sung in four parts, the Tenor and Bass being led by the Priest, and the Soprano and Alto by the Girls of the St. Anne's. The same Girls sang 43 Carol Services in St. James's, English Martyrs, and Carmelite Church. We loved learning the Masses and have undertaken to do one a month at English Martyrs during Lent we are singing Mass X, and are busy preparing Mass I for Easter. In the Parish Magazine here, we were spoken of as "sweet voiced and highly trained children", which of course quite set us up. But we were even more pleased why are remark of one Priest, who said we were "Liturgical Minded"

(Margaret Beckwith 13)

COUNTRY DANCING AND NATIONAL DANCING. Having you use of a hall, belonging to Wesleyan Church, we have great opportunities for dancing which we all love. We know 38 English country dances, and about 20 of other nations. The schools here were lately Classified into (a) proficient (b) good (c) learners. You will be pleased

– 97 –

to know that St. Anne's Girls were Classified as proficient, with one other London school.

"One up for Vauxhall." (Ada Bosworthy 14)

ENTERTAINMENTS. At Christmas time, we had a jolly party with good things to eat and games and dances. We also saw the pantomime Robinson Crusoe and included the famous Conjuror Gingalee. Besides these two big events, we were entertained to the pictures by our Captain Andrews- a big friend to us. We saw "Boystown" and enjoyed it, though most of us had a little cry too. Another excitement was a party given to those who have been faithful to the church singing. Father Barrett was our host in the Jacobean restaurant.

(Betty Elligott 14)

THE NEW CATHOLIC YOUTH SOCIETY. In Vauxhall, you are so used to a splendid Youth Centre, that you cannot realise what a thrill it gave us when one was commenced in Reading, in February. All between 14 and 18 are eligible, and some of us liked it so much, that we have continued and enthusiastic attendance. We are full of ideas-we are to have a dart board, Table Tennis, games, library, etc.- We are also going to have cookery, tap dancing, singing, shorthand, and even a "Brains Trust." In the summer, we hope to have cycling Club, swinging, Tennis, hikes and picnics- aren't we ambitious? It was when the article in the UNIVERSE. "City of Boys and Girls," was read aloud to the members, and we knew our own Vauxhall was a leader in the Catholic Youth Movement.

(Marie Spanswick 14)

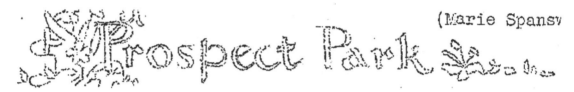

During her first few weeks on evacuation we spent our days in Prospect Park. It became the open air school or hundreds of children from London. It was a great novelty to us and we all enjoyed it. I don't think the teachers were quite so happy. I heard sister trying to cheer one of them up, by saying.

"Anyway you have lovely fresh air." and the reply was.

"I have had enough fresh air to last me till the end of my life."

Let me tell you a little about the Park. It is the largest in the south of England, and is 120 acres in extent, situated in the highest part of Reading, and is very open. There are pitches for netball, football, cricket, Bowling Green. I expect in London, we would call it a common. Nature takes its own course in this Park. There are no notices saying keep off the grass, no flowerbeds all over the place. Instead, bluebells and primroses grown in the woods and you can walk on the grass without being ordered off. There is a mansion on the hill where the family, who used to own the land, resided. Since the park became Crown property, this mansion is a refreshment place. In all seasons, Prospect Park is beautiful but most of all, I like it in spring, when the buds are coming out, and the trees begin to lose their look of loneliness. The grass gets its soft velvety shades back again, and birds begin to seem their souls of gratitude.

(Pauline Brackstone 12).

ooOoo

Extract from "The Advertiser's Weekly"
(without comment lest we be accused of boasting)

In August 1939, 19 year old Stanley Fisher left for training with the R.N.V.R. I'll be back in a fortnight he told us all

But within a fortnight young Fisher was en- route for the Mediterranean in the anti-aircraft Cruiser Coventry. Able seaman Fisher has now been awarded the Distinguished Service Medal for the gallant conduct when the "Coventry" went to the aid of a hospital ship "Aba", as she was being attacked by a German planes of Crete, last May. 18/5/41

He was in a gunner director tower when a bullet from an attacking Junkers passed through the body of Petty Officer Sephton and wounding Fisher although mortally wounding Sephton carried on setting a magnificent example to Fisher who was also able to carry on thus maintaining the efficiency of the director.

Sephton was awarded a posthumous VC for heroism that may well have saved the "Coventry" and the "Aba"

Fisher joined the advertisement staff of the "Daily Mail" as an office boy at the age of 16 after leaving the Salesian College Battersea. His widowed mother heard of her son's award from his colleagues, on the "Mail." She said.

"I only heard of Stanley's part in the action off Crete when some Boys off the "Coventry" came to see me. He never said anything in his letters. He was in hospital in Alexandria for six weeks, but he is at sea again in a destroyer now. Fisher's elder brother a Sub Lieutenant R.N.V.R. Was lost in one of H.M. Ships last May.

[Authors Note:-Sub lieutenant Cyril Barnsley Fisher died 6/5/41 H.M.S. CAMILO]

ooOoo

HIS THOUGHTS
by Pamela Moore

Gaily coloured butterflies flitting from flower to flower, the melodies of the birds singing in the foliage of numerous trees and the air breathing of roses, spring freshness the loveliness of life everywhere.

Former pilot officer Anthony Benlow was sitting in a bath chair for the first time since his crash in Scotland. He was thinking very deeply and at the same time drinking and simple splendour of an old Sussex cottage set in an old world garden.

Life... What is life?...Nearly had my light put out, I suppose it's a wonder why am still in the land of the living.... June....Eight months. Eight months! Can't be?....And only just beginning to sit up and take notice.....Doesn't seem so long ago....Eight months. Yes, a few miles from our base when the engine gave out. That sickening feeling in the stomach, the heart in the mouth...Down, down, faster, faster, round and round then deep oblivion,

No use thinking about that now. Lucky for me we didn't come down in Germany. It had been a large scale raid on Hamburg that night fires everywhere, at times we were even flying through smoke. We dropped our bombs.....Lord, I hope they dropped on the target. Hellish this war....Why can't we live in peace?

"Doctors tell me I shan't be right for ages yet.....He addressed a piece of ivy that was swinging to and fro in the gentle breeze. Life's just like you, good luck, bad luck, sickness, health peace and war, lastly life and there."

Strange thinking it over....We all set out full of beans, there is a certain queer thrill in the idea of courting death and daring the unknown.

Jimmy Turner, (what a chap) painting slogans on before we left. Forever dancing and making the Girls danced too! He had a different one each night and broke his heart each time one let him down. Sentimental Jimmy! How we used to pull his leg.... Now there is no more Jimmy to Joe with about his flirtations. I expect there are many Girls too, who will be a little sorry that there is no more Jimmy amuse them with his antics.

Edward Dennaby, our dear old idealist. That feeling in his presence of being on one's best behaviour. What was it? That noble brow, a wayward lock of hair falling across it, those penetrating eyes or the finely curved mouth or perhaps most slender sensitive hands which drew notes of wonder from his violin. He hated the idea of war, but loved his England. He looked for all that was a beauty in life. Yes, why did he have to die in the ugliness of war?

Paddy O'Rouke with his Irish temper and laughing Irish eyes, forever finding himself in some scrape or trouble.

Many's the time we had to dig him out... And what he was going to Hitler! A proper fighter with no thought for himself, but of getting the job over quickly and settling down in his Emerald isle.... A pity he could not continue the fight, for he was the true type.

Helmouth Scarnberg, usually known as Harry. An Austrian born in England, he had become a British subject, he was fighting for liberty and that people might enjoy freedom, but half his heart was in Vienna. He would almost sob when Edward played his violin, especially the lilting Viennese waltzes. He loved his wine and drank to life that people might enjoy it as he did; a fascinating chap of a very mixed temperament, one minute gay, the next in dreams of its own making, but who got on well with everyone. Be true lover of life who was finding out the mysteries of death.

"They were a grand crowd." He thought on. Of the good times they had had together....I wish I could have continued their work for them, but I am out of the war for good now, I suppose. I feel a bit of a twirp while the other fellows are going to it. Still I suppose lucky... Yes very lucky."

His attention was suddenly riveted a live little figure coming through the yew trees. Tousled brown curly hair, eyes with two little devils dancing in them, a cute little turned up nose, a mouth, a sweet little mouth that could pout, smile, quiver and generally melts one's heart, simple pale blue dress, two arms that tenderly clutch a Mass of red and green roses and two sandaled feet stepping jauntily along. It was Stella. She left off singing as she came near and smiled that beaming smile which said. "I love you- isn't it a glorious day, you are feeling better? A slight concern, and then-"Isn't life really grand?"

She struggled to put all the roses in one arm, gently pushed his hair of his forehead, kissed it and a red rose dropped in his lap, whether by accident or not.... She then proceeded to put the roses in a coloured bowl humming her favourite tune "Rustle of Spring."

Yes, Stella would make their home a shiny star in a topsy-turvy world. Perhaps they would be able to teach others that so much happiness and peace starts in the home, if every home had those ideals....At this point he fell asleep. Stella, who had been carefully watching him fetched a little stool and leaned her head against his knee. She too, had her dreams.

ooOoo

The IMPORTANCE or being ACCURATE
by Owen Porter.

The narrow high street in the village of Burrow –under –Slough was almost deserted on a quiet sunny afternoon as Mrs. Tim's arrived to do her bi-weekly shopping.

The only signs of life were Mr. Carter the village butcher standing in his doorway and a cat sunning itself on the windowsill of the "Beehive" the village local.

Mrs. Tim's advanced down the high street, greeted Mr. Carter, which he returned and remembering that it helped the rations if you were friends with the tradesmen, commented on it being a fine day. She went into the shop and saw Mr. Carter was excited about something.

"Did you 'ear the plane last night Mrs. Tim's.?" Said he.

"For sure." She replied. Wasn't him that was afetching me from me bed ad so late ad all."

"Aye." Replied Carter, "Me and Joe was just aleaving the Beehive, yonder when we 'eard 'un. Joe says to me. There's Jerry." says he, "an' no warnin'." Why we might 'ave easy been blown up in our beds for all we'd known."

Mrs. Tim's was not going to be outdone by this.

"Yes Mr. Carter I heard him swooping over me House and I never had time to get under me Table if he'd dropped his packet then. Me sister, she came down from London last Thursday you know, she was so shook up be it, she be going back to London today, to see her doctor, she suffers with nerves. She came over all funny afterwards......

Later Mr. Jones was talking to the carrier from the next village..... "Aye John, that jerry we ad last night. 'e swooped over 'ear. And Mrs. Time's sister go such a right, she's garn back to London to see a doctor."

"Poor dear, she'll probably be a nervous wreck for the rest of her life, 'ave to go to 'ospital, 'ome broken up and all. "Said John sympathetically. Mr. Carter agreed.

With these planes flying around, dropping bombs, 'an no warnin' why me an Joe were comin' out of the Beehive.......

The Carrier on his daily rounds told this story so many times, getting so worked up, that by the time he'd finished his journey the tale ran something like this.

"Well Mrs. Dean if it hadn't been for Mr. Carter's presence of mind he and Joe would 'ave been killed stone dead, they had no warning, down come that plane and let's go of a couple, Carter pulls Joe down in the road, so they were all right, but Mrs. Tims sister, well, they've taken her to 'ospital in London......

Mrs. Dean's husband according to custom called in at the "Banstead Arms" for his drop of "Mild" about closing time that night and had a chat with Fred, the barman,. To him he told the story.......

'As 'ow me wife 'eard that bloke Carter an Joe Field, the plumber 'ad been near killed last night when at Burrow, an as how two women Mrs. Tims 'an her sister 'ad both been rushed to 'ospital."

"They must have been badly knocked about Bob." Said Fred.

" That they was." Responded Bob. Injured for the rest of their lives I reckon., but Carter and Field were worse, they were both out in the open 'an were flung all over the place." A tall thin young man leaned across the counter, and spoke to Bob.

"I'm a reported from London. Can you give me any details about this plane crash?"

"I reckon as 'ow I could like." Said Bob. But I gets might thirsty-like when I talks." Bob decided that two unexpected drinks were worth a good story. "Well Mister it was like this 'ere. We all of us 'eard jerry going over last night, and Fred and me 'eard a big wallop, sometime after thy'd gorn over."

Fred nodded he would fill in the details later.

"I ses to Fred, I ses. I reckon that's a jerry down over be Burrow –under Slough! That's a village some twelve miles over the hill. Well this morning as ever was John the Carrier comes in an' tells us as 'ow this bomber came down on Mrs. Tim's farm, blowing the House down 'an' badly wounding Mrs. Tim's and 'er sister, an' old Carter the butcher and Joe Field the plumber, But. This was Bob's masterpiece. "It weren't no Jerry it were British Bomber one of them they calls a Wellington. I seed it afterwards with me own eyes".......

Ten minutes later he was phoning his report:

"British Plane outward bound on bombing raid over France, crashed at Tim's farm Burrow –under- Slough Sussex, at about ten 'o' clock last night. Four people injured. Two seriously. Houses down and damage to farm buildings. Explosion heard for miles.

In the office of the DAILY FOGHORN

"That new reporter sent in a good story to-night. Bill." The editor looked up from the cartoon he was studying.

"Did you get it through the censor? Its dangerous copy to handle you now old man."

"Sure. I promised to be a good boy and put it on an inside page, in small caps. There's such a thing as freedom of the press Newton."

"Okay. Go ahead, you had better head it 'Bomber down in Sussex."

A few nights later. "Germany Calling... Germany Calling.....A Report has reached Berlin to-night of the success of one of our fighters over England a few nights ago. On reconnaissance over the English coast the fighter encountered a British bomber on its way to Germany. After a brief combat the British plane was shot down in flames. A report afterwards appeared in the English Press states that six people were killed in the industrial town of Burrow –under- Slough when the bomber crashed on a row of Houses. Apparently the English are not safe from their own bombers.

So ends the story. It is not true, but you have heard, and repeated dozens of them. Next time you hear a story check-up first, before believing it, or passing it on.

ooOoo

FELLOW PASSENGERS

By Joan Trenery

I have often passed the time away, whilst on a tedious train journey by studying my fellow passengers. Often I have come in contact with the prize bore of train journeys. He is the seemingly bluff hail fellow well met sort of chap who immediately plunges into a record of <u>his</u> blitz nights of the heaviest bomb that fell near him. Of the fiercest incendiary on <u>his</u> roof. Of the largest plane that just skimmed over <u>his</u> House. Of his magnificent courage and "sang froid" through all these great experiences. This tale is told many times and each time it is garnished with a little more colour and completely less true.

As a bore, this chap had a good companion in the tall angular lady who with tightly compressed lips just "sits" and never a word, though her sniffs are very eloquent when one asks for a window to be opened or permission to smoke.

My particular bete noire he's a breezy young man who has been everywhere had seen everything and has all the moves of the war mapped out to the nearest detail and who implies mysteriously that he knows someone who he's a relative to a fellow who in turn he's friendly with and someone at the war office. I hope I am not of a violent disposition, but I have very murderous inclinations towards these folks. Have you met them?

<u>Afterthought.</u> I wonder what kind of fellow passenger I am?

(Now, now, Joan, let sleeping dogs lie — Editor)

ooOoo

Written to the memory of the priests who led the existence of hunted criminals, risking starvation, torture and death in order to keep the flame of faith burning in England during the reign of Elizabeth and the Jacobites. Especially to the memory of Francis(little John) Owen who contrived most of the secret holds and hiding places in catholic houses which afforded sanctuary to many a priest pursued by Topcliffe and his gang of fiends.

Off all the ancient country houses now standing in England, perhaps Harvington Hall contains the most interesting collection of secrets. it is a great gabled pile of redbrick and sandstone standing against are background of sombre trees and surrounded by the dark waters of the moat.

Harvington Hall is in Worcestershire. it lies a mile and a half from Chaddlesley Corbett near the main road between Kidderminster and Bromsgrove and it now belongs to the Catholic Diocese of Birmingham. It was in such a state of decay that rigorous restoration as destroyed much of its charm but the romantic spirit of a bygone day still lingers on. Anybody is allowed now to explore the old place echoing rooms, you wonder what tales of excitement and hair -breath escapes the crumbling walls would tell if only they could speak.

to a surveyor who wished to measure up the Hall, the place would be a nightmare, the close apart from secret passages and chambers and falls floors, it is a perfect tangle of staircases and corridors and doors leading off at all angles and no to floor levels are alike.

Let us begin our tour of inspection by crossing the bridge and entering the main gateway where if we turn our eyes right, we will see in the wall a slot about 7 inches wide. This was used as a recess for food or communications to be collected by the person in the hide built in the angle of the wall between the gateway and the courtyard. In those days there was an iron plate with the ring to tie up a horse fitted over the hole in the wall and the person in hiding was able to bolt it on the inside. To get to this hiding place we have to go into the house and climb the main stairs to a room on the first floor which is known as the "reception room." This is a long low room with a beautiful fireplace and on either side of this fireplace are doors, both exactly alike. One is an ordinary cupboard, but the other opens onto a few feet of passage and the whole floor lifts up disclosing a small room some ten feet below. There is a tiny fireplace in there and between the fireplace and the wall is the whole for the food to be passed.

Let us now take a winding stairway to the top of the house. Put on your rubber plimsolls because we are to do a bit of rafter climbing and you will probably slip and break your neck. Hurry. Here we go. don't you think the smell of rotting wood work and mildew and the dark corners and shadowy twists in the staircase make funny quivers run down your spine? I forgot to mention that father John Wall the last priest to be caught and hanged in England sheltered here and was caught near here...

And wasn't Topcliffe a beast! Perhaps he's in Hell and he sometimes wanders around here to inspect some of the secret rooms which deprived him of many a victim. We may meet his ghost in a minute ... all right I'll stop it. we are at the top now in a perfect mass of attics, standing before a great confusion of doors and passages, to the right is a room still known as a nursery and beyond this is the chapel. They have put in a big modern alter now because Mass is occasionally said on the spot where the original alter stood. This is the big one, but Harvington's first alter was a little portable one and if you will look at the skirting of the wall facing the window, I'll show you where they hid it when spies were about. That's it, that little notch that looks like a flaw in the woodwork. Kick on it hard - that's it. Now see the middle of the floor rising like a trapdoor. In there they hid the Vestments and all the sacred things. It is empty in there now, but we will not put our hands in there. Just say a small prayer and close the floorboard lid down again. Above the chapel in the lath and plaster of the Gables in the very apex of the roof, are the remains of a perfect little secret room with the runway through the rafters. Here we do a spot of rafter climbing. The walls of the attics are flimsy partitions which do not reach the ceiling so by stepping from one roof rafter to another, you can cross the whole house without touching the floor or passage. all along this elevation path are signs of secret places where a fugitive could pause for breath and reflection. Restorations had destroyed the evidence of the secret way down to the ground floor and the moat, which is a great pity. We won't stop to cross the whole house via the wooden beams, so let's down to another part of the attic where there is a remarkable hiding place fewer than five solid -looking stairs. Two of these steps are movable and beneath them is a cavity large enough for a man to hide in. It is a tiny room with a door that was once very solid and this leads down to a room six feet high and five feet by nine. This little chamber was contrived by putting a false ceiling in the Butler's pantry below. There was a mattress roughly made from weeds out of the moat found in here and it is believed Father Wall slept on it just before he was captured.

There is a little room on the first floor known as Dr. Dodd's library and there are two cupboards in it. The walls are made of brick laid between wide oak uprights. One of these wide beams of would tip up on a pivot and can be bolted from the inside. This is and entrance to a long tunnel leading under the moat and ending near Gallows Pool.

There is another room known as the South Room. On the left of this is a small scullery with a modern sink. The whole of this floor lifts up and reveals a chamber of about six feet deep and six feet square. Jump down into it and you will see a square hole in the wall two feet or so above the floor level. Look through this hole; you will see a deep shaft which runs from the roof to the chamber below ground level. Put your hand into the shaft and you will feel a rope which is guided by a bracket in the wall to work a pulley. The big wheel is fixed in the roof. This shaft is hidden from the outside by daub and wattle and thick beams. in those old days before the greater part of a shaft had fallen in, anyone could squeeze into the shaft and lowered themselves down to a room that gave exit onto the moat.

These are but some of the mysteries of wonderful old Harvington Hall but were these indeed the left, could one ever tire of exploring these time -worn rooms and passages?

Can we help admiring or even envying the nerve of our Priests of those days? Never let us forget what they did for the Faith in England. And you Francis, little John Owen.....You were indeed loyal to your Faith, faithful to your ideals, and heroic in the way you took your torture and death.

ooOoo

THE DAFFODILS.
From out of the cold dull grey winters span
You come, an early messenger of spring.
Awakening interest anew in man
A joy alike to beggar or to king
A flash of colour in dull city streets
Waving carpet spread in rule fields
To gladden every knowing eye it meets
Or in whatever bower its fragrance yields
Might not these be sweet messengers of God?
To lift our mundane minds to higher things
And in the calm that contemplation brings
Strike Fountains in our minds and Aaron's rod?
Well might I live a life of joys thrills?
While I see beauty in the daffodils.

STUFF and NONSENSE

Mrs. Stuff, our new needlework teacher was, before her marriage, a Miss Taylor. Her mother's maiden name was Cotton and her grandmother's was Holland.

Such a combination of names set the conversation going one evening, on these lines –
"A real joke isn't it? "
"What is, I don't cotton on."
"Never mind, it's immaterial."
"I think you want muslin."
"That's where we don't see eye to eye."
"Oh I see the point right."
"It's about time you tacked on."
"Oh don't be a wet blanket"
"Darn you! Shear off."
"I will, this is getting threadbare."
"It certainly is patchy."
"Yes. We've got you taped "
"Sew long."

ooOoo

St ANNES ANNALS
FEAST of St ANNE
JULY 1942

An article published in the July 1942 Annals - (author unnamed possibly the Editor.)
Illustrates its purpose the Club Magazine was intended for, entitled:-

ooOoo

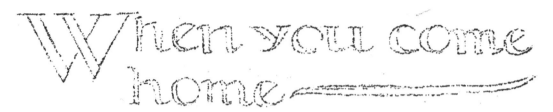

When you come home

It is easy to forget when compiling a magazine that it is mainly for those who are miles away and who like to know how things are going back home. Of course the old place isn't what it was in your time. Not by any means. After the war you can come back and say" I told you so I knew you couldn't have done without me."

We are waiting for you, if we are still here, to come home and put the place on its feet again. But that's going to make a senior Club of it isn't it? Because you're getting old of cause. Awkward!

The Club always was and must remain primarily a Youth Club. That means that older groups must come on different nights from younger ones, unless we can get sufficient accommodation to allow separate groups to meet has different rooms on the same nights. The Settlement Council has kindly placed some more excellent rooms at our disposal, thanks to Miss Walsh, but that means for obligations for the Club to meet. If it is laying the foundations of a good Club for the future it is worth taking. At the moment as fast as we expand and take on more liabilities so we seem to lose our assets in the shape of old members. One after another they are called up so, doesn't forget to pray that we shall be able to keep going until you return and incidentally mention our debt to your affluent friends. In the meantime we are doing what we can to further Catholic Youth work beyond the parish boundary. A Priests Study Group of some eighty members from four different dioceses meets here monthly to study various aspects of Catholic Youth work. \ They organise retreats for Boys and Girls and are holding a course at our Club for training Catholic lay-folk as Club leaders this is being attended by 160 people. Following this there will be a retreat and perhaps other developments. This of course is not just to advertise the Club but to help others to work for those who leave Catholic schools. Local Youth centres are springing up by the dozen but they are mostly pagan affairs and our young people are becoming pagan. We must show that Catholics have something better to offer than morally, intellectually, and socially. Yes, when you come home there's still a full-size job waiting for you and more fighting to be done- of a different kind.

<u>SUNDAY APRIL 26th</u>. Empire Youth Sunday.
We contributed to the world-wide of observance of this day by holding a Youth Rally in the Church; every seat

was filled. Father T Dullahan. S.C., Gave the address speaking of the part "Youth" was playing and was to play in the world, and stressing the necessity for return and strict adherents to Christ's teaching in order to achieve progress. Afterwards we were "at home" to the visitors. Entire Club building filled to suffocation with visitors and members wearing beaming smiles and fighting tooth and nail to procure cups of tea from perspiring "canteen duty" members also wearing beaming smiles!

April 28th.

In future the Club will close on Tuesday as. So few members turned up on that night that it's not worth the opening.

May 2nd.

The Dramatic Class entered an extract from "KING LEAR" (act 1 scene 1) for the Stuart Headlam competition. The adjudicator's report- most encouraging.

May 4th.

To-day we lost Barbara Abram and Hilda Smith to the Land Army. We wish them, as we wish all our pals in the services, the blessing and protection of God. And the luck to find a "cushey "billet!

WHIT MONDAY May` 25th.

As a result of a suggestion made a month or so ago a concert and social (members only) was held in the hall this evening. Though compiled somewhat hastily the programme was greatly enjoyed and was followed by community-singing and dancing. If all those enthusiastic members who said they would sing, dance, or recite, etc., when the show was first muted had stuck to their intention instead of "thinking better of it" the organiser's task might have been a good deal easier! Condolences offered to performers who addressed microphone confidentially expecting the words to boom from loud speakers. Failure of some due to impossibility of purchasing battery on BANK HOLIDAY.

Land Army claims yet another Club member. This time Eileen Blessington that stalwart upon who rested much of the responsibility for the printing of the last issue.

May 26th.

Guild of St. Agnes invades Boxhill much to the alarm of local military.

May 27th.

Workmen in. Last year's "blitzing" has necessitated major repairs to hall.

May 29th.

After repeated postponement we were privileged to hear Madame Fachiri who gave a violin recital lasting for over 1 ½ hours tonight. After playing works of the great Classical composers she ended with a number of requests. The recital was thoroughly enjoyed by all present, And in response to popular demand. Madame Fachiri announced that she would play for us again on August 7th. It seems that charm and glamour is not so much the prerogative of women, or of women and Club chairman!

May 30th.

Some of the Girls paid a visit to "The Manor" Epsom. This afternoon. Madeleine Taylor "Maddy" to a friend's must have been wearing a more than an unusual vacant expression for she was asked by one of the inmates "Do you sleep in the dormitory, or have you got a room?"...**Report as follows/-**

NETBALL and all THAT

By Maureen Ney (Captain)

It can be said, I think, that netball during the past season, was successful, in spite of certain lack of enthusiasm during a spell of bad weather. We entered two teams in the L.U.G.C. league, Pella reaching the finals and Howard also do very well. All the netballer's wish to thank Mrs Gibbs who turned up every Saturday, hail rain or snow, and put in a lot of hard work coaching both teams Thanks also to Mrs Oettinger, of the Girls School, who helped to coach Pella for the finals. Unfortunately, the cup was lost to the opposing team, but still - there's always next year. Come on St Anne's

When the netball season has finished, Mrs Gibbs invited the party of netballer's and Keep- Fitters to the "Manor" Epsom, where she is drill and games instructor. The "Manor" Playing fields are large and well-equipped and we were made extremely welcomed by the staff and girls. The first item on the programme was a game of netball which we thoroughly enjoyed because we won. We then had a lovely tea in the large hall, after which we return to the playing fields we played rounder's in front of a large and appreciative crowd who were pleased to shout advice at both sides, indiscriminately. By this time most of us were gasping for breath, but the "Manor" girls seemed quite unshaken. Out came the High Jump apparatus so not to be outdone, we re- gained our breath and "jumped to it", and believe it or not a few managed to clear 4 feet, to say nothing of 11 feet in the long jump. Later in the evening. Of course, all good things (and times) come to an end and it was time to go home, so wearily but happy, off we went. We had a most enjoyable afternoon and eagerly looking forward to another visit, which we hope will be very soon.

ooOoo

Diary Cont./-

May 31st.

Club Committee meeting. Ssssssssh! Letter posted up on the notice board from Iris Noakes she seems to be keeping cheerful. Best wishes from us all Iris! For the benefit of new members Iris is no relation to the famous or should one say notorious Joan!

June 12th.

Eileen Smith joins the ATS best of luck Eileen! If you have to do any marching, let us know and we'll forward some roller skates!

June 13th.

C.O.M. Outing. About 32 "Children" went under the wing of the redoubtable Father Koch to St, Muar's Convent Weybridge. Spent time playing games of the "rounder's" variety and finished up by tearing madly to the station to catch 8.30 thinking it to be the last train. (Last train actually circa 10 p.m.).

Report as follows:-

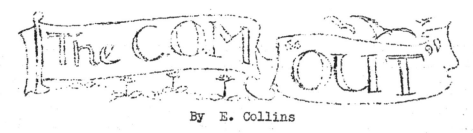

By E. Collins

Sunday, 14th June was the day chosen for the C.O.M. outing and St Maur's Convent, Weybridge, kindly agreed to have us for the day.

After a hectic journey we arrived at the Convent gates full of that feeling of anticipation which is the hallmark of all the C.O.M.O outings. We were ushered into a small but very impressive waiting room and our eyes were drawn immediately to the centre table on which reposed a huge brass bowl containing some of the most exquisite roses we had ever seen. Suspended from the ceiling, just above the roses, was a quaint little lamp, its framework being of wrought iron fitted with glass windows. The walls were oak panelled and there were several delicately carved chairs and tapestried seats. Somehow, we knew from the first moment we were in for a splendid time.

The Mother Superior greeted us kindly and took us along to the day school, which strangely enough was known as St Anne's. This was to be our "camping" or rather "dumping" ground and as soon as we had parked OUR things and changed into our gym shoes we decided to have lunch straight away

Lunch was laid in the garden a beautiful place with gentle sloping lawns and borders of many coloured flowers and towering trees. What a sight met our eyes! three long tables each covered with a snowy cloth and containing bowls of rich creamy custard and refreshing looking rhubarb, While at the far end of each table were dainty services of delicate hued China.

After lunch we did offer to wash up but the nuns wouldn't hear of it, they sent us off to the rounder's field where everyone excelled themselves whether they cheated or pulled off a rounder with ease and grace. Of course, the winning team was the one that had "played the game" all through and this fact was re-rammed home to the losers. I believe we lost most of the tennis balls we took with us, thanks to his Reverence, who with a mighty sweep of the arm, sent many of them spinning into space and consequently out of bounds. Still we made a patched up peace and plumped for hot rice.

During this exciting game there occurred a most unfortunate accident. Somehow or other, Father's head got in the way of the cricket ball, for suddenly the air was rent with a mighty crack! What a cosh was delivered to the temple! The first part of the nut-cracker suite being completed, it was decided we would play a less dangerous game. So we started "Warny."

We were a dishevelled lot by the time we went to tea. Several photos were taken during tea and we hope they turn out all right, especially the one in which Father Koch is supervising the bread and butter spreading competition, lorded it over the busy ones as if he was used to watching others work and thoroughly enjoying same.

Tea over, we made ourselves ready for benediction during which our celebrated choir gave a fine rendering of the plain chant "Salve Regina." The chapel, though small was very lovely with the alter softly radiant in the light of many candles.

After benediction two of the nuns showed us over the boarding school. The dormitories were the essence of good taste, Especially one that was decorated in green and cream. Each bed was surrounded by curtains of green folkweave and at the foot of each bed were tiny white stools with carved legs and green seats. There were green hand basins fitted into the wall, One to each bed and these were topped with glass shelves and shaped mirrors. The beds were covered with beige and brown quilts, The whole room was light and airy and in fact, a perfect dream.

The classrooms are not very large, but they were inviting and delightful and all of us wish we were young enough and lucky enough to be pupils at St Muars for it really was a schoolgirls dream come true.

When we had finished going into raptures. We played rounder's again until we were abruptly interrupted by "Des" our President who came flying into the field with the announcement that if we wanted to catch the last train(which left at 8:45) We'd better get cracking as we'd half an hour's walk to the station and it was then 8:10. We have never moved so quickly in our lives and were forced to take a hurried leave of the nuns who of course, understood and we arrived at the station with minutes to spare.

Needless to say we were as stiff as pokers for the best part of the following week. But were unanimously agreed that it was well worth it as we had experienced one of the most enjoyable days in the annals of C.O.M. history.

Diary Cont/.
June 14th.
Majority of C. O. M. Staggering about sadly in need of "crutches!"

Hear that Barbara and Hilda are keeping each other company through communal bouts of "flu." Happy daze!

ooOoo

A STRANGER IN LONDON

By JOHN MOSS.

One Saturday in March, I found myself on his majesties service in the heart of the empire, and for about six months too... What a break it meant for me, a grand opportunity to look around this famous beloved spot, seeing the things I had only heard and read about.

Prior to this, I had wangled a few weekends in London. You know it kind of thing; a night at one of those much appreciated hostels that provide a home for Servicemen on leave, and if you bring your mates, by the time you've finished eating and sleeping, with a dance probably on Saturday night, church on Sunday morning, and a show in the afternoon It's time to be on your way home again.

No wonder then that I am now really seeing his great whirl of happiness and sorrow, beauty and ugliness, which is London. At this present time, too, London means more to us, for it stands as a symbol of sanity and freedom in a world gone mad.

My first three all was to stand in front of Buckingham Palace, my thoughts going back to the death of King George, the abdication of King Edward, and to our little crowd around the radio at home to hear that wonderful account of our present King's Coronation to hear the BBC announcer, along the route of the royal procession of a describing places which I have since been privileged to visit myself. Buckingham Palace is but one of the places. At school I was always fascinated by stories of the Tower of London and its mysterious doings. And I have not only seen its but had been inside and examined it thoroughly. I can only say that I have now been to such places as the "Odeon" "Madame Tussauds" and have danced at the Hammersmith "Palais De Dance" and the "Astoria." Yet not so long ago back in the office, I remember how we use to read the West End programmes and listened to Oscar Rabin's broadcast from the Hammersmith and sigh. If only.

Hearing so much about the seat of our religion in England, I promised myself a visit to Westminster Cathedral. I have since had the privileged to serve there at Mass and Benediction several times and while serving their on Palm Sunday I saw Cardinal Hinsley for the first time.

Among those memories of good times I have badly, and good friends I had and made last but not least, are the good people at Saint Anne's Vauxhall. When I first arrived in London by I enquired about a Catholic Club in my neighbourhood and was told that there was a Social in the local school once a week. Going back to the "digs" after one of these with one of the lads I had met their he invited me to go along to Saint Anne's. I said I would probably pay them a visit so he told me how to get there. I left him at that and continued on my way. After a few minutes I was surprised to hear him a running back to let me into the great secret.

'There's just one point.' He said. 'There may be a bit fussy about letting you in but just say that you are a Catholic and you're being alright. I have often smiled since to myself at this advice. Anyhow, that week found me at Saint Anne's.

What a fine place it is. What a grand crowd you all are. I really am grateful to you all for making me so welcome. I went into the Club that night a complete stranger but when I said "goodnight" I had made friends among you. Since then, I have become more and more attached to the place. At times I find it hard to believe that I am anywhere but in my own Club in Salford Cathedral. It is fine to be in the Club just like the one at home, though so far away, and to be greeted with the same familiar "Hello Johnnie" like a lifelong friends. Yes, I'll be sorry when the time comes to the view of but I won't forget you. It seems strange to be able to thank the war for anything but trouble and unhappiness, yet if it wasn't for the war I wouldn't have had any of these things to be thankful for, and speaking for myself, so far at any rate, I have had many more pleasant experiences than unhappy ones in the Services. But war is not a pleasant thing. Some of you have had your share our sorrow as the result of it and may I express my deepest sympathy, but we are all affected by in some way, even if we had been spared actual sorrow

So for all our sakes, let's hope he will not be very long before we can look back on it as. "Just another memory" To all of you I send my very best wishes always and sincerely thank you for the grand spirit of friendship and hospitality we have shown to.

'A stranger in London.'

The foregoing story bares testimony to what the Club really meant to Members and also Strangers alike.

ooOoo

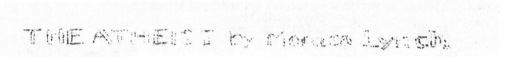

He is never happy
For he has no God
He has never heard His voice
Or trod the paths He trod.

His life is not enjoyed
His world is sad and dim
All is dull and void
No Eternity for him

And then his soul is cast upon th' Eternal shore
He meets the God "that isn't" then sees His Face no more.

ooOoo

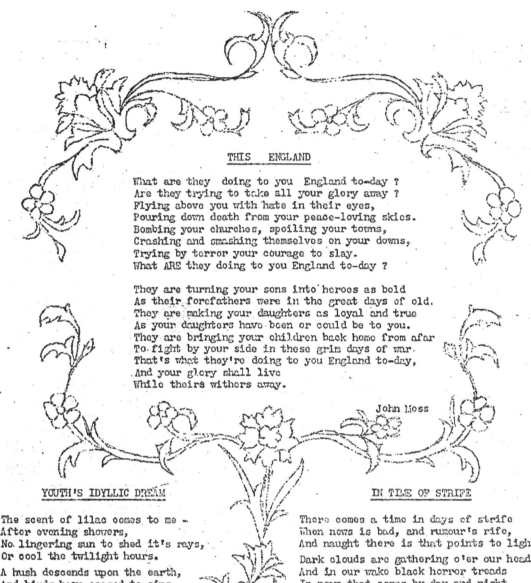

THIS ENGLAND

What are they doing to you England to-day ?
Are they trying to take all your glory away ?
Flying above you with hate in their eyes,
Pouring down death from your peace-loving skies.
Bombing your churches, spoiling your towns,
Crashing and smashing themselves on your downs,
Trying by terror your courage to slay.
What ARE they doing to you England to-day ?

They are turning your sons into heroes as bold
As their forefathers were in the great days of old.
They are making your daughters as loyal and true
As your daughters have been or could be to you.
They are bringing your children back home from afar
To fight by your side in these grim days of war.
That's what they're doing to you England to-day,
And your glory shall live
While theirs withers away.

John Moss

YOUTH'S IDYLLIC DREAM

The scent of lilac comes to me –
After evening showers,
No lingering sun to shed it's rays,
Or cool the twilight hours.

A hush descends upon the earth,
And birds have ceased to sing,
In treetops high some yawning beak
Preens now a feathered wing.

I drowse, and, dream of former days
Of rippleless life's stream,
Oh! would that we could but resume
Young Life's idyllic dream.

Frank Barry

IN TIME OF STRIFE

There comes a time in days of strife
When news is bad, and rumour's rife,
And naught there is that points to light.

Dark clouds are gathering o'er our heads,
And in our wake black horror treads
In news that comes by day and night.

We wonder what can yet betide,
And hope for aught to turn aside
The warfare from this troubled sphere.

But keep your courage, still be proud,
There's silver lining to each cloud,
So hope and pray till victory's here.

Frank Barry

ooOoo

"When do we dance?"

By Mary Lams

From the cafe next door come the strains of an orchestra and the rhythmic thud of dancing feet. It's the Monday night "hop" of the Tank Corps who are billeted there. (Dancing every Monday says the handbill. Admission 1/-) Ladies free). And here at home, glancing through yesterday's SUNDAY TIMES, An article by Monsignor Knox on "Idleness" catches my eye. That and the sounds of dance next door set me thinking a little on the questions of leisure. From the time we first heard a Nun at school say "We shall have to account for every hour of our lines" we must all have wrestled a bit with this problem. But even Nuns have a set time of the day for recreation; that thought is always a comfort. Yes we must have time to relax. What with going to it and keeping at it, we need not worry about having too much time to ourselves.

But it's possible, reminds my uneasy conscience, to get up early and do a good days work and still be slack. "Choosing the less important of duties and doing it first is one of the commonest ways of idling." Says Monsignor Knox. An uncomfortable thought. We sit by the fire for another few pages, when we know we ought to get to bed; we have another few minutes after the alarm has gone, though this will mean a hurried breakfast or none at all. Even lazing by the fire when we ought to take a walk or going to the pictures when we go out dancing will give us better recreation and much-needed exercise are ways of taking the line of least resistance. It's all very hard, being strict with ourselves, yet it's always necessary if we're going to be any good, and it's vital now, for we've all got to get tough with ourselves (and we haven't done that yet)if were to win this war.

That dance is still going on. The piano's stamping out, "What more can I say, tum, tum-it-tum-tum." I'd like to go. but I can't. Instead of washing my hair another night, I sat over my favourite evening newspaper reading the "Courts Day-By-Day" and the collar of my one suitable dress is washed and ironed - but not sewn on. So I think I'll just take a bath and get to bed.

ooOoo

OLD POPPA

By Pamela. A. Moore.

"Ha Ha." Chuckled old Poppa, hunting round for his collar stud. "Isn't life strange?" He hummed a merry tune and did a little dance round the bedroom.

The entire Household was a bustle, people rushing round and bumping into one another. The excitement? A Wedding. Poppa could hear the "Oh's" of rapture as the bridesmaids buzzed round the bride "like a lot bees" thought Poppa he could hear his wife shooing the people away from the door as they came to take a peep at the bride, and then, quite unlike the rest of this happy to us bustle, he heard quiet sobbing.

Well, well Pierre fancy a big boy like you crying."

"I - I find your collar stud Monsieur, here it is." said a strangled voice.

"Thank you sonny, now come and tell Poppa all about it."

"My beautiful Yvonne she-e marry your son Eric Pierre going to be so lonely without my beautiful sister, Poppa, he sobbed. What am I to do I wish I were a man."

"Now don't you worry your little heart sonny auntie and Poppa are going to look after you. Yvonne won't be away long, and why, it won't be long before you are a fine grown up man."

"Then Poppa, I will be a soldier one of General De Gaulle man right hand." Poppa smiled at this quaint English.

"No-o nor Madam, she is so kind to me, and would think I and grateful for her kindness."

Poppa finished his toilet brush to Pierre, put their button holes in place and was feeling very pleased with his reflection in the mirror, when the door opened very quickly and in strode a tall young man, a sergeant pilot in the RAF.

"Only gosh, dad, did you feel half as bad as I to? Do you think Harry's got the ring OK? Crumbs! Another half an hour yet! Hello Pierre you don't look very happy."

"Oh you ver happy Monsieur Eric." Replied Pierre with a watery smile.

"Come on Eric don't look so worried, it's nearly time you were at the church. Said Poppa giving him a gentle shake towards the door.

Now Pierre I think you can run along too nine, you can come and kiss Yvonne before you go he added seeing the child's face change now go on Eric its unlucky to see the bride, as Eric made to go with Pierre.

Go on dad bunkum he gripped his father's hand and out he went.

Poppa gave his coat one last pull straightened Pierre's wayward lock of hair and went in to the adjoining bedroom.

Old Poppa lived his own wedding all over again, when he went into the room and sore the girl in the bridle array. Grace, beauty and simplicity of most becoming apparel the girl, his only son and chosen for his wife.

Sufficient to say that old Poppa felt a faint flow of youth and very proud when he led her to the Alter and his wife couldn't resist a slight tear, while Pierre inwardly choking kept a brave smile on his little face, when after they were pronounced man and wife he saw Eric taking her out of his life or, so he thought.

They had a little party and the radiant couple went on their honeymoon. Pierre went to bed early after his emotional day and while Mary Poppa's wife busied herself with the wedding presents Poppa sat back in his chair with his chief friend, his pipe.

Three years ago he owned a little boat. "London Pride" was its name he did quite a nice little business with pleasure trips. Then came the war, Luckily he had saved an adequate sum of money, so that he and Mary did not want. Then so unexpectedly had come that trip to Dunkirk. Old Poppa never could remember how it came about, how one night he was sailing with a lot of other small craft over the channel.

It was a sultry night a red glow from the south the stars glistening and every now and then the sky lit up as a shell burst or a bomb fell. At the break of dawn, He would never forget as afterwards he told his wife. "Our Boys thousands of them being bombed to blazes by Gerry. Fires flaming into the sky a black pall of smoke lying low over the noise of dive bombers and bombs, machine guns and cannon fire, a merry hell on earth. Our job was clear, to rescue as many as possible. I grabbed a few fellows swimming in the sea they were half dead, and coming along a human chain of men was a little boy hanging on to a youth. I bundled them in and turned round for home sweet home. One of the fellows I had rescued wiped his brow and said "Cor blimey proper picnic out there ain't it mister?"

"Are we doon hearted," cried and burley red bearded Scotman

"No." they all shouted

"Coom on then reel out the barrel."

I went over to the little boy who was whimpering at the side of the young man

"Have a piece of chocolate sonny."

"Er not speak much English Monsieur, we are French."

The young lad took off his hat and a Mass of curls fell on his shoulders. To my amazement it was a girl.

"Good God child! Do you mean to say you have gone through that lot?"

"I had to Monsieur, my mother and father are dead killed when a bomb fell on our House, then of course had to look after Pierre and we made our way to Dunkirk, this was the only way I could escape from the Germans, so I dressed as a boy, and Monsieur I can never repay you for your kindness." She dropped her head and went in to a deep faint. About nineteen I judged her looking down. What pluck! We wrapped her up and Jock took Pierre onto his knees to comfort him.

We were machined gunned on our way back and may I be forgiven for what I said then,

We managed to pull the girl around and he was the first one to see the dear old shores of England, yes, and that brave girl went down on her knees and we all knelt down too

Deo Gratias. She murmured and sobbed on my shoulder.

Poppa smiled in his comfortable chair. The rest of the story is simple. Poppa took the two of them to his little House and his kind hearted wife mothered them. Until one day that son of his came home on leave and had to fall head over heels in love with Yvonne, and take away the valuable help she had rendered Mary. But she would make Eric a splendid wife and they still had Pierre to keep them company in their coming old age who though timid looked as though he would become another Eric, "Life is strange." said Poppa out loud.

"What did you say?" "H-u-m Oh! Nothing dear."

oooOooo

By Rosemary Martyn

"---- And of course, wound up Donald Hilton looking intently at his evacuees, I know none of you have taken Lady Whiteheads brooch, but it has disappeared and the old Lady is terribly said about it.

Codfish, tall and skinny and the eldest of six from Whitechapel looked at the other five. Although he was the best scrambler within miles of Hilton manner, he had his own interpretation of Meum and tom(myer an'yourn) and he decided that if one of these kids had pinched that brooch, the little yet Was going to give it back.

Donald leaned on his stick. He knew in his heart that none of these kids had taken the brooch. She was very old and had a habit of putting things down and forgetting where this favourite roach was worth a fortune. He gave a sigh and turned towards the door of the playroom. For a second is eyes rested on Vera Violet Perry. Known as Winkle. She was a pretty little thing, like the palest pinkest rose of June. Her fair curls were soft and silky and her big eyes were cornflower blue. Winkle had never been known to "muck abaht" in church or to tell lies or lose her temper. Everybody said she was an angel. Yet in spite of this Miss V.V. Perry fitted in perfectly with the other five, and indeed, Whitechapel itself would not have been complete without her. Still looking at Winkle, Donald made a request.

"I am asking you youngsters as a very special favour not to put the wireless on for the news."

Six pairs of eyes opened wide. then came the chorus

"Why"

"Never mind why. Do as you are told, and keep your eyes open for Lady Whitechapel's brooch."

Donald departed and Whitechapel was alone. Ikey Mo' looked at the clock on the wall. It was exactly six o'clock, so he made a dive for the wireless. Before he reached it The Cock Sparrow put our foot and he measured his length on the carpet. Before he realised what had happened the Codfish was kneeling on his chest.

"Yaroo!" yelled Ikey Mo'.

"Nah listen 'ere, you son of Isaac." Snarled the Codfish." I got a lot to say to you. A first a'vall you let that radio alone, see?"

"Oood'yer fink you are?" Sneered Ikey. "Some blinking Sunday school ma'am?"

"No." Replied Codfish, taking the unfortunate Ikey's ears and raising the little Hebrew head a few inches off the floor. "I'm the little Shepherd of kingdom come, and yer a little crook. Gimme that brooch!"

"I ain't pinched a brooch."

Ikey Mo was of the seed of Abraham right enough and he was always out to make what he could. He was also a little sneak, known in school as the "nark." But he definitely was not a purloiner of precious stones and he knew no more about the missing brooch than the other five.

Codfish let go the Hebrew's ears and, with a thud, Ikey Mo's head hit the unsympathetic floor. He set up such a yell that Mrs Green the housekeeper rushed in.

"Well I never!" Said the horrified Lady. "Well I never!"

Ever since this mob had been thrust upon her not unwilling shoulders and in spite of the "well- I-nevers the children had adored her and took notice of what she said. A few moments later the outraged feelings of Ikey were soothed and the Codfish sufficiently lectured on bullying, although the latter young gentleman thought what he thought.

As the days slipped by, however, it became apparent to even the Codfish, that none of his fellow -evacuees had got the brooch and sorry as he was he put the matter from his mind.

Lady Whitehead, however, was becoming more and more fretful as the days went by. During the past few years she had grown very irritable and scolded everybody she came in contact with. She had hated the children being in the house and since the disappearance of the brooch she had taken a violent dislike to them and stayed in her room as much as possible.

It was almost two weeks after Donald's strange request about the wireless, when the master of Hilton Manor sent for Winkle. She found him in this study looking rather pale, his "hoppity" foot propped up on a low stool.

"Good morning, Winkle." He began

"Goo morning Mister Don."

Donald seemed to have difficulty in finding the right words or there appeared to be something in his throat that was trying to stop the words from coming. The child sensed that something was very wrong and her heart began to beat rather painfully.

"Winkle, "Said Donald at last. "You are a brave girl, aren't you? "

"I--I hope so." Replied the child in a small voice.

"Some of us have to be very brave sometimes." Donald sighed glancing at the foot of the stool. "We mustn't show the world all we feel inside."

"N-n-no."

"Nearly two weeks ago, Winkle, your daddy's ship was sunk and I'm afraid everybody on board was lost."

She did not burst into tears. He saw her little white face that seemed too small for the great blue eyes. Those eyes were dry but there was an expression in them that he would never forget.

The only emotion she showed was the clenching of her hands till the knuckles gleamed white. She was telling herself at big girls don't cry and she mustn't cry in front of Mister Don. But the ache insider was getting bigger and bigger, so she hurried from the study before it got too big ...

Outside the door, with no one to see, that tears could run in rivers and one could cry "daddy daddy."

"Cry!!!" baby! Cry baby 'ardin cried for a fardin

It was an Ikey Mo' on the prowl and Winkle was just the right size for him. He liked tormenting Winkle because she never retaliated.

It was a changed Winkle this time however. Of all the people in the world to see her face go "sloppy" Ikey Mo' was the last one she wanted for a witness. All Winkles' grief turned into a white fury.

"You -you snoopin' spying little yid."

For a moment, Ikey Mo' was too surprised to speak. He gazed in wonder and admiration. Nevertheless he got over his surprise and dashed towards her.

"Why you little monkey, I'll flay you alive!"

Winkle raced down the corridor with Ikey at her heels, "Beast Fool!" she shrieked as he ran.

"Let me git you." Roared Ikey Mo'. "Come and be flayed alive and thrown in the pond."

"Beast!" roared Winkle as she darted into the garden. He caught her by the stinging nettles and ducked her in them until her arms and legs were covered in big white bumps. Then like lightning, she shut out her hand, grabbed Ikey's nose and hung on until he was bent almost double, then with a strength lent her by fury, She kicked him on his nether end and sent him Head - over -heels into some current bushes.

By the time Ikey picked himself up, Winkle had taken refuge in a greenhouse. The door was shut fast, but there was a missing pane of glass. Looking round for a suitable missile he saw a hose and a convenient tap. Next moment a stream of water poured steadily into the greenhouse.

"Beast! Fiend! Fool!" shrieked Winkle. She ducked under a shelf and came face to face with a huge daddy longlegs. "Help, Murder!" She darted to the next corner and saw a great big eye that belongs to a ghost "Police!"

Ikey's luck was then out, he was attacked in the rear by an irate Gardner and whilst he was pausing to gently rub his tender parts, Winkle darted towards a house. In the playroom, she found Ikey's shell; she leaned out of the window and threw it at him. The little Hebrew did a jig of frenzy and dashed into the house. That shell was the apple of his eye.

Winkle raced up to Lady Whitehead's bathroom and found a heavy silver box. With a business like look, weighed it in her hand...... leaned over the banister's and dropped it on Ikey's head. He sat slowly down. Whitechapel and Mrs Green rushed up at that moment. They gathered up Lady Whitehead's second-best dentures and her lost brooch. Mrs Green picked Winkle up and carried her up to bed.

Meanwhile, Lady Whitehead was cleaning her various bits of jewellery which as Donald pointed out should be deposited safely in the bank. She had settled down with the little brush and duster when she realised that she had forgotten the little tube of Kizz which made the diamonds sparkle much brighter. She was about to press the bell when the Codfish pushed his way into her presence and laid the brooch on the table. Had the Codfish being a nice-looking boy with a clean face and good manners, the old Lady would have grabbed the brooch in her usual ungracious manner, but being perverse, she beamed at him and he grinned back sheepishly.

"My dear boy, I am so very grateful!"

"'Sall right. You're welcome. Anyfink else I can do for yer?"

"Well I'd like a little Kizz. Said Lady Whitehead.

Codfish felt his face burn and put two fingers underneath is grubby," But After all" he told himself "The poor sites got one foot in the grave." He leaned forward, gave her a pack on the cheek bolted leaving her beaming like a schoolgirl.

Some hours later Donald limbed to Winkle's bedroom. He found her lying in her bed her hands clasped behind her head, the blue eyes open, two pools of mystery and a white little face.

"Winkle dear, I have just received a telegram from your mother. Your father and his mates were picked out of the sea and are all safe and well in Italy. And, Lady Whitehead is taking you all to a circus tomorrow! "

Winkle flung her arms round his neck and burst into tears.

ANSWERS TO COUGHDROP CORNER

By M.A. Chance

1. Who was known as the Wisest Fool in Christendom?
a. Charles II
b. Napoleon
c. James I
d. St Francis of Assisi

2. Isaac was Abraham's:
a. Son
b. Brother
c. Grandchild
d. Nephew

3. The following is a list of birds, plants and butterfly. Can you say which are which?
a. Yellow Rattle   c. White Leghorn
b. Camberwell Beauty   d. Essex Skipper
e. Mountain Ringlet   f. Red Campion

4. The verse that begins: "Drink to me only with Thine Eyes" is from the pen of:
a. Longfellow
b. Shakespeare
c. Ben Jonson
d. Belfe

Mrs Itermards husband and 12 sons were home on leave from the Army (who could ill spare them. She sent her youngest offspring to obtain Seven pints of liquid refreshment. The child had a three pint jug And a five-pint jug. The barmaid (an offhand woman) told him to help himself. There were no measures about but wonder boy brought back the exact amount, and he used only the two jugs in doing so. How?

For answers See end page.

END PAGE
ANSWERS TO COUGHDROP CORNER.

Question 1.- James I
Question 2.- Son
Question 3.- Bird:c. Butterflies: b,d,e
Plants: a, f.
Question 4.- Ben Jonson.

Mrs. Itemard's Beer: First of all the W. B. filled the five-pint jug he then filled the three-pint one, from this and having drunk(for he was a hardened youth) this as soon as he poured it in, he put the remaining two pints into the three-pint jug. It was then a simple matter to fill the five-pint vessel and trot home.

ooOoo

St. Anne's Annals

19 42

Christmas

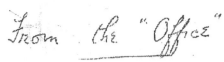

From the "Office"

Sorry we are late with this issue. Even if your copy reaches you after Christmas you will know that our thoughts and prayers were with you. If it gets to you in time, we wish you a happy Christmas and a happier and more peaceful New Year. May all those parted families soon be united?

The Club is still jogging along in spite of the war. Most of the members are taking a really active interest and that aimless "whiling-away-the-time atmosphere of the Blitz days is disappearing. It is cheering to see the needle workers gathered round a blazing fire in the Sewing Room making dolls for Christmas or the boys in the Craft Room quietly making wallets and things as girls chatter away while making their bags and gloves. The concert party is about to emerge from the chrysalis stage. The orchestra is finding its feet and the choir is spreading its wings, like the Christmas Angels. The musical hour is still held on Sunday afternoons and the Drama Group is about to do JANE EYRE. The girls are doing well at Netball and the Boys have entered the C.Y.C. S.W. London Football League. Table-Tennis matches are a regular feature for boys and girls and the Discussion Group still makes Parliament look silly each week. A good sign is the increase in junior activity. Fifteen aspirants were enrolled in the C.O.M. Bringing its total up to well over fifty. The Saturday dances are still good and the Sunday Whist Drives continue. The Ballroom Dancing class is popular although Keep-Fit needs recruits. There's more Club gossip in the Diary. The Clinics are better than ever and need workers.

It's always a pleasure to see old faces when on leave or to hear from you. It's grand to know that we have so many trusted friends. You older ones know what a tussle we've had. The youngsters take things for granted. The debt is still £3000. Archbishop Amigo kindly paid our overdraft last year and lent us £1000 at 1%. Yearly interest our yearly interest is now only £85 so we should make some more progress with the dept.

I cannot close without thanking; those of our present members who are working as hard to help asked to carry on. The team spirit here is something to be proud of, and no one works for personal thanks or glory. Without boasting, for visitors remarked on it. The atmosphere of the Club is truly Catholic. May it continues throughout 1943 and long after you have returned. God bless you and bring you all back safely

Yours in Christ.

Adolf. P. Koch.

10

DIARY
BY: — FRANK BARRY

August 5. Lillian Lewis one of our old members died today R.I.P.

August 7. A return visit was paid by Madame Fechiri. The violin recital was thoroughly enjoyed by us all and we are anxiously waiting to see if our Chairman can arrange yet another visit. I expected repercussions when Madame

Fechiri praised our high taste in music but so far nine inch cigarette holders and velvet trousers are still unknown in the Club. Longhair seems to be the order of the day however.

August 9. Club outing to Beaumont College we left the train at Staines and finished the journey on foot by the Riverside. The going was very warm and the sole place of refreshment encountered end' route was immediately relieved of all available liquid food. After reaching the college we had a brief rest and snack. We then wandered onto the spacious playing fields and proceeded to enjoy ourselves. The rain did its best to dampen our spirits but the boys emulated the ducks and continued to enjoy their game of cricket. After tea and vigorous towelling - we all joined in what would have been a gentle game of rounder's, if everybody had held onto their bats!

 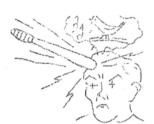

We tramp back to Egham and to round off the day our train whizzed through Vauxhall and dumped us down at Waterloo. Back at the Club: between muffled gasps of pain as we move our weary limbs we tell all and sundry what a wonderful time we've had. Mad Dogs and Englishmen go out in the midday sun!

August 10. We were entertained by a rather unusual type of lecture tonight. It was on Practical Psychology and Miss Masterton was the lecturer. Most of us are worried over the sanity of everybody else now. I is keeping my opinion to me!

August 12. Terry Bates pays us a visit. He is still stationed in Scotland and the land of Heather and haggis. Seems to agree with him.

August 15. "The Manor" was again Besieged by a girls today. The fun and games were enjoyed by all and thanks must be given to Mrs Gibbs for making the trip possible.

August 16. Feverish activity in the Club. Carpet laying, piano shifting and offensive sweeps in the corridor herald the return visit of a famous personage and who could it be but the one and only Solomon. He gave a recital played duets with is brilliant pupil Miss Gwen Byrne. Club members now refuse to speak to anybody unless half-a-crown is paid in advance for the privilege.

August 21. Many weird noises have emerged from the library during its long and varied history but a new record was set up this evening. The scene was the first meeting of the Violin Class and if we didn't become geniuses in a night we did at least have a good time.

August 22. Mr Barr took a party of us over Westminster Abbey. Being in such good company we were able to visit remote parts of the Abbey which are out of bounds to ordinary visitors. When Mr Barr played the organ for us we were thrilled to bits.

August 26. General Meeting of the Club. Chief points which were proposed and carried were as follows: An extra sixpence to be paid monthly by all members in addition to the nightly subscription of 1d., each class to have an organiser and every member to belong to at least one class.

August 31. Classes restarted this week after the usual break during August. Most of the classes are well attended but all of them could do with fresh blood. Why not join one or two and get to know your fellow members better?

September 4. Six new members joined the Apostleship of Prayer this evening. The rules are simple and cost only 1d. Per month. Delphine Venturi will be pleased to expand more fully for all who are interested. The members of the Dramatic Class have suddenly become extremely secretive. They refuse to divulge what they are preparing to show at Christmas and only talk with their hands over their mouths.

September 11. The noises from the library have now reached a degree of stability and it is whispered that a tune has actually been distinguished now and then.

September 13. Another Nuptial Mass for Club members this time it was for Tom Stock of the Royal Navy and

Agnes Greer. Agnes must have imagined the wedding was on Monday but she made it! Heartiest congratulations to them both.

September 18. Jerry Ney honours us with his presence. He is still stationed in the same place. If he stays there much longer we will have to send him a wire when the war is over.

September 20. Retreat for girls at La Retraite Convent Clapham. Ghostly silence in the Club until they return. I think there should be a retreat for the girls every week!

September 25. That close secret of the Dramatic Class seems to have spread somewhat. There must be a common informer in the Club.

October 11. Youth Leaders Conference arranged by the "Priest's" Study Group was held this afternoon. Further meetings are to take place on the second Sunday of each month.

October 18. Fourteen members of the Club went on a hike to Epsom. After striding out for some miles it was annoying to find ourselves back at the starting point. Undismayed we carried on and eventually reached Leatherhead. Incidentally I don't think Robert Bruce was one of Sheila Hagerty's ancestors - she certainly doesn't like spiders!

October 24. The boys played their first football match at Parliament Hill Fields today. The game was against St. Aloysius and resulted in a win for St. Aloysius 5-0.

Grand reunion of all members at the dance tonight. Peter Perla Bernie O'Sullivan and Owen Porter appeared in khaki and Frank O'Sullivan represented the R.A.F., not to be outdone the fair sex had Iris Noakes of the A.T.S. present. Each had varying views of service life but at least they all looked well on it.

August 31. The girls played their first game of netball against Vauxhall Young People. Very close game resulted in a win for the girls 11-10.

November 7. Another netball victory for St Anne's. This time against Mildred Fitzgerald Club at Paddington Recreation Ground. The score was a handsome one of 22 – 6. Nice work girls, keep that net vibrating.

The marriage of Gwen Putt and Vic Wise took place today. Both of them have our very best wishes.

November 8. Football matches against John Kirk Club at Brockwell Park. John Kirk were the victors 4-1.

November 11. Thick fog descends upon the neighbourhood. The few people who managed to reach the Club just had time to collect a compass and set a course for home. It is rumoured that some members penetrated into darkest Camberwell and have been interned for the duration.

November 12. Terry Bates breezes in once again. Will everybody please note that his red stripe signifies promotion and not vaccination?

November 29. A retreat for the boys was held today. In fact a retreat for the boys and a treat for the girls.

Footnote. For all data that has been omitted I apologise. For that which is incorrectly stated I bear full responsibility. For the small portion that is correctly I breathe a sigh of relief.

ooOoo

There are two parts to Jerusalem, the modern city and the ancient city. The ancient city is surrounded by a wall, and life inside the ancient city is like that of the older part of Cairo. The streets are tiny and narrow the houses all shapes and sizes and the smell far from pleasant.

One Sunday, after Mass, I decided to go on at all with some people from the Y.M.C.A. - and we started out in a car. Our first stop was the Garden of Gethsemane with the famous Church of all Nations. The church has twelve domes presented by Catholics of most countries in the world. It was built in 1921 and is of course, comparatively modern. The only part of the original church is a place of very fine mosaic flooring. There is a piece of rock some five feet square in the middle of the alter which is believed to be the spot on which our Lord said his prayers.

Just a few yards from the garden, is the tomb of our Lady. Leaving the church of all nations, we went down the long road to Jericho, past the tomb of Lazarus, the birthplace of Our Lady. And the Inn of the Good Samaritan. There are quite a lot of these roads in Palestine running down the mountains. They remind me of the scenic railway at Margate. We came at last to Jericho, a very ancient town and very dirty, we didn't stop but went straight through till we came to the River Jordan which was also muddy and grubby.

Our next move was to the Dead Sea for a swim. All the time we were travelling downhill and on the run from Jerusalem, we had dropped from 4000 feet above sea level to 1000 feet below sea level and the pressure on our ears was pretty heavy.

I shall never forget swimming in the Dead Sea. It is impossible to sink as you have a job to keep your feet underwater when you are standing up! And once you get on your back, you float about for hours. The water is very salty and if any of it gets into your eyes, you are blinded for 15 to 20 minutes. If you try to dive in, your head is the only part of you that will go in the water. It is not hard to believe that there is nothing living in the Dead Sea.

Leaving the Dead Sea we setback for Jerusalem.

Next day, we went to the city of Tel Aviv, the most modern town in Palestine, And on the way, We travelled along the seven sisters Road. Which is one of the most famous roads in the world. Here we passed orange groves, and say many hundreds of oranges and the scent of them it's something that perfume manufacturers have not discovered. Here again, the tiny streets and square houses. There is a huge Church marking the spot where our Lord was born and it is in the possession of three different denominations. The Greeks, the Armenians, and the R.Cs. Each part of the Church is very lovely. On Wednesday we went to Mount Calvary, which by the way is a very steep hill running right through the old city. This Church again, is in possession of the three denominations, though the key is kept by a Muslim. Jewish people are not allowed to enter the Holy Sepulchre church.

Immediately inside the Church is the Rock of Unction or what is believed to be the place of Our Lord's anointment. High up on the Church on the spot now occupied by a Greek Churches alter is a place marked that is believed to be the actual spot where the cross was erected. In another part of the church is the tomb of our Lord. This is definitely recognised as the most holy place in Jerusalem. In this church too, is the chamber where the true Cross was found in the fourth century.

Upon leaving the church, we wandered through the old city to the Wailing Wall. There were plenty of whailers there and kicking up such an awful dent, that we didn't stay. We went to the mosque of Omar which is built on the site of Solomon's Temple.t They say the inside is the most beautiful building in the world, but we were not allowed inside. It was a feasting week and only Moslems were let in. From here we, who went to the church built over the house of the death of our Lady. Then onto St. Peter's. Excavations here have revealed Chambers many feet beneath the ground and are believed to be the rooms of the high priest Cephias. In the church we saw the actual dungeon where our Lord spent his last night.

On Thursday, we went to the Lake of Galilee, 120 miles from Jerusalem. We inspected the wall of Jacob which is still in existence then went onto Nazareth, which is a sacred place, and so on. It was lovely there, having lunch by the lake and then we had to see about the journey back to Jerusalem, because our few days leave were almost finished. I'm hoping to go again one day.

God bless you all.

TOLD BY THE FIRESIDE

"Tis a story they love to tell in Ireland, thought is the story of how the warm arms of an Irish maiden held the Infant King, and how Christ was cradled on an Irish heart while Mary slept.

It seems that Bridget was the sweetest and loveliest young woman in all Ireland. The grace of Patrick's Baptism had awakened in her eyes the stable in Bethlehem and in her heart the carolling of the Angels -when God gave her a vision and a dream.

Tomorrow at the Christmas Mass she would open her soul to the infant Saviour for the first time. Tomorrow she would share him with Mary. What did it matter whether his godhead were hidden in the swaddling close to disguise of a white host? How she would love to feel is small hands clutch her fingers; to hug the warm softness of his cheek to hers.

His Children waiting for his worshippers. But Bridget did not kneel. Woman's heart was too full of pity for the scene. Before her on the rough floor, travel stained and utterly exhausted, lay a young man sleeping heavily. Near the manger her back resting to hear his baby cries and gurgles. Would tomorrow never come? Would she lift to welcome the divine baby?

Around her, but the more faintly Bridget's eyes closed ..... Then opened again.

The rough stone walls of a room faded into the grey dim lines of the hills of Bethlehem. In front of her a cow track led to the dark entrance of a cave. On the path below her, Shepherds was hurrying away with tidings of great joy. All now, she would hear the last exaltant echoes of the Angel Song. With quick steps she hurried to the mouth of the cave - and paused. Surely she should kneel and adore. Heaven was here, buried in the cold shadows of the cave. God was amongst h on easily against the cold surface of the rock, sat Mary.

Her weary dark ringed eyes made her look older than 14 years' shoulders sagged as if they bore the weight of the heavens? But tired as she was she would not leave a precious charge in that crude manger. Her frail arms fumbled and caressed her child. The holy child the Infant God.

Bridget looked and marvelled. Out of a heart mingled with pity and love she whispered; Mary, you're tired indeed. Well you might be, macushla that 'tis all you did and suffered ere you bore your Joy. T'was many weary miles you carried him under your heart, wandering from housetop house, tired and frightened, with the door slamming in your face – And Him. And after all that, the cold comfort of this dreary cave on this wintry night. Alone, macushla, you bore your child, for what use is even a good man when a woman's great hour has come? No woman took Him from your arms to bathe Him and wrap Him against the bitter wind. That too, you did alone. Mary machree, you're weary, but you can sleep now mavourneen, if you'll let me.... If you'll trust me... if you're. Oh! Mary can I....?

Then tho' under her sleep laden lids, Mary smiled, and Bridget knew that she would not refuse. Instantly she was on her knees by Mary's side, making with her cloak a couch for the tired young mother and receiving into her eager arms the Holy Babe. So, while Joseph and Mary slept with exhaustion.

The son of God was cradled on an Irish heart and soothed by an Irish lullaby.

Sure, of course, the vision faded with the night, but wasn't the coming to her Himself that morning in the "Christ-Mass".

With acknowledgements and apologies to Frs. Thurston and Lord, S.J. and all the Saints and scholars who have handed down to us the "Vision of St Bridget."

ooOoo

On a Sunday morning at four o' clock when I was little more than a youngster. I descended a coal mine for the first time. I came of a mining family, and my forbearers had been miners as far back as I could remember. Nevertheless, the thrill of entering the cage and going down, down, down into the earth for the first time, was a feeling I shall never forget.

Arrived at the bottom, about half a mile underground the air appeared to cause a certain compression on our ears, owing to the forced method in which it was put into the mine. My next move was to make my presence known to the two clerks in the small office, and that being done. I was to travel on what is known in the pit as the travelling way. A very long walk. I arrived at the little cabin where I was to work on a drawing of an engine to be used for haulage work. This little place was really a cave cut out by the side of the travelling way and its dimensions were equal to those of a small living room. It was whitewashed and the roof was supported by large iron girders, which gave me a sense of safety. In the front of my compressed asbestos helmet, a four-volt electric lamp was fixed. For a short while I rested, then I set about my work in real earnest and worked on steadily for nearly three hours.

Then suddenly I heard a thundering noise which is very often heard in the mine but the nearness of this rumble alarmed me, and looking towards the doorway, I saw that dust was pouring into towards me, which made it obvious that it was a fall of stone. Waiting only till the air became clearer as the dust settled, I made my way to the door and looked out onto the travelling way. As I feared, my way back to the shaft was blocked by the heavy fall of stone and I realise that everything depended on the extent of that fall. How long I was to remain a prisoner, I did not know, and knowing full well that I was trapped like a rat in a trap, my predicament was not too good at all. I must admit I was scared, and knowing the disadvantages underground, found it difficult not to panic, so I took out my lunch and began to eat slowly listening intently for the slightest sound. It must have been only an hour I crouched there in a silence like that of the grave, while the air became hotter and hotter and I knew that soon breathing will become difficult. Perspiration began to run down my face and trickle off my chin, and a very long hour crept by again until I thought my head would burst. By this time I was parched and longing for water. I crawled to the edge of the debris-And even to this day, I don't know why, and when I was all but giving myself up for finished, I heard a faint thud. I listened again intently and heard the unmistakable noise of the rescue party as they worked to get to me. Such hope, that gave me strength then to hang on as a drowning man hangs onto a straw.

My light went out and I was in darkness that seemed to sit on me, but not for an instant did I take my eyes off the spot through which my rescuers would come. Every minute seemed an eternity, but at last a hole appeared in the rubble and a voice task if I was O.K. I tried to speak but words did not come, then water was handed in and I drank it in one gulp.

Two days later, the travelling way was cleared and all was as usual in the mine. I went down again and finished my drawing and planning and that district today works regularly and produces a fine amount of coal.

ooOoo

... Way in a secluded corner of Warwickshire, stands an old house surrounded by a moat.it is not large but it is a gem, and the memorial to the Jesuits and Recusants who risked their lives for the Faith.

"Baddersley Clinton" long before penal times belonged to the Catholic family Ferrers. They own it to this day and are still Catholics. This house bears traces of priests hiding on a large scale. Father John Gerard held meetings there in secret and the hiding places were contrived by his faithful servant Francis (Little John) Owen.

During Elizabeth's reign, death was meted out to any Catholic Priest found in England, so young students were quietly sent to the seminaries abroad, ordained and smuggled back. In one period alone, out of 252 of these young priests, more than half were caught an executed. In this house the Jesuit Superior had his H.Q. and it was the scene of a thrilling search by persuivants in 1591. It happened one morning when seven priests were at Mass. In Father Gerard's own words...." Next morning at 5 o'clock went Father Southwell was beginning Mass; we heard a bustle at the back door. Then we heard oath's and cries as the faithful servant withstood them. Father Southwell, guessing what it meant, quietly took off his vestments and stripped the alter while we collected all our belongings, so that nothing might be found to suggest a lurking priest. We did not even wish to leave our boots and swords about, and we were anxious about our beds which were still warm, so some of us turn them over so that the cold part would deceive any who put their hand on them to feel. Thus while the enemy were bawling and shouting outside, and our servants were keeping the door, we profited by the delay to stow ourselves away in a secret place underground where we stood with our feet in the water all the time. Then the leopards were let in. They raged about, peering into all the corners with candles and drawn swords. They took four hours over the business and failed in the search."

Had this raid been successful, and the Jesuit Leader caught then it would have set the cause completely back. These entire priests were eventually martyred.

In the base of the West Wing is a tunnel running its whole length. It is lighted by loopholes and at the far end is an exit onto the moat. This tunnel was obviously the sewer of the house, but it had afterwards been converted into a hiding place because undoubted secret ways have been made into it. This was a common arrangement and can still be seen in some country mansions. Owen saw the possibilities of converting it and there is ample evidence to show that he was responsible for the work here.

His first problem was the disposal of sewage, and this was overcome by building on the square turret to the wall outside the tunnel. The steps leading to the tunnel were thus hidden, as also was the exit to the moat. This latter was achieved by fitting a huge stone slab into vertical grooves in the walls which could be raised or lowered, portcullis fashion,by means of counterbalancing weights in the thickness of the walls.

Directly above the slab is a pleasant panelled room which was a priest's room. The door is exceptionally thick with huge bolts and there is a trapdoor in the ceiling leading to a hiding place in the roof. The window seat can be raised in this room above the tunnel, and the stone bottom inside the seat can be raised to reveal the way into the tunnel. When the loopholes had been blocked and camouflaged the water of the moat was raised and no one suspected that the underground place existed. No wonder Father's Oldcorne, Southwell, Gerard and Co- related that they stood up to their ankles in water.

There are many secret places in "Baddersley Clinton" including a priest hole in the roof among the flues. Not many years ago this was discovered when some repairs were being carried out; a warm little place among the rafters lined with smooth plaster and furnished with two benches large enough to hold six men.

There is another hide in the same stack on the ground floor; a spacious one at the side of the fireplace, but nobody can find a way in to this one.

Beautiful "Baddesley Clinton" one of the oldest an loveliest of our country mansions, and very well preserved. Occasionally, the house and grounds are thrown open to the public, but it looks its best in the evening when the sun sets behind it's time worn gables and its outline stands mellow against the golden sky. Whilst her noble walls stand, "Baddesley Clinton" will be a monument to the priest - those magnificent sportsmen whom she sheltered for the Faith.

ooOoo

This YEAR OF GRACE 2042 AD. by PAMELA MOORE.

Mrs Merany now nearing her 70th year stood looking at door of St Anne's universal Club.

"H'mm, altered bit since I was last here." she said aloud.

"Has it?" said a voice behind her.

"Why yes." she replied, turning to see the smiling face of old father O'Rory. "Well, fancy seeing you here John- I mean father, I thought you were in Rome. Dear dear? I really can't get over seeing you hear."

"I couldn't fail to recognise you Mrs Merany that is your married name isn't it?"

They both went back the many years since they were boy and girl at the Club.

"Well what about coming in and having a look around the old place. It certainly has seen some changes." said the priest

"As a matter of fact." replied Mrs Merany. "I was trying to make up my mind when you spoke, only hearing so many young voices I thought they would resent an old lady's intrusion."

"Nonsense."Why it was being rebuilt before I left. Strange that I should come back and look after the youngsters."

Again they both recalled the happy days of long ago.

"How about the 'Quiet Room' said Mrs Merany "or least used to be called the 'Quiet Room' even in my mother's time. The name always amused me."

"I'm afraid it's in an uproar at the moment as we are preparing for Christmas 'Do's' we still call it; 'Quiet' although it never was nor is very quiet."

At this they both laughed and as they walked down the corridor they watched the comings to and fro of the young people as they dashed about with all manner of brightly coloured festoons. They went into the 'Quiet Room.' It had not altered much. The furniture was different but still cosy, and the feast of Christmas had not gone out of date like so many other nice customs. Boys were on ladders, whilst girls handed the gay decorations and masses of Holly, giving instructions, criticising and condemning and demanding to be allowed to do it themselves. But the boys just waved them off. There was a burst of laughter as a mass of prickly Holly fell on an unfortunate boy's head (quite accidentally of course). A girl's voice came out of the din: "It's no use sitting there looking the essence of misery Helmut, I can't think why you worry so much about concert music. I think it's beautiful and melodious." But Helmuth did not appear to agree

"Helmuth," explained Father O'Rory, "Has composed some music for our concert but he doesn't seem to think it's any good. He's one of those who need a great deal of encouragement."

"Does he live in these parts?" asked Mrs Merany.

"No he comes with a few others from Germany, in fact we get them from all parts of the globe now. Club members take them to their homes, if they are able (for the health Department won't allow overcrowding these days),if not we put them up here at the Club. Their countries in their turn invite our young people. It's all part of a great educational scheme and works very well."

It seems strange that in my mother's time everyone was fighting everyone else, and what Chaos and destruction it caused. She often told me the tale of the Club and what they called the 'Blitz.'

"Well, let me show you the rest of the building." said Father O' Rory. He took her to the great gymnasium, quite the finest on this side of London. One side of the hall was entirely made of glass to let in plenty of air and light, and everywhere was the finest modern equipment. They then went to the hall below, which was used for dancing and a theatre. By pressing the series of electric buttons rows and rows of seats came into position. Just then, however, the curtains that draped the glass were artistically hung and wherever there was a square patch, Holly and evergreen were being put. Up at the far end of the hall could be seen a busy crowd of people painting scenery.

"Excuse please." said a voice behind Father O' Rory's shoulders.

"Yes, Franz?"

"Please come and view the scenery for the nativity play Papa.

"Very well, Framz. Let's have a look Mrs Merany and tell him what we think of it."

Mrs Merany thought well of it.

"Now." said her guide, "you must come and see a little bit of ground outside."

The little bit of ground proved to have a skating rink, which was a swimming pool in summer, a tennis court and a small but lovely garden even though the English climate had improved with the times.

"In the summer also." he said "We have at our disposal and old Manor House which some poor old Lord who couldn't pay his income tax in the great World War left to three of our Clubs. But most of our young people fly off to America or Europe during their holidays. As you can see, both in Town Planning and Foreign policy nowadays youth is given preference."

Mrs Merany cast one more glance at the graceful skating as they went inside and marvelled at the wonderful things that had come to St Anne's. They went into a series of rooms all of which had the different uses and then into the Printing room.

"Oh dear." said Mrs Merany, "Do you remember those silly little verses I used to write for the old magazine?"

"Well I thought they were excellent verses." said the priest gallantly. They both laughed at this secret shared from old.

"Now we will go into the Library." said Father O' Rory. Let me introduce you to our two librarians, twins Amaryllis and Christopher. Perhaps you would like to show our visitor some of our latest books."

"Certainly." they cried and jumped to it.

"They're very keen on their job." she whispered.

"Efficient librarians are traditional here. "said Father O' Rory.

The twins showed Mrs Merany some of their favourite books and she noticed how different the spelling was. There was no unnecessary letters. She looked round the library.

"You haven't many books dealing with history have you?"

"We have no use for it, at least, not much." replied Christopher. "Who wants to know how many wives Henry VIII had, or which war kill most people? It only rekindles old hatreds when people read how much territory they used to have and haven't got now."

"But surely." said Mrs Morany. "That's not all there is in history. One is able to correct previous mistakes."

"No." said Christopher with a determined look. "We live in the present and the future, and we solve problems as we go without looking back."

"Don't you like to look back on the history of the Club, its founder?" She said. looking up at the portrait on the wall.

"Well there is that to it." said Christopher following her gaze.

ooOoo

What is a suffragan ?
  (a) Someone in pain
  (b) A Bishop or.
  (c) A woman who fights for her equality.

St. Anthony of Padua belong to:
  (a) Cannons regular of St Augustine
  (b) Friars Minor.

Can you place the following Dickens characters in their right books:
  (a) Mr Larry.
  (b) Seaforth
  (c) Mrs Haversham
  (d) Quilp.

There is a plaque on the front of the pulpit in St Anne's church. is it of:
  (a) the sacred heart
  (b) the good Shepherd
  (c) St John the Baptist

How many of the confessionals are double sided.
(a)one (b) none (c) two (d) all

Is there a statue of St Anne in the church? If so where is it?
Who knocked off the nose of the statue on the pulpit?

Is it right or wrong to give a couple of coppers to the Salvation Army. If it is wrong. Why?
(Please see answers on back page)

ooOoo

WHAT'S YOUR QUERY, DEARIE ???

If you have a problem or a secret care or woe, write to me. No charge.

When water comes on "points" what shall I do about a bath? I feel I must have my bath occasionally.

Oh don't worry about that. Just get two bowls of water, knee in one and wash your feet in the other. This is a nice easy position for picking out the splinters in ones feet.

I am tired of life. What can you do about it?

Nothing my friend. Of course, I could shoot you, but I am not tired of life yet. Might I suggest a long walk on a short pier?

I suffered dreadfully with hiccoughs have you a permanent cure?

Why yes. Stand in the middle of Kennington Cross and put out your tongue till it touches the ground, then tread on it with the left foot whilst you put your other foot in your coat pocket. You should never have hiccoughs after this.

Which is the best way to get fat?

Before the war you could go to the butchers and buy it All you can do now is to jump from the top window or roof and you'll probably come down "plump".

Can you tell me the difference between a drunken man and a fool?

Yes a drunken man can always get sober but a fool can never get wise. And by the way one fool makes many.

However can I be cheerful when so much suffering and death is going on in the world?

One smile for the living is worth ten sighs for the dead.

How can you stop a bus when you want one in the black-out?

Oh just put out your foot and trip it up.

I suffer very often from boredom, what can I do?

Begin to realise that there are many other people in this world besides you. Take a little interest in their pleasures and troubles and lend a hand here and there. The time will not be so heavy on your hands then.

When are they going to ration powder?

Which powder? Boracic, baking, toilet talcum, tooth, Steadman's custard, washing, soap, curry, Keating's face, dusting, lemonade, egg, liquorice, Sieditz or gun?

Next year I am going to be better. I shall be less self-centred, and lazy. I shall have more patience with people who annoy me and to bear with those who make me lose my temper... to turn the other cheek, so to speak. To remember that a gentle answer turneth away wrath and to.....

So sorry dear, but there is no paper left!

ooOoo

MOUNTAIN PEACE AT CHRISTMAS.

Out of the valley, away from the plain.
Breathing the air of the mountains again.
Far from the city, its noise and its grime.
Its hustle and bustle and swift race with time.

Into the quietness, up, up to a peak.
Where beauty is soon and silence can speak.
And bells may ring out from steeple to steeple.
The mountains the mountains bring peace to the people.

Out of the valley of grief and despair.
Away from the presence of sorrow and care
Up up to the mountains, the peaks of the soul.
Where minds find their healing and hearts are made whole.

Eyes blinded with fear now look ye above
And gaze on God's mountains the peaks of His love.
The peaks of the soul are the heights we must seek.
When the bells may ring out from steeple to steeple.
At Christmas the mountain bring peace to the people.

ooOoo

ANSWERS TO COUGHDROPS.

1. A Suffragan is a Bishop consecrated to help the Bishop of the Diocese.
2. St Antony, belongs to both.
3. Mr Larry. A TALE OF TWO CITIES
4. Seaforth. DAVID COPPERFIELD
5. Miss Caversham. GREAT EXPECTATIONS
6. Quilp. THE OLD CURIOSITY SHOP
7. The statue on the plaque St John
8. Two of St Anne's confessionals are double sided.
9. Yes- it is on the left hand side outside the choir.

The name of the person is only known to a few and she's asked us to see nobody else 'nose'

No. – The. S.A maintain that baptism is not necessary for salvation, and as it most definitely is, we must not help them spread this hearsay.

ooOoo

St Anne's Annals

July 1943

THE LAST WORD.

To our great surprise yet another issue of St. Anne's Annals appears. We thought it had died a natural death. This number is a request number demanded by older members clambering for news from home and those at home are glad to supply the demand. But do members who are away realise how much we who are at home clamour for news of them- their travels, the sights they see, and their doings(as far as these can be revealed)? The next issue will be in December and we want it packed with Arabian Nights Tales and anything else the censor will let through.

We are most grateful to those who have so kindly written for this issue and we dare to hope for more good things from the same pens. What a treat it is to here from old friends. Miss Mary Blessington, our long suffering Stencil-Cutter, Miss Frances Desmond our chief Artist with Elio Pasquini and the whole faithful staff willingly put their inks, paint, needles and grey matter at your disposal. Our gratitude goes out to all of them and especially to our zealous editress Miss Rosemary Martyn. They are glad to do it if you will bring a little happiness to those who are so far away. So you see, you're not forgotten, and if your name appears in the next issue as a contributor you will be remembered more than ever.

Dec. 18.

The Dramatic Class gave a fine performance of JANE EYRE perhaps the best for a long time. It was especially adapted for them by Miss Dale. The proceeds went to the Prisoners of War Fund.

Dec 20.

"Comrade"Fr.Fitzgerald gave a lecture on "Communism v Catholicism." In spite of the discussion that followed nobody saw "red" We could do more of this type of Lecture by this type of lecturer.

Dec.30.

Something in the air. Girls and Boys borrowing rags, bones, hairpins and what not. Everybody getting ready for the Fancy-Dress Party. The three prizes were well won by Arthur Pearson as "Old Mother Riley" the funniest. Delfina Venturi as "Salvage" the most original and John Noakes as the "Spirit of Christmas," the prettiest.

Jan.3. 1943

Much noise in the 'Quiet Room' which is again the scene of great festivity. Tables spread with jellies, sandwiches, home-made cakes and Christmas Pudding. It is one of the famous C.O.M. parties. Everybody is in High spirits (Mr. Hyde thinks some are too full of "spirits") (Now then, Phil, people who live in glass Houses.....ED.)Tea, games, eats, sing-song, eats and we call it a day, crawling home to bed, tired but happy.

Jan 3.

Tim Laidlaw and Pat Alleyne Married today. Congratulations and years of happiness! Now for a quiet Club. They is living at Plymouth.

Jan 6.

We held a "Bidofado" tonight. The Concert Party did most of the "bits" – cheery ditties. Monologues, and funny skits and the rest of us saw to the "DO" Empty cups and cake stands.

Time to take off Party frocks and start Classes.

Jan.12.

The Boys have begun a Boxing Class. Perhaps this is where the Girls should start a First Aid Class.

Jan. 18.

A few members hiked to Caterham today and returned to the Quiet Room fireside aching but 'appy! Violet Crickmore called up for munitions.

Feb.14.

Retreat for Boys the second of its kind, held at the Club. We hope the Boys enjoyed the conferences as much as they enjoyed the teas.

Feb 17.

The walls of the Quiet Room are bedecked with pictures with various types of international dancing Idea: to create discussion. Result; almost blood-shed. Pictures come down.

Feb.28.

A good crowd of Girls went into retreat at St. Vincent's Convent today and were even better when they come home.

(Better than what? Ed.)

Mar. 1.

From now on the Boys meet every month to discuss their Club affairs on the second Monday and the Girls on the first Monday. This should give every member a chance to air his or her views and make suggestions. The Club has also become a "Twin Club" rather than a mixed Club. I.e. Boys and Girls Club running side by side, meeting jointly as required.

Mar. 8.

A new covered way or corridor has been declared open. It encloses the path from the Club to the House and gives the place a very prosperous look. Also a New Catholic library started for members.

Apr. 4.

A Catholic Youth Rally was held at Notre Dame Convent Southwark and we were well represented. After the speeches we sat down to a very nice tea. Then each Club produced an item towards a two hour concert. Of Course like every Club there, we thought our effort the best and we congratulate the Girls on providing a fine play.

Apr. 6.

Father Madden starts Junior Boys Club on a Tuesday's. Let's hope it's as successful as the junior Girls Club.

Apr.11.

Hike to Oxshott. No one lost apart from the whole party being lost. Strange that the starting point should keep popping up everywhere. No aches and pains this time. Keep fit helps happy hikers.

Apr. 27.

Kathleen Stock joins Land Army. Bob Skinner also disappears – War work.

Apr.29.

An Aquarium has come to brighten the Club and provide an interesting hobby. What is there about an aquarium that evens a half-wit witty? The fish must thank God for the gift of silence when they hear what the poor fish outside are saying.

Talking aquatic – John Kennedy is in the Navy now.

Apr. 30.

Elio Pasquini and William Bogazzi attain 3rd. and 6th. Place in the N.F.B.C. Drawing Competitions. Congratulations.

May. 2.

Our heartiest congratulations to Madeleine Deverill and Ernie O'Sullivan who were married in St. Anne's today.

May. 8.

Our team enters the C.Y.C. Netball rally at Wimbledon and wins all matches except those which count. A Good Effort anyway.

May. 9

Charlie Putt married Maude Broome at St. Anne's. Many years of happiness Please God.

May. 16.

Ramble accompanied by Special Reporter.(q.v)

The following report./-

The C.Y.C. Ramble [17] by FRANK BARRY

Bright and early on Sunday 16th. May the select six start their journey to Engelfield Green for the combined ramble for Catholic Club s in S.E. London? We trained to Egham and I think it was quite an achievement that we arrived there without boarding one wrong train.

Having a couple of hours to spare we inspected the countryside and gave vent to our feelings. Some of the locals eyed us with suspicion but as we felt quite normal we didn't worry unduly. The country air soon gave us an appetite and we sat down and ate our sandwiches. This was rather a lengthy business has anybody who has seen the Taylor's lunch will agree!

Josie Taylor decided she knew the way to Inglefield Green which probably explained why we were rather late in arriving. So as we arrived we paid a visit to the church. After everything had been critically surveyed we entered the Club. Here we disposed of our few remaining sandwiches and had a welcome cup of tea. After lunch two of the Girls became our guides and we walked along the riverbank. Perhaps walked is rather misleading because most of the time was spent in what I can only describe as lethargic repose.Such an abundance of inactivity made us extra lazy and we caught the bus back to tea. This was a grand meal and earned the gratitude of the entire Club's present.

We all attended Benediction in the evening and it was good to see such a packed church. A special sermon was preached and enjoyed by everybody.

A social occupied the rest of the evening. At last we had reluctantly to take our leave and thanked Father Preedy for his hospitality. We had all enjoyed ourselves to the utmost and resolved to pay another visit him and not-too-distant future.

Diary Cont./-

May. 18.

Discussion Group decided to study old London, so made a trip to Lincolns Inn Fields. This proved interesting. Now we know how many "pubs" there are in a "square mile"

JUNE 2.

Another Nuptial Mass Joan Terrance and John. O'Leary this time. We wish them every happiness.

JUNE 8.

Sister Marie wrote and produced. "Scenes from the Childhood of Jesus." A crowded hall appreciated it and enjoyed most of all the Tableaux by the tiny ones. A collection was made for the Red Cross.

JUNE 10.

Day out to Boxhill. Went in wrong direction of course but got there eventually by bus after a push up the hill with great gusto, we sat down to rest, very eagerly, every few yards. The thought of tea got us to the top at last. After which games and the train, with usual rush.

JUNE 12.

Anne Bremer joins W.L.A. to save National food situation. Good old Anne. We hear that Terry Bates has gone abroad. Howard Saunders boxes for Club at Charity show and beats opponent. Other entrant's not so lucky but put up a good fight.

JUNE 13.

Latest Club craze is Indoor Cricket but the Boys can't stand the racket. The Girls are too rough By the way the Boys have not lost a single Handball match yet.

JUNE 14.

Whit Monday and Purley Downs. In Spite of the rain a great time. Another party went to Egham. Both have fine time in the Quiet Room that night fighting out which had finest day.

JUNE 18.

Baby Show-phew! Thanks to the members who helped and ex-members who entered babies

JUNE 22.

The Discussion Class, and others, visits Brockwell Park Open Air Theatre to see Ballet. More of such visits are planned.

JUNE 23.

C.Y.C. Dance for Catholic Club s in S. E. London. It's nice to see joint activities for Catholic Clubs.

JUNE 27.

Outdoor Procession at Meadow Road Convent. Some of our Boys were enrolled in the Guild of the Blessed Sacrament.

Mr. Thorne elected Warden for the coming year.

JUNE 28.

Harry Ward says goodbye to join the Army.

JUNE 29.

18 of us went to a violin recital at Wigmore Hall by Madame Fachiri (who has been to the Club to give concerts) and were lucky enough to get 12 free tickets for another one next week. These needed no pushing.

JULY 3.

Quite a flutter at the dance. Our first Coloured Band. What Music.

JULY 4.

Hilda Smith up for the day. We have been delighted to see old faces from time to time as they come home of leave. Those have included Barbara Abram, Jean MacDermott. Mary Fitzgerald of the Land Army. Helen Ludford, Monica Lynch, Monica Vanstone. Of the W.A.A.F.(by the way Helen L. and & Monica V. will soon be Mrs.) Eileen Smith, Julia Amer, Iris Noakes of the A.T.S. Joyce Stratton, of the W.R.N.S., Nurse MacDermott, Douglas Clarke, Joe Alleyne, Ted Lock, Pat Bryan and Frank O'Sullivan of the R.A.F.(Frank is now in Canada)Ernie Brewster, Ernie O'Sullivan, Owen Porter, Jim Nicholls, Pat Bailey, John Cullen and Peter Perla (both now abroad)from the Army, and Tim Laidler, Tom Stock, and Gerry Wickings of the Navy.

Pat Deasy is now a P.O.W. in Italy. Steve Cain and Pat Gaygan have been wounded (the latter rather badly) we all wish them a speedy recovery.

Future Plans:

We are entering for the C.Y.C Sports at Beaulah Hill on July 25. Imagine about 15 Boys and 24 Girls all out to bring back a nice silver cup to adorn our walls for a year.

St Anne's Feast will be celebrated by an entertainment by any concert party and a full length play by the Drama Group unless are called up the night before.

The C.O.M. goes to Weybridge on July 11. For their outing and the Club Mixed Outing to Boxhill on August 8th.

This year an experiment is being tried. We have taken an old farm-hostel for a week in North Devon, from September 4th. To 11th. So think of us down by the sea and imagine what might have been but for Mr.Schikelguber!

Stop Press!!

NEWS JUST RECEIVED THAT JIM MASON & JOHN SMITH ARE SAFE. P.O.W.'s IN SINGAPORE AND JAVA.

EXTRACTS FROM A LETTER RECEIVED BY A CLUB MEMBER FROM A SOLDIER ABROAD.

29th. January 1943.

What a surprise I had today when I answered the call come and get your mail.

I was given your magazines. I had given them up as lost, but when I imagine. Is that being so interesting they were read by everyone who handled them and route .....

I have glanced through the magazines that come to the conclusion that your club is something which is going a long way in helping youth. I really can no longer consider myself as a youth, but rather getting on in years, especially under the stress and strain of this tropical existence. Well, that's rather beside the point though.

What I want to say is, that the onus of another war rest on the new generation and they should be made to vow that they will ensure peace for all time. We are doing our bit with the same hopes as they had in the last war, but have every hope that another shadow will not fall in another 20 years' time

I have shown your magazines to a pal of mine, and he was interested to the extent of suggesting writing an article between us. You and the club can have the pride of knowing that you have given an interest to a few in a barren and godless country. For a year or more we have been roaming, and one feels completely out of touch with God.

Try to imagine a country totally void of churches and nothing to relieve the materialistic point of view. Vast plains very sparsely populated, mostly barren, excepting where a stream runs, surrounded by mountains of rock rising some 7000 feet, there was snow on the top. It gives one a sense of fertility but our good old British humour saves us from going mad

I do hope I'm not writing too seriously?

It is now two years since I left that "Spectred Isle" I'll and have met nearly every national there is. It is surprising or perhaps natural how they love their own country, and how they set us, the British, on a very high level, the thing which we do not really want to accept.

So time marches on, I must close now, awaiting the next edition of the magazine and all news of dear old Blighty Cheerio.

ooOoo

From time to time during idle hours my thoughts often turn towards "The Club" particularly Saturdays (as today) and I look back with pleasure on the many hours I spent dancing with, or drivelling and delighting in the society of the many friends I made there - so once again I have decided to write and this time it would seem that my intentions are to be fruitful: I could here make the point that I also am fruitful having well eaten over my share of bananas and oranges etc. Since leaving England but I'll say little on this subject for fear of causing too much envy in the breast of those over 6. Before it arises though I would like t dispel all false illusions that life is a idyllic existence of palm trees, soft sands and even softer-eyed sophisticated sirens! At the moment my share of the desert contains more dirt than the smoke laden atmosphere of London, and I share it with every variety of insect, etc., from the common ant to the tortoise passing through the stages of scorpions, lizards, mosquitoes and flying beetles of 'the bus ticket size'! Kit inspections are often awkward as it is usually difficult to distinguish between Sammy the snake and my spare laces, or Cuthbert the Chameleon and my Coal Tar(Q.M. variety) - but Nil Desperandum"

We are aptly recompensed by plenty of sunshine for about 14 hours a day of late, also we have had plenty of opportunities of sea swimming so all in all have no real complaints.

Although censorship regulations are still strict and I am not allowed to mention all I should like to - I can however mention some of the places I've been to. Cape Town was the most hospitable of all and the people there did their utmost to ensure that all of us had a thoroughly enjoyable stay Sunrise over table Mountain is a thing to be seen as it is so impressive as to defy description by pen and ink particularly as wielded by me. It was more like a masterly oil painting then any cameras could produce. The Rhodes Memorial has a quiet dignity and overlooks a panorama difficult to equal anywhere. The little I saw of India was not particularly impressive; the "Gateway" looks statelier on a picture postcard than in fact–Though that applies to almost anything to a greater or lesser degree. In Iraq I visited the capital Baghdad but the days of Magic Carpets and Ali Barber have passed away and Western-styles are in great evidence here though whilst combining East with West the difference is more marked than anywhere else I have seen. Camels, Donkeys and rickshaws vie with high powered Automobiles For the right of the road-men wear anything from sacks to Saville Row suits. Pale faced Pharisee women (their skin is the whitest in the world)! Mingle and contrast with the black veiled sombre looking Mohammedens - truly a cosmopolitan city with every colour, race, creed represented: Mosques next door to Music Halls and swing music from cinemas clashes with snake charming rhythm (Eastern style) from the ill lit cafes where the locals drink strong black coffee and smoke the Hubbly-Bubbly- the most notable place of architecture is the Arch of Ctesiphon just outside the city. In its heyday the civilisation of these parts must have been a great one as per many exhibits in the Museum - the most notable being the skeleton of a woman buried more than 4000 years ago and sunk into her neck bones is remains of the necklace she wore- also for her use various cosmetics, rings, bracelets etc.,. Other utensils considered necessary for her adornment in her new life, all of which were buried with her. Basra itself is best soon forgotten but not far from it is the reputed area of the Garden of Eden between the Tigns and the Euphrates and at one spot the natives point out a tree as being the one from which the Forbidden Fruit was plucked. I also pass through Ur where Abraham was born and trees have been found there as far back as 5400 years: the remains of Babylon - Hanging Gardens etc., are of course world-famous but in building this city Nebuchadnezzar's workman were too efficient and thoroughly defaced all traces of the 7000 year old City of Kish from where it is thought arose the first Sumerian Dynasty after the flood - traces of the flood have incidentally been found hereabouts.

At Kirkuk now a flourishing oil town, is the tomb of Daniel and site of the "Everlasting Furnace" even today one can still scrape the ground and a flame or jet of steam will hiss forth - the ground still contains many natural chemicals which years ago probably burned as a furnace. Syria I saw but did not explore.

The Trans Jordan Desert consisting entirely of blackish boulders for as far as the eye can see and stretching for over a hundred miles is a very unusual site but not the best comfortable site for sleeping. The River Jordan was distinctly unimpressive. Situated between deserts is Palestine truly described as a Land of Milk and Honey? Here I visited Jaffa not compatible with the oranges of the same name! And Jerusalem and Bethlehem where I spent most of a leave I was lucky enough to get. Tel Aviv the counter part of Brighton only more so-Gaza and Beersheba – and Bethlehem I visited the "Church of the Nativity" built over the spot of the Manger and Crib of Christ's birth. The modern city of Jerusalem is very up-to-date and to step through the gates into the Old City is like putting the clock back several hundred years at one twist. To Christians the most important places in The Old City are the Via Dolorosa and the Church of the Holy Sepulchre. A Church is erected over the spot of each of the Stations of the Cross: the last five Stations are incorporated in the church of the Holy Sepulchre. The Jews have their Wailing Wall and the Mohammedans the Mosque of Omar in which is an Urn containing 2 hairs said to come from Mohammed's beard! Just out of the Old City on the Mount of Olives is a Garden of Gethsemane in which is built the Church of all Nations. It is a beautiful Church built over the Rock of Agony and subscribed for by all principal Christian Nations. It overlooks the beautiful Valley of Jehoshaphat in which it is thought the final Resurrection and Last Judgement will take place. There is also the Chapel of the Ascension build over the rock from which Christ Ascended into heaven. I did not see much of Egypt but did cross the Suez Canal in a rowing boat! Not particularly spectacular but I don't suppose many people have done it!

Can't tell you much more at this moment but my Cooks-all -in Tour is not yet finished and I expect soon I might be studying more modern history? I hope everybody at the club is well and would like to be remembered to them all and hope to see them all again soon .... All best wishes to everybody - Dennis Smith.

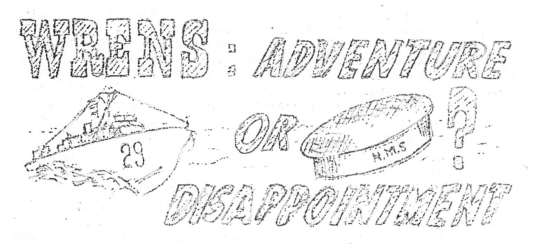

WRENS : ADVENTURE OR DISAPPOINTMENT?

A private in the Army was once asked what he thought to be the secret of a happy service life and he replied.

"To enter into it with a spirit of adventure and never to lose the spirit, and then you will take everything good and bad in your stride."

It was that thought uppermost in my mind that I entered a W.R.N.S. training establishment in London on a glorious summer morning of last year. I certainly felt very strange as I knew nothing about the W.R.N.S. and very little about the Navy, except that which I had learned in history studies, but on that morning I indeed felt very privileged to be serving with those "that go down to the sea in ships." but I did not feel strange for very long, as I was one of 300 who entered on that day, and the officers and wrens of the establishment by their kindness and understanding soon initiated us all into service life.

That was a year ago, I felt the nursery of my service life after two brief weeks and since then I have had a very gypsy -like existence. The superintendent Wrens words that we were in the service not to get but to give all that we could, have indeed meant something. That is why the words of the Army private seem to me to be the only way of making a success of service life, because it is in so many ways a life of detachment. For that reason it offers us unique opportunities for improving as spiritual status which otherwise the majority of us would be too lazy to impose upon ourselves. I refer chiefly to the discipline and obedience two commands of superiors which are demanded of us.

I have many happy memories of my life in the nursery and in my various quarters and stations. I remember the afternoon of my enrolment when five of us walked through London for the first time in our uniforms, feeling as if we were equal to Nelson or Wellington for courage and valour after we had saluted for the first time, although on close examination we found that we had acknowledged not a naval officer but a hotel commissionaire!! Then there was the day when we made our first train journey as Wrens.

We were all very security-conscious and a poor unfortunate Wren who was to join us was almost reduced to tears because even though she had tried for a quarter of an hour to prove to us that she was no fifth columnist, we refused to tell her our destination. It can be fun peeling potatoes at 3 a.m. and well can I remember those days. It was in the winter, and many times whilst plunging our hands into icy cold water at that unearthly hour, we asked ourselves why we had become Wrens, and cursed our colleagues for having such large appetites, declaring with muc self-sacrifice that we would willingly go without.

There were amusing incidents too connected with my particular work as a radio operator. Our crew suffered one severe blow to its pride when one of the members fainted when we first went on watch, thus showing that the days when women were trained in the gentle arts and swooned on every possible occasion have not completely vanished.

it's a happy life to be a Wren, but to keep it so, the spirit of adventure must not be lost, otherwise even the constant moving from place to place will become wearing and the life that was looked forward to will be a disappointing experience. It's up to us, if we maintain an adventurous spirit we shall indeed be glad that we are helping in the fight for justice and freedom for this land that shows what loveliness can be. "This England!"

ooOoo

WHITE AFRICANS & BLACK BY FATHER CHATTERTON

As one crisis succeeded another before the actual outbreak of war, and the prospect of German boots tramping over the whole of Europe came nearer and nearer actual realisation, people began to ask themselves how a war would affect them. Most of us expected lots of bombing and grim U-boat warfare. These expectations have been in some degree fulfilled, but for most of us the war has provided one surprise after another. Thus I imagined myself spending the first few years of the war in an air-raid shelter, trying to look calm, whereas in fact I spent a good deal of my time elsewhere trying to keep cool.

Such is the unexpected course of things that towards the Autumn of 1941. I found myself looking over the side of a ship in convoy at a whale, described by a native boy as "him smoking Sir." We were on our way to Freetown in Sierra Leone. A voyage from England to W. Africa in wartime is not altogether pleasant. You are overcrowded in your cabin, and have to put up with hot nights and the good old fug. The long slow voyage makes you realise what an enormous continent Africa is. On you go, day after day, knowing that if your ship were turned to eastwards at any point she would run into the western shore of Africa. However, eventually the day comes when you get into tropical rig. It is a relief after trying to survive in a stiff collar and English clothes-and you know that your destination is almost reached.

The harbour of Freetown is magnificent and can take a very large number of ships. To the South run the hills which give Sierra Leone its name; they are quite beautiful yet strangely dark in the piercing brilliance the tropical sun.

No sooner do you put your foot ashore then you are besieged by countless little boys and girls after pennies- that are your first impression. And what next? I think the weird, tumbled-down "chicken-house-like dwellings, made out of bits of tin, wood and rubbish. The people seem happy, sitting about all lazily haggling over odd looking goods offered for sale. But here one must be careful; Africa is a very large place, there is such a variety of tribes and people are that any generalisation is bound to give a wrong impression. The population of Freetown alone is made up of a mixture of some thirteen different tribes: they do not speak the same language or have the same customs or standards of education; some are poor, some wealthy, some live in very Comfortable houses and others in very uncomfortable and squalid Huts. But it is beyond me to tell you all about these (to us) strange peoples indeed. I shall send you a book called "White Africans and Black" for your common room table. So that you may see for yourself from some good

Illustrations and a story something of what the West African peoples are like.

It is strange, Isn't it, to think that one evening you are taking a cup of tea with a fellow in St Anne's club and another within a few months intervening: In the canteen in a strange, hot and smelly old Freetown.

ooOoo

TRIBUTE from a GENIUS

I had been watching the old fellow all the way from Crewe. He sat opposite me in the dusty, third class carriage, peering through thick rimmed spectacles at a large volume.

He must have been a great student with well-developed powers of concentration, for all the noise and the chatter of his fellow travellers and all the swaying and hurrying of the train left him completely undisturbed.

It was not until we had passed Watford that he looked up.

"Excuse me boy." He piped tapping me on the knee." Are you by any chance a Catholic?"

"Yes," I replied, rather shaken at the sharp and sudden turn of conversation.

"Well read this lad." He said, thrusting the book at me, and pointing a long bony finder at a paragraph: Which began at the top of the page. Wondering, I read:

"There is not, and there never was on this earth, work of human policy so well deserving of examination as the Roman Catholic Church. The history of that church joins together the two great ages of human civilisation. No other institution is left standing which carries the mind back to the times when the smoke of sacrifice rose from the Pantheon, and when the leopards and tigers came bounded in the Flavian amphitheatre. The proudest royal houses are of yesterday, when compared with the line of the Supreme Pontiffs. That line we trace back in an unbroken series, from the Pope who crowned Napoleon In the nineteenth century to the Pope Who crowned Pepin in the eighth; and far beyond the time of Pepin the August dynasty extents, till it is lost in the twilight of fable. The Republic of Venice came next in antiquity. But the Republic of Venice is gone, and the Papacy remains. The papacy Remains not in decay, not a mere antique, but full of life and youthful vigour. The Catholic Church is still sending forth to the farthest ends of the world Missionaries as zealous as those who, landed in Kent with Augustine, and still confronting post-hostile Kings, with the same spirit with which she confronted Attila. The number of her children is greater than in any former age. Her acquisitions in the New World have more than compensated her for what she has lost in the old.

Her spiritual ascendancy extends over the past countries which lie between the planes of the Missouri and Cape Horn, Countries which, a century hence, may not improbably contain a population as large of that which now inhabits Europe. The members of her communion are certainly not fewer than 150 millions: It will be difficult to show that all the other Christian sects united amount to 120 million. Nor do we see any sign which indicates that the term of her long dominion is approaching. She saw the commencement of all the governments and of all the ecclesiastical establishments that now exist in the world; and we feel no assurance that she is not destined to see the end of them all. She was great and respected before the Saxon had set foot on Britain, before the Frank had passed the Rhine when Grecian eloquence still flourished in Antioch, when the idols was still worshipped in the Temple of Mecca. And she may still exist in undiminished vigour when some traveller from New Zealand shall in the midst of a vast solitude, take his stand on a broken arch of London Bridge to sketch the ruins of St Paul's."

Scarcely had I finished that paragraph when we pulled into Euston station.

"Don't you think that is a great tribute to the church? The old fellow asked as I handed the book back to him.

"It's certainly the greatest complement I've ever read," I told him especially when one considers that it was written by Lord McCauley just over a century ago when Catholicism was not enjoying its happiest days in England. And the fact that McCauley was not a Catholic makes the tribute even more striking."

By the time I had said that mouthful the old chap had been swallowed up by the crowds on the platform.

There and then I decided to get McCauley's essay on von Ranke's. History of the Popes. And believe me I found it well worth reading.

John Cullen.

Do you Remember when "Yes, we have no bananas!" was ONLY A SONG?

SHORT STORY

"Portrait of a Dreamer" it was called. Hailed by critics "as the picture of the year." "Masterpiece", connoisseurs and buyers jostled the each other to see it. It depicted a young man of about 20, seated at a piano, one hand lightly caressing the keys, the other holding a pencil, with head thrown back finally featured face, before him laid a half- finished sheet music, while clearly great music was passing through his brain. But the making of the picture was in the eyes; misty, deep brown eyes which defied description yet which told the whole story.

A middle-aged ordinary -looking man sat in the Academy watching the reaction of the viewers. That his picture should attract such different types gratified him not a little for those eyes had taken him year to paint. A couple of art students were arguing about it. "Richard and I used to argue like that." He thought. A young boy, holding a much worn violin case stopped with his mother.

"Just look mother a dreamer with wonderful dreams, composing music for the world that people might find great joy in happiness and a little comfort in sorrow. He is thinking that people might love one another through music, and forgive each other. Er you think I shall ever be able to play with such expression that people may feel the power of the Masters?"

Mother and son passed on. Mark felt in his pocket and pulled out a crumpled pencilled sketch. Mist came before his eyes and his mind went back ...

It was a hot June day. He was climbing the garden wall to peep at his new neighbours. Imagine his surprise to see a boy about his own age, with a mop of brown curly hair, doing much the same sort of thing.

"Hello." he said, "What's your name?"

"Mark, What yours?"

"Richard."

What a whacking they both got hours later for spoiling their clothes, but what friends they had become! Later, in their youth, they had both toured the Continent, Mark for his painting, Richard for his music. Richard loved children and composed many pieces for them, loved their friendliness and trusting innocence.

"Mark. " He said one day. "I'm going to compose a work and put my whole soul into it. God has given me this gift and I want to use it in the right way. It must make people love and forgive, Happy and carefree, workers after their toil must know its beauty. It must portray ideals. But what a hopeless dreamer you must think me."

Now Richard was gone...Yes. The wall again.

Marks eyes cleared. He got up and hurried after the young boy and his mother. Presently the boy was telling him... "My mother is English; my father is Italian ....drowned .....My music lessons have stopped ....."

Mark often goes to the Academy to note his young protégé's progress he often says to himself," your dream must come true."

Pamela a Moore.

At this time of the year, when the very well-known series of Promenade Concerts is just commencing, it would appear fitting for some courageous and very humble club member to say a few words about these concerts.

Of course, to the perverted minds of the individual jazzman, these concert on nothing but madness (as the bus conductor said to us one evening whilst travelling to the Albert Hall. "Yer all looked doped when yer come out") but to the genuine music lover it is an experience unforgettable and beyond all the subtle words of poetry.

Sir Henry Wood, the distinguished conductor, inaugurated the promenade concerts forty-nine years ago. Through all these years they have become so immensely popular that the music loving public declaim: "they are now a national institution." It is indeed a very fitting tribute to Sir Henry's undying energy.

These concerts run for a period of eight weeks that is from approximately 1st. of July to 31st of August. During that time some 6000 persons attend every night. Of course, this number increases substantially when the program is a highly select one.

The programs are divided into two parts, the first is usually devoted to works of the famous classical composers such as Beethoven, Tchaikovsky and Wagner, the second part of the works of less well established composers and moderns. Certain programs devoted entirely to the works of one composer. For example Monday is Wagner night, Wednesday is Bach and Handel night, and Friday is Beethoven night.

The most popular programs are the ones devoted to the works of the mighty Beethoven.

A typical Friday evening programme is as follows:

Symphony No.1

Piano Concerto No.5 "Emperor" Overture Leonora No 3

IN MEMORIAM - SERGE RACHMANINOV.
Funeral March - Chopin
Symphony No. 3 - Rachmaninov.

The above program actually took place on Friday 25ᵗʰ June. It was indeed an excellent one. The works of the finest composer ever, placed with those of one of the most virtuoso pianist of our time, presented a very moving picture.

The hall, as usual was crowded to the point of suffocation. A burst of applause as a leader of the orchestra come in, and then a further, but more sustained, burst as a conductor came on amounts of rostrum.

The Symphony was well played, and gave us a picture of Beethoven in his lighter mood. The Concerto was really impressive, truly giving credit to its nickname "Emperor". The Overture was very beautifully performed, the trumpet call (off stage) was simply stupendous, and the famous rush of violins at the end of the piece was wonderful, indescribably wonderful. That concluded the first part of the programme.

The second part of the programme was rather more sombre. The Funeral March presented a picture of magnificence, and the Symphony whilst rather syncopated, was very pleasing.

Thus ended another Promenade Concert, a true successor to the previous ones and an inspiration to those to come.

Long made the Proms live. Long may music, the art of arts, live to give us the greatest of all pleasures.

COUGHDROPS

Life is like that. A gas range explodes and blew a husband and wife through the window. It was the first time they had been out together for five years.

A Navy gunner just came home on leave. When his wife went out one night she left him a parting reminder "To be sure and keep the fire going. When she returned the fire was out and hubby was sleeping in his chair. Just to get even, she yelled "FIRE" as loud as she could. Hubby leapt to attention tore open the oven door, rammed in the cat, slammed the door and cried "Number One Gun Ready SIR."

They had a bit of excitement at Henley the other day. The control tower got a message. "Cadet Jones to tower: My fuel gauge shows empty what'll I do?" The operations officer, envisaging a plane helplessly circling the field, rushed to the mike screaming: "Take it easy, son, don't get excited! Where are you?" Came the reply. "I'm sitting in my plane down on the flight line. I haven't taken off yet."

One day the Colonel walked into the kitchen... "ATTENTION" the Mess Sergeant shouted. All snapped to but the new recruit Cook. "What's the matter?" asked OM "why don't you stand up when the command is given?" "SIR" the cook explained "I've just started this recipe, which says don't stir for 25 minutes."

H.G's Walking down a London street the other day, had the laugh of a life-time when they saw a second Lieutenant – dash around the corner and high-tail it down the street after a bus - a woman chasing him with a hairbrush!

Hitler's hair is said to be turning grey. --- What's he worried about it won't last long.

A sailor and his girl were strolling through the park. Spring was in the air, etc.; the damsel looked up soulfully and sighed. "There's romance in the sky romance in the clouds romance in the sun!" Muttered the realistic Sailor. "Say, sister isn't there any romance within walking distance?"

Our spy on the continent cables that 1944 Nazi tanks will have 4 speeds in reverse.

The Navy's newest recruit shouted. "Man overboard." Engines were reversed etc., when the young "Matelot" reported. "Sir I made a mistake when I said man overboard. The Captain quickly called for full steam ahead, muttering naughty things about recruits. But a third time the recruit came up. – "Perhaps I should explain Sir, that it was one of those nurses."

Howard Saunders

ooOoo

POETSCORNER

SOMEWHERE IN ENGLAND
You loved him you married him
Now you have to wait
Until the war is over and
There is an end to hate
You said you would prefer to be
His wife for just a day
The not to have his loving arms
Before he went away.
And will you do your duty now
To write him every night
To pray for him and dream for him
When you put out your light
You are a brave determined girl
You keep your chin up high
To watch the battle fronts to hear
The thunder in the sky
And surely God will keep him safe
And bring him back to you
                    H. Saunders

WHAT MAIL MEANS
I try to pass the mailbox
And hold my head real high
I know there's not a letter there
And I just want to cry
It's so long since you've written
I expect to hear each day
But I've only had two letters
All the time I've been away
If you only knew my longing
Perhaps your write more often

The way I want you to
A letter such a small thing
But it's bigger than the sea
When it's one that you have written
And sent with love to me.

J. Moss

ooOoo

ENVY

Lilies with the flaxen face
Poppies flaunting his and Grace
Rosebuds dimpling in the sun
Have no worldly ease to run
Swayed by breezes washed by rain
They've no earthly toil or strain
And when another life I start
A life wherein I have no heart
I pray O God that I may be
A little blossom on a tree

A.J.L.

ooOoo

BRUSH UP YOUR LITHURGY

Distinguish between Gradual's and GREMIALS: Missales and Missiles:
Aspersoria's and Aspros: Chasubles and Capsules: Maniples and Mandibles: Predellas and Prelates: As and Antiphon: Pew and Pewter: Girdles and Gurgles.

ooOoo

BRUSH UP YOUR BIBLE

What Old Testament dog wagged his tail and why?
Who had a talking donkey?
Prove from the Old Testament that dogs are partial to women.
What hero of Israel proved that empty headed chatterboxes are a menace to human life?
How can you show that all bald headed men seldom rise in the world?

ooOoo

A GRUMBLE

Having been a member of the club for some years now I think I can speak with more than a little authority regarding the atmosphere of the club. For some time now there seems to have been a lack of spirit and sociability which although it may pass unnoticed by members, must be very apparent to newcomers. How many can honestly say that they know everybody in the club? It is obvious that you cannot be everybody's busom pal but it is the duty of all members to be good mixers and not split up into small groups as though the rest of the club was beneath one's dignity.

It is extremely hard to be chatty and at ease with a complete stranger but even a few words will help to make a person feel at home. The number of would-be members who have been literarily frozen out of the club must be enormous.

With just a little thought for others and very much less egoism St Anne's can once again become a model club. So what about it fellow members?

ooOoo

SOME ADDRESSES

Trooper Patrick Deasy 10600930 P.G.66 PM 3400 Italy
Denis Smith (as on letter)
Miss C Hutt."Littlecot" Lostwithiel Cornwall.
Ldg. Radio Mech. John Moss (R.N.)P/MX117651,H.M. L. S. "Skeena"
c/o. G.P.O. LONDON. Doonfoot. Nr. Ayr. SCOTLAND.
Rev. J. Chatterton. R.N., Royal Naval Barracks. DEVONPORT.
L.A.C. Birkett D., 339326, 33.W.V., R.A.F., M.E.F.
1330029. F. Parsons. L.A.C., R,A.F. M.U. LAGOS Oshodi. B.W.A.F.

JACK GREER
5118453 Sgt.J. N. Greer.
R.A.S.C.,Q(A,E)Branch.
G.H.Q.,M.E.F.

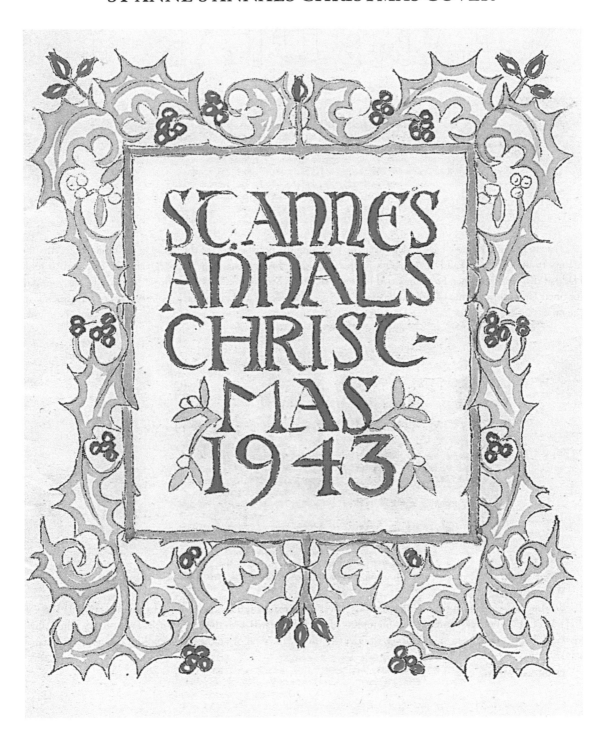

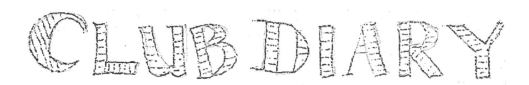

CLUB DIARY

Saturday 24th. July

True to promise we now have a nice silver cup adorning the polished top of the piano in the quiet room. Thanks mainly to the efforts of Paddy Coyle high-jumper, he floats through the air with the greatest of ease and to John Haddad that scarlet runner. St. Anne's tied for top place with Streatham. Well done Boys! It certainly was your day for once. Good to see Ernie O'Sullivan keeping up the old tradition and giving such a *commendable* performance in the mile.

Sunday 25th. July.
Red letter day magazines are out. Hey you, take your turn in the queue, you'll get your copy if you stop shoving.

Wednesday 29th. July.
Bustling and banging in the hall all this week. Fever pitch reached today reason, the last rehearsal of "LILIES OF THE FIELD." All the cast going round mumbling under their beards with the exception of Frank Barry, who knows his words backwards. The man is a marvel, wonder whether he has swallowed the book whole or if he is just made that way!

Friday 30th. July.

Several people roaming around and looking as though their last hour had come, including Father and Mr. Bailey. Between them they have a totally transformed the stage and we now look through French windows onto a peaceful scene of flowers and trees and sky. Black cloths can be very realistic at times.

This necessitating the removal of part of the back wall thus giving an additional source of entry. The play went off very well indeed and £7.00 was raised for the settlement. Frank Barry must be congratulated on his fine portrayal of a country vicar. Everybody remarked that it was the best performance yet. Further performance to be given in September, if the cast can manage to remember their words all that time.

Saturday 8ᵗʰ. August.

Outing to St. George's College Addiscombe. Terrific muddle over journey, but arrived safe and sound, just in time for lunch. Many thanks to the Father's for given us such a lovely time!! Their orchards were too good to be missed!! As for the blackberry bushes on the "wild land" at the back - the memories of those haunt us still.

Monica Vanstone today plighted her troth to Jim Frouton congratulations Mr. and Mrs. And all good wishes.

Wednesday 11ᵗʰ. August.

Ernie O. Sullivan goes abroad today. Let's hope it won't be long before he is home again. May God bless and protect him.

Sunday 22th. August.

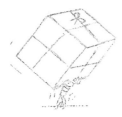

Rosemary Martyn presented four plays today and the way those youngsters "put them over" shows how well they had been trained. All excelled themselves, and we were quite captivating by the little pageboy who staggered onto the stage with a box almost as big as himself. We are looking forward to some more treats of this kind, so what about it Rosemary?

Tuesday 24ᵗʰ. August.

Boys play Westminster at Table Tennis and won 13-4

Saturday 28ᵗʰ. August.

Six brave pioneers go to prepare the ground for the would be holidaymakers at Bumsley Farm Hostel.-------
Report as follows:-

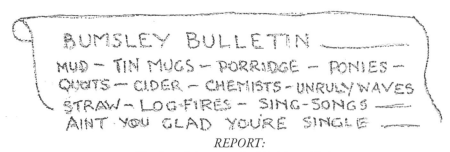

BUMSLEY BULLETIN _____
MUD ~ TIN MUGS ~ PORRIDGE ~ PONIES ~
QUOITS ~ CIDER ~ CHEMISTS ~ UNRULY WAVES
STRAW ~ LOG-FIRES ~ SING-SONGS _____
AINT YOU GLAD YOU'RE SINGLE _____

REPORT:

The first of the many: by Madeleine Taylor.

A short walk 1½ miles, a sharp climb over a sort of Mount Everest with cases full of lead, brought us to the farm. After a high tea we decided to explore some of the inviting paths got lost and nearly missed supper. Retired to bed, carefully padding our tenderest parts with any tufts of straw that happened to be in the mattresses.

SUNDAY: Rose early, to get a little rest before our 8 mile walk to Mass, all feeling a little horsey. Climbed Beacon Hill in steady downpour and commenced to foot slog. To our surprise, car gives us a lift to Lynton. Two early now, so we indulged in swings are putting in local park and nearly missed Mass. U.S. Army band meets us swinging "Adeste Fidelis". After Mass we explore Lynton and Lynmouth and a "paddle" which practically meant swimming with all our clothes on. Hence to walk home through pouring rain, picking blackberries and singing lustily, seemed quite a dry affair.

Diary Cont./-

Monday 30th. August.

We lose Reg. Connor to the Air Force and Harry Ward to join the Army. Good luck to them both.

Further report as follows:-

BUMSLEY BULLETIN Cont./

MONDAY: Early breakfast, and away to sea, just 2 miles off. This time taking costumes. Towards lunchtime, we thought we'd ask where it was, approached lonely cottage, and were sent back to almost where we started from, to walk in opposite direction. Arrived eventually, but too rough to swim. After lunch, discovered the Hunters Inn. Thought it was a mirage but a scrumptious tea reassured us. Went home to de-carbonise our shoes. They called it mud.

TUESDAY: Woody Bay today. Started early, but were late when we left the Hunters. Did some commando stuff, straight up the face of the cliff but it was worth it. At the top the sun was just breaking through and the sea looked as though it was on fire! The cliffs were white and grey with purple heather and yellow gorse. We all stood silent, just looking, the only sounds were of seagulls screeching and waves breaking on the rocks below. We walked down an 18 inch path with a drop down one side to investigate two piers marked on the map, having visions of tea pavilions and slot machine. These proved to be too stone jetties with not s sign of civilisation. Had a glorious swim which made us crave more than ever for tea. Found a fresh water stream pouring down a mossy bank, and literally "fell in."

WEDNESDAY: To Ilfracombe; hook or by crook. A wet and weary walk to Coombe Martin: and bus from there. Most of the time was spent in a café. A quick look round, and bus back to Coombe Martin to trek seven miles home. Though the spirit was willing the flesh is weak, so we hired a taxi.

THURSDAY AND FRIDAY: Our turn for Orderley Duty. Short visit to the she village,i.e. three shops, one church and a few Houses. Disentangled our plaits (first time for a week) and made frantic preparations for the others, and get some fish and chips before meeting the "party proper."

Diary Cont./-
Saturday 4ᵗʰ. September.
Club very quiet and peaceful us all its noisiest members under the care of Father Koch are on holiday at a farm hostel in Devon. We lose Pamela Moore to the W.L.A. and "Biff" has also joined the tillers of the soil somewhere in England.

ooOoo

BUMSLEY BULLETIN Cont./-
B. THE PARTY PROPER. by. Violet Crickwood.

Saturday: The "Main Party" arrived at Barnstaple at 4.20 pm except a certain Miss. B. We played "Humpty Dumpty" on a wall, waiting. The foresaid Miss B.turning up eventually we bundled into the Bumsley bus and were dumped at the cross roads. Eventually after a high climb and many rest we arrived and having crossed a slab of stone bridging the Heddon Water, we found ourselves in the old 16ᵗʰ century farmhouse. After the "scrum" for a bed or bunk, there followed a general upheaval unpacking and bed-making. Above the noise of everybody talking at once, came the welcome sound of the gong, and all trooped down to high tea. After tea, partaken from enamel plates and tin mugs, some took stock of our surroundings, whilst others improvised a "chapel" in the barn. We sat round the log fire and sang songs, and very soon after a supper of cocoa and sandwiches retired to bed, very tired and very happy. Mass at eight in the chapel.

SUNDAY: Along a lovely walk to Heddon Bay past and moors of purple heather and home again for lunch. Lazy afternoon a lazy afternoon in the field. strolled in village in evening for cider at "FOX AND GEESE."

MONDAY: Another walk to Heddon Bay. Some of us standing in the sea, unexpectedly got very wet. In the evening we all trotted along to the "HUNTERS INN" singing all the way there. We waited in vain for some cider, and sang all the way home again: and played against for the rest of the evening.

TUESDAY: Up early, Marion Wright, ready for a long walk to listen. We set out your sandwiches, as apples are lots of good cheer, marching in step with the music of rioting by the young men(?) of the party. After a happy day at Linton it more or less (they would not serve one of a young man in the Club as he was not old enough) he was decided, that the aged and the weary should go back to Parracombe by bus. They were all given the luggage to take home. And the unfortunately, the conductor forgot to tell them where to get off, they were taken almost into a Barnstable and had to tramp many a weary mile back with the luggage.

WEDNESDAY: Birthday of Our Lady, she was duly honoured in the little "Chapel." Pony riding, games and little parties going about on their own.

Not without testimony, about a dozen of us decided to try the far famed pastimes of pony riding. Three ponies were available and the rides were of two hours' duration.

Bernard, Joan and I made up our party. The facetious remarks which were passed, we received with a tolerant smile. Dolly, a peculiarly wild pony fell to my lot, and having mounted, we set off- at least, they did, for Dolly would not move despite all my efforts. She simply would not stop eating grass, and it was only after I had kicked and lashed her vigorously that she made any attempt to move.

Until the moors were reached, we maintained a walking pace but after that, we made an exhilarating speed, sometimes trotting sometimes cantering and even occasionally galloping. At first, being known as a "greenhorn" I was jolted up and down by Dolly with merciless consistency till my very ribs seemed near bursting point. Relief came, however I suddenly discovered the knack of rising in the stirrups with the horse in such a way that bumping was cut out. In this way riding became a beautiful smooth motion and a real pleasure.

When the Heath had been crossed, we arrived at the hills overlooking a place called Woody Bay. The view from here was remarkable. On the far horizon, the mountains of Wales rose up to meet the clouds, whilst the sea from our lofty height seemed as if it were frozen and motionless. To the left and right Moors was steep hill slopes covered with trees we rode slowly along in an atmosphere that one is serene and content, and then off we dashed along at a stony path. As we wended our way home we sore for the first time, the wonderful picture given by the heat and the hills in the setting sun. Yes, I can say quite honestly that I thoroughly enjoyed my first attempt at only writing.

By Rudi Perla.

PS. Quite honestly? What about you when you stopped to hold an open a gate and Dolly walked on and left due on the gate, Rudi?

THURSDAY: Some went into Barnstable and the rest had as sunny day by the sea. We had tea in the garden of "Kittitoe Guest House," we appreciated the beautiful China and new bread.

FRIDAY. Last day in "Glorious Devon" and last look round the village gathering blackberries and heather, the last "glass" in the Hunters. Some neighbours came in the evening to join in her sing-song round the open number log-fire.

SATURDAY: Everybody up early, bags and cases packed. Twenty-nine of us gathered round Edna and Dorothy who had looked after us so well and sang "for they were jolly good Fellows three cheers." We pick up our luggage and march up the hill to get our bus. A walk round Barnstable, lunch at various places, restaurants or fish shops according to fancy, then train home

We shall think of that lovely holiday in Devon for a long time to come.

ooOoo

Diary Cont./-
Saturday 11th. September.

Today heralds the return of the wanders from thee sunny south. Rupert Brook's poem "The Great Lover" adequately describes everybody's feelings about it- especially if read with tongue in cheek. Normal life resumed at Club. No more peace from now on!

Friday, 17th. September.

We learn that Frank Barry has to go into hospital for a serious operation your prayers for his recovery please.

Monday, 20th. September

Today it was decided to start a gramophone Record Club and a Book Circle. Members to pay 2p per week which entitles them to a free choice of book or disc in turn. Records can be swing or Classic according to taste. Club assisted by contributing a certain percentage towards the cost.

Friday, 24th. September.

Reproduction of the LILIES OF THE FIELD was to have taken place today but owing to the unfortunate illness Frank Barry the principal character, it has to be abandoned.

Sunday, 26th. September.

Peter Katin! A name to be remembered, for although only 12 years old he plays the piano with the brilliance and accuracy of a true artist. And can he sing! And eat too. Seven of the Club's buns in one go isn't in it!! Many thanks to Mr. Barr and Peter's parents for making it possible for us to hear a genius in the making.

Friday 1st October.

Dramatics our resumed again under the very capable her leadership of Miss. Chown. Play decided upon being THE CRIME AT BLOSSOMS so those concerned have a busy time ahead of them. Time limit for learning words, six weeks! Where's the Sal Volatile! They've all fainted!!

Tuesday 5th. October.

Good heavens who's this? Why, its Madie Taylor returned to the fold after an absence due to illness and believe it or not, she's gone blonde in front, or is it her halo in the making! The Devon Sun must have been strong!

Friday 8th. October.

Table Tennis match between St. Vincent's and ourselves. We lost.

Saturday 9th. October.

Mrs. Agnes Stock presented her husband with a baby daughter today. Congratulations to both and all good wishes to Ann Kathleen.

Tuesday 12th. October.

First attempt at the English Class with Father Koch as head. Nearest attempt to a "Will Hay St. Michael's" we'll ever get. The new teacher soon put the pupils in order and learned a lot!

Sunday 17th. October.

Young ladies about to be called up, receive very good advice from Dr. Letty Fairfield and Father Rochford at a conference for Girls.

The Girls beat Camberwell at netball 25 -3

Tuesday 19th. October.

After last week's frantic effort at an English Class, we have at last been sent a gift from heaven in the person of Mrs. Dearlove. The syllabus is very interesting and includes a study of the English language. This Class is most enjoyable so don't be put off by the high fallutin' title. Come along and enjoyed yourselves and learn to speak proper.

Sunday 24th. October.

Several Club members paid a visit to Saint Alban's to see Frank Barry. He is recovering from his operation and we were glad to see him looking much better.

The Boys won their football match against St. Vincent's.

Friday, 29th. October.

Boys beat St. Vincent's at a Table Tennis match.

Sunday 31st. October.

If you should pass by the new Quiet Room on the Sunday evening and hear hilarious shouts issuing forth, don't wonder what on earth's the matter. The reason for such merriment is that under the new order. Sunday evenings are now Social evenings and much fun and laughter can be had out of playing such games as "Proverbs", and "Adverbs" "The Spirit Passeth", etc. Why not join us and enjoy your Sundays!!!

Tuesday 2nd.November.

The Young Boys Club is going strong. Members have much difficulty in making themselves heard.

Tuesday 8th November.

A staggering bill has come from the Tate Library for missing books. Will all those who have ever borrowed any books, search their shelves and cupboards to make sure they've not got any of them. We should also be grateful for the return of any old football kit, which has been borrowed.

Wednesday 9th. November.

Camera given by Rosemary Martin realised £2. To go towards meeting the Tate Library bill. The netballers and footballers have been very busy again this season and have thoroughly enjoyed their games. Many thanks to Mrs. Gibbs who is also at the Club on Saturdays for netball whatever the weather. The Girls have won a goodly number of matches to date and the Boys have scored the winning goal so many times that we suspect them of praying to St. Jude. Table Tennis matches on Fridays and Sundays have been well supported and if the resulting scores have not always been in our favour, the comradeship and friendliness which has arisen between the other Club s and St. Anne's is all that really matters.

V've Le Sport as they say in our Parks. We are always glad to hear from our members who are serving with the forces whether oversees or still in England. Familiar faces are forever welcome and we have received visits from such people as: Barbara Abram - woman expert in tractor driving among other things. - Hilda Smith quite a a hand at milking cows – Anne Brewer and Pam Moore- our cabbage and potato supplies is assured- Mary Fitzgerald -who usually manages to come home "in the wars,"- C. Riffoni now a Tiller of the soil and E. Blessington who manages to get home every weekend and is as keen netballer as ever –

E. Smith A.T.S. pops in every three months or so and looks fine and Mrs. Enid Lynch W.A.A.F. comes in occasionally as does Mrs. J Minton(nee Badger). Arthur Blessington has come home after a year abroad having volunteered as a paratrooper: news derives from time to time from F. Parsons, T. Bates, F. O'Sullivan, E. O'Sullivan, J. Moss, Peter Perla, P. Polombo, D. Smith and D. Clerk.

We learn that Frank Barry who is convalescing in Warwickshire has now developed rheumatism and so will not be coming home until Easter or thereabouts. All our sympathy Frank, you are having a stiff time. Ernie May, we are sorry to hear: has had to go into hospital for a rest cure, please God here would be when us again

We would wish all our readers and members are very happy Christmas and New Year.

E COLLINS.

ooOoo

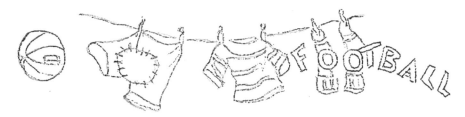

FOOTBALL

BY BERNARD DRIVER (Capt)

Absent members must still wonder if St.Anne's still runs a football team, and whether it is a successful team.

For their benefit, we append below,the result of their matches to date. The team is of course, essential a young one and one of our greatest handicaps is that we are unable to play the same team each week.

As ever, the defence is good. The weaknesses is in the attack as we lack the regular centre forward and right wing. Nevertheless every game played has been very keen and fast.

We are still In the C.Y.C. League S.W. Section and are mostly meeting old rivals.

On Sunday, November 27th. we visited St. Mary Magdalens Mortlake and played our best and closest game of the season to date. Afterwards, we were royally entertained.

If any Members ever look in at the Club and feel like a game we will do our best to fit them in.

In conclusion on behalf of the team I send best wishes to all old playersAnd hope they are getting plenty of sport.

RESULTS UP TO DATE

St. Annes	9...	St. Mary's	4
"	4...	St. Mary's	4
"	4...	St. Vincent's	2
"	2...	Holy Ghost	2
"	1...	Streatham	2
"	0...	Mortlake	1.

ooOoo

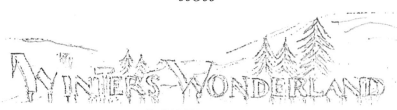

WINTERS-WONDERLAND

By PAMELA MOORE.

Peter and I donned our winter coats when Cliff and Pauline knocked. As had been our long custom, the four of us were to walk the seven odd miles to Landey for Midnight Mass.

We exchanged greetings and stepped out into the bitter night air. For hours the snow had been falling thick and fast and was now falling in a few wispy flakes. Pauly and I chatted about our Christmas shopping, presents, new clothes and how they fitted, while the Boys snorted as though to say "Girls all over! That's all they think about; clothes." Nevertheless while we talk read definitely heard them mention new overcoats, and new silk shirts. Soon the conversation flagged, Pauly found her way to Cliff's arm and, while I measured my stride with Peter's silence fell upon us.

The stars shone brightly in the blue black velvety sky, and the crisp snow crunched under feet. We were walking through Christmas card land. Over little bridges where the stream had frozen below. Along hedges with fairy cobwebs, past trees whose branches, laden is snow, held in strangely beautiful and sometimes grotesque shapes, past lonely cottage with a few bright lights making the snow glow wherever the light fell. Probably I thought, some loving parents were filling their children's stockings with toys, chocolates, fruit and nuts. We cane to a village with a quaint Church perched on a hill, and my imagination ran riot. I could see the villagers wending their way up to the little church whose bells pealed merrily, the women dressed in long cloaks and hoods, the men in their three-quarter high hats, wide cloaks and long boots. Sleigh bells were jingling sweetly and carriages a with the horses hoofs making but the slightest sound of the soft snow were making their way to that same little Church on the hill to Midnight Mas in the days of old.

"Look where are you going?" Shouted Peter, as I negotiated a telegraph pole and they laughed at my dreams.

We had yet another half-hours walk so we took to singing carols and, arm in arm we strode along with GOOD KING WENCELAS, ANGELS, KING'S AND SHEPHERDS. By the time we reached Landey we were short of breath and tingling with warmth that comes from exercise. We made our way to the little Church dedicated to "The Queen of Angels.", found our benches in the warm candle-glow, and prepared for Mass, The choir was at its best, and I could see that everyone was filled with the spirit of Christmas. After Mass we visited the Crib, and as we left the Church, I turned to look once more at the brightly burning candles, flowers and ever-greens and at the Statues welcoming the Child King, the wonderous night, long, long ago!

"Let's go home our castle way." Said Pauly, upon which everyone agreed. The castle had been our playground for years, at first for frolic and later for study. We knew at castle-history by heart. As we rounded a bend in the river, there it stood high up on the bank with a background of tall pine trees, gaunt dark.

"Looks a bit creepy." Whispered Pauly. We marched boldly up the stone steps to the Massive oak doors, and Peter placed his eye to one of the many cracks.

"What do you see?" I asked.

"Why spooks! yes spooks of bygone ages. Jesting and revelling. The lord of the castle is entertaining; the wine is flowing. Ah! And here comes the great boar's-head leading the procession of joints and delicacies. Ho! Ho! shouts the lord on his dais. Eat, drink, and be merry! More music Jesters more foolery, laugh my merry maidens and gallants."

Plop! A well-aimed snowball from me, caught him on the ear, and then began a good old snowball fight, Pauly and Peter versus Cliff and I.

The fight took us well towards home and before long, we were sitting around a huge crackling log fire drinking steaming hot cocoa and munching crisps, buttered toast. When I made my way to bed the choir's GLORIA IN EXCELSIS DEO ET IN TERRA PAX was ringing in my ears and my heart was filled the spirit of Christ's Mass in Ye Olde Merry England.

ooOoo

EAST AND WEST
BY
JOHN CULLEN.

Have you not seeing the gentle, waving palm,
At the eventide beside the Indian shore;
Nor seen the Indian Ocean, placid, calm,
Whipped up by galeinto tempestuous roar?
Nor seen the dawn's first flush of snow-capped peaks of Himalayas;
Nor seen the Holy Ganges where it seeks
Across sparse, sweltering plains the distant sea?
Nor have you viewed with fascinated eye's
The coloured markets, spices, silks, and dyes
Thronged with black natives, ragged, poor, unshod?
Have you not seen the wanderers Hand of God?
Ah! But I've seen the smiling fields of Kent,
And Orchard boughs with rosy apples bent
A thatched cottage on a winding hill
Where bees, and buttercups, and peace live still;

A rustic window with an antique vase,
Where skylarks sing amid the fading stars
Where scent of hay, new mown, does please the sense,
Rose-frames porch, and crazy, broken fence,
Cool stroll at evening, neighbours friendly nod,
Yes, I have seen the wondrous Hand of God.

ooOoo

KILLED IN ACTION.
By HOWARD SAUNDERS

It happened last night....or had you heard...
With all your problems sure he tried
Perhaps there wasn't the time to no know
That last night ... A soldier died.
It was no one of importance.... Just a boy
Perhaps you might remember him,
The paper boy a few years back.
I think they used to call him Jim

Tough job he had.... There all alone,
To hold that knob as best he could
Specially when there wasn't to hand
The ammunition that there should.
They say t'was great... the stand he made:
He saved the lives of scores of men
With arm hung limp along his side.
He stemmed the drive.... Again and again.

He ran clear out of cartridge clips
And as the yellow tide rolled past,
He waded in with one good fist,
He is the only weapon.... At the last,
He beat them off as man gone mad
And calling back along the line
For the ammunition he knew full well
We never would get through in time.

His thin lips muttering a curse
At the devils swarming him there
While in his heart, for us at home, and
He framed, muttered, a silent prayer.
I guess it was no pretty sight
They've found while morning light was dim
Drowned in his own life's blood
That world within the throat of Jim.

They say he will get a Posthumous "Cross"

And I guess he knew just what it meant
To give in full for the things he loved...
Not just a measly "ten per cent",
Oh come now....sure, I hadn't thought
To disturb your calm or give you a fright
It only thought you'd want to know
For it happened.... Just last night.

ooOoo

DID YOU THINK
By JONNIE MOSS

Those slim grey ships slide out from shore
Said then they go and passing on
Those ships were in your mind no more,
Or of laughing Boys who manned them
Did you think as they steamed away
Just where they went or what name did
Or if they'd see dawn another day
After they had left the Harbour mouth
Clear of the land, way out of sight
But it ever occur to you
That they may already be in a fight?
I do like the many who just except
The daily rations and grumbled too
With never a thought for the men out there
Who gave their lives to bring them through?
"Admiralty regret to announce the loss....!"
You've heard the voice on the radio say
Did you shrug your shoulders and then remark
"So what they launched three more today!!!"
But many brave lads were also launched
To a world way far beyond the blue
They loved their lives- but gladly gave then
That others may live-including you
They seldom make the headlines bold
With a little fuss they do their work
For King- for Country- and Mankind
Facing the grim odd which they never shirk
Yet many scorn them, many shun
And it hurts them if you only knew
To feel with most they rank so low
Branded- "a rough unholy crew"
That's why so often when they're ashore
Our Sailors seldom seem to care
When they offend or what they do
To past a few short hours they're there

Yet when the bugle call shall sound
And God shall come all the men to judge
Whose soul I wonder them will show
The smaller all the greater smudge?

ooOoo

THESE I HAVE LOVED

By MARY CHANCE

The first start of evening hanging in the trembling sky
The Moon glimpsed through the twigs of a leafless tree
A flash of understanding with a child, and children
themselves warm and eager
Music-God's most generous gift, and the wonder of words in
poetry
Heathered hills and quite primrosed valleys
A lone train whistling through the soundless night
Dusty sunbeams and cottage gardens
Well-formed hands and well dressed women
Foghorns heard across the dirty London Thames
The smack of leather flung against willow
And cats- mysteriously things who full well know they were once
held divine
The sinking into sleep and remembering dreams on waking
Kilted men marching and some people's smiles
The hallowed peace and security felt in old Churches
The flicker of a fire-lit room and young roses.
The rumbling throb of organs and waves of love
The shape of horses
The distance splendour of high Mars, and the weekday Mars
That makes the whole meaning clear.

ooOoo

LAUGH THIS OFF BY *Paddy Coyle*
1. The highest honour Scotsmen can confer on anyone is the Freedom of the City.
2. Sixpence for that coat-hanger. Too Much.
3. A moth is a Scotsman's favourite pet in the house because it only eats holes.
4. Will you give me a penny? What for? For being good. Can't you be good for nothing like your father?
5. Can you tell the difference between a tram and a taxi? No! then get a tram.
6. The saddest story of the month is about the Scot who paid 15/- for a room in a hotel and dreamed he was sleeping in a park.

I WISH YOU ALL LUCK THERE IS AND ALL YOUR HEART'S DESIRE AND ALL THE MONEY IN THE WORLD I DON'T REQUIRE.

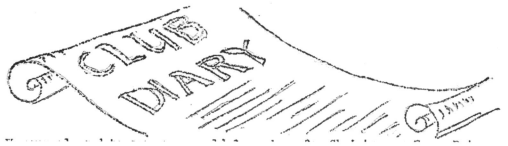

We were pleased to see so many old faces home for Christmas. Terry Bates and Arthur Blessington from North Africa. Barbara Abram, Eileen Blessington, Ann Bremer, Pamela Moore from the Land Army. Also Carrado Ruffoni.

December 31st.

A universal hubbub wild sounds and voices all confused.

Club party a great success. Fancy dress numerous and original. The prizes were won by Evelyn Collins-a shepherdess-the prettiest. Delfina Ventura-Black Market-the the most original Adolf Perla- Red Riding Hood's Grandmother-the funniest.

Father Koch representing the LAW and tried to keep order. Congrats, to Arthur Parsons and Phil Cullen on its organisation.

January 2nd.

C.O.M. Party. A scrumptious tea in spite of rationing.

Father Koch did a hat trick by producing Christmas Pudding to finish it off. Fortunately the party ended before all the furniture was broken owing to a new game- "Musical Air Raid!"

January 3rd.

We returned to Classes and normal life again after the Christmas holiday.

January 5th.

We're certainly enjoying ourselves, three parties in one week. We were very enjoyably entertained by the concert party and we congratulate them and Mr. Hyde and all their hard work. They seem very well versed in Pub-Crawling! We now know where they spend their time when not at the Club. The Hall was beautifully decorated with coloured candles (which did not drip on us this year owing to the ingenuity of Mr. Bailey and Damien) and the waitresses picturesque costumes added to the effect.

January 8th.

We heard that Frank Barry who has been in hospital since last September was very ill. We had Masses sent for him and hope that you will all pray for him. He is now at Nuneaton too far away for us to visit him.

January 16th.

Rosemary Martyn presented a children's plays which were a great success the attendance was excellent in spite of the thick fog. The sum of £3.7.0. was collected for the dept.

Eileen Smith and Monica Lynch (nee Chance) were home on leave. We congratulate the latter on obtaining her second stripe.

January 22nd.

Girls beat Balham Holy Ghost at netball.

January 24th.

We were pleased to see John Kennedy on leave looking none the worse for his Torpedoing experience.

After causing a great deal of trouble and having numerous interviews Phil Cullen, condescended to start work at the Air Ministry. Little did they known what they have let themselves in for.

January 29th.

Elie Pasquini and Harry Ward home on leave, both looking very well.

January 30th

We invited several football and netball teams from other Club s to a social evening. The concert party entertained us once again. We ended the evening with dancing. Plenty of food floating round, our members have not heard of rationing. Boys have suffered their worst defeat of the season from Mortlake 10 -2.

February 4ᵗʰ.

Adolf Perla went into hospital today. Peaceful days ahead.

February 5ᵗʰ.

Adolf proved too much even for the hospital authorities. They set him loose today. Girls defeated Mortlake 28 -2.

February 8ᵗʰ.

Boy's with the help of one of the despised Girls team beat Mortlake 14 – 11 at Table Tennis.

February 18ᵗʰ.

The Dramatic Class presented "Crime at Blossoms." We congratulate all members for their performances specially Evelyn Collins and a Ron Villard who had so much to learn. The hall was packed and £6.7.0 was collected for the debt.

February 20ᵗʰ.

Boy's conference given by and Father Fitzgerald. St. Anne's were represented by 10 members. Girl's spent the afternoon buttering and jamming buns for them to eat.

February 25ᵗʰ.

We were delighted to see Danny Berkett home again after 3 ½ years in the Middle East. He's looking very well and needless to say he's pleased to be home

February 27ᵗʰ.

Girl's made a day's retreat at the Club.

Report as follows:-

REPORT OF THE RETREAT
BY *Phil Collins.*

Sunday Morning February 27ᵗʰ. No light of the number of Girls in various parts of the Club busily preparing their task for the day.

It was to be a Boys Retreat for the Girls and each one and one small job to perform during the day. The rota been prepared beforehand.

We began with 10 0'clock Mass in the Oratory. Mess in the oratory! This seemed only one of those true events of which we dreamed. But here, it was really taking place, and it's very sanctity filled the little Chapel with renewed warmth.

Father Warner S.J. gave the retreat. Deep knowledge of his well chosen subjects together with striking fluency of speech and interesting similes made the conference excellent and instructive.

To hear the Stations on the Cross in the large hall, then another conference. At 1.00 there was dinner(which by the way was delicious) I think someone forgot to get up and began to serve, or something of that nature, but apart from drowning Father Koch's voice(whilst reading in during dinner) with the scrape and scratch of soup spoons it passed uneventfully.

Afterwards there was spare time for a quiet reading or perhaps a visit to the Chapel. I believe that someone was overheard to say that "silence is indeed golden."

At 2:40 there was another conference followed by the Rosary.

Tea was at 4.o'clock. This again was very enjoyable and there was a conspicuous absence of soup spoons.

Our excellent day closed with Benediction, one which impressed us all very much. I still love to picture the little Alter silently aglow with the flickering of candles and the once Monstrance majestically radiating a magnificent of multi spangled light. And over all the tranquil atmosphere the faint mist of incense.

ooOoo

Diary Cont./-

February 29th.

Boy's won their Handball match against St Christians Peckham 11-1

March 2nd.

We started a Scout Troop for Boys over 11 and hope it will be a success.

March 3rd.

Photo's received from Frank O' Sullivan now in the Bahamas, the travelling around and seems to thrive on it. Members so impressed by the performance of "Crime at Blossoms." flocked to join the Dramatic Class

March. 4th.

The Netballers beat West Norwood 38- 2.

March 6th.

We heard with deep regret that Paddy Hyland had died of wounds received in Italy. R.I.P.

March 10th.

Rudy Perla once again on holiday, informs us most solemnly that it is only for six weeks this time.

March 13th.

Queer noise in the Club. Joan MacDermott be 'ome on leave from the Land Army.

Ernie Morgan left to join up. We wish him the best of luck.

March 14th.

Paul Palumbo taken prisoner in Italy and escaped while waiting for transportation to Germany. Brave Paul!

March 15th.

Heard from Barbara Abram- the backbone of the Land Army says she is busy ploughing, harrowing, drilling, etc. Also they have several new calves. We hope Daphne appreciates the honour of having one named after her.

March 16th.

Boy's beat St Mary's Lambeth at handball 11- 4.

March 21st.

After a fortnight's hard work by Father and Mr. Bailey, the quiet room is a masterpiece of interior decoration. Unfortunately it was seen by a few members as it was blitzed one hour after being finished.

March 22nd. CLUB RE-BLITZED.

REPORT ON BOMB DAMAGE as follows:-

The dismal occurrence of the wailer was becoming quite familiar, and when it sounded at one 'o'clock on the morning of March 23rd. it not only did us out of a bit of beauty sleep. But heralded the advent of a big and beautiful bomb which buried itself in the lawn of the Club.

Rich black soil was scattered far and wide; worms and debris covered the roof and windows of the Green room and library. A big tree lurched against a wall. The very large crater contained a miscellaneous collection of articles, such as chimney stacks, bricks drainpipes and pocket handkerchiefs. Through two gaping holes in the walls of the Settlement part of the Club could be seen the deplorable state of chaos inside.

Our Quiet Room scene of so much fun in the past had gone, so we went to work to turn the Oratory into a Quiet Room. Furniture was dusted. Some of us swept over the floor, others washed the floor, others polished the floor, others walked dirt over the floor and the rest just walked behind them with a duster. However, in a short time the place was habitable.

Then we decided to dig a path round the crater, and whilst we were digging and indignant air-raid man stalked in demanding tom know why he had not been told about the bomb. Someone muttered something about having run short of paper and envelopes. Then a crowd gathered around to watch. When one of them wondered aloud.

"What's happened here?" She was told sweetly.

"That one of us had dropped a sixpence and we were looking for it"

The big hall was next on the list, some of the young ladies of the CLUB scrubbed the floor and others polished it. By the end of the week things were nearly ship-shape. At the end of two weeks things were as they were, but for the crater. But even craters have their uses. Ours served as the burial ground for the "tooth" Bernard Driver had extracted some six months before.

This "tooth" was buried with great solemnity and pomp one Sunday evening after Benediction. Bit by bit and piece by piece the Club was cleaned and polished up. The most notable thing of all was the cheerful way in which everybody turned to and the spirit of comradeship and loyalty of the Club members which any amount of bombs can ever destroy.

ooOoo

Diary Cont,/-

March 23rd.

Fred Parsons home after 18 months in West Africa.

March 27th.

Tommy Stock home once again after an eight month trip to Canada USA and Mexico which he enjoyed.

April 1st.

Netballers beat St. Mary's Clapham and Southwark C.T.C.

Hilda Smith home from the Land Army on leave, still loves it.

April 5th.

Girls will be pleased to know that they can eat and drink without fear of finding Bernard Driver's tooth in their tea and cakes, as he has buried it with a full ceremonial and more mourners on the edge of the bomb crater. Deo Gratias.

ooOoo

VERY TOOTHSOME *(I don't think)*
Being the true story of Bernard Driver's tooth.
By One who nose.

Many stories have been written of many things, but I doubt that if any story so original or perhaps so boring has ever been written about so unimportant a thing as Bernard Drivers tooth.

He was an insignificant person to look at; a whelp of a lad and entirely unglamorous, evening with his mouth shut- which it seldom was. But therein lay there germination of an awful our as you shall soon here, dear reader.

Many of Drivers friends had great powers of attraction by means of the eyes, perhaps by means of the hands, but most common of all, by means of the tongue. Alas! None of these had Driver. He was backward in these methods and in his mind he longed for some mystic attractiveness that would surpass all these. But still, at the age of 17 he found himself on the shelf. Lack of courage and charm made him a dull fellow, and all the people of the parish passed him by unnoticed. The lad's ignoble brain rebelled at this and his mind grew more and more conceited and more and more to scourge his mind to invent some outstanding characteristic which he could bring to bear on the multitude, but try as he would, the only characteristic he can muster was than unbearable toothache.

For many days the young whelp would not visit his dentist, but with the pain driving him more and more insane, he at last slunk into the hospital and at eight o'clock one Sunday night and had a tooth extracted.

Some devilish instinct caused him to demand the dentist for his extracted tooth with which the good humoured tooth-puller complied. Little did the obliging fellow realise how much trouble it was going to cause!

A scheme now formed in Drivers brain. He belonged to St. Anne's Club Vauxhall. A Club where good living young Christians conversed over tea and national milk cocoa.

He joined in the interest and activities of the age, such as ballroom dancing concert party and melodrama and is very friendly with all the members whilst his brain hit upon a malicious scheme to win his popularity and admiration from those ready friends

Many people were gathered round the inevitable tea and beverages that appealed to them, and were talking about each other as was the custom of the time, when the evil fellow whipped out his carefully preserved decayed tipped tooth with its three long prongs and held it aloft for all to see. A ghastly silence fell; one of those silences that throb with fear and bewilderment. Eyes popped out, mouths dropped open and faces registered horror. Then after a tense moment, women screamed out and men made for the door. Many people were trampled out of shape. Many disappeared never to be seen in the vicinity of St. Anne's again.

And what, you may ask, is becoming of Bernard Driver? That infamous lad may be seen only in brief occasions cowering quietly along the ill-fated Harleyford Road, obviously haunted by the spirits of those who might have been his lifelong friends!

Such them are the powers of a preserved extracted tooth. The moral being, never, ask the dentist for the tooth he has pulled!!!!!

It might interest you to know too, that Master Driver is just had two more teeth extracted. Look out.

Diary Cont./-

April 7th.

Pamela Moore and Corroda Ruffoni home, also Eileen Smith who we congratulate on becoming a Corporal.

April 10th.

Twenty-seven stalwarts set out for Purley Downs where we had a very enjoyable day. Played the usual boisterous games and came back half dead.

Report as follows:-

On Easter Monday, Club members went for a ramble.

We started out after the 10 o'clock Mass. Bound for Purley Downs. At the Oval we boarded a tram and the entertainment was given by our "Enoch" who took on the job of Commentator. On one occasion when she sighted three of our party were going by "bike" she yelled. "Look. Look. Look" and all the tram passengers, apart from our party, jumped to their feet and hung out of the window!

Arthur Parsons handed around "Gob-stoppers" They did not prove very effective.

At the terminus we turned left down a Road leading to the Downs; it also led to a Pub where the thirsty ones stopped for a quick one.

Whilst we were walking slowly along and admiring the, Father Koch described a Café. He said it was a beautiful little place whose wooden walls were covered with a wonderful collection of pictures. We decided to eat our lunch in this charming place. When we eventually arrived at its door, however, we found the café was closed. A few kind words (?) from Father Koch to the owners, however, and the door were unlocked, unbolted and un-barricaded and we all trooped into a converted barn. Re were some weird pieces of art about and some of the prints on the walls were pretty. I for one. Enjoyed my spam and a view of Loch Lomond!

After leaving there, we walked through an avenue of trees, from whence we could see the aerodrome. We walked along narrow paths crawled through gaps, gingerly stepped over barbed wire and down slopes into a valley. Down here we decided to play "indoor cricket" as Bernard Driver and Arthur Parsons picked sides. After a few slight arguments we played in real earnest. It was a rousing game, cheats versus liars. The Liars won! They had the loudest voices!

At some ones suggestion, we found a nice bit of lawn and played some soothing games as "Kingy" "Warney" "Cockaroosha" and "Tin-can- Tommy"

By this time, we were all feeling the need for a nice cup of tea as we strolled. Into the town to a nice café and had tea and bread and jam. Afterwards our party broke up into three. They discussed plans; the three cyclists peddled off.

Others waited for a bus so that they could go back to the Club and make tea all the others hiked back over the hills and dales.

We picked a comfortable tram in which to sit ourselves for the homeward journey. Mick and Mary went to sleep, and of course our "Enoch" did her funny turn! This time she dropped her case down the stairs, but the obliging person it fell on. Picked it up, and threw it up without a murmur. Good old "Enoch!"

When we arrived home, we were full of vim and vigour in spite of a few aches and pains.

We are all agreed that there must be a few more of these rambles during the good weather.

ooOoo

Diary Cont./-
April 11th.
Spent the day regretting we had been so energetic yesterday.
April 12th.
Annual General meeting. It was agreed that the past year has been a successful one. All Classes going well the Boys were well placed in the football league, and the Girls were top in the C.Y.C. S.E. Netball League and second in the SW league.

The new committee Elected were:

George Belcher	Evelyn Collins
Paddy Coyle	Phil Cullen
Jack McAuliffe	Francis Desmond
Ron Miller	Rosemary Martyn
Arthur Parsons	Joan Noakes
Steve Sage	Marie Perla
Damien Welfare	Delphina Ventura

April 15th.
Party of 18 went to see "The Song of Bernadette" and came back favourably impressed.
April 16th.
Girl's Table Tennis match. We won 18 - 7 against West Norwood.
April 19th.
Look out for a big Naval event soon. Bernard Driver has joined the Navy. We wish you every success and hope he will be happy and as new life.
April 21st.
Congratulations to Joan Minton (nee Bagder) on birth of a son Christopher John.

April 22nd.

Ron Pawson home after 2 ½ years in Canada, where he has acquired a wife, and intends to return as soon as possible. We wish them every happiness.

April 23rd.

Father Koch and a band of enthusiastic workers cleaned and distempered the common room. This experiment proved so successful that they intend to do the whole Club "IN TIME." Rosemary Martyn catered most lavishly for their appetites; they're willing to do it again, if only for the eats.

Report on the decorating. As follows:-

When Father Koch first said.

" Lets spring clean the Common Room. " There were cries of.

"Spring Clean It? Why. It isn't dirty!"

The following Saturday, six Girls and a boy were to be disillusioned.

All arrived at the Club before 10 am dressed in their oldest clothes, complete with mops, dusters and aprons. One bright spark even had a hoover neatly tucked under her arm. They were all firm believers in –the better the day, the better the deed! And were all bent on doing some dirty work;

Rosemary was soon firmly installed in the kitchen, where she began preparing dinners for ninety (sorry I mean nine!) while the rest of us, led by the Reverend Father, set to work on the Common Room.

By lunch time, we had stripped the room of furniture, and swept dusted and washed everything, including the ceiling.

No time was lost in washing for lunch; we simply wiped the dirt from our hands and removed small portions of mud from the regions of our mouths, and marched into a delicious lunch, all of us smelling strongly of turps and paraffin.

If you want to enjoy a dinner, get Rosemary to cook it and spend a few hours before hand scrubbing walls and floors.

In the afternoon began the task of getting the place distempered and the furniture put back. This developed into a race against time.

We were again called to halt by Rosemary. This time for tea. We have still not found out whose birthday it was, but we enjoyed the iced cake al the same. During tea we introduced Father Koch to that old song." When father painted the parlour." Until he said.

"Let us cease this boisterous hilarity---" or words to that effect.

By the evening we had finished. In fact, we put all the furniture back as well and made the room so tidy, that several members walked in and after looking all around simply remarked.

"What a funny smell of paint in here!"

ooOoo

Diary Cont./-

April 24th.

We lose another member. Teddy Mayhew has left to join Bernard in the "Royal Arthur". We wish them the best of luck and hope he likes life afloat.

April 25th.

The party went to Chessington zoo where they thoroughly enjoyed themselves. Much to the disgust of members who didn't go, we were not mistaken for any of the animals and returned home without any difficulty.

Report as follows:-

CHESSINGTON ZOO.

by M Taylor

The fact was that ten of decided that we non-too well so we decided to take a day off and spend it at Chessington zoo in order to recuperate.

We started at 11.39 from Vauxhall. By the time we reached Chessington it was very warm and ideal for a lazy day, when we reached the zoo after a leisurely stroll from the station, we paid a visit to some of the animals, but we stayed longest in the Parrot House. There was something familiar about it; in fact, they caused most excitement, probably because they could shout and scream louder than we could:

It was not long before we found a quiet spot in a large field where we settled ourselves comfortably to each our lunch. Then after a spell of spam, ham and idleness, the fun really began. We had swings see-saws, slides, merry – go -rounds and anything else we could see, after that we had a thrilling ride on the "Ghost Train" and went into the circus. It was time we had a rest and it passed a couple of pleasant hours watching the horses, ponies, elephants and (some-what) beautiful (?) girls rather doubtful clowns.

We had rea after the circus then made another trip to the swings. Somebody discovered a rocking horse, and then the fun started with a vengeance. I think the least sad about this the better, all I know we had sore seats and bow legs by the time we started for home.

Outside the circus we found an old horse bus that made journeys backwards and forwards from the station so we all clambered up onto the top deck. I do envy the people that always used to ride in them.

When we arrive back at the Club, we were thoroughly tired and hot, but revived after a refreshing cup of tea,

I must say we felt far from recuperated the next day – especially when we sat down!!!!

ooOoo

Diary Cont./-
April 28th.
Sgt. Frank O'Sullivan home after 18 months training in Canada USA and Bahamas.
April 29th.
Congratulations and all best wishes to Sgt. Julia Amer on becoming Mrs. McDonald.
April 30th.
Congratulations to Jim and Monica Prouton (nee Vanstone) on the birth of a son Michael Edwards.
May 10th.
Congratulations to the Netballers on had been second in the C.Y.S. S.W Netball League.
May 13th.
Netballers beat Deptford 15 – 3.

May 15th.

Boy's monthly meeting. John Haddad elected Sports Capt. Ron Miller elected Swimming Capt.

May 18th.

Pleased to hear from John Moss once again. He is one of our most faithful correspondent.

May 19th.

As the Scouts are proving so successful we started the Club Pack for Boys under 11. We wish them the same success.

May 20th.

C.Y.C. S.E Netball Rally. We congratulate the netball team on winning the cup. We now have 2 cups and hope to add to them in the near future.

We were very sorry to hear that Peter Perla has died of wounds received in Burma. Please remember him in your prayers.

Congratulations to Daphne (nee Abram) and Ernie Smith on an addition to their family Damien James.

May 22nd.

At the Girls monthly meeting. Evelyn Collins was elected Rambling Capt. Joan Noakes Sports Capt. Madeleine Belcher Ballroom Dancing Organiser. We decided to enter the Ballroom Dancing Competition at Cowley institute.

May 28th.

We were invited to a social at Mortlake. 23 members went and thoroughly enjoying themselves.

May 29th.

On Whit Monday, owing to traveling conditions, we decided to keep clear of the trains and we went to PURLEY, again where we returned happy up worn out.

THIS IS A PHOTO IN THE ALBUM TAKEN POSSIBLE 1944
JUST STATING "THE CLUB"
By the house shown in the left side background
it appears to be a Club outing possibly this is PURLEY

Tops of Bill Bailey's & Fr. Madden's head at rear
Some other very young faces are
Dennis Lynch -Tom McAvoy- John Macdermott.

ooOoo

Diary Cont./-

June 1ˢᵗ.

About 34 members of the Guild of St. Agnes invades Boxhill.

Report as Follows:-

BOXHILL with the C.S.A BY Peggy Knight.

The weather, which had been so lovely over Whitsun was disappointing on the morning when the Guild of St. Agnes was going to Boxhill, but as we left St. Anne's at 1.o'clock, the sun appeared from behind the clouds, and as we got out of the train at Boxhill station, he was smiling quite sweetly down on us.

I had seen Boxhill from a distance, but had never been to the top and I must confess that the climb appeared formidable, but it was easier than it looked, and we reach the top with the loss of only a little breath. There we found an open space, and we all set ourselves down to admire the view and stay out hunger with the rolls with which Father Madden and so amply provided the party.

Hunger appeased, the youngsters under Rosemary's protection set off for the swimming pool, while the staider members remained too admire the view until teatime! We had a very nice tea at the Killarney Tea Rooms, about ½ mile past the swimming pool and then we made our way back to the top of the hill and played rounder's until the weather, failing us at the end of our day, caused us to make our way to the station and our earlier than we had intended.

The journey down the hill was rather more difficult than the ascent, especially as most of the Guild had a arms full of dog-daisies and rhododendrons, but we made it with only one mishap, and that fortunately not a serious one.

ooOoo

Diary Cont./-

June 4ᵗʰ.

Two of the oldest members Fred Parsons and Eileen Blessington were married today with Nuptial Mass. We wish them every happiness.

June 11ᵗʰ.

Corpus Christie Outdoor Procession at Meadow Road Convent. Very pleasing to see the Club so well represented, even Father Koch should have been satisfied.

Saw Maria Palumbo who told us that Paul is now in hospital in Alexandria. We wish him a speedy recovery from his wounds.

June 25ᵗʰ.

C.Y.S. Ramble at Eaglefield Green. 30 members were able to go and of course they all knew the way and as usual lost themselves. They were found, however, by Father MacDonald who gave Phil, Marie and Adelina a lift, but as was to be expected, the car broke down under their weight. They all went touring and after dinner, and from what we can hear it's more by luck than judgement that they were not all drowned.

June 26ᵗʰ.

Elie Pasquini on leave looking well. His training to be a Pilot.

Ernie O'Sullivan has been in some tough fighting in Italy but has now stationed 2 miles from Rome in. He hopes to get an audience from the Holy Father.

Denis Smith is quite well in Alexander having the rest after fighting in Italy.

The Record and Book Circles of doing very well indeed. We have bought 9 records and 24 books since last October.

We are sorry to say Frank Barry is still in hospital. Please remember him in your prayers. He is unable to write and appreciates letters from anyone. Address:

Welfare Nuneaten General Hospital Nuneaten Warwicks.

We would like to remind all members in of forces that we have an album in which we are waiting to display the beautiful portraits so please forward some.

Joan Noakes.

ooOoo

FOOTBALL *Arthur Parsons.*

Well boys, we have done better football this year than any other before. At the end of the season we are fourth in the C. Y. C. (Senior) league.

Although we had quite a few tough games, we want some of them which is much better than we have done in the past.

We may not have done as well as the netball team, but I think we can pat ourselves on the back.

I will be very grateful if you will search your home for any football gear as this is borrowed and must be returned. If it is not return, we shall have to play in their birthday suits next year.

NETBALL. Lily Coffey

The netball team has again had a successful year. Our efforts were crowned with a C. Y. C. League cup for S. E. League and we came second in the S. W.

With members getting married and called up, we shall soon need some reinforcements, so how about it?

BOYS P. T.

There are a few persons who have achieved perfect physical fitness (almost). Quite a few persons turned up every other day bar Thursday. We would welcome them with open arms and break them in gently. (Especially those with pugilistic instincts).

We have a very fine handball team owing to the unfailing zeal, zest and vitality of the present team.

Due to call up we could do with some fresh blood (not to be spilt). We are very fortunate t in having a good PT instructor like Mr Bryley, but alas! All boys being boys, he gets some rather cheeky remarks, but takes it in good fun. Therefore boys, try to be a bit more angelic in the near future.

P. Coyle – Handball Captain

S. Sage – Secretary – without portfolio.

A. Miller – class organiser.

KEEP FIT.

This is a nice large class. Large in number, (I mean). We are keeping our figures nice and trim (we hope) with the drill and the dancing and games

HAND CRAFT

Although this has been changed from Thursday nights to Wednesday, the classes still very enjoyable. It is it is better really, from a sociable points of view because i.e instead of getting straight home afterwards we can join in the community singing that everybody enjoyed so much.

CONCERT PARTY. Phil Cullen

We are doing very well in this class and hope to put on a show for the feast of St Anne. We could still do with some more new members. All the more the merrier!

ENGLISH. Arthur Parsons

Thanks to Mrs Dearlove, the English class is most interesting and an entertaining. There is nothing.

And it embraces many interesting matters.

ooOoo

I have been asked to give you an idea of life in the land Army, so I will kick off by disillusioning some of my readers.

Contrary to many popular beliefs, members of the W.A.L. do not spend their days sunbathing and showing off them breaches.

Land girls work in all branches of agriculture such as milking, general dairy farming, tractor driving, rat catching, market gardening and fieldwork.

I am one of the common field workers employed by the War Agricultural Executive Committee, in a hostel with about 18 other girls. We are usually sent out in gangs of six or 10. A lorry and coach, conveys us to the various farms where we have to work.

About this time of the year, the main job (not a very popular one) is hoeing cabbage, potatoes, kale etc., and of course when the sun shines, (literally).

Next is the time that we all enjoy most; gathering then the harvest though it means working until 9 o'clock at night and often weekends as well. We first have to stack the corn, and then several days later loaded onto the wagons. The loads are then carted to the end of the field and built into ricks until they can be thrashed. We always compete to stack the corn on the wagons so that we can ride across the fields on top of the load

November is not a very popular month. We spend it picking up acres and acres of potatoes.

My particular gang of girls were thrashing for the best part of the winter. By the way, thrashing means beating out the grain from the corn. The actual thrashing is of course, done by machine. We help to feed the machine and build the straw's stack.

Planting the potatoes, cabbages, etc,.This work for March and April. You can guess that they potatoes weren't planted too thickly.

We usually arrive back at the hostel at 6 o'clock in the evening and then of course everyone dashes round to get clean once again and get some dinner. As a hostel is situated 5 miles from the nearest town, and it doesn't happen to be a bus service to this particular town, one can't exactly go places in the evening, though we managed to amuse ourselves. We hire a coach to take us to town on Wednesday evening so that we can go to the local dance or cinema.

Maybe I should mention here that we regain touch with civilisation at the weekends. After we have finished work at noon on Saturdays we are free to go home but we must be back by 10:30 Sunday evening.

On the whole, I think that the majority of girls enjoy life in the W.L.A. I know the girls in my hostel do.

I do hope that those of my readers who have informed me that they can do to or three times as much work as the Land Girls are going to spend their holidays working on a farm. The country is in great need of these magicians!

PS can anyone tell a poor land girl how to prevent her face becoming like the beet-root when the sun shines?
Bremer

ooOoo

July 1944
By Frank O'Sullivan.

A few years ago I remember learning the geography of Canada and its people.

This war presented me with an excellent opportunity to see that country and to meet some of its 11,000,000 inhabitants.

On reach the Dominion, the first impression one receives is of the vastness. Although used to journeys occupying hours, here y last for almost the equivalent number of days. It takes six days to travel from the east coast to the west coast of Canada by train.

The scenery varies immensely during a comparatively short journey. Nova Scotia and New Brunswick-almost entirely bush country parts of it almost impenetrable. Prince Edward Island very agricultural and thickly populated;

Quebec- A land full of beautiful lakes and mountains. The flat land there is largely rock strewn and fit only for cattle grazing.

Ontario; flat futile agricultural. In its Southern parts (e.g. the Niagara peninsula) peaches cherries and apples are in abundance. Further west laid the province of Saskatchewan, Manitoba, Alberta, British Columbia containing within their boundaries the prairies and the Rocky Mountains. Not having seen the latter provinces, I'll not venture any opinion regarding their respective merits.

Being a city dweller, I'd like to convey a few impressions of some cities you've heard of but not seen.

OTTAWA. In the province of Ontario is the Capital.

It contains the various government buildings and offices. It's not very large judged by English standards, having around 100,000 inhabitants. It is modern and very pleasant indeed is a walk through the parks alongside the canal. A visit to the Houses of Parliament is something that will live long in one's memory.

MONTREAL. - In Quebec is the largest city in Canada having 1,999,999 people. Situated on an Island, the city itself is built around a mountain- Mount Royal- on top of which is a huge cross which is illuminated at night. The city contains many large and beautiful buildings, new and old. Among these buildings perhaps the most beautiful is Notre Dame Cathedral with its religious museum- a favourite spot for tourist.

QUEBEC-, From which the province gets its name, overlooks the St. Lawrence and has 175,000 people. It is the most historic of all Canadian and its narrow cobbled streets still remain reminding one much of old London. The Citadel- bounded by its own stone walls is the residence of the Governor - General. Nearby, is the famous Chateau Frantanac, With the recent conference held here, these two buildings have been witness to many historic events beginning with the invasion of the city by Woolf in 1776.

TORONTO & HAMILTON – In Ontario, lie further West, their buildings being reminders of the influences of nearby America. The Cathedral of St. Michaels in Toronto is I think, one of the most beautiful I have ever seen.

ST,JOHN. – New Brunswick is a city not to be overlooked, boasting a population of 60,000. They are largely comprised of descendants of the first English settlers in Canada.

No account of the geography of Canada itself would be complete without mention of the Niagara Falls. There are two falls at Niagara – a fact little known I think to most Englishmen. The one most frequently seen is the American Falls at Niagara. Larger and perhaps more beautiful are the Canadian or Horseshoe Falls. Shaped as their name implies.

The Canadian people are varied in descent and in temperament.

In the Eastern Provinces of New Brunswick, Prince Edward Isles, Nova Scotia and Ontario, the people are largely of English or Scottish descent. They are friendly and hospitable, being very proud of their ancestral connections with the" old country" as they so often call the British Isles.

The Province of Quebec is the largest in Canada. Largely French speaking. Its people are deeply religious-though the sections of some French Canadians, would perhaps give the lie to this statement...Kit is unfortunately, very backward in comparison with other Canadian Provence's. The standard of education outside the cities is very poor and in some parts is non-existent.

Travelling to the western provinces of Alberta, Saskatchewan, Manitoba and British Columbia– the people become more and more like the typical Englishman. They are, I'm told very hospitable and nothing seems to be too much for them to do to satisfy a visitor's needs. The majority of them have emigrated from England within the past fifty tears.

With the advent of the aeroplane as a means of transport, the apparent vastness of this country is being somewhat diminished. To anyone with a lust for adventure.-

Canada offers endless opportunities.

Maybe a combination of those two factors will help Canada attain during a short period, the same degree of development that has been achieved by her neighbour, the U.S.A.

ooOoo

The first starry flowers of the almond blossom flushed and shy against black branches.

The soft clinging touch of a child's hand; the innocence and beauty shining in the clear depths of a baby's eyes.

The music of the wind on a high hill–top and the graceful sweep of the valley below with the cornfields all a–ripple like the wild sea waves.

The pearly beauty of the Milky Way on a warm, still summers night and the murmur of the sea in the distance.

The thrilling sight of a bird in flight, dipping and soaring on outstretched wing.

The blue dusk over the river, with the lights twinkling on the embankment.

The light of greeting in the eyes of a friend and the warm welcome of mother and home after a long journey.

The brilliant colours of autumn and the sweet smell of earth upturned by the plough.

Dewdrops all a–glisten on the spider's web, and due-spangled grass in the light of early morning.

Hikes and outings with a crowd of friends with cheery banter and merry quip.

Re-reading of favourite books before a roaring fire, and the sweet comfort of one's own bed after a weary night on fire– watch.

The cool dim quiet of a little church after the noise and the bustle of the busy world.

Christmas and the glow and the joy and the hope and the peace of this happy festival.

Snow–laden branches sparkling and ethereal in the light of the winter moon.

The soft radiance of candlelight. Skies opal–lined delicate and distant.

The exquisite grace of the valley and the poetry of motion.

The lumbering playfulness of puppies and the quaint capering's of kittens.

Kew in springtime with cherry blossom thick and clustering might fairy foam.

St James's Park and the lake view from the Palace side.

The golden warmth of the summer's day, heavy with drowsy murmuring of, bees; skies seen through leafy branches; the cool chattering of a little brook and the scent of new – mown grass.

Clouds, gold –edged and the wild ecstasy of storm and tempest. Seas lashed to fury by the wind and rain, foaming and eddying, leaping and drawing in fiendish delight.

These things I cherish, Born of earth and sea.

God's handiwork; a taste of heaven – to – be.

By Joan Noakes & Phil Cullen.

The Club.	"A land of settled Government A land of just renown. Where freedom broadens slowly down. From precedent to precedent!'	Kingsley.
Arthur Parsons	"Thy voice is a celestial melody'	?
Bishop Brown.	"And still they stared-And still the wonder grew. That one small head could carry all he knew."	Goldsmith.
After any Club Outing.-	"….'n'; how Are your arms, n'legs, n'lungs, n'bones a feeling now?"	Mansfield.
Father Koch	"His years but young, but his experience old, His head unmellowed, but his judgement ripe."	Two gentle-men of Verona.
Ron. Miller	"It would talk, Lord how he talked	Beaumont & Fletcher
Phil Cullen & Marie Perla.	"Their conversation was brief and their desire was to be silent	Juvenal
Steve Sage	"A Cheerful look, makes a dish a feast.	Herbert.
Adeliegh Perla	"Seen by rare glimpse, pensive and tongue tied.	Juvenal
Mr.Bailey at 10pm.	"They dwindled, dwindled one by one. And may I say that many a time wished they were all gone."	Wordsworth.
Edna Ward	With gentle yet prevailing force, Intent upon her destined course.	Cowper.
Jean Simmons.	"Lady of Silence."	J.S.Elliot.
Mr. Hyde	"A little nonsense now and then relished by the wisest men"	
Father Madden	"E'n though vanquished he could argue still.	Goldsmith

L...y C....y	"Scorn delights and live laborious days"	Milton.
Bunty	"...as frank as rain. On cherry blossom."	E. B. Browning.
Evelyn Collins	"Most excellent accomplished lady."	Twelfth Night.
George Belcher.	"Deferential Glad Gay.be of sure.	J. S. Elliot.
Mary Kennedy	"So sweet the blush of bashfulness. E'n pity scarce can wish it less	Byron.
Mrs. Dearlove Bernard Driver.	"With these conversing, I forget the way." "The little tyrant of his field withstood."	Gay
Barbara Abrams	"So buxom blithe and full of face. As heaven had lent her all his grace	Pericles I.
Paddi Coyle	"What is this life so full of care We have no time to stand and stare."	W.H. Davies.
Rudy Perla.	"The quiet voice that always counselled best	

RYMES WITHOUT REASON
By George Belcher.

Georgie Belcher some limericks tried
And these he handed in
I've given them place
To use up a space
Though his efforts I'd much rather hide.

There is a Club at Vauxhall
And some of its members are tall
Some short and fat
Are often joked at
And some, just go there, thats all.

There is a young school girl called Lil
Who isn't as clever as Phil
For school she don't like
Work gives her a fright
Poor Lil's skill (against Phil's) will look ill.

There was a young fellow called Addie
Who often gets into a paddy
At times with his paw
He will make you feel sore
So I think he will make a good daddy.

There is a great tall guy called Arty
Who often gets sour and tarty
He gets into moods
With the Girls and their snoods
But he's always the life of the party.

There was a tall smart guy named Jack
Who wore a suit like a sack
One day while out walking
And doing much talking
He stopped at a bar for a snack.

There was a dark chappie called Slim
Who when he would shaved liked a trim
He was fond of a ball
And he played in the hall
But the price of glass made trim Slim grin.

There was a young lady called Chance
One Sunday in church tried to dance
But would little Boys flee
From that Sacristy
When with candle-sticks round she would prance.

Do you remember young Barny
Who had a pal called Ernie
They both joined the Navy
To get their hair wavy
I hope they come home nice and curly.

We have a young girl as our editoress
Who thinks she is something like Good Queen Bess
'Cos she's always in bed,
That's why our poor Club mags in such a mess.

ooOoo

– 182 –

GLORIA IN EXCELSIS DEO
SAINT ANNE'S ANNALS
CHRISTMAS 1944
ET INTERRA PAX HOMINIBUS

CLUB DIARY
by Maddalene Belcher

JUNE 26.

Thanks to the flying bombs, Pat Laidler is off to Newcastle. Now we can look forward to a bit of peace.(Joke)

THE REST OF JUNE.

Owing to continuous attacks by "flying bombs". The classes are to close for a longer summer vacation. The Club, of course, will carry on.

July 22.

A strange young lady in the Club! Oh no it isn't- it's our own Edna wood with a perm! And doesn't she look glamorous too! We like it very much Edna.

July 28.

Bernard Driver home on leave. He likes the Navy, but prefers other places sometimes. We hope they make the tea to suit you Bernard. We couldn't please you with ours at the Club! And how far can you spit now?

August 3.

News from Ernie Morgan who is in France. Good old Ernie, we are glad you are safe and well. Take care of yourself, good people are scarce.

August 4.

Bernard Driver buzzed in and waltzed Arthur all around the hall, by a way of saying farewell. Cheerio Bernard for a little while. We shall all look forward to your next visit.

August 7.

As the official sports day at had to be cancelled by the authorities on account of the "Doodlebugs", we decided to have our own sports day. Joan Noakes and Paddy Coyle made a splendid job of organizing the races and fun. It was held today at Beaulah Hill, and the weather was beautiful. Everybody enjoyed themselves immensely and crawled home tired but happy.

August 8.

All armchairs occupied by those feeling stiff after the energetic day before.

August 9.

Mary Dudley looked in at us. She is on leave and looking very well.

August 12.

John Kennedy home on leave after eight months at sea. He is enjoying life on the ocean waves.

August 14.

Another letter from Ernie Morgan. He says he is working very hard these days, in fact harder than ever, but he manages to get a bit of football practice in now and again, in his spare time. That's right, Ernie, you do all you can in the football line, and then come home and kick a few goals for St. Anne's.

August 19.

For brave stalwarts braved the rain and set out with a trek cart from the Club to rescue a gas stove from a bombed House somewhere. The job was successfully carried out, but they were mistaken for Gasmen on the way home by people who, needed repairs! It could have been worse; they could have been taken for looters whilst removing the stove.

August 26.

Bernard Driver home again, because his home was blasted by a flying bomb.

Sept 2.

Douglas Clarke here for a dance. Home for one day.

Sept 3.

Party congratulations to Evelyn Collins and Frank O. Sullivan on their engagement.

Sept 11.

The Perla family that from Oxford where they have been staying for several weeks. Our one and only Teddy Mayhew on leave from the Navy.

Sept 14.

We lose another member to the forces. Steve Sage this time. We hope you will enjoy life in the Army, Steve. Lots of good luck.

Sept 18.

General Meeting - Arthur Parsons elected to Table Tennis Captain Jack McAuliffe Vice Captain.

Lily Coffey Girls Table Tennis Captain. Madeleine Taylor Vice Captain. Adolf Perla has been elected to the Boys Committee.

It has been decided, in order to make things more comfortable for every Club member a new scheme been put into operation: On first and third Sundays there will be a social. A real social, where you dance and play games with everybody. This might break up the set that has formed a separate little dancing Club of its own.

On the second and fourth Sundays, there will be a Whist Drive.

Whenever there is a fifth Sunday in the month it will be given up to indoor games or lectures. This will be an excellent way in which to welcome back ex-members.

Where's the evenings are to be kept for Club members under twenty-five, and Thursday's for the Boys under twenty-five. Ashtead has become a reality at last. To everybody's joy, Father Koch broke the news that we were to move in on Thursday. Plenty of elbow grease was ordered so that we could get down to the paintwork and dirt.

Classes restarted this evening. Very good attendance for the start.

It is nice to see Fred Parsons again.

Prayers for Frank Barry who is being moved to Bath. He has been ill for a very long time, but his friends are always thinking of him and remembering him in their prayers.

A Bazaar has been discussed and planned for an early date in December, so get to work all of you!

Sept 21.

The moving job to Ashtead was a great success. All orders nicely carried out. All furniture carefully carried in, so nothing was broken and the two young ladies who rode in the back of the van thought they were on top of the world instead of what-not.

Report as follows:-

OUR
COUNTRY HOUSE
by Phil Cullen

Without doubt the greatest adventure the club has yet undertaken is that of obtaining suitable place for use as a holiday house for all London Catholic Clubs

The idea was hailed as "excellent" and "just the very thing." The theory stage passes quite smoothly. Putting theory into practice however, was most certainly no matter of ease. Little imagination is needed to form an idea of the numerous difficulties of obtaining a suitable place in the midst of a world war, and despite prevailing dearth of houses of any description; reality as ever, prove most grim. This was April 1944.

In those apparently far off days, Club members may have been seen in clusters, ploughing through and dust "For sale and to let" columns of various newspapers, people began to think up all sorts of friends "that may know of something". Many varied ideas were set forth but all of no practical consequence. Then Father Koch really got down to business, and somehow, after much work, worry, travelling to and fro, interviews, correspondence, discouragement, prayers and fasting, and very much patient waiting, we heard that the project had materialised. At least, a house had been located which would prove suitable, but very much remained to be settled before any final decision could be made. Permissions had to be gained, all sorts of people had to be consulted, some had to inspect the place, and others had to approve of it. Then the stolid, unbending solicitor world at to be approached, and continuously urged onto greater speed, a thing hitherto unheard-of. There was also much alteration and repair to be accomplished, before the house could be inhabited by 20 or so youngsters in holiday mood; and lastly, by no means the least of the main hold-ups, struggling to the fore, and standing obdurate as ever, was the major problem......... Money.

Even this was overcome. After much more worry and waiting sufficient cash was secured to justify and getting on with the job thanks to Bishop Brown and Archbishop Amigo. At length it was settled that we may move in at the end of August, when and if we could get a van.

The much postponed holidays were hastily arranged half days and even lunch half–hours were filled with shopping expeditions of many kinds. The task in hand, to find furniture, curtains, carpets, and the Hundred and one other essential items, in these days of points and permits was colossal. We all became most domesticated, even the boys; and many of St Anne's Club members may have been seen parading the shops, obviously well trained in the art of careful speculation; only to return to club with a mental note of sizes, prices, qualities, lengths and even which was the best assistant to approach. Here Father Koch, the trainer and bargain-hunter in chief, sorted out all the evidence, and most often went off him to get goods, "just to make sure!" After many minor adventures, some quite enjoyable," and others "... not so bad when y're only watching" (to quote a gang of hard–worked boys, at the point of trying to manoeuvre a gas–stove through a small gate) the essentials were gathered in from their devious sources. Stand up and bow, boys!

Then all was ready. The eagerly awaited moving day dawned on Thursday, September 21. About half a dozen Clubites got the day off. First thing in the morning, some were again detailed off, bargaining. Some tied up, some took to pieces, various articles of furniture, ready for loading straight into the van, and someone popped off to get the house open, aired, and to rub off the top layer in general...... system.

4:15 that afternoon saw the giant pantechnicon pull-up at Malden Lodge, complete with six 'ites in the back. The fun began. Pillow and light bundles were aimed very accurately up through the bedroom window, where some obliging, long-suffering soul tried to catch them. Mattresses assumed legs and a whole line of multi-coloured stripes could be seen coming up the stairs at the double. Bed–ends, springs, carpets, tables, crops and brooms, were transferred with amazing rapidity into the house. As soon as all was neatly dumped, a nice cup of tea went down very well, as the girls discussed whether blue went with brown for the lounge, while the boys wondered if the walls would stand awash. Tea over. Things began to take shape, everyone worked like trojans, and by the end of the evening, the curtains were up, carpets down, and the lounge was complete, even down to a vase of flowers (home grown) on the table. The inevitable meal ensured. Tired but very satisfied, we called it a day.

Something attempting, something done!!!

ooOoo

A VISIT to ASHTEAD
by Lu Roe

On a certain Saturday afternoon in the month of September, I arrived at Victoria station puffing and blowing, intending to catch the 1:55 train, only to find the gates closed and the train just about to leave. Incidentally, I had had no time to get my ticket so I just looked very imploringly at the Ticket Collector, whereupon that worthy opened the gates and after having listened to my hurried explanation of the absence of my ticket, let me through. In the course of tearing along the platform, from a certain carriage I noticed several hands frantically waving, not the least, conspicuous of which, were Madeleine O'Sullivan's and Delphine's. By a stroke of good luck I managed to fall into a garage, or rather, perhaps I should say with the help of two of the girls who dragged me in just about one second before the train started. However after several rude remarks (not all deserved) including those of a certain Miss Desmond, I was at last able to sit down and collect my thoughts.

On arriving at Ashtead about 4 p.m. Going across the common we met a familiar figure on a bike, clad in clerical attire, (three guesses please), with several loaves in his basket. After exchanging a few words with him, we went on our way and soon arrived at a large mansion, then called "Maldon Lodge," now St Anne's Country Club." The house rather took my breath away, as although I had no idea what to expect. I hadn't dreamed of such a lovely place. The room which appealed to me most was the Front Room, which looks out onto a lawn where there are some lovely trees to which two are particularly striking because of their beautiful contrasting colours, one, a copper beech and the other, a golden horse chestnut tree. After having gone round the house and the garden, somebody made the very welcome suggestion that we should have a "Cuppa" we refreshed ourselves with the said "Cuppa" and some nice fresh buns, produced by Fr., (to which we did full justice), said goodbye to Fr. who had to get back to Vauxhall, and then got down to the graft. We were of course all appropriately equipped in slacks, overalls, etc. And we soon wired in with washing paint, cooking, painting doors, and all the various jobs which are involved when one has recently moved into a new house. At 7:30 pm or thereabouts, Doris came tripping in, (she by the way was assistant cook to Des), and announced that supper was ready. This consisted of a very appetising meal of Rabbit Pie and vegetables. We finished with coffee and cheese straws. After supper we all went to phone Fr. (was that call really necessary? – I'm sure he must have been quite bewildered at the connection at the other end). We then adjourned to the front room where there was a nice log fire and amused ourselves in various ways, including a nice sing-song (Evelyn played the piano very nicely). Thank You! We were all quite ready for bed when the time came and apart from the fact that some sweet kind person had placed a nice cold Talcum Powder tin in my bed. I had a fairly good night and slept well.

The next morning we went out in the icy dew to Mass at Fr. Leake's little church. The short walk back was quite enjoyable, as although it was very cold, it was also dry and bright. After a very nice breakfast (one must pay full tribute to the cook) we again set to work until dinnertime, and having partaken of same, we prepared for Mrs Gibbs who had promised to come to tea. I think she quite enjoyed herself and seemed very enthralled with the place. Anyway she seemed quite sorry to go. Some of our party had to go back on Sunday night, much to their dismay, which left three of us with the housekeeper. We sewed curtains until bedtime. The following day father came to lunch and suggested we all went for a walk in the afternoon. The weather was lovely and we came back feeling on top of the world. On the last day of our weekend, Tuesday, we finished off our various jobs and reluctantly left the London after very jolly stay at Ashtead.

ooOoo

Sept 23.

John Kennedy came up from Chatham on a week-end leave. He is waiting for another boat, in the meanwhile, he thinks Chatham is the worse place on earth. Cheer up John!

Sept 25.

Harry ward is home once again for a few precious days. We are glad to see him looking so fit and well.

Sept 30.

Glad to welcome Tom and Kathleen Stock. Congratulations to Kathleen on her engagement.

Oct 1.

Our first social. A complete success and thoroughly enjoyed by all.

Oct 7.

Steve Sage on his first leave.

Oct 8.

The Whist Drives went with a swing. Guess who won first prize? Only our own one and only Phil Cullen! Poor old Phil, bet your life wasn't worth living!

Oct 21.

News from Frank Barry at Bath. He is enjoying a glass of Guinness every day now. Doctor's orders of course.

Oct 23.

Bombastic upheaval in the Club. Pat Laidler has come back once more.

We heard friend Anne Bremer prescribing a "rocket bomb" at such length with much detail, but we hope our old Pat won't chase off again in such a hurry. After all, nothing worse than a rocket landing your breakfast egg, Pat!

Report as follows:-

LONDONDERRY AIR by Pat Laidler.

According to friends of mine, I have travelled more than all the rest of the club members put together since the war began of course, with the exception of members in the forces. I have therefore been ordered to write a few lines about my journeys.

Most of you know that I lived in Plymouth the six months, and from there I went to Dundee. Then to Newcastle and back to London. There is no need for me to dwell on these journeys because it would take up too much space, so I will tell you about my latest trip to Londonderry.

Thanks to the Flying Bombs, I found myself in Newcastle once again waiting for a telegram which would take me on to Northern Ireland. Eventually everything was settled and I arranged to leave Newcastle at midnight. I hired a taxi to the station and felt very much alone leaving the house at that hour. Feeling very fed up, I found on arriving at Carlisle at 2:10 that the connection was late. It was very nerve wracking waiting alone at that hour in the morning, so seeing a girl by herself, I started to chat to her and found that she was also going to Ireland, and I thought we would be companions for the rest of the journey. However, when the train arrived at Stranraer, I had to leave her and find the Immigration Officer. No–one seemed to be able to help me and all was noise and confusion. In the end I went along to the Naval Officer and after he'd examined my telegram and identity card, he showed me where to get a train and a sailing ticket. Obtaining these, I was very vague as to where the ship was, and whilst trying to find out, the officer appeared and took my case. Then everything seemed simple.

The ship loomed up in sight and I walked up the gangway. Evidently, I was the last person on board as everything seemed peaceful. The Officer left me in the care of a sailor who took me first to one man who checked my telegram and gave me another with my description, etc.,that would bring me back. Then I went to have my case examined I had heard terrifying tales about the Customs but had thought with luck that I might be able to keep my diary with me, so had taken a chance. The result was that I had to wait while the man looked through it. He asked me if I'd put anything in it about the raids. I told him "I didn't think so." He informed me that "This wasn't the time to think–I should know!" Then he showed me a page referring to the bombs – I said. "Oh yes, that's when I was bombed out!" Thinking he would have pity on me and let me keep. No such luck, he kept my diary and gave me a slip saying if I travelled back that way I would have my diary returned then. I was then dismissed and told to sit anywhere, so I sat next to a WAAF and enquired of her in it was possible to get tea, and found that only breakfast was being served, so I trotted into the saloon for breakfast. The waiter took ages to serve, but eventually I ended up with sausage, beans, egg and toast. I struggled through best part of it and had just finished when I felt the ship start to move. I watched a few people walking about and it seemed easy, so I got up and managed to get back to my seat near the WAAF. We were all advised to keep a life–belt handy, but I hadn't settled down for more than a few minutes, when I started feeling peculiar, so I turned to the WAAF and at the same time she informed me that she was feeling very sick. That started me off. The sea was choppy and one glance at the waves lashing the side of the ship made me feel worse so I decided to go below to the cloakroom. Everybody was making for the cloakroom too. I need not go into details, but I was unable to leave the cloakroom till the ship stopped at Larne. Even then, I was still feeling very sorry for myself. It was rather fortunate for me that everybody else was feeling groggy, or I would not have arrived at all.

Arriving at Larne I gathered all my goods together and I found that the train was due at Belfast about 12:00. From there I caught the connection to Londonderry which was my destination.

On the train to Derry I shared the compartment with an elderly couple. The woman slept most of the time, but her husband gave me his opinion of London–I only occasionally got a word in. However, as we were nearing Derry, he was very kind and pointed out various places. The particular thing I remembered was the Hills of Donegal stretching along for miles. The scenery was very beautiful and then I realised why so many songs and poems are written about Ireland.

At about 4 o'clock, the train at last stopped at Derry there I was met by Tim who seemed to think it was a huge joke when I told him I had been sea-sick, we arrived at our digs which were only a few minutes from the station. I did not like the look of Derry nor the house where we were to stay for a few days. After tea we went to the ship and the guard allowed me to go on board as it come on to rain. I was a bit scared as I had had quite enough of ships, but following Tim I managed to find my way to his mess quite safe and sound. All his pals were pleased to see me and I'm afraid I made some of them a bit homesick. They gave me tea in a big mug and we sat chatting for a while. Then we left the ship and went for a walk around the town. Tim pointed out the Derry Wall and the Guildhall, I was not very impressed with Derry however, the next day being on my own, I went to the food office managed to lose myself. But everybody was helpful, so I eventually arrived back.

On the Saturday we moved to a house where I was supposed to do my own cooking, etc. I was not very happy there and the people were not very friendly either. I was very disappointed not to have got into the Free States, but the nearest I could get was a little place called "Strabane" sweet little place nice and clean and the people friendlier than at Derry.

Just as I was settling down, I received news that Tim's ship was in Liverpool. Shortly afterwards I packed my goods again ready for the journey to Liverpool.

I was dreading the thoughts of enduring the sea again, but the journey was quite uneventful and I was a good sailor and arrived in Liverpool at 7:00 in the morning. We only had two days in Liverpool and then returned to Newcastle. But the call of London was strong by this time.

I was so happy when I arrived at King's Cross Station that I knew how much London meant to me. It is impossible to explain one feelings, but there is something about London and I was overjoyed to see it again.

I must say I enjoy travelling, but would prefer it under peace – time condition. So here's hoping will have peace this time next year.

God Bless you all. Happy Christmas.

ooOoo

Oct 25.

Jonnie Moss popped in to see us all whilst passing through London. He is now a Petty Officer. We congratulate him on his promotion. You will soon be an that Admiral at this rate!

Oct 29.

Interesting talk given by Mrs. Stormont, Probation Officer. It was mostly about Holloway. If we miss any of our Girls, will know where to look for them.

Report as follows:-

A Night at the Police Court by Kathleen Amer

On Sunday, 29 October, Mrs Stormont, Probation Officer of the

Great Marlborough Police Court, came to the Club and gave us a very enjoyable account of Police Court proceedings, and told interesting stories about some of her cases.

When we were all comfortably settled round the Common Room fire, Mrs Stormont began her informal talk by describing the routine of the person who has been charged. The prisoner is kept in the police station all night and next morning bundled into the Black Maria which calls at other stations for other prisoners. The Black Maria is partitioned off into compartments and the prisoners are locked in. We were all amused by the way some denominations took the oath. A Jew keeps his hat on. Before the war a Chinaman was allowed to wring the neck of a chicken, now he breaks a saucer or blows out a candle. Catholics can take their oath on the Douay Version if they care to ask for it.

There was quite a heated discussion where we learned that the prisoners had to give up coupons for the uniforms! The uniforms at the women's prison in Holloway are slate grey and very full and reached down to the ankles. Prison life did not sound too terrible really, it just means being deprived of liberty and been locked in your cell at half past four.

Mrs Stormont told us about a suicide, a boy who stole from gas meters, a girl who had a perm and no money to pay for it. She told us of a boy who made good, but most of all, we loved the story of Old Maggie. Poor Old Maggie was seventy-two and she had been in and out of prison since she was eighteen for being drunk. She was well-known in Great Marlborough Street Police Court and into every Good Shepherd Convent in the country, but in spite of all the trouble she gave, she was rather a lovable old soul, and when one night the siren sounded, and Maggie dashed off to the shelter and got run over and killed, there must have been a few people to mourn for her.

Thank you Mrs Stormont for a very entertaining evening. I feel sure some of us wouldn't mind a little sojourn in Holloway, because if the wardresses are like you, it will be too bad!.

ooOoo

Nov 1.

A few of us, along with Father Koch and Mr. Bailey went along to Ashtead for the day and worked like Trojans, whitewashing, distempering and generally cleaning up until the House looked like a palace.

A story as follows:-

Phil and the Hill by J. Taylor

For the sake of those who have not heard the story of Phil and the bus, I will try and describe what happened. While staying at Ashtead, a party of us decided that we would like to go for a bus ride to Mickleham. Having boarded the bus, we left Father Koch to pay the fares and enquired the stop for Mickleham Down. He was told that we got off at the "Running Horses". After what seemed to us a long time, Father ventured to enquire the fellow passenger how much further we had to go he was informed that we had had it we should have got off at the stop we had just passed. We tumbled down the stairs of the bus, led by the Rev. Father, as we were making our way slowly up the hill, he jumped off, shouting words of encouragement to us to do the same. Joan Noakes jumped off; so did Lily Coffey and I, Mary Chance eventually plucked up some courage and made the jump. Phil looking rather like the boy in Casablanca, stood fast on the deck. We waved poor old Phil a fond farewell as the bus gathered speed and disappeared round the bend of the hill. Being kind–hearted souls, we decided not to go back to the "Running Horses" to await Phil's arrival, but to walk up the hill to meet her. Can you imagine our surprise when a bus speeding in the opposite direction (towards the "Running Horses") had Phil on the running board! We let out a whoop of delight and nearly collapsed with mirth! What to do next was a major problem. Should we wait at the top of the hill, or again go to meet her? And risk My Lady Cullen, drive past. Eventually we decided to walk and Phil who had had enough of buses by now came striding up the hill to meet us!!

ooOoo

Diary Cont./-

Nov 3.

Cupids been at it again! Our beloved Delfina has become engaged. Congratulations!

Nov 10.

Letter from Denis Smith in Rome. He has visited all the wonderful Churches and buildings there.

Nov 16.

George Belcher called up for the Army.

Nov 18.

Steve Sage and at the dance. Bob Suterb back from Russia.

Nov 15.

On Wednesday, November 15, the only Catholic member of the Norwegian Parliament visited the Club and gave an interesting account of his country and the Gestapo.

Nov 20.

Teddy Mayhew home. He likes life in the Navy, but hates making his own bed.

Nov 27.

Bernard Driver home again. He is on a draft leave this time and going on a Corvette. We wish you luck, but don't get seasick.

Dec 1.

Lots of Bustle and Excitement. Everyone's getting things ready for the Bazaar. Well not quite everyone. Some still have never heard of a bazaar apparently.

Dec 2.

The Bazaar was a magnificent success. Everybody thoroughly enjoying themselves. The Bishop gave a short speech and picked the winning tickets for the raffles. You could have heard a pin drop when they drew for the bottle of whisky!

The grand amount of £150.00 odd was collected for the Settlement dept.

Dec 4.

A reporter in the Club. Look out for St. Anne's in Headlines.

We had a short General Meeting which was enjoyed by all. We discussed forthcoming attractions, the results of which will be published in our next issue.

Happy Christmas to all our members, at home and in distant lands, and peaceful New Year.

ROUND THE CLASSES

NETBALL. According to the scores, we have not done very well at this year, so far. We have had some very good games, however the standard of the opposing teams has been higher than last year. Bunty – Captain.

FOOTBALL. We have not done so well this year at football, but are hoping and praying that we will win at least one game and not score any more goals for the wrong team again. I wish St Anne's team would turn up on time too, if it isn't asking too much on a Sunday afternoon! Arthur Parsons.

HANDCRAFT. Although it has been said that handcraft classes is more or less the "Refuge of Sinners" I feel sure that we all enjoyed it very much indeed – I know I do, even if I am fond of dancing. Most of us who go to this class would still come even if the dancing class stopped, but although we think the lovely work and embroidery shown us by our present instructress is wonderfully interesting to learn, we still prefer leatherwork

Betty Ainsworth.

KEEP – FIT. This class is more enjoyable than ever before. It is a nice class and not too large, but there are still a few vacancies for anybody wishing to join. It is more tiring than dancing, and such more fun.

CONCERT PARTY. The concert party are slogging away. Sweet girlish voices and dark brown basses (voices I mean) are strained to the last chord on Wednesday evenings. They all come out merry and bright, so they must enjoy it. We are looking forward to the entertainment too!

CHOIR. We are looking forward to the carols again this year. Recruits are wanted to give up some of their time and part of themselves for the Honour of Our Lord.

JUNIOR GIRLS. It is very gratifying to notice the wonderful attendance these youngsters put in, not only on Monday evenings for games, but their religious duties as well. They are on their toes at the moment, planning costumes to wear at their fancy dress party a week after Christmas.

COMMUNITY SINGING. What is nicer than to gather round the fire with your best friends and sing your favourite songs?

ENGLISH. A very interesting class. Such a pity more do not attend. It covers such a lot of interesting subject, or should I say "uncovers"! Almost everybody reads books, so surely a great many people would enjoy this Tuesday evening class, which deals with all manner of subjects and discussion.

BILLIARDS. There is a very nice room. A very nice table. A very nice captain. No team.

DRAMATICS. At the moment of writing it is only a matter of days to the performance of "Daddy Long–legs." With regard to perfection and character–building it is now or never. The delay in production has been mainly due to enemy activity, which caused the evacuation of some of the junior members of the cast and also the temporary cessation of L.C.C classes. Another setback being that the loss of male members to the forces, and not uncommon occurrence in these days of war. However, despite these setbacks the play goes on, thanks to the untiring efforts of Miss Chown whose patients and advice have been a source of edification to us all. A word of appreciation must be given to those of our newest members who have worked so hard during the year. Their efforts have been greatly responsible for the rebirth of enthusiasm in the class as a whole.

Meanwhile here's wishing all their ex-members in the forces every good wish for Christmas and we hope it will not be long before they are "treading the boards" with us once more.

Evelyn Collins.

ooOoo

MOTHER by Madeleine Taylor

Does it ever occur to you that when we are asked to name their favourite possession, we talk of books or jewellery or gifts that have no special value but the most loving lasted possession is forgotten.

It is some–one we have had from the cradle, whose name is the first word we learn to speak. Some–one was always with us and teaches us from early days the difference from right and wrong. Who is out nurse in illness both of mind and body and loves us in most any mood – she makes excuses for each moan and grumble.

Who when we used to run and fall would pick us up and kiss us and because she had kissed us we were better. The same one we would run from school to tell our tales and pranks to, who used to hug us and murmur "Don't grow up."

Then there were her surprises; she spent her days in planning them, just to hear that childless "thank you mummy."

And later she was there to hear our trouble and our sorrows. She never seemed to weary of giving loving words.

As we grew older, she grows older too, and love for her grows until at last nothing can surpass it.

And yet, when we are told to name and dearest possession, we forget this God- sent gift of love "Mother."

ooOoo

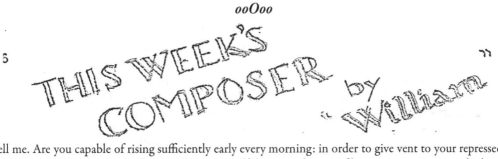

Tell me. Are you capable of rising sufficiently early every morning: in order to give vent to your repressed desire for good music? That is, are you willing to permit yourself the great pleasure of listening to a program which embraces the music, not only of the more depressing type, but also music that encompasses all that is most truly melodious?

A music that carries one's thoughts to very disturbing heights.

Of course, perhaps you do not understand what I have written! Well have you ever troubled to peruse or shall we say, rather look at the "Radio Times"? Not merely the pages showing the times of the sundry programs which cater for the members of the Services, but those showing the programs set aside for the entertainment of us poor and humble civilians? Glance at the first few lines. Now then, 7:0 a.m., Big Ben. The News. Program Parade. 7:15 a.m. The Daily Dozen.(This item should tune everyone up for the next [ubiquitous?!] Programme). 7:30 a.m. This Weeks Composer.

Ah! This is indeed a programme of programs. The program which introduces the all willing to sink to such depths, the music of all composers. The adjective "all" suffices.

The object of this program is to place before the public the music of all forgotten composers such as Byrd, Cherubini and Diabelli, also that music of all recognised composers which has never achieved even modest popularity.

Therefore, those of you with sufficient energy (that is, those who live an enthusiastic existence) who cared to rise at a more than respectable hour, and switch on that piece of furniture, which you have taken for granted for so long that you have quite forgotten its presence, tune into the Home Service, and you will then be in a position to listen to a program which will give you much food for thought. You will in fact be in the unique position of knowing a little history of each well–known composer. Also you will become acquainted with the works of the not so famous composers. Further, you will be able to see for yourself how the matters strived after and achieved the title of "genius". How they gain knowledge and experience as each work succeeded the other.

Naturally, as you know. The most sordid part of most things is describing the details of it. But in a situation such as the present, one is justified in assuming that the task is not of such a nature that it demands one's complete highly intellectual attention.

Some weeks ago the composer selected was Verdi. As you are, no doubt, aware Verdi is the greatest exponent of Opera.

Opera, as created by the Italian School. It is sometimes said (a great controversy still rages over this matter) that Wagner is the greatest exponent, but this is not so, as Wagner did not write Opera, but Music Drama, which is another thing.

Verdi was not a composer of beautiful melodies strung together by so many bars of recitative alone, but also one whose unique senses of the dramatic served him so well that even today, when dramatic values have changed, one is still able to feel very much thrilled by such scenes as head of Act III of "Rigoletto" or the trial scene from "Aida".

In Verdi one sees, at its finest, the way in which a composer is capable of rising to full maturity by learning from mistakes previously made. In studying his Operas one sees how he progressed from being a mere writer of beautiful melody to one who gave a genuine character to the protagonist.

One of Verdi's finest Operas "IL Finto Stanislao" was a complete failure. "Nabucco" was a huge success. Even so, "Nabucco" whilst being fine in its way, as none of the qualities of say "Rigoletto" or "Aida" the music of the last two named works is so wonderful that to attempt at the description would be wholly futile.

"Aida" is surpassed only by "Otello"(an adaption of Shakespeare's "Orthello") and "Falstaff"(an adaption of Shakespeare's "The Merry Wives of Windsor").

"Verdi's" last two alone entitle him to a place amongst the "great."

In all, Verdi composed about 26 Operas a Requiem in memory of the poet A. Manzoni, a Te Deum and, strange to say, a Quartet.

Whilst my attempt at the description of "This Weeks Composer"is totally inadequate, perhaps it does not convey a little of what is said. That is played depends entirely upon the circumstances of the particular case.

The pleasures one can derive from listening to this program is unique. Especially at such an early hour, since one's mind is extremely clear, and consequently able to absorb with great facility all that is said and played.

Whether you are captivated or not by my humble words, I venture to recommend,with much diffidence, that you try out my suggestion.

Rise early, you will gain immensely in the long run both physically and mentally.

ooOoo

LAUGH THIS OFF
by Terry O'Leary

Little girl, why aren't you playing with that nice dolls house I bought you? I've let it furnished to my friend for sixpence a week!

Mary, did my eyes deceive me, or did I see you in town last night wearing my new Macintosh?
Yes Mamm. I didn't want the rain to ruin your new frock.

Good you show me the dog that won the championship cup for the best watchdog. Sorry he was stolen last week.

Then there was the one of the blind beggar who had a card round his neck bearing the legend.... Don't be ashamed to put halfpenny in, I can't see!

Boss: The job of cashier is worth £10 per month.
Applicant: "One couldn't get very far on that."
Boss: "it is not intended that one should!"

Bridegroom: "Do send the train bearers away.
Bride: "My dear, I cannot. They are the dressmaker's children and they do not let go of the dress until it is paid for."

Then there was the case of the hotel proprietor who put in the following:- This delightfully attractive Hotel is so especially suited to persons in need of peace and quiet at thousands flock here every summer to enjoy this solitude.

My son, I am awfully sorry to hear you are at the bottom of your class. That's all right dad, they teach the same things at both ends.

Two places the internal combustion engine has brought nearer to each other ----this world and the next!

A monologue is a conversation between an Income Tax Inspector and a farmer.

A lovely dress fabric, madam. We have it in other shades-Great Mist twilight and Schoolboys Hanky.

A deputy once mislaid his speech. After some time, it was found in a chemist shop where he had left it. In the meantime the chemist had made it up for an eye wash.

The New Year is about the only new thing tax payers are likely to see for some time.

You said that parrot I'm bought offer you would live over a hundred years – well it died the day after I bought it!.... Er the hundred years must have been up!

ooOoo

T.. M.G ".... "This immense glorious work of
the foreign intelligence" Wordsworth
B.r..ra D..v.r "Fair sweet and young." Dryden

M.... T....R "Work space, space space." Wordsworth

G.o.g.e B.l.h.. "And it we would speak true
Much unto the man is due." Maxwell

Ashstead "Here is the pleasant place
and nothing wanting is..." Drummond

F.an, B.r.y "Wit may flesh from fluid lips." Byron

T.. C h.i. "But those unheard are sweeter." Keats

D.r..S..p..d "Angels, when you your silence break
regret their hymns
to hear you speak." Dryden

The Club after 10 p.m "How perfect was the car Wordsworth

M.r,. h.n.. "But children you should never
and let such angry passions rise
P..L C....n to tear each other's eyes."

Ashtead any mealtime "We are all the hollow men. "T.S. Eliot

D.l.i.a en.u.l "That foster child of silence
and slow time." Keats

M.g.a..n B....h.r. "Graceful and useful
all she does." Cowper

M.ur.. Go..d..g "Her voice no touch of harmony
admits irregularity deep
and shrill by fits."

The Night "My temples throb
of the Play my pulses boil... Hood

T.rr. O'...... "See sweet his voice
see smooth his tongue." Mickle

The Bazaar "The wealthiest men amongst us
is the best Wordsworth

J.s.e Ta.l.r. "No morning tools and
severed my useful arms." Clifford
English Class "Some mute inglorious Milton
Here may rest." Gray

ooOoo

A happy Christmas to all our members,
A wish that may sound strange,
Though the world is full of strife,
Old memories do not change,
Christmas always stood for peace,
The joy and goodwill to,
Wherever you are in the world today,
May expressing reach out to you.
The troubled world once saw a start
And footstep did not cease,
Until they stood before the throne
The little King of peace.
Those of you who are with him now
Big peace for this world and then,
The grace for everyone to live
With love for our fellow men.
Rosemary Martin.

ooOoo

DEC. 11.

C.O.M. Annual Election. Joan Noakes was elected President. Committee for 1945:- Francis Desmond, Edna Wood, Delfina Ventura, Philomena Cullen Evelyn Collins and Rosemary Martyn.

DEC. 15

Performance of "Daddy Long Legs". It was very well done indeed. Congratulations to all the cast on the loyal way they supported each other throughout the rehearsals when "doodles and rockets" were at their worst---or should one say and best?

Madie Taylor was an excellent "Judy" and the juniors were very impressive as orphans.

Noble collection of £10.00.

Mike Plant's reflects.

In December 1944 I was in the Club Hall with my cousin Pat Thomas, when Toni Maconi jumped up onto the stage, immediately he took off the record playing on the big record player and announced.

"Listen! Glen Miller has been reported missing., He was on his way to Paris on a plane that's crashed. (Glen Millers plane was lost on December 15th. En-route to Paris to make arrangements for his Band to perform to Troops over the Christmas period.). Toni then sorted through the recodes and put on Glen Miller' s 'In the Mood' And as a reminder of his swing music. That the Club danced to.

DEC. 17.

Nice quiet evening in the Club. Boys C.Y.C. Retreat we hope I have some more of these!

DEC. 26.

20 of us visited Ashtead for the weekend recording more fully, by Olive O' Sullivan).

As Follows:-

By
Olive Wood.

We arrived at Vauxhall station on boxing morning; some of us not quite recovered from the effects of Christmas day. On the way down, we were serenaded by the snores of a certain young lady well known to you all.

From the look of the countryside, we were certainly having a white Christmas though it didn't snow. We eventually arrived at the House, lustily exercising our lungs in the true Christmas manner.

We welcome a cup of hot coffee, prepared by the cooks. One of our number,(Arthur by name) was to hang up the mistletoe this however was the only used by certain sailor (you know what Sailors are).

Next we discovered that we had a newcomer. A kitten.Sandy by name and sandy by colour.

After doing what we could our way of Housework-very little-we sat ran a fire in the lounge until we heard a gong sound for dinner. By this time, some more visitors had arrived. So we all trooped into the dining room together. We thoroughly enjoyed our dinner,although the custard was burnt. Congratulations to the cooks. (You must give praise where it is due. After dinner came an afternoon cup of tea, then we played "Truth or Dare" and other games.England son's certainly did their duty.After this we adjourned for tea. In spite of the fact that a beetle was going the round of the table, we enjoyed it very much especially the iced cake supplied by "Bless". This cake was decorated with candles for Philomena's birthday.

Then it was suggested we should wear each other's hats. Some of the boys looked very girlish in turbans.

We then decided to play a few quiet games like Consequences Barber's chair etc...

Then came community singing with the accompaniment of that master of the piano - Bernard Driver. By this time we felt in need of a restorative which was supplied by Father Koch.

Then two people (no names) wanted to know how to play postman's knock and were soon instructed by the expert. (Yes you've guessed it, Bernard of course!) After this we had some more refreshments in the shape of sandwiches.

Glancing at the clock we saw that it was time for some of us to return home so we set out reluctantly for the station with full naval escort. While we waited for the train, we sang some good old songs. We eventually arrived at Vauxhall singing and made our way home, tired, but I think we all enjoyed ourselves!

Diary Cotn./-

DEC. 31.

Club 's New Year's Eve fancy dress party. The dresses were better than ever this year, and though members are always begged to bring only enough eats for themselves and their own guests we again seemed to be knee-deep in sandwiches and Swiss rolls! So the common room was turned into a buffet and tea was made at intervals. Prizes were offered for the prettiest, the funniest and the most original dresses but everybody was so good that it was decided to vote for the three lucky ones. Mary Holmes won the prize for the prettiest-a peasant. Eileen Parsons was the most original and she was "Treasurer oot" Rosemary Martin was the funniest she came as Bessie Bunter.

Energetic games followed. It was funny to see a handsome young Roman partnering "Bessie" in a game of musical bumps and taking good care that she sat on the floor good and hard when the music stopped! A shy Egyptian lady was coyly peeping at a set of traffic lights and a noble looking "Chinks" were hobnobbing with a "Tweedledum and Tweedledee"! "Day" was dancing with "Night" and "Smash and Grab" was hand-in-hand with "Black Market." It was rather surprising to see a delicate "English Rose" using so much "punch" in a very rough game known as "Breakthrough."

We were very sorry indeed when midnight came. Whilst we were singing "Old Lang Syne" there was a loud crash as a rocket fell nearby and in a good many minds was a prayer that we should all meet again safe and sound in the near future.

JAN. 3ʳᵈ.1945 Third. annual Bit-of-do the hall was a perfect picture of festivity. Tables looked lovely and so too did the waitresses in their gay dresses. Lots of food as usual and heaps of mince pies and Christmas pudding.

The Guild of St. Agnes did a funny little play that went off very well and then the concert party entertained with soles and monologues and funny sketches. Hearty congratulations to Arty and Co. for a happy and amusing evening.

JAN 7.

C.O.M. Party. There never was any party at any time so much looked forward too for enjoying as this one. The Vauxhall C.O.M. parties stand alone for quality. The tea was magnificent and everybody had come, not because it was their duty to support the table, but they came because they meant to enjoy themselves. And he came to have tea-and they ate (I'll say they did!!) Even honoured guest and the mighty once in the seats of the exalted at the posh end of the Table- but if you were, but it was just too bad!

JAN. 23.

We gave them a social and invited other Clubs and the concert party obliged again

FEB 6.

Very eventful evening, Sir Shane Leslie paid the Club a visit. We all had a very interesting talk with him and he showed us the engagement ring of Mrs. Fitzherbert. His great grandmother was her adopted daughter. Mrs. Fitzherbert was the real wife of George the Fourth. He also has another claim to fame, being the cousin of Mr. Churchill.

FEB 15.

Boys beat Kings Own at handball.

MAR 1.

Bernard Driver home again on the first of a series of embarkation leave. Ron Miller joins the Navy. Eileen Bunting leaves the Club and takes up nursing. We wish them both got speed.

MAR 10.

Opening day at Ashtead.Archbishop Amigo and Bishop Brown performed the very impressive ceremony of Officially opening St. Anne's Country Club and blessing it. Almost every member of the Club was there and amongst the visitors was Lady Holberton and Mrs. Dearlove. It was a grand day in the history of the Club and we know that everybody who goes there to stay for a holiday is assured of a excellent home away from home. We heartily congratulate everybody who made, not only that day, but the House too, such an outstanding success.

MAR. 11.

Girls retreat. We began off badly by arriving late at Holy Rood House. But we tried to atone for it like taking almost no time at all to don black veils and creep into the chapel. It was a success full day, and we sincerely thank Mother St. Mildred and the other mothers who looked after us so kindly and so well. We also thank the President of Holy Rood House C.O.M. for "visiting" us at teatime and invited us to their forthcoming play. Lots of larking about on the bus coming home.

EASTER MONDAY

Day at Ashtead. Rousing game of rounders, much argument. Splendid tea at Malden Lodge. Train home. Stiff joints.

APR. 4.

Another distinguished visitor at the Club. Bruce Marshall, author of "All Glorious Within".

APR. 6.

Annual General Meeting. Proceedings began with Father Koch in the chair. Some arguments on the treatment of newcomers which was eventually settled before blood was shed. A satisfactory year on the whole, and members warmly congratulated each other on keeping to the Club in spite of enemy action. All reports and decisions being made and all other business coming to an end. Father Koch thanked the retiring committee and the new committee was then elected.

COMMITTEE 1945

Joan Noakes	Phil Cullen
Lily Coffey	Rosemary Martyn
Madie Taylor	Marie Perla
Barbara Driver	Arthur Parsons
Damian Welfare	Adolf Perla
Tom McEvoy	Pat McMonagle
Peter Stork	Jack McAuliffe.

APR. 28.

The Club's first week's holiday at Ashtead began. Those left at home can picture what it will be like once they all settled in. We know the little larks of Phil Cullen and Mary Chance- and we can only hope the Holly is not as prickly as it was last year in the Autumn! Such a waste of time sewing up the buttonholes on Phil pyjamas - she hasn't any buttons on them anyway.

MAY. 1.
Trams strike
MAY 4.
A party of our girls waded through the rain and went to Holy Rood House to see a performance of "The Martyrdom of St Cecilia" It was a first class performance and very reverently done. The performers spoke very clearly and their costumes were really Roman. We thank them for a very enjoyable evening.

MAY 8. VE day. Iron Crosses now being plentiful, a couple should be awarded to Arthur Parsons and Jack McAuliffe for rowing four (not to small) girls along the river for four hours.

Report as Follows:-

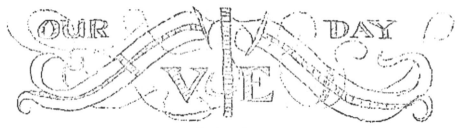

By Anne Bremer

It was during my journey home on VE day I saw the first wave of VE spirit. All the villages were hanging out flags and bonfires were being built on village greens. My train was full of soldiers and Sailors all singing at the top of their voices, and it was quite clear they had celebrated very well although for them the war in Japan was still on.

It was marvellous coming out of the Underground Station and hearing all the ships sirens on the river sounding... And seeing the multi-coloured flares being dropped by the planes overhead. The reflections in the sky of the bonfires reminded me of the blitz and I could not believe that it was finished.

In the evening I went along to the Club to see how all my friends were taking the news. Everybody decided that we should all go to the West- End later in the evening, but the first thing they wanted was a bonfire in the Club garden before we set out. By whoodling and coaxing, we eventually persuaded Father Koch to let us light a bonfire on the bomb crater in the garden.

Within a few minutes the biggest bonfire in the district was crackling and blazing like fury, and there were many willing stokers piling on forbidden fuel until things became too hot for them. A small bevy of beauties (no rude remarks please) gave a a song and dance in the firelight, the choirmaster and chief stoker being one and the same!(What a number of trades one leans in the navy!)

The more select members of our community chose to dance in the hall to the radiogram. At nine o'clock we all assembled in the common room to hear the King's Speech. The King was duly toasted with tea whilst our more valiant numbers carried buckets of water to put out one of London's best bonfires.

Then we all prepared to go West (literally of course). We did arrive at the Strand eventually where we had to dodge the rockets been fired at Nelson by the Ack- Ack girls. Here we lost some of our party. Crowds of people were wearing ridiculous hats and making the most weird noises with anything could you could make a noise with! The thickest crowds were round Piccadilly, but the fireworks kept the people moving and even the police were kissing everybody and anybody! There were people up the lamp posts and everybody was insane on an insane night. It was just like a mad dream, but finally we found ourselves outside Buckingham Palace which was a blaze of light. It was now just before midnight and the thousands were shouting:- "We Want the King".

He suddenly appeared in Naval uniform with the Queen who was dressed in white with her jewels sparkling in the light, on the balcony. They were greeted with many loud cheers. After a period they returned indoors and we made our long weary way home.

We visited many parties in the streets on our way back and big bonfires were still blazing and there was songs and pianos and drums and dancing.

Footsore and weary we bid each other farewell and crept home each one of us no doubt with a failing that we should never forget Victory in Europe.

PS in any of you are feeling sorry for us because all the milk bars were closed, we'd like to mention that we remedied that a couple of weeks later.

ooOoo

Diary Cont./-

<u>MAY. 21.</u>
Hike to Purley Downs. Very enjoyable.

<u>MAY. 22.</u>
The Guild of Saint Agnes disturbed the peace and quiet of Boxhill, making the most of along, happy day out.
<u>MAY.27.</u>
The Guild of St. Agnes gave a performance of "Children in Uniform". The audience thoroughly enjoyed it, and the youngsters themselves seem to be having the time of their lives. The spirit of good comradeship is very strong in the St. Anne's Guild of St.Agnes. A magnificent collection of £11. 5. 0. Bravo the Guild.
<u>JUN. 1.</u>
We receive the papal blessing, sent from John Kennedy.
Many Thanks John.
<u>JUN. 10.</u>
Thirty attending the Empire Youth Sunday C.Y.C. Mass in the ruins of St George's Cathedral.
<u>JUN. 17.</u>
Second performance of "Children in Uniform" very good. Not a dry eye in a place. We congratulate Theresa Clinton won her song "Only A Rose" beautifully sung.

JUN. 24.

Hike to Oxshott.

JUN. 30.

Congratulations to Tom Stock. A son. Michael Anthony.

JUL. 1.

A few dozen children filled the coach and sailed are off to give the Nuns at Effingham Hall the pleasure of their company for one and the most infamous outings they have every year. We hear the Nuns gave them a good send off with hearty hand waving them off- and even threw rose petals after the coach. They must have been glad to see the back of the C.O.M.

Report as follows:

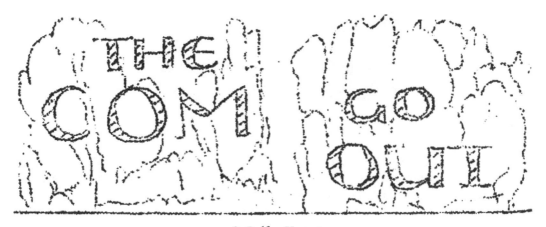

By Delfina Venturi

We had been warned that Sunday, 1st of July, was the date fixed for the Children of Mary outing, and as you all know, the President expects every child of Mary to be there, or elves! So it was arranged that we would meet at 10:30 outside the church.

Everyone came prepared for a lovely day out, and a hike before we had previously been told that we were in for a 3 1/2 mile walk, after leaving the train, but, low and behold, there was a coach waiting nearby, which, we were told was for our use,(a coach, mind you!) How this was procured, no one knew, and, no doubt, will for ever remain a mystery to us,(careless talk costs lives) you know!!

The coach was a 32 seater but there were 38 of us so there had to be a little mental arithmetic to see how to seat everyone, eventually there were only two people standing. We started off after much hassle and bustle, about 10:45 never before had there been such a noise made in Harleyford road, everybody seemed to be in the best of spirits, laughing and joking.

Our journey was very pleasant and enjoyable, the country was at its best, entered, for no apparent reason army lorries that seemed to be of special attraction, whether they had an unusual sort of bonnet or motor or because they were decorated with enable leave one and couldn't say. We were very lucky too, cherries were handed round, 10 each, then five, they were black ones and meaty too, that the two occupants that was standing, came in as wonderful targets for a halt the cherry (hogs) pips. The place chosen was the convent, near Effingham hill run by the religious of Christian instruction, we arrived there at 12:30 Nuns came to meet us giving us a most hearty welcome, telling us that we had the entire place to us disposal also that we could swim in of all and the ponies would be available for us to ride at 2:30.

Lunch was at 1.o'clock, sandwiches were munched, tea was provided to drink with our sandwiches, bowls of loganberries(or were they raspberries?) were brought in, very scrumptious they were too! After lunch, a few girls swam in the pool, enjoyed themselves, and came back, with most gorgeous hair styles, plaits, long bobs, yes even "Edwardians". The remaining few, sought the playing fields, "rounder's" seemed the most favourite game, but before teams had been fully chosen, we were informed that 3 ponies and 2 horses were ready. Everybody was shy to ride at first, but after a bold dash by a couple of brave people, horse riding became very popular, and in no time at all, was in full swing, and been thoroughly enjoyed by all, until it rained "cats and dogs", which made most of us go inside to view the House. It was a lovely House, the rooms so unorthodox and beautifully furnished, and decorated (which by the way is done by the Nuns themselves), you felt that each room you entered, couldn't possibly be better than the last, but in most cases it was. The gardens and fields, surrounding the House were most beautiful, there were so many varieties of flowers, making such a wonderful splash of colour, that he had to be our breath away.

We had a grant tea followed by Benediction at 5:30. The chapel was quite big with an number of gaily painted statues all round the Alter looked beautiful,(you know how Nuns decorate them usually).

After Benediction we played "rounder's" until almost 8.45 pm lemonade, sandwiches and cakes were served, then everybody prepared themselves for their homeward journey, snaps were taken, the Nuns came to see us off, we gave them a rousing cheer, told them how we had enjoyed our day and thanked them for their hospitality and kindness.

The coach was invaded, it drove down the drive, the Nuns running from one field to another in order to cheer us and throw rose petals at us.

On the way back, a the rain had simply fell down buckets full, but nobody bothered themselves about it, we had a lovely day and felt for the beans are you able to cope with anything, even our English weather, and that's saying something!!! We just kept on singing (did I say singing?) Sorry!! Anyway the driver enjoyed it and people in bus and tram queues seemed quite envious of us. We arrive back at the Club, tired, but very happy at roughly I should say 10.00.

Three cheers for Effingham, so that we shall be invited again sometime.

ooOoo

Diary Cont./-
<u>JUL. 9.</u>
Mary Dudley put her head round the door. Nice to see her again.
<u>JUL. 13.</u>
Barbara Abram looked in. Looked well.
<u>JUL. 14.</u>
The boys beat St. George's Cathedral at cricket. 106 against 47.
<u>JUL. 15.</u>
The Guild of St. Agnes go off to Engelfield Green for the day. Judging by the balls, bats, swimming gear and colossal packets of food and sweets they intended to enjoy themselves in a big way
- and did.
Josie Taylor.

G. B. S. Report

At the Corpus Christie general meeting, Mr. Thorn was re-elected for a further term as Warden of the guild. Proposed donations to be played from a surplus Guild funds, received unanimous consent.

We are happy to say that over the last two or three years there has been a steady improvement in membership, resulting in a much more inspiring turn out at monthly communion.

During the early war years and membership steadily shrunk until there remained but a token force of Guildsmen to keep the banner flying in Vauxhall. Since that time gradual return of old members and steady campaigning among the Youth of the parish has led to an increase in members and a spiritual reawakening which augurs well for the future, when we hope to see <u>all</u> our old members at holy Communion in company with a majority of the men of the parish.

All the men, and boys under 14 who wish to join the Guild should apply to the Clergy or to Mr. Thorn. We are all was happy to welcome new members in the firm belief that a flourishing Guild can do much to strengthen the Faith throughout the land.

ooOoo

Letters to the Ed.

Dear Clubmates,

It seems, and I suppose it is, very long time since I was able to enjoy your company at St Anne's.

Much has happened to me since I left for Nuneaton on November the eighth 1943. Life seemed very dreary during the ten months I spent at Nuneaton. Lying for months without treatment and seeing my folks once in a "blue moon" was a great tax on my spirits. It was then above all that I realised what staunch band the friends I had at Vauxhall in the club.

The cheerful letters I received and the knowledge that I was remembered in your prayers were just a tonic I was needing to help me through the darkest days I ever want to face.

Things brightened somewhat when I was moved to Bath and since coming to London last November and being able to see everybody again, life has been worth living. Progress is extremely slow, but the fact remains I am progressing. We pray that the day will dawn when once again I shall be able to grace–or disgrace the club with my presence.

Being so long in hospital is a dreadfully dull business but at least, one gets used to the routine. I have met all sorts of interesting people and made many friends. The nurses are changed fairly frequently and this is rather unfortunate in some respects. Just when you find a nurse who has something worth talking about, she's changed for another, a grim – looking female whose only interest in life is stuffed birds! Doesn't give a chap a fair chance, does it?

Although I have been away from the club so long I always follow its activities with great interest. Numbers have varied according to enemy action and calls to the services, but the old place kept going all through the darkest days and now that peace has come in Europe there is a greater chance to reach a higher standard than ever before.

The magazine has been a great help in keeping in touch with events and I have been most impressed with the amount of humour in the past few issues! Itma seems to have nothing nowadays.

The acquisition of the house at Ashtead promises to provide many happy hours for members in the future. All those who were at Belsen (sorry, Bumsley) with me will appreciate what a boon it will be to have a hide-out so near London. The local pub is quite handy I'm told, so let's hope supplies are equal to demand!

I am always please see or hear from any of you, so make a note of my address and spared me a few minutes now and again.

May God bless you all
Yours sincerely,
Frank Barry

ooOoo

"Do you like Opera?"
"No" you answer. "I don't like Operas"
Why?"

"Do you like Opera?"

"No." you answer. "I don't like!"

"Why?"

"Well, it's so dreary. It doesn't mean anything. The singer shouted at the top of their voices, and then, one can't hear the words anyway. And well"........

Thus, one hears all the common prejudices, also much of the abuse levelled against Opera as being pretentious frivolous, absurd, etc., etc... But let us pursue the argument just a little further. Let us ask and hypothetical confirmed hater (?!) Of Opera.

Have you ever seen or heard an Opera? And he will invariably answer. "Well. No. Not exactly." He will generally appear rather distantly, that Opera is so dreadfully boring. Such a fag to listen to. And yet, he knows everything about it. Naturally he's an expert!

That's the trouble with the vast majority of individuals; they believe themselves to be sufficiently competent to pass judgement on that which the greatest minds have produced after years of hard and exacting work. On that, which not even individuals of a learnered intelligentsia humility, have every dared to pass judgement.

However, these individuals are not so far the decade that they are incapable of salvation one is never too old to learn, and I can assure you with all sincerity that if you are willing to devote your exceedingly versatile minds to developing that part of your brain which has apparently remained dormant, you are still capable of musical salvation.

Have you ever given way to that in its applicable desire to feel the breath of a wonderful melody from one of the arias of an Opera? It is a great experience. It gives you fresh life, sends new blood coursing through your veins.

You have no idea what a great pleasure it is to listen to, say, the quartet from Act three of Verdi's "Rigoletto", the "Prize Song" from the "Mastersinger" by Richard Wagner or something as superbly exciting as the "Toreador's" song from the Opera of Opera's "Carmen" by George Bizet. It is such beautiful music, one feels, that in his own way, each of the composers must have put his whole heart into their composition, fired with the honest desire to create something worthy of bequest to prosperity.... And prosperity is not just a question of a few words in some never read History Book, it is something which concerns you and me; that music was bequeathed to us, to enjoy over and over again. But do we enjoy? No, we asked much too clever, such stuff is for individuals who live in the clouds; high – browse they are called, I believe.

No these high-brows do not live in the clouds, but above them, where the sky is clear, where they listen to the finest of all instruments, the human voices. Away from all thoughts of the microphone. The microphone is only required by singers who cannot sing!

As I have already said you are not incapable of being in a position to assist in the cleansing of the defiled alter of great music. In fact, you can be one of the main assistants in the disinfection, if only you really used your intelligence and, instead of turning your highly polished noses up (?!) When you hear the word mentioned, you really listen to the music (you cannot dislike a thing you have never heard or if you have heard it, never listen to), and appreciate the art of singing without a microphone. Take it all in, it does not matter if the words fail to reach you, after all you can always read the text of the Opera before or after the performance, that, I do believe, requires but little intelligence. And, you know, it's the music that matters in Opera.

I further point which draws much criticism of Opera is invariable difference between the story and what one sees on the stage. For example, when you are witnessing the performance of an "Opera" such as Puccini's "La Boheme" one has to realise that whilst the story gives it that mini is consumptive, it does not follow that the singer taken the part should be so. In fact, as a rule, the suggestion is quite the opposite.

Surely, we can forget the facts and use our imagination. The use of one's imagination is, after all, very stimulating. We like our letter colleagues who only too well appreciate the full – throated melodies written by the then inimitable Puccini.

I hope that my very poor words will stimulate your possibly (unconscious) insatiable desire for Opera. If I have suggested in that, it will be a very pleasing thought.

William.

ooOoo

Do you remember when............
Bishop Brown said I don't know?
Father Koch took the dancing class?
Father Madden was called Blondie?
Delfina Ventura was tall for her age?
Damien Welfare smoked tobacco?
Madeleine Taylor was as gentle as a lamb?
William Bogazzi was a swing fan?
Phil Cullen played a fairy in a pantomime?
Bernard Driver had an Odol smile?
Josie Taylor knew the right answer?
Ron Miller's voice was sweet and low?
Lily Coffey was a worm – fancier?
Terry O'Leary preferred male company?
Marie Perla won a jitterbug contest?
Arthur Parsons was satisfied with half–pints?
Anne Bremer was anaemic?
Frank Barry.

ooOoo

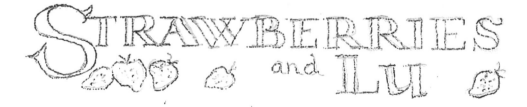

I've a great admiration for Lu
Who slept under a tent and wasn't blue---
For the country's good cause
She distributed straws
Between strawberry plants in a queue.

Her bedroom was not all that she wished,
For the wind and the rain as it swished
Blew the tent in and out.
In a rage she would shout:-
Oh why did I come – I've been dished!

But she stayed and she saw the job through
And the strawberries will now fall as dew
On the straw she had laid
The patient is paid
I wonder who'll eat them – not you!

Francis Desmond.

ooOoo

There is a story now current, though strange it may seem
Of the great Adolf and his wonderful dream.
Being tied of his exploits he lay down in bed,
And amongst other things, he dreamt he was dead.

He then in the his coffin was lying in state
With a guard of brave Poles who mourned at his fate.
He wasn't long dead, when he found to his cost,
That his soul like his soldiers had gone to be lost.

Upon leaving earth, to heaven he went straight,
And arriving up there gave a knock on the gate
But St Peter looked out in invoice loud and clear,
Said. "Go away Adolf, we don't want you here".

"Well", said Adolf, "That's very uncivil-
I suppose after this, I must go to the divil."
So he turned on his heels and away he did go
At the top of his speed to regions below.

But when he got there, he was full of dismay.
While waiting outside he heard old Dick say
To his imps. "Now look here boys I give you a warning
I'm expecting Adolf down here in the morning
But don't let him in, for to me it's quite clear

He's a very bad man, and we don't want him here.
IF once he gets in to be no end of quarrels,
In fact HE'LL corrupt what's left of your morals!"

"Oh Satan dear friend." poor old Adolf cried,
"Excuse me for listening while waiting outside-
If you don't let me in where else can I go?"
"Indeed," said the Devil "I really don't know."
"Oh do let me in, I'm feeling quite cold."
Said Adolf most anxious to enter Nick's fold.
"Let me sit in the corner no matter how hot."
"No." said the devil "No certainly not."

Then he turned Adolf out and vanished in smoke
And just at that moment, old Adolf woke
He jumped out of bed in a shivering sweat
And said. "That's a dream I shall never forget.
Then I won't go to heaven I know very well,
But it's really too bad to be kicked out of hell!

Kathleen Amar.

ooOoo

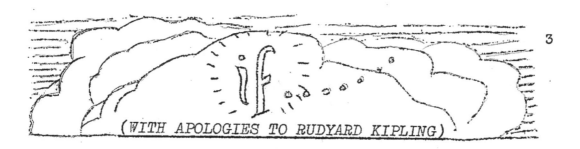

(WITH APOLOGIES TO RUDYARD KIPLING)

If you can keep your head when all the clubs
Engaged in place and Mags and bits of do's,
If you can undertake to sing or so or dramatize
And learn to read and write, air your views and criticise.
If you can play ping-pong, shopsnap, and darts
Or do keep fit canteen and (dear me!) Learn your parts.
If you can play at soccer and get treated like the ball
Get well bashed the boxing and not feel hurt at all:
If you can take your crocks back (and other people's too)
And lend a hand with washing up and not show that y'r blue
If you can dust and polish, clean windows all mend chairs,
If you're the type that's suited to odd jobs or small repairs,
If you can run a jumbled stall – sell tickets for the dates,
If you can pair up curtains and make oddments into sets,
If you can go to Ashtead on your half days off from work
And turn a hand to gardening or do anything (but shirk),

If while you're there you eat and laugh and grow proverbially fat
Then came graciously take the insults (so painfully due to that),
If you can bear to hear it said of a job that's taken days
If you want a job done properly – do it yourself,
as I always says.
In fact if you are capable of any sort of job
Read through the rules; fill in a form and then just pay a Bob.
Now if despite this, to join you still intend
Then all the club is yours, and everything that's in it
And which is more, your qualified for membership my friend!

Phil Cullen.

ooOoo

Laugh please.
By
Nobody in particular.

He: "I say, is it possible to love two girls at the same time?"
She: "Not if they know it!"

The shop- walker seen a very harassed young man, went up to him.
"Looking for something in gents clothing, Sir?" He asked.
"No." Replied the young man, "Something in women's clothes I have lost my wife."

Mr. Workshy. "I wish something would turn up, don't you?"
Mrs Workshy. "I certainly do. What about starting on your
                shirtsleeves?"

A householder confronted two burglars in his house.
"Don't mind me," he said, "I'm only sleepwalking!"

Betty's uncle counted the cherry stones on the edge of her plate.
"I see my dear you're going to marry a rich man." He remarked.
"Yes uncle," she replied, "But I had to swallow three stone before I could get him!"

A man asked the office boy who stuttered if he could see the manager.
The office boy replied YYYes SSir,wwhat nnname shshall I ssay SSSir?"
Mr. Charles Chesham of Chichester." Answered the man.
PPPleas SSIR ccould yyyou gggive mme aa ccccard. Ttthe mmmanager wwwill ttthink I'm ppplaying tttrains!"

ooOoo

..R.A. D. R.VE.	"That gaunt and toothless thing!"	T Clayton
J.C. M.AC..F.E	"Waking or sleeping. Does he even hear?"	Wordsworth
RO..M.R. M. .TY.	"She was a Phantom of delight."	Wordsworth
BUMSLEY	"And the attending and spreading of straw for a bedding."	Belloc
D.AM.E. W..FA..	"Keep my countenance I remain self-possessed."	T.S. Elliot
J.AN N.AKS	"Type of the wise who saw, but never roam".	Wordsworth
PRE-ELECTION	"Each (for madness ruled the hour) would prove his own expressive power."	W Collins
J..E AR.L...	"Thy notes flow in such a crystal stream."	Shelley
R.. MI...R	"A soft responsive voice."	W Collins
CLUB RAMBLE	"Meandering with mazy notions."	Campbell
E..E,N P.R..NS	"For every why, she has a wherefore."	Butler
OL..E O'..LL.VAN	"I'm playful and gay as a kitten."	
M...LE.N. O'..LL.VAN	"Rich in saving common."	Anon
DRAMATICS (at the moment)	"But fly our path our feverish contact fly, "For strange the infection of elemental strife."	Arnold
ANN. B..M.R	"What a speck is she dwindled into."	Lamb
F.TH.. K..H (at Ashstead)	"It is not linen you're wearing out but human creatures lives."	Hood
F..K B.R.Y	"I put my pleasure in a pint of ale."	Belloc
ASHSTEAD HOLIDAY (1st. in May)	"My dear it rains, it hails its snows!"	Anon
C...IT.., ME..ING	"We grouped together and avoid speech."	T.S. Elliot
TO ALL	"I give the toast across the world, and drink, it, gentlemen the club.	Belloc

Phil Collins and Joan Noakes

ooOoo

POST WAR 1945 ---

THE BEGINING OF A NEW ERA.

In August 1945. The end of the War brought a - New era in the Clubs History. After ten (10) years' service from it's founding. Father. Adolf Koch, a very active, respected friend and stalwart Club LEADER, was to leave St. Anne's to become a Parish Priest in Blackfen Kent. There no doubt to carry on his good work in the Youth of his new Parish - The same Spirit that he had instilled in St. Anne's. He was to be replaced by Father. Robert (Bob) Madden, who had already been serving alongside Fr. Koch during the period of the war years.

It was also a time when the demobilisation of thousands of the Forces, was underway. They the serving personnel were only too pleased to return home to an uncertain future, to face unemployment and a Country about to try and reconstruct the ravages that the War had caused. Within their ranks, were old members of the Club, who had been overseas and by then, in their early twenties. Upon their return to the Club, love tristes with the older Girl Club members "Girl meets Boy" were rekindled. Inevitably they found (apart from sports) the mood had somewhat changed and possibly not to their way of entertainment.

Fr. Madden as Club Leader, assisted by a new incoming Priest Fr. Leahy, took over the mantle, to continue and carry on Fr. Koch's good work. With the task of melding the old with new Club members, changes had to be made; the need for producing ANNALS took a back seat: as they were extremely time consuming to produce and their purpose had been fulfilled. It is also possible that the previous old team changed, as did the method to produce such articles, as can be seen in the new versions available from July 1946. Scripts covers and art-work all came out blue. Although scanned (for the purpose of inclusion), the art work reproduction is somewhat scanty; as can be seen in the following two ANNALS: It is possible to assume that the 1945 and the 1947 issue was never produced (hopefully someone with prove me wrong).

Within days after the end of the war, the Cold War began. Conscription into the forces continued, possibly with two factors in mind. Employment of young Men, and due to the problems of the reoccupation of war torn countries, caused the requirement of Servicemen to be called upon, to control the flood of refugees and displaced persons, specifically in Europe. With the pending breakup of the British Empire, all males upon reaching the age of 18 were conscripted and doomed initially to 18 months in the services, which in January 1948, change to 2 years National Service. For the Club, it was the continuation of recycling of male members, subsequently this effected many girl members, who were going out with their man. To some extent, due to this upheaval the membership of the Club tended to evolve every two years. The following is a list of a few of those members who were conscripted.

NOWADAYS IT IS CALLED A GAP YEAR? BACK IN THOSE DAYS OUR GAP WAS TWO YEARS
(These are just a smidgen of members who were conscripted to serve King / Queen and Country)

Paddy McMonagle Army UK	Jimmy Richardson. Army/Parachute Regt.
John Healey Army India ?	Keith Ager. 1945-47 ? Army.
Tom MacAvoy Called up?	Lou Ager RAF UK
Bert MacAVoy Called up ?	Mike Plant. 1948-50 Army West Africa
Bert Thomas Army.?	Pat Thomas. 1949-51 Army Canal Zone
Dennis Lynch Navy?	Brian O'Sullivan. 1950 -52 RAF. UK.
Eric Blackburn Navy.	Harry Spanswick. RAF 1951- 53?
Phil Frost 1951-53? Army UK	Mike MacDermott Called up?
Derek Rivers Called up?	Arthur Course. 1952-54 Army. Germany
Roy Summersby. RAF UK	Tommy Wilberham. 1953-57 RAF Egypt
Don Skinner Called up??	Mike Higgins Called up?
Jimmie Rankin Called up?	Joe Dixon Called Up?
Derek Beamish. 1954 -56 Army UK.	Phil Darcy 1954-56 Army Kenya.
Eddie Buchan Called up 1954 -56?	Joe. Plant. 1955-1957 Army Malaya

Kevan Lewis 1955-57 RAF UK
Brian Jenkins.1956 -58 Army UK
Maurice Green Called up??

Kenny Richardson. 1955-1957 ?? UK
Johnnie Manzie Called up ??

Plus many many others....

ooOoo

Fr. Bob Madden also realised that there was a necessity to engage the older members with their own Club, and formed the Over–Twenties. 'The Pella Club.', and to ensure that the Older Members were provided for, Thursday night was their night. A Magazine called, 'THUMP' (This Has Unique Memoir Percussion), was produced, as seen by the transcribed 1948/49 Christmas Issue. Fr. Madden was also Chaplain to the Variety Club. A Charitable Institution. Bob saw another opportunity to invite the Artiste, Singers, and Radio Entertainers, to visit the Club and open a function and perform their act. In the late years of the 40s and early 50's. It was the beginning of a new and exciting period of time. In supporting the Club, those Celebrities appearing at the London Palladium, would visit and entertain Club members on a Saturday or Sunday Night Social. (They appear under a separate heading.) In the early 60's a shield was created, inscribed with the names of the Clubs President – Vice Presidents – Honorary members and Committee members from 1946 -1954.

PRESIDENTS
Rt. Rev. W.F. Brown Bishop of Pella
Sir Alec Guinness.

VICE PRESIDENTS.
Miss A. Shelton. Elected 1948
Mr. V. Hyde Hon. Mayor of Niles Mich. USA 1951
John Gregson 1953

HONORARY LIFE MEMBERS
Danny Thomas. Apr. 1950
Max Bygraves Jan. 1951
Gaynor Hyde Feb. 1951
Steve Race Apr. 1951
Billy Daniels Mar. 1952
Danny Payne Mar. 1952
Jonny Franz Mar. 1952
Joe Mathews Mar. 1952
Dr. J. B. Lawless Mar. 1952
Dick Shaun. Mar. 1954

CLUB LEADERS
Adolf Koch 1935-1945
Robert Madden 1945-1952
Charles Byrne 1952- 1954
P. Boulding 1953- 1954
P.G. Pearce1954 -

Father Robert Madden
Club Leader. 1945 - 1952

St. Anne's Annals

THE JOURNAL OF ST ANNE'S CATHOLIC YOUTH CLUB VAUXHALL. S.E.11.

JULY

4ᴰ

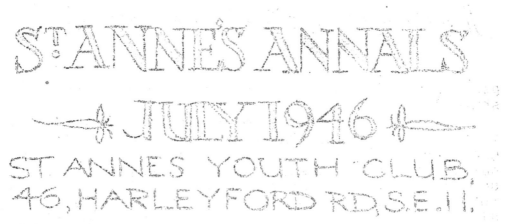

St Anne's Annals

July 1946

St Annes Youth Club,
46, Harleyford Rd, S.E.11.

Since the last issue of St Anne's annals war has ceased and we faced the task of reconstruction.

Our victory celebrations stand as but the first milestone on the way to real peace. As we progress step-by-step led us give a special place in our prayers to those who died. With God's help, to ensure that much sacrifice will never again be needed.

Frank Barry an old member writes in this issue on life in hospital. He has been on his back for some years, but we are pleased to learn that there is definite hope of his recovery.

Club members could do a great deal to assist this by writing or visiting him. He would like nothing better. The address is:

Frank Barry Ward (B) St Stephen's Hospital
Fulham Road S.W.10.

The editor wishes to thank all contributors to this issue and to point out that these pages are open to all. Contributions on all subjects are welcomed

ooOoo

Taking Stock *by Father Madden*

In Club life every year brings its own problems but 1945 – 1946 opened with more than its share.

Father Koch has become a parish priest it is difficult to imagine the Club without him. It had grown up around him. Through the wall years he had cared for it and nursed it back to health after two separate bombings. The tone, the spirit, the feeling, the "character" of the Club - whatever it was that distinguished St Anne's from so many other similar organisations-had depended on him. And now he was gone.

Some of the older members who had held prominent positions, and done much good work in the past, were becoming restless. They found it difficult to adapt themselves to the new regime. In the event, they gave up the struggle and sought more congenial Club-life elsewhere.

The passing of the bombing danger, and the return of the evacuees were largely responsible for a sudden increase in the number of younger members. The newcomers were very welcome, but, on account of their numbers, were a little difficult to absorb. However, the goodwill of the majority, guided by a loyal committee, was to be a great help in overcoming this difficulty.

The recurring problems of rationing, the shortage of sports gear and of all kinds of equipment remain. But most of the members seem fairly satisfied. Club functions-parties, hikes, outings, socials, plays,-are crowded, often overcrowded.

Yes, we can look back on these last 12 months with some degree of satisfaction. Please God, next year will be less difficult, but not less satisfactory.

ooOoo

<u>COMMITTEE MEMBERS 1946</u>

S. Talbot Hon. Sec.	A. Bremer.
P. Cullen.	P. Daly.
V. De Troia	M. Mulvey
T. Marconi.	D. Welfare.
B. Driver.	R. Perla.

CLUB DIARY FROM: July '45 TO: June '46

<u>July 29th</u>.

Splendid performance of the young person in pink produced by Father Koch. Terry O'Leary in the male lead: Margaret Freeman at very short notice the leading lady. Both really excellent strong supporting cast.

<u>July 30th</u>

After a short Committee Meeting, it is announced that Father Koch is to leave Vauxhall to take a Parish of his own- Blackfen, near Welling Kent. News received sadly. We feel that we are about to lose a very very personal friend. We do hope and pray that he will find his new task a happy one and that we remain in the Club that he has created will still continue to aspire to those ideals which he has always strived to attain.

<u>August 12th</u>.

Farewell party to Father Koch. Every section of the Club aid in making evening memorable £45 was collected and a spiritual okay made up. Both these were presented to the 'Gaffer' on behalf the Club by Arthur Parsons.

Evening a success, but one or two understandable tears.

<u>August 15th</u>.

We welcome Father Leahy to the parish and hope he has a long and successful stay in Vauxhall.

<u>August 27th</u>.

Return of the Guild of St Agnes from a week's holiday at Maldon Lodge, the Catholic country Club at Ashtead Surrey. Full of stories about pillow fights, dancing in pyjamas ghost stories in the dark play reading, and a table tennis tournament that lasted well into the night. They are all deeply grateful to Father Koch, who bought them each a bunch of flowers to bring home with them.

<u>AUGUST 30TH</u>.

General meeting. Father Madden takes a chair for the first time as the Club Leader. Having introduced himself, squashes rumour by outlining plans for continuance of Club largely as heretofore. The problem of age limit to be studied but otherwise held over pro tem. Father Madden indicates during his address that he desires the younger members (boys particularly) to become more active in conducting the Club, and would encourage any display of initiative.

It remains to be seen whether our younger members will respond to this invitation.

<u>August 31st</u>.

Three young members of the Club print their own newspaper Response!

October 5ᵗʰ.

Parish presentation to Father Koch after a short concert presented by the C.O.M. and the C.B.S. jointly, featuring an excerpt from a "Midsummer Night's Dream" together with various items including a swing trio formed by some of a younger members: A cheque for £50 was presented on behalf of the parish to Father Koch by Bishop Brown after an excellent speech by Mr Johnson. Vauxhall's oldest Parishioner.

December 1ˢᵀ.

Bring and Buy sale held today. Stalls loaded with all sorts of rarities. Novelty provided by Mr Tony Quinn, the famous the outstanding event in the form of an expedition – "The Trooping of the Colour"-of miniature soldiers. A great success thanks to all that helped. Over £200 raised for the settlement Debt.

December 20ᵗʰ.

The Carol singing venture. While a group of our members awoke echoes win within a 3 mile radius of St Anne's (total proceeds £6.10.0.) The choir visited Ashtead with the idea of clearing the debt on the house. But owing to heavy rain the choir ended up rather unhappily sitting round the lounge fire singing the carols to themselves. Proceeds nil.

December 31ˢᵗ.

New Year's Eve fancy dress party great success first prize won by a 'horse'- Barbara Driver and Olive O'Sullivan.

March 20ᵗʰ.

Bishop Browns Diamond Jubilee- see special report elsewhere. As follows:-

The outstanding event in the parish since our last issue has been our beloved Bishops Diamond Jubilee 60 years a Priest. 60 years, most of them spent as Parish Priest and friend to the people of Vauxhall-working always for their good, rejoicing in their happiness, sympathising in their sorrows. A real friend indeed.

His Lordship came to Vauxhall 54 years ago, to start a parish. He had high ideals. Only the best he could get would be good enough for the serving of God. Surely he has succeeded even beyond his expectations. Despite setbacks, he went on and still goes on-a shining example of untiring levitation to a noble purpose.

By Bishop Browns especial wish there was no Diocesan Celebration. He asked only the prayers of his friends everywhere. Nevertheless, Parish festivities were arranged and the Bishop received many presents. On entering the church to say Mass Elgar's Ecoe Sacredos' beautifully sung by the schoolchildren. After Mass the Bishop received the Press then read numerous telegrams and messages of greeting.

In the afternoon an entertainment and presentation by the schoolchildren proceeded tea in the Library with several old friends including some former teachers.

A reception in the Hall ended the day. The youth Club concert party gave a short selection from their repertoire and the Bishop was presented with a cheque from the parishioners.

His Lordship departed to the strains of 'For He's a Jolly Good Fellow.' looking rather tired but we hope, feeling happy at these humble efforts of his people to show their love and appreciation.

ooOoo

Diary Cont./-

March 24ᵗʰ.

More money raised towards clearing the Debt by the performance of 3 act "The Joan Danvers" – a drama. Quick work this- 10 weeks from first rehearsal to performance.

March 31ˢᵗ.

A stir is caused in the Club by the petite, famous daughter of famous parents.

The convert, who talked on Catholicism and the stage and afterwards answered all our questions. See report elsewhere.

Report as follows:-

A most moving experience was related by Miss and Carson, the distinguished actress daughter of Sir Lewis Casson and Dame Sybil Thorndyke when she visited the Club on Sunday, March 31st.

Once been unable to disembark the company performed George Bernard Shaw's 'St Joan' on the foredeck of a boat-with Miss Casson in the title role-to an audience composed entirely of soldiers. The Cast played in their everyday clothes without make up or properties. Searchlights illuminated their stage against the darkness of the night. The sea and the spellbound audience that was incredibly beautiful leaving (said Ms Casson) an unforgettable picture in her mind.

She went on to outline the adventures of the company of which she was a member during the war years-travelling through England Scotland and Wales, taking the theatre into tiny villages and out of the way spots to people who hardly ever if at all seen a play. They would perform for 2 or 3 nights in any place large enough to hold an audience, then be off the next morning sitting in the back of a van full of scenery and props. On these journeys all manner of subjects were discussed but the most frequent topics were politics and religion.

Ms Casson feels that these debates probably helped to clarify a growing desire for the true faith although at the time she had not come to the crossroads.(She has since become received into the church)

Local children borrowed to play Lady Macduff's child in Macbeth sometimes caused unforeseen difficulties. One child, on the stage, was completely unconcerned when told of it's 'fathers' death. On another occasion a child burst into a flood of assumed tears much to the astonishment of Anne Casson playing Lady Macduff. The audience were treated to the spectacular of Lady Macduff trying to quiten a bellowing child out of the corner of her mouth!

Ms Carson spoke for an hour and a half, and that the end of the extremely entertaining talk stayed for quite a time in conversations with members of the Club. The extra ordinary zest for life and great personal charm one our whole-hearted admiration. We offer her deepest thanks for a visit that will be long remembered

ooOoo

Diary Cont./-

April 7th.

Dance hall becomes a cinema.

Father G Williams accompanied with an explanatory commentary the showing of a film on the Mass entitled 'The Perfect Sacrifice.'

A Technicolor film made in Hollywood, this is its first public showing in this country. The effect of this dramatically simple film, which shows just exactly what the priest is doing at the Alter, somewhat marred by one or two 'technical hitches.'

April 10th.

A party of ten or eleven go to the King's Theatre Hammersmith to see and In the Title Role of Bernard Shaw's 'St Joan.' Afterwards privileged to visit her in the dressing room. Definite high spot this.

April 18/22ⁿᵈ.

28 Club members spend the most enjoyable Easter weekend at Ashtead. Joined on the bank holiday by 60 fellow members who spend the day with them playing rounder's and whatnot.

May 12ᵗʰ.

Annual outing very lucky for weather. We travel by coach to Bracknell Bay on the south coast. Swimming for the brave, but most contented themselves with rounder's and cricket.

May 26ᵗʰ. Another very successful play. This time a comedy 'Baa Baa Black Sheep. Eileen McMonagle and Terry O'Leary in the leads. A few more plays like this and the Debt will soon be cleared.

June 1ˢᵗ. Tubular steel armchairs in the Common Room in place of basket-and easy chairs. Long-standing complaints from the girls that old basket chairs tear stockings. Few of them seem to wear stockings. Cream and red steel chairs seem popular. As progress!

July 7ᵗʰ.

Stag party at the Club. Boys quite gay, girls away on annual C. O. M. Outing.-This time to St Teresa's convent Effingham, Surrey.(Near Dorking)the journey-by coach(or 'Sharybang' to quote a bystander)-unnecessarily prolonged by the drivers unfortunate habit of losing himself. It is perhaps worth noting that the coach stopped(for redirection) frequently within walking distance of a 'Halfway House.' Many of the C. O. M. Return home in the evening with a high colour. During the day the girls went on horse riding played tennis on the convents grass court, and enjoyed a calling did in the swimming pool. Poor Olive fell in! Fresh picked raspberries and cream for tea will be long remembered as high spots of a grand day. Report as follows:-

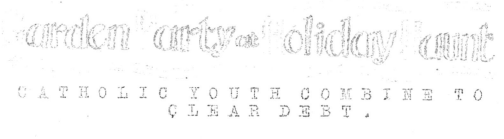

There was 'all the fun of the fair' at Ashtead Surrey this weekend.(Writes our Roving Reporter)

Malden Lodge, the Diocesan Holiday Youth Club run by Fr. Koch went 'gay' with the grand garden party and fate, organised by the Ashtead associations a group of willing workers drawn from all parts of the diocese, to aid in clearing the debt(£1750)burdening the Club.

The spacious grounds of the Lodge, the tall trees gently shading the lawns formed an ideal setting for the gaily coloured stalls and sideshows; Roll the Penny, Hoop-la, Darts, Wheel of Fortune, and others.During the afternoon raffles were drawn, while the warm sun made the thought of refreshments very popular with the visitors-the 'paying guests' -at the party(estimated at about 200) who came from a widely separated districts to support the venture.

Several of the stalls and raffles were provided and by groups from the outlying districts one, from as far away as Northampton.

The whole affair was an example of truly cooperative effort on the part of Catholic Youth. It is a pity that so few of our own Club members were present to help raise the takings over the £40 realised. Apart from a donation from the Club, St Anne's little in evidence.

ooOoo

BLACK BLACK MARKET

Comment from   REG CONNOR 196909 F/o Connor.
                      R.P.Air information ACSEA Comm Flight
                      R.A.F. Tengah Singapore. MALAYA.

I've just been reading about the food cuts at home. One article points out very rightly too, that rations most able to supply food are not doing their full share. From what I gather Mr Attlee thinks that irrespective of home shortages Britain should take the lead in this humanitarian gesture. He is not, to my mind, giving sufficient consideration to the fact that Britain can very easily become one of the most have not nations herself. One thing out here in Singapore is a black market I do not hold servicemen responsible, the quantity of goods involved is far too large could it be possibly be weak administration?

ARABIAN NIGHT-AND DAY

From Bernard Driver RP3 C/JX539241. 28 Mess HMS LONDON
                      C/o GPO London.

We are stopping only 24 hours here in Aden, and I am going ashore later on when the sun goes down.

At the moment, I am having the hottest time of my life the sun is scorching everything, and the heat seems to be shimmering across the water. The rocky peaks behind the port are completely void of vegetation and burnt a dark brown stop the natives ashore black as ink how much is dirt and how much is natural colouring is an interesting point.

I am playing tug-of-war and a copy for the radar team. Though this keeps me fit it diminishes my much prized and well beloved paunch. Such a pity-I have worked hard to build up. I'll see you at the end of July.

HOSPITAL HOSPITALITY - OR WHAT HAVE YOU?

Have any of you ever been in hospital? You haven't? Well then, fill your pipes girls, a new fellows get out your knitting, gather round and I'll tell you about it.

The day starts with a bowl of water and a request to look lively stop. Open one eye, that middle of face and dry on towel, going off to sleep again during the performance. Half an hour later dawn breaks....

Breakfast arrives at 7.30 a.m. kingdoms may come and kingdoms may go but porridge goes on for ever. One man managed to dodge it 3 mornings running. A tablet has been erected to perpetrate his memory.

Morning papers and mail are next on the list. Surprisingly how one can have so many friends and so too few letters. Wriggle into comfortable position just in time for the nurses to come and strip the bed. Doctor arrives and expresses surprise that all the patients are still alive decides to wait for a few days before informing insurance agent.

Dinner up. One man asked for roast beef and Yorkshire. Nurse becomes alarmed and calls Doctor. No coffee and cigars to finish with so make the most of hot milk and Wooodbines.

Sink into brown study and gaze at wall until teatime. Lettuce is never served with this meal more than seven times a week.

The quiet of the evening was broken only by supper at 6:30. Bedtime is at 9 o'clock and as the lights go out people who haven't said a word all day start a conversation with their neighbours.....

Drop off to sleep and dream of the day is when the only ward we know was a girl under twenty-one.

Frank Barry.

ooOoo

Madeleine and I found ourselves, on a very wet Saturday morning, at Croydon awaiting a 6 seater Anson to take us to Colinstown Dublin. Our first ever air trip!

It was with very mixed feelings indeed that we presently made our way to the big monoplane that was to carry us safely-we hoped across the Irish Sea.

We clamoured into the cabin and settled in our seats uncertain whether to feel excited at the prospects of flying or apprehensive of the prospects of being air sick. Kind friends had made a point of telling us all about airsickness, and how, on the American airlines the air hostess hands every passenger a large paper bag as he or she enters the plane....

The engines roared into life as a cabin door was closed and locked(who cared about it being locked-we wouldn't have to get out until we landed..... With luck)

gently bouncing the plane turned and taxied slowly into position for take-off, I turned and grinned at Madeleine and she grinned back-this was it!

The pilot gave it the gun-as he called it-that we gathered speed. In a moment we were racing across the open airfield, the engines roaring, the pilot tensed in his seat. We fixed our eyes on the trees ahead rushing to meet us; then, abruptly, the bouncing and vibration ceased, our forward movement became quite smooth and the advancing trees began to shrink and passed away beneath us. We were flying!

I press my nose to the window and saw the country speed out like a relief map then thick cloud blotted out the view. At various times the pilot gave us our location with height and speed but we saw very little because of the bad weather.

We soon got used to being in the air and were not really sorry when we were told 'We're landing'-we were eager to see what Ireland was like.

Since that landing-quite safe-we've fallen for Ireland, especially Glendalough near Avoec in the Wicklow Mountains. There we rowed across a mountain lake and climbed into the historical 'St Kevin's Bed'-near this spot is Enniskerry, with the battle scene to 'Henry V' were filmed.

We can recommend Ireland for an enjoyable holiday(whether you flight over or not)!

ooOoo

A VISIT TO THE ETERNAL CITY

I was one of 5 lucky ones the board as ship to be allowed to spend 4 days leave in Rome. It meant a 5 hour journey from Naples but it was well worth it.

We reached the rest camp outside the Rome area too late in the evening to do more than make one or 2 arrangements for our stay and then turning for some much needed sleep.

Early the next morning we went to Rome, and into the Vatican City- 'A city within a city.'

We visited museums and galleries and saw most wonderful paintings and sculptures, the Vatican library and the famous Sistine Chapel with its awe-inspiring paintings by Michelangelo. I could only walk around gazing in quite admiration.

Then came the really big moment-the audience with the Holy Father.

We filed through the bronze door into the St Peters-and after climbing a multitude of steps arrived slightly breathless at the Sala Clemenstine where the audience was to be held. There were many Allied servicemen there: we joined them and waited.

Then the great moment came.

Heralded by the soft tinkling of a bell. His holiness appeared, preceded by a number of the Vatican Guards. Everybody knelt silently as the Pope, dressed in white, walked slowly to the throne we rose to our feet and listened as his holiness addressed us, first in English and in French and Italian, saying how happy he was to see so many of his faithful flock from all countries, stressing the universality of the church, and expressing the hope that the time would not be too far distance when peace would come and we would all be reunited with their families.

Once again we knelt as the Holy Father blessed us and remained on in these as he walks slowly from the room.

An ambition of my life had been fulfilled it was an experience never to be forgotten.

John Kennedy, tall redheaded, and rubicund: at present serving with the Royal Navy - now stationed at Chatham- hopes to be demobbed shortly. While on the leave of which he writes procured and sent home to Club Apostlic Blessing, which, framed, will hang in the Club room.

ooOoo

It was a glorious summers day and Jimmy lay on his back in the field under a large tree. He had served Father Smith's Mass that morning, had been to holy Communion and now, whilst the others were playing some way off, Jimmy lay thinking.

"So there you are." The priest settled himself on the grass and propped himself against the tree to light his pipe.

For some time there was silence. The sun seemed hotter than ever. The sky was blue and clear and the only sound was the distant calling of one boy to another in the distance.

"Father." Said Jimmy suddenly. "I've been thinking about your talk last night."

Every night Father Smith gave the boys a talk as they sat around the fire last night he had spoken to them on holy purity and had laid special stress upon the importance of clean minds and hearts. He had told them that it was always possible to tell a boy or a girl who treasured this virtue. And he warned them of the importance of practising control over their eyes, which he had called the windows of the soul. Sometimes it is very hard, he had told them, but they must remember that they were keeping themselves clean and pure for our Lord-and that he would help them if they tried hard.

"What about it Jimmy?"

"Well." said Jimmy. "I know it's all right for you, a priest, but if you worked with crowds of others who joked and talked about rotten things I wonder if you would find it easy to keep bad thoughts out of your minds?"

"Of course I wouldn't Jimmy. But where's the harm?"

"Well that's a sin isn't it?"

"It can be, certainly-but it isn't always. You see Jimmy-strictly speaking there's no such thing as a bad thought. It isn't the thought which is bad-it is we who are bad. Let me explain.

When we speak of bad thoughts we refer to those things which from childhood we have learned are too private to talk about in public - bodies and the functions of these bodies. We all know about these things, but we know it is wrong to talk about them unnecessarily. But although we don't talk them-they really are good, because God made us and all he makes is good. Such thoughts can only be bad if we keep them in our minds for a bad reason. You can't prevent the light from coming through the window and so you can't prevent thoughts coming it into your mind-if you hear people say rotten things. But you can stop the light from getting into the room by pulling down the blind and in the same way we have to stop the thoughts from straying into our minds as soon as we know they are there it is only if we do not try, that they become bad and sinful. If as soon as we know they are there we try hard not to give in to them, then there will be no sin, not good to give in to them, then there will be no sin whatever happens. Sometimes it is very hard but still keep trying. Think of something else-something exciting, and when you succeed say a little prayer. When it's all over your Phil so pleased with yourself that your quite forget that God is pleased with you too."

ooOoo

NOTES & COMMENTS
by "The Analyst"

<u>HATS ON IN CHURCH.</u> Women are still expected to wear hats in church, but it is becoming quite common to see bare headed women-normally young women-at services. I learned recently that in the early church it was strictly customary for women to veil their heads since only women of loose character went bareheaded...

<u>SUGGESTION</u> A Club member came up to me the other day to enquire what the general feeling would be about hanging in the Club picture of its founder(Father Koch) I couldn't say what the general feeling would be because so far as I know the subject had never been broached. My own view is that it will be a nice gesture of esteem, but I pass it on what do readers think?

<u>HO THERE GARDENERS!</u> It is over 2 years since the last bomb landed in the Club precincts. It is reasonably certain that no more bombs-other than atom bombs will be sent to us - so it would be if a good thing if we put in a little time making the garden more shipshape. Don't be put off by people saying that they are going to rebuild it all so, why worry? It will be a good while before that happens.

<u>GOING GOING..</u> It seems that the concert party has finally reached the end of its tether. A pity. Mr Hyde(class instructor) with a few stalwarts, worked hard in the past, but lack of support will kill anything....

<u>CAPTAINS PLEASE NOTE.</u> Many of our members in the forces visit the Club when on leave. Most of them took part, an active part, in the various sports before they were called up. Why is it, then, so rare for any of them to be offered a place in the team for the

next game? A little unselfishness needed here.

<u>ANOTHER SUGGESTION.</u> It is amazing how little the average Londoner knows about London out seldom natives go sightseeing. Why not organise expeditions to places like Madame Tussaud's, the tower, St Paul's Cathedral, the George Inn and the Roman baths?(There is beer at the George and water in the bath's) before the war, organise parties were allowed to tour film studios and many of the larger industrial firms permit group visits. And museums

and galleries are not nearly as dull as those who haven't been would make us think. What about the trip upriver in a Thames steamer?

HOWDY NEIGHBOUR. St Helen's parish hall, badly damaged in the Blitz has been repaired. The youth group there can now function normally. Perhaps the sports captain's would like to stimulate a little friendly rivalry by throwing out the challenge or two.

DRAMATIC FOLD UP. After a gallant effort to keep things going minus Mrs Chuttleworth the senior dramatic group are 'resting.'

TAILPIECE a professor of Greek tore his suit and took it to a tailor named Acidopolus, from Athens. Mr Acidopolus examine the suit and asked "Euripides?"

"Yes," said the professor. "Eumenides"

Toni Marconi,(CRICKET CAPTAIN) says"..." The bats need renewing, but otherwise no grouse. I'd like to thank the team. They've shown fine spirit. This season, 4 matches played, 4 Won. – Last- return with Baskerville won 112/69. Bert MacAvoy 29 not out.

SWIMMING. is in the doldrums at the moment, but Tony Richardson plans to stir things up.

NETBALL FLOURISHING. Our Girls placed 2nd in league at the end of season. Want some more recruits if anyone'd like to join in.

TABLE TENNIS. 15 matches played 15 one. Awarded Catholic Youth Confederation shield.

TENNIS. - New venture. Keen crowd of players and beginners meet twice weekly only practice yet, but may compete later.

FOOTBALL -Played 15 16 lost 6 drawn 3. Among notable scores beat SVP team 8 -1(Leslie Green 6)

ooOoo

A 'ST ANNE'S ANNALS' reporter eavesdropped on a recent conversation between C. O. M. Pres. Phil Cullen and new spiritual director Fr. Leahy about the.

CHILDREN OF MARY

Spir. Dir,..." What's been happening lately tell me all!"

Pres. "Well there was a retreat organised for Palm Sunday at Ashtead - then found to be too near to Easter and scrapped. But 24 turned up for the May procession.

Spir. Dir." Not bad that only 12 missing!"

Pres. "We've split the C.O.M. up into groups now, you know. There's the Eucharistic group about 5 girls pay a short visit to the Blessed Sacrament each day. Another group studying the Scriptures. They are on St Mark's Gospel at the moment, there is a 3rd group, the Apostleship of Prayer. We teach catechism when required, organised by monthly socials through the winter and on occasional weekend retreats. Now and then we throw a party or fix up an outing just to liven things up a bit.

Spir. Dir. "You sound like a Publicity Agent."

Pres. "I'm sorry it wasn't intentional; but it's not a bad idea to publicise sociality a bit. I construed suspicion that there are good many girls in the parish who could join in. There is only one main rule, so simple that no one need ever break it, to receive holy Communion once a month.

Spi. Dir." That is not terribly hard, is it? We must see if we can do a bit of recruiting..."

ooOoo

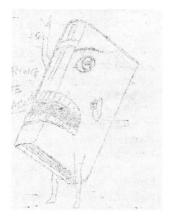

<u>OVERDUE BOOKS</u>: whilst many fresh books are constantly finding their way into the Club Library, through kind gifts and the Book Circle. Quite as many, are continually finding their way out through members forgetfulness.

Do please, search your own bookshelves to see if you have any Club books that are long overdue.

Books should only be kept for 2 weeks unless renewed.

ooOoo

St. Annes Annals

THE JOURNAL OF ST ANNES CATHOLIC YOUTH CLUB VAUXHALL CROSS

6d

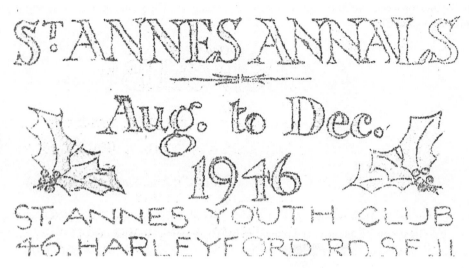

ST. ANNES ANNALS
Aug. to Dec. 1946
ST. ANNES YOUTH CLUB
46, HARLEYFORD RD. SE.11

We of St Anne's Club owe a great debt of gratitude to the American Catholic Welfare Committee, under the chairmanship of Msgr O'Boyle, for the help that has been given generously to us.

In August of this year a grant of £100 drawn from money donated by the people of America, was awarded to the Club to assist its recovery from the ravages of war. (St Anne's was Blitz three times).

This grant has done much to help' and we offer to the members of the American Catholic Welfare Committee-and through them the people of America are heartfelt thanks for a net of kindness and generosity which leaves us for ever in their debt.

During the last two months the Club has been visited by several of his Majesty's inspectors in connection with a proposed Ministry of education report on youth work. Without exception they expressed satisfaction at the way in which the Club is run, and its general standard of achievement.

A happy Christmas to all readers:

A GOOD CLUB?
by
THE CLUB-LEADER — REV. R. D. MADDEN.

What sort of thing makes the Club a good Club?

Successful teams?......... comfortable premises?.... Charming members?

No, they all help, but they are not altogether necessary. A long run of successes can easily develop smugness and inability to lose gracefully. Many a fine Club is going up in dreadful premises. Charming members are sometimes quite useless and very selfish.

One of the chief characteristics of a good Club is I think the spirit of service.

The spirit that brings a girl regularly for her duty night in the canteen (three hours of hard work alternating with boredom.

The spirit that makes a boy see through to the end any job a has undertaken.

The spirit that drives members to be faithful and punctual in attending the classes even when they feel a little tired, or when the weather is bad, or when some temporary counter attraction offers itself.

The spirit of service is essentially reliable and unselfish and helps members to realise that they are serving, not an individual or their own ends, but they course: immediately that of the Club community: ultimately, of Jesus Christ

Is St Anne's a good Club?

ooOoo

July 7th.

C. O. M. Out into St. Theresa's Effingham. The girls certainly enjoying themselves. Arrived back at Vauxhall to find the Club going strong. To our utter amazement to BOYS are doing **the Washing Up!**

A weekend retreat at Beaumont 1946?

July 8th.

Another member home on leave this time George Belcher he tells us he thinks he can stick Germany for another year.(Letter from George on another page- Ed)

As follows at end of Diary:-Letters

July 14th.

Tonight is social night. More members than ever are attending the Sunday socials. Arthur Baker from Fulham entertains us with his guitar and rocky mountain singing. We welcome another new member- Pat. Kowalski, a Polish sailor. Pat is a medical student at University tutorial College. We hope you will enjoy is membership of the Club, and in later years but back on it with pleasure.

July 21st.

Our outing to Beaumont College. Perfect 'Go as you please.' The majority of the boys are playing cricket, a few have gone rowing; whilst the girls are exhausted themselves at rounder's. Are tea!.... What's this? Word is being passed round 'to drink the tea quickly to avoid the taste'! Before we finally set foot for home to attend benediction. The pleasant surprise; an all BOYS choir which we all enjoyed(it made a change). It only goes to show that boys CAN sing. How about joining OUR choir boys?

Back Row: Jock Mackay -John Sheppard- Sheila Mahoney -Girl?- Rita Bremner -Fr. Bob Madden – Pat Kowoski-
Dennis Lynch /
Barbara Spanswick - Toni Maconi - Paddy McMonagle - Tom MacAvoy- Eric Blackburn- Mike Mulvey.
Kneeling: Mike Plant -Vera De Troia - Vic Le Grande -?
Sitting: Harry Spanswick - Mary Martinelli - boy? - Bert Thomas? - Tony Blackmore - Tubby Smith -Pat Thomas.

Diary Cont./-
July 22ⁿᵈ.
Father Leahy started his holiday
August 4ᵗʰ.
Arthur Baker is here again to entertain us. After much persuasion Pat Kowaski sings in his native tongue. Bob says home on leave. The RAF hasn't quietened him down.
August 19ᵗʰ.
We thought readers would be interested in a Club members rather exciting personal experience. Here is her own description.

August 19th '46 by TERESA CLINTON

Nineteenth of August. Was a red-letter day in my short life; the day fixed for my broadcast.(My father had written, earlier, to the children's hour department, I was given an audition and engaged to appear in a young artist's program), and at 2:45 I entered Broadcasting House to attend the rehearsal at 5 o'clock.

The intervening minutes were spent in the vestibule where I watched many people passing to and fro, wondering whether any were famous broadcasters are just ordinary members of the staff.

At 3 o'clock (precisely) I found myself in the presence of Miss Mae Jenkin ('Elizabeth'of the Children's Hour) the Young Artistes' producer, who welcomed me very kindly and introduced me to the accompanist. I sang five songs of which. 'To be Near Them', 'When Daisies Plod' and 'The Kerry Dance' were chosen.

I was now free until 5:25, so I took the opportunity for a walk along Oxford Street where I had tea before returning for the fray.

Strangely, I didn't feel at all nervous, just very excited.

Back in the studio I sat facing a big clock watching the hands creep steadily towards 5:25 – my own zero hour (for the program had already started, being sent out from another Region).

Miss Jenkin beckoned me forward and after a word of encouragement I faced the microphone.

The red light glowed; I heard the first announcement; then the opening chords of my music. I took a deep breath, and – I was 'on the air.'

I say my three songs, and can dimly remember Mr Jenkin moving up to the microphone to announce each one.... And then it was all over.

There were handshakes and congratulations, and then I was once again outside broadcasting house, just one of the crowd busting by, none of whom were concerned in the least that I had been on the air. But after all, why should they be?

ooOoo

Diary Cont./-

August 21ˢᵗ.

Father Madden On Holiday. He Feels He Needs It!

September 5ᵗʰ.

Steve Sage 19 Days Leave, with the news that he hopes to be demobbed in six months.

September 14/15ᵗʰ.

The Convent Of Our Lady Of The Cenacle, Hampstead Have The C. O. M. for a weekend retreat. Club social this evening spoilt regrettable occurrence at end.

September 17ᵗʰ.

John Kennedy demobbed today from the Royal Navy.

September 20ᵗʰ.

New Dramatics teacher comes to sir senior group into activity after long 'rest'. name, Miss Esther Williams.

September 22ⁿᵈ.

GENERAL MEETING. The following have been elected for the sport side of the Club, as Captains.

NETBALL-MARIA BREMER FOOTBALL-RUDOLF PERLA. TABLE TENNIS-PAT BUTLER. BILLIARDS-PADDY MCMONAGLE.

The Editor of this magazine appealed for help in the work of preparing and printing the 'ANNALS' though there are typist and artist among members of the Club, few seem willing to come forward with offers of help... How about it folks?

Saturday night dance admission fees increased from one 1/6d to 2/-. "jiving" has been banned altogether from the Club. during the month of October the Club will be closed on Sunday evenings as a punishment for some very bad behaviours during the social on September 15ᵗʰ. Friday's to be 'bazaar night – everyone to work in preparation for the bazaar on December 7ᵗʰ

COMMITTEE MEMBERS 1947

S. Talburt Hon. Sec.	M. Bremer.
J. Denneny.	E. McMonagle.
R. Perla.	E. Belcher.
L. Green.	J. Healy.
J. Kenney	

ooOoo

September 29ᵗʰ.

Outing to Camber Sands. A perfect day, enjoyed by all. Most of us slept through the return journey.(See "Camber Sands" by George Bulline on another page) As follows:-

The sun was shining brightly
As it does in foreign lands
When we climbed aboard our motor-coach
And made for Camber Sands.

The streets of London as we passed
Gave way to fields and trees.
We knew that every mile rolled by
Was one less to the sea.

At last the coaches halted and we saw on
every hand.
A waste of hills and valleys
all composed of shifting sands.
The briny looked inviting so.

We donned our swimming suits.
Then trode upon some pointed stones.
And went back for our boots!

Emerging from the ocean next
Our sandwiches we tried.
And sandwiches they were all right.
For sand had got inside.

We tried our hand at beach quoits
And a game of rounder's too

And never a dull moment passed Until as stay was through.

At nightfall came the coaches,
We return to London's roar
But one and all would fain return.
To Camber Sands once more!

<u>October 12th</u>.
Frank Farmer home on leave, a regular visitor. Netball team beat Mitcham Athletic 25 – 3

October 13th. "Poison Pen"(3 set play) was this evening staged in the Club by Miss Rosemary Martyn. The play was quite well received, though some thought it in bad taste. The silver collection amounted to £6. A raffled bottle of whiskey(proceeds £7.10.0) was one night Mrs Bows of the parish.

Football team beat Balham 3 -1.

Cast of one of the Plays Actors –
Some not recognised - others: Pat Kowaski Marie Perla John Macdermott Anne Hendy -Fr. Healy

October 26/27th. Girls weekend at Ashtead. Everybody "let their hair down"(see "QUITE WEEKEND" on another page)

As follows:-

On a very rainy Saturday in October Nine of us (all Club members) invaded Waterloo station and boarded a train that took us all the way to Ashtead without breaking down (Carmel was with us). The 'Pioneer Corps' (including the two leaders) that went the previous evening managed to miss two trains; eventually caught the wrong one and landed at Tolworth. They did not disturb the peace and quiet of Maldon Lodge 'till' long past bedtime on Friday.

However, after a very righteous lunch one party complete but for Eileen and Helen, retired to the fireside in the lounge. We were busy discussing general topics when they arrived. Apparently they had forgotten the way (as they said) and visited the local constabulary to enquire. Maldon Lodge was at last discovered by the noises of our quite discussion.

After tea, as some of us serenaded the neighbours on our way to church, the rest occupied themselves in making apple pie beds.

The mischief was discovered by Phil and Anne (our two leaders) who on their return noticed suspicious looking lumps in the beds. After justice had been done all 'tuck' was brought down to the lounge where Phil made a pleasing sight seated in the centre of the floor surrounded by apples, pears, oranges, grapes, biscuits, cakes and cream buns–to say nothing of the assortment of sweets.

The feast was really Babs delayed birthday party. After everyone's sweet-tooth had been satisfied there was a general vote to play 'Murder'. After many screams and 'murders' there followed a cabaret.

Eileen and Helen (suitably padded) obliged with an opera, the origin of which was as much a mystery to the singers as to the audience.

From the realms of opera we were transported to those of ballet, danced by ballerina Phil, Carmel and Marie, no professional dancers could possibly hope to imitate the grace and poise.

After the ballet we were so weak with laughter that we only just managed to crawl up to bed.

Sunday dawned, and the rain was still pouring down when we sallied forth to early Mass.

After breakfast we dived for our favourite seats by the fire in the lounge and planned the C. O. M. Social. Each item as suggested was rehearsed, including the community singing, which was helped by Carmel's song-book and sweet melodious voice. (To hear her singing' Nelly Dean' is an unforgettable experience).

During the afternoon four brave members defied the weather and went for a short walk. They enjoyed most in seeing, on their return, the toast being made in front of the glowing fire.

After tea Helen and Eileen taught us all to dance the 'Ampstead Way'. Ashtead has surely never before heard so much singing and laughing.

We played 'Consequences'; very funny because we decided to see only the names of people connected with the Club.

Then came the time to depart after another marvellous weekend at St Anne's Country Club.

Still in very high spirits and much to the amazement of other travellers we continued as singing and dancing in the waiting room on Ashtead Station. A train drew in; and all the 20 squeezed into one compartment, serenading the porters at each station through which we passed.

At Vauxhall we tumbled out and made for the Club (always a happy landing ground) for the finale to a weekend that I know my friends and I will always remember.

ooOoo

Diary Cont./-

<u>October 28th</u>.
Teddy Mayhew home after service in the Pacific.

<u>November 1st</u>.
Table Tennis Cup presented to Pat Thomas as representative of St Anne's Table Tennis team at the C. Y.C. Dance held at the Manor Place Baths Clapham.

Now stands(with others) on show in Common Room.

<u>November 2ND</u>.
NETBALL team beat Christ Church 19-9.

<u>November 3RD</u>.
G.B.S. gives their first social of the winter season this night. Songs, quiz, games and dancing. This evening we had the pleasure of meeting father Madden's brother.

Football team beat Streatham Squires 10-1. Les Green scoring nine.

<u>November 9th</u>.
Netball team beat century youth Club 21-4 and sitting12-9.

<u>November 10th</u>.
Football team beat S. V. F. Clapham 10-2 Les Green scoring eight Great guy, great guy!

A variety concert staged in the Club this evening by the still at school of dancing, with girls from the age of 3 ½ years upwards taking part. During the evening the dole was raffled, and one by a very shy young man.

<u>November 11th</u>.
Father Madden's mother and brother paid us a farewell visit this evening before going back to Ireland. It was kind of them to show that such an interest in the Club. We would like to thank them both and offer them a United could wishes.

<u>November 14th</u>.
Barry Jackson home on week-end leave. Hopes to get home more often in the near future. Fred proud home for 11 days leave.

December 7th. Bazaar and sale of the work this afternoon. The work weeks tastefully displayed on stalls ranged round the hall, and jostling crowd of local people moving around looking for bargains and finding them. Hectic, but successful afternoon, over £200 raised.

ooOoo

LETTERS TO ED.

14870086. Spr. G.P BELCHER. No2. Pln. 104 A.T. Coy Royal Engineers B.O.A.R.

Sir, I have just received your July issue of St Anne's annals among some books in a family parcel.

I enjoyed every minute of it, Some of the typing was poor but readable.

Having just come out of 'dock' myself, I thoroughly digestive Frank Barry's article. A military hospital is about the same!

I quite agree. with the analysts suggestion about the picture of the Club's founder Fr. Koch to be hung in the Club. I sincerely hope this suggestion is carried out.

Best wishes from a reader and Club member in Berlin'

GEORGE BELCHER

(Many thanks' glad to hear from you, George-Ed)

ooOo

o

FIRST XI Played three. WON three.

St Anne's   v. Balham 3-1

"   v. Streatham 10-2

"   v. Clapham 10-2

"   v. Building

Apprentices 10-1

(friendly)

SECOND XI

ST. ANNE'S   V. Westminster 6-0

As the results show, we are having a very good season up to the time of going to press. Everybody is of the belief that this is the best team St Anne's has put in the field, although the average age of the players is only 17, the main reason for our victories is a very good team spirit and keenness on the part of the players.

The chief contribution to the success of the forwards has come from Les Green, a centre forward. (Has 23 goals to date), ably supported by the rest of the line, who have served him with the ball whenever the chances are arisen.

Among the defence we are very fortunate to have Tony Maconi and Anthony Jones as fullbacks. These two have broken up many an attack on our goal, and we believe they'll to the best backs in the league

John Healy

ooOoo

ANNALS NETBALL

September 28TH. SURREY COUNTY NETBALL RALLY

Something very extraordinary happened, the team arrived late and so missed their first match. The second match was with St Peters, our team won 4-1.

The third – Nonesuch School – another triumph for our team 13- 0. The last match – Regents Street Polytechnic- resulted in a draw 3-3.

October 5th. LONDON UNION NETBALL RALLY

Eight girls from Club, full of energy and good spirits went to Paddington recreation ground and succeeded in winning their first match against Wyndham Club.6-5 and drawing with Christchurch.2-2

LEAGUE MATCHES
SURREY COUNTY LONDON UNION
Mitcham Athletic Christchurch.
Oct. 18th. WON 25-3 Nov. 2nd. WON 19-7

Century Youth Club. Wyndham Club
Nov. 9th. WON 21-4 Nov.9th. WON 12- 9
MARIE BREMER

ooOoo

JOHN HEALY IN INDIA

As I stepped off the ship the first things that caught my eye were the buildings. Such contrast has to be seen to be believed. On one hand are impressive buildings of the shipping agencies, and the houses of the white people and higher classes of India, and on the other of the houses of the lower classes – farmers, dockers and the like, who work for a monthly wage that would only keep us for a couple of days.

Eight or 10 people live crowded into one small mud hut, without lights, drainage, or sanitation.This is no doubt one of the causes of the short life of the majority of Indians.

From Bombay I journeyed across country to the great army base at Doolali one of the finest army camps in India. I stayed for quite a time here, on the plains, where most of the great farms are situated.

This belt of flat country is nearly 2000 miles long and 400 miles wide, and in the summer months is one of the hottest places in India. The temperature reaches hundred and thirty° F. between March and June. One has to drink anything up to 14 pints of liquid the day, including half-a-pint of salt water to replace the body salt which is lost in perspiration.

There are more cattle in India than in any other country in the world, but due no doubt to the primitive farming methods the milk yield is very low. The cattle are not housed in the dry spell but just left to roam the plains.

As I travelled across India into the hills of Bihar the scenery changed from sun baked earth to thickly wooded hills.

Sleep was now made difficult by the mournful cries of the jackal, the scavenger of the country. Smaller animal life abounds and the presence of snakes, lizards and scorpions with knife like stings formed one of our chief worries. Of the big game, most of which is confined to the south, the Bears are most interesting especially when seen at play.

The one thousand two hundred mile train journey from Bihar to Jhansi on the edge of the Sind Desert, took five days to complete. Never were the shortcomings of Indian trains more evident to me. Especially the nasty warmth and the hard wooden seats which run the whole length of the train.

It was in Jhansi that I first visited an Indian bazaar. What a colourful site it was, with everything on sale from a toothbrush to a dressing gown. Hundreds of natives were milling around whilst Tonga's and rickshaws twisted and turned to get in and out of the crowds. Cattle being driven here and there, dogs barking, beggars crying out for baksheesh, and merchant shouting their wares all added to the variety. It was here that the unwary British soldier could pay fantastic prices.

My next stop in place was New Delhi. Here the long straight roads and the water fountains, the excellent buildings and above all the Vice Regal Palace combined to make New Delhi the finest and most modern city in India.

The Palace, which took seventeen years to build and cost £1,000,000, stands in three hundred and sixty-five acres of grounds and has a wonderfully kept gardens.

It was New Delhi, on Christmas Eve that I had the good fortune to see Lord and Lady Wavell and hear a carol concert given by an R.A.F. choir.

On the way back from Delhi to Jhansi went on to Bombay and from there came at last to England and home.

ooOoo

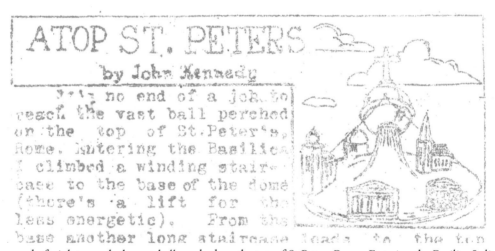

It's no end of a job to reach the vast ball perched on the top of St Peters Rome. Entering the Basilica I climbed a winding staircase to the base of the dome (there's a lift for the less energetic). From the base another long staircase leads to the top of the dome just under the ball (of bronze), reached not by stairs, but by ladder!

Recovering breath after this climb (420 ft up from the ground) I looked around the ball, with narrow openings at intervals all round.

I tried to see through one of these openings but felt so certain that the ball was toppling with my weight that I hastily retreated to the centre. Regaining my nerve I tried again and peered out over the city of Rome and the country beyond.

Among the beautiful buildings within view of the Victor Emanuel Memorial, the Palazzo di Venetzia, the Cathedral of St John Lateran and the Coliseum. From another opening could be seen the Parthenon and the Appian Way. Through another the River Tiber and the Palace of Justice.

I looked below to when minute dots past and light, and out between the buildings... People passing through the city! What looked like slow moving carriages were really fast cars!

It was wonderful. I felt as if I were in another world, looking disdainfully down on the troubled earth.

From the ground, the clouds are far away. Here, I felt that I could reach out and touch them.

I felt on top of everything while my exultation lasted; as it passed I turned my attention to the guide book to read that the ball was put up by Sebastien Torregiani in 1593, is over our-hundred feet from the ground and supports the weight of the nine-teen foot golden cross, the very summit of the Basilica.

The cross has been climbed by workmen, but the Vatican authorities do not allow visitors to do this. I needed no real restraining, I was not sorry to get down to earth, in more than one sense, but even so, it was a wonderful experience.

One can get some think of John's experience in England, (though the Associations are not quite so holy)?

At High Wycombe,Bucks. There is an old church standing alone on a hill. Perched on the top of its tower is a hollow 'Golden Ball' from the inside of which one can see all the surrounding countryside with the town of High Wycombe looking like a model beneath one's feet.

The church was built by a Sir George Dashwood around about 1769, and legend has it that the Golden Ball surmounting the tower was used for the meetings of the notorious 'Hell-Fire Club' of which Dashwood was founder and president.

The 'Hell-Fire Club' was a society of noble 'young bloods who, sated with the pleasures of the time, turned, (it is said), to devil worship for a new thrill.

Stories are told locally of their doings that make the flesh creep. Nothing now remains to prove or disprove these stories, but an ascent into the Golden Ball even in these modern times is hair- raising enough; it involves climbing a short ladder suspended, more or less in space!

ooOoo

ALL IN A DAY'S WORK.

HILDA SMITH, an old Club member, joined the Women's Land Army during the war, and since that time has grown to love the life on the land so much that she does not want to return to London, and is quite happy to remain working on a dairy farm. We print here an account of a day in her life. She writes:-

I was awakened this morning by "Anna" the big red cow that has recently carved. She was pacing up and down inside the rails of the home-field mooing all the while.

I dress quickly for quite often in a cow can hear her calf bellowing she will try to jump the gate and maybe hurt the other which, in the morning, is full of milk.

It was nigh on 6 o'clock but the boss had picked me to it. He was downstairs and had already put the kettle on. After a cup of tea we started the machine and began the milking.

First, the cows others are washed and the formula drawn (to see that it is good) then the suction units are fitted whilst we prepare the next cow.

I fed the small calf – two weeks old – with half a gallon of 'mischief's' milk then turned to "Anna". From her thirty-six pints of milk I fed her calf, which had been taken from her the first day after birth.

We have to let the calf suck her fingers while guiding her hand into the bucket for calves naturally push their head upwards to suck after two or three days, however, should be shoving her head into the bucket and almost knocking us over.

With Stocking's milk we fed two more three month old calves. They all get a little cattle cake and some good hay. Milking ended, I washed the cooler etc., in cold water and let the cows out into the field.

After breakfast I spent an hour washing the dairy kit in boiling water, then set to work cleaning out the cow sheds thoroughly – a job that lasted until dinnertime.

Two of the others have started to cut the grass – please God it will be good weather until we get it in safely.

I realise now why it is that the farm worries me so much even the weather. We have been glad of no rain as it has kept our cows in grass – the only source of food for them now but we long for a spell of fine weather to increase the hay yield, especially as next winter we shall be short of cattle – cake.

After dinner I joined the rest of the workers hoeing potatoes. (Why do thistles and other weeds grow where they are not wanted).

It took me all my time to keep up with the others and now and again I saw the boss to apart of my road to help me.

Just before tea – time I left the hoeing to feed the ball the cows in their stalls. The trick of tethering is to give each about handful of cattle – cake and then look sharp about doing it while the cow is eating.

Tea – time over, the cows were milked again. The boss believes in twelve-hour milking intervals because it helps to allay disease in the cows! Others and is more comfortable for the animal.

"Anna" gave from both milking's about 6 gallons – her efforts were rewarded with a little more cattle – cake.

We fed all the calves, and then let the cows out once more into the open. Then followed the usual washing of all the dairy kit and the sweeping out of the cow shed.

I took some water to the bull but it failed to satisfy him. It was that little extra bit of hay he wanted to finish up with!

Then the cats had to have THEIR drop of milk.

After all that the rest of the time is my own until bed – time, which brings me up to this moment when I'm sitting finishing this account of an ordinary day in my life as a farm worker.

Let me just add that I wouldn't change this life now for anything. I go to bed each night tired out but content in the knowledge that I have done a really good day's work' and what can be better than a contented mind?

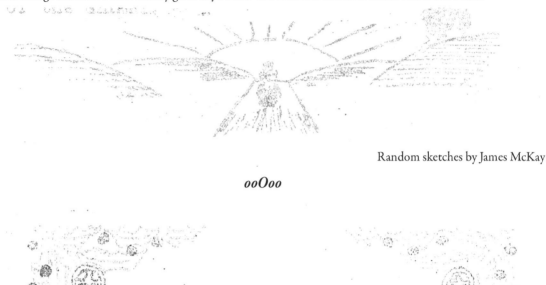

Random sketches by James McKay

ooOoo

OF FAITH.

(A Sonnet)

'Tis vain to trust in human things or friends.
Or put one's trust in empty things of earth.
For all these things, yes, all of them have ends.
And men is prone to fickleness from birth.
That he who will, persist in human ties.
Until such time as passed to show and prove.
That craft is not a stranger to allies.
In whom was centred all his faith and love.
For we poor men, descendants of the first.
Who fell so low through weakness and sin,
Will ever hope and wait and always thirst.
For time and lasting friendships to begin.
Oh! Trust in no one, only trust in him.
Who suffered to redeem us all from sin!

TERESA CLINTON

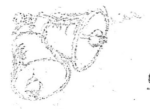

CHRISTUS NATUS EST.

They came to the gate in the chill of the evening.
The crowds had subsided, they entered alone.
They had tramped from far Juda, to do Caesar's bidding.
But welcome, to shelter and warmth, there was none.

A star, the Kings Herald, hangs o'er the mountain.
All nature is silent, the earth bare and wild.
In yonder cave, lowly, with creatures of burden,
Lies aarth's Lord and Saviour, Messiah,- a child.

Mary, his mother, looks thoughtfully on Him.
And lovingly hushes His murmuring stirs.
His baby eyes open, she smiles at them gently.
Those eyes that ere long will in suff'ing meet hers.

She watches Him sleeping so quiet and peaceful.
She ponders the mocking and buffeting crude.
The pangs and the torments, the path and the writhing.
That soon He must suffer – and she at the rood.

Hark! Angels are joyous, the heavens are glowing.
This child is to succur Man's destiny poor.
Ring out, oh ye bells, to proclaim Him and praise Him.
Two words, lost in darkness the light he'll restore.

PHIL CULLEN

ooOoo

Too sunny to ride to the office... I'll take a stroll through the park. I hate to see all those buses lined up waiting for passengers.

Ah! Here's the newspaperman; let's see what the latest news is...

LAST PERSIAN TROOPS MARCH OUT OF RUSSIA

... It's a time everybody stopped bullying the poor defenceless Russians....

ARABS ASK FOR JEWISH COLONY IN PALESTINE TO BE DOUBLED

... Wonderful to see the world in such harmony...

AMALGAMATED NYLON GOES INTO LIQUIDATION

Not surprising really; none of the girls seemed interested since black woollen stockings came into fashion...

Lunchtime already! I must hurry along to the canteen before they run out of span these York buns are so tasteless.

Time for a 'quick one' I think.

"No thank you Miss. I won't have a bottle of whisky today. I'll have a pint of Mild instead. Here's sixpence – keep the change."

Homeward bound at last. Must drop this poor down – and - out a shilling. He's been out of work ever since the Black Market was disbanded.

What's that bell ringing? Oh dear! Is the alarms; time to get up. Still, it was fun while it lasted, and dreams do come true...

Sometimes.

ooOoo

Guild of the Blessed Sacrament
by A NEW RECRUIT.

I write this article from the viewpoint of one who has joined the Guild only recently and had been asked to write an account of this parish organisation.

After a few enquiries into the nature of the Guild and the so called obligation. I decided to join, being duly excepted in time to be present for the Annual General Meeting held somewhere about the feast of Corpus Christi, of which a new Committee for the current year was elected; the new Warden been Mr R Perla under whose leadership the Guild is progressing and endeavouring, to return to its peacetime standard, a rather difficult job in this period of re-adjustment.

The retiring Warden was Mr Thorn, who had so ably guided and kept the Guild going during the war years.

Meeting are held at present, on the first Sunday of every quarter. Matters usually discussed (I find) are the Intention for the month's Mass, spiritual help for members ill or in need, methods of assistance in parish affairs in general, and at every meeting so far, the problem of more support from the men of the parish has come up.

Some of the older members are rather sceptical of the non-interest shown by the majority of parishioners. Of course, there may be other commitments, but only in scattered cases.

Where are all you ex–Serviceman?

There must be a lot in the parish, yet only one or two in the Guild. How about introducing into your own parish the spirit that prevailed in Catholic Forces Groups abroad? Here's your chance – take it!

We welcome all prospective members who are willing and keen. The Guild is open to all men from the age of 14.

Young lads! Don't be turned away by any impression that it is some sort of old men's Association–far from it. Youth is well represented on the Committee.

On the other hand we need a lot more of the older men to add their experience to the Guild and thus make it truly representative of the parish.

Now, a word about the "obligations", which are in reality part of the normal life of a Catholic. 8 o'clock Mass and Communion on the first Sunday of each month, Benediction on the third Sunday of the month. Meeting every three months. Annual procession on the feast of Corpus Christi – and that's all! Can anyone possibly consider that as too much? No. Then why not join – now!

Think it over and apply to either the Rev. Father Madden (Guild Spiritual Director) at the Presbytery, or to the Warden, or to any member of the Guild.

ooOoo

STAR of DAVID

Charles Cowen our newspaperman Club-member contributes some notes of interest to all Catholics on the religion in which our Lord was born; and from which Christianity is the natural offshoot.

In the course of duty as a reporter. I was present at the induction of a new minister at the Brixton Synagogue in Effra Road. It was the first time I had entered a synagogue and naturally I was keenly interested in everything.

The service took place on a Sunday, and was introduced in the presence of certain civic officials, together with the Mayor of Lambeth, and various members of his corporation. Clergy of the Church of England had been invited, but they graciously decided on the grounds that they were holding services of their own which they could not cancel.

No Catholic clergy were asked.

Induction does not mean ordination, but installation in the new 'parish'. The new minister is not a rabbi. He is by virtue of his studies and training qualified to preach Scriptures and administer the faith, but has not yet been granted the favour of that position.

In the Jewish faith there is, strictly speaking, no such thing as a ordination. The Rabbi holds the position of the learned and to the community but does not normally conduct services. He is a teacher and lawyer rather than a priest and is not expected to preach except on certain special occasions. There is here a parallel within if the Non-Conformist meets where the reader is merely a studied minister of the group appointed by them to administer the Faith.

The strange custom to Christian men is that of wearing a hat in the place of worship. To the Jew it is correct, and if any person should omit to bring a hat with him he will find a number of small skullcaps, from which he may borrow.

Fortunately I had a hat.

Something that might amaze the self-assertive maidens of today is the segregation of women from men. Only men are permitted to enter the main part of the synagogue, the women taking their places in the gallery above, whence they witness the service, in which only men may take part. This segregation arises from the sense of propriety once prevalent in the East which regarded as immodest for women to appear in the presence of males other than near relatives.

It becomes very obvious during a service that the congregation are doing a great deal of the work, owing to the fact that there are many responses. During the solemn part of the service, prayers are chanted by the Canter. The Canter is generally chosen not with regard to his religious knowledge, but for his singing voice, which needs remarkable strength and clarity to sustain anything resembling tone after hours of chanting in Hebrew (a guttural language).

While there is little resemblance, generally between a synagogue and a church, there are certain similarities.

At the eastern end of the building – the front – in the 'Almomar'. This approximates to our alter; a richly carpeted platform, which is approach by at least three steps.

Behind this is the most important part of the whole building, the 'Ark'.

You have probably read in the Old Testament of the Ark of the Covenant, in which Moses kept the tablets bearing the Ten Commandments. It was then a richly wrought box of precious woods and metals, essentially portable, for the Tribes of Israel were Wanderers without permanent houses or 'cities of stone'. In present days, the 'Ark' which holds, as it did then, the scrolls of law, is an alcove in the wall of the building, richly draped, and covered with a large curtain bearing the 'Nagen David'– the device composed of two intersecting triangles resembling a star, which has become as much a symbol of Judaism as the Cross of Christianity. In fact, though it does not have a definite meaning right across, the 'Nagen David' may be found within Jewry-in approximately similar places; even descending, as has the symbol of Christ's, to be in worn as a trinket around the necks of young ladies.

Strangely, nobody seems to know how it originated or what precise significance it has – not even the new minister, when I approached on the subject.

Before the Ark is kept burning a perpetual light called the 'Hor Tamid'. This is symbolic of the revelation which God has given to the world through the 'Terah' or Law, a copy of which is contained in the Ark.

It will be seen that there is a precedent for the light that burns in front of the Tabernacle throughout Catholicism, significant of Christ within.

When the world is troubled, Gentiles say. "I'll bet the Jews have a finger in this".... Corner these people and they will reluctantly admit. "I suppose there are some good Jews". Believe it or not there are. I make no apology for Judaism, being a Catholic, but if it realised that in order to completely observe the rules of his faith a Jew must comply with six hundred and thirteen precepts which cover every motion of his daily life from waking, when he is considered unclean in the eyes of God, to the time he finally retires and says a prayer which begins. "Into thy hands O Lord I command my spirit." It may account for the number of lapsed Jews who are Jewish only by race.

ooOoo

By the time this is read. The Hotel strike will be over, I for one had a little enjoyment from it.

A spirit of curiosity and the novel experience, I suppose, tempted me to go to the phone and ring the Staff – Manager of a strike – bound Hotel.

"Are you taking on any hands?" I enquired.

"Yes". Came the reply." Be here inside an hour and will fix you up".

I went and found the Manager.

"What can I do for you, young man? He purred.

"A night's work."

"Well, we have only washing up at 2/- an hour".

I accepted and was given over to a greasy youth who escorted me to the chief washer – up; my boss for the evening.

As we went into the kitchens my nerve almost failed, but this spasm past. The chief 'soul–lion', a pleasant man called Phillips, told me to change my things in a tiny room and don an apron. On returning, a fellow in khaki greeted me with.

"Bon jour Mousieur."

"Bon jour Mousieur. Comment allas vous"

I replied, not to be outdone. He then relaxed into the vernacular and I learned he was a commercial traveller with plenty of spare time.

"In my last job." he said. "I was making £4. and £5. a day in tips."

Another gentleman possessing a very cultured voice had been reduced to this dishwashing through ill – health. One fellow a medical student of 19, who was raising funds, said.

"Why didn't I do this during my vac?"

The most interesting person, a regular member of the staff; was a little fellow who normally worked in the pantry kitchen.

Washing-up was fairly simple; all metal utensils were clean. The large things were placed on a belt which went through a monstrous washing – machine in which they were subjected to boiling water under high pressure. On reappearing they were practically dry. All the cutlery was placed in wire baskets and raced through a sink of soap suds and then clean water – some wiping was necessary in this case.

At 9:30 p.m. dinner arrived and I was presented with a large plate of roast duck, peas and potatoes, followed by tea and some ice – cream scrounged from a chef.

At midnight by finished.

"What time did you start?" I was asked.

"Six." I replied.

"We'll say five." Replied the other and gave me 14/-

As I left by the back door I was confronted by fluttering banners reading.

"Catering Workers on strike."

I must confess, I felt a little uneasy.

ooOoo

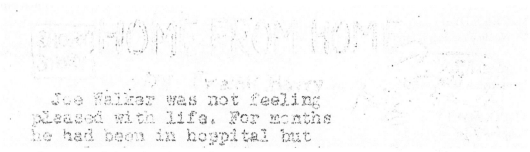

Joe Walker was not feeling pleased with life. For months he had been in hospital but now, alas, he was due for discharge, three days before Christmas. He thought of his lonely lodging and the prospect of eating his Christmas fare alone with only memories for company. Strange how we had grown so fond of hospital life during his stay. He remembered how awkward he felt when he was first brought in. Living by himself had made him lose touch with communal life and it had taken him some time to settle down in the large ward. Now, however, he was completely at home with all and sundry, and the days were filled with laughter and companionship. He viewed returning to solitude with a heavy heart.

The following morning he left the hospital and trudged through the snow – carpeted streets towards his lodging. Throngs of happy people jostled him as they eagerly searched the shops for Christmas fare and presents.

He shivered unhappily and wrapped his coat tightly around his sparse frame, quickening his pace. As he stopped at off the curb there was a warning shout behind him. He tried to jump back but was knocked down by a passing bus.

Several hours slipped by before he regained consciousness and looked around. He blinked in amazement, refusing to believe his eyes. The scene was one he had come to know so well during the past months. Familiar faces passed and repassed his bed as the nurses went about their duties and he recognised several of his fellow patients. He smiled contentedly as he lay back. It was nice to be home again....

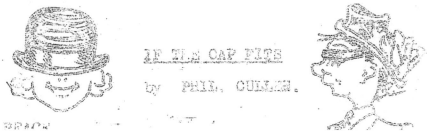

PEACE

Yet much remains,

To conquer still, peace with her victories

No less renowned then war. New foes arise.

Threatening to bind ourselves with secular chains. Help us to have free conscience from the past.

Of hireling wolves, whose gospel is a paw.

Milton

THE CLUB.
"Gay sprightly land of mirth, and social ease."

Goldsmith

F.T.E. L..HY
"Mix your sage ruminations with glimpses of folly, this delightful at times to be somewhat insane."

Horace

J.CK M.AU..FFE
"I didn't reply, I was thinking of other things."

Hilton Brown

M.R, KE.N.DY
".... No simplest duty is forgotten."

J. R. Lowell

O.LV.. S.LL.V.N
"her sprightly looks, a lively mind disclose."

Pope

THE COMMITTEE
"long tutored in what to do,
why, and which way to do it"

E.V. Knox

THE MAGAZINE
"after proper preparation,
and profound examination,
they wrought it out with exclamation."

J. K. Stephen

GENERAL MEETING
"Moan. Brethren moan..."

Hyperion

TENNIS-ITES
"Six precious souls and all agog
two – through thick and thin"

Cowper

F.ANK. AR.Y
"cheerful in converse, smart in repartee"

Sir. C.H. Williams

J.H. K.NN.D
"social, cheerful, and serene."

IsabelLa

F.T.E. M.DD.N
".. Go where I may, rest where I will
Eternal London haunts me still.."

Thomas More

MA..E.P.RL.
". That voice, majestic and elate"

Keats

ERI.? PE,ER & BER.
".. And they laugh, but obey
When the word has come forth from the wise"

E.V. Knox

R.DY.. ERLA
".. From grave to gay, from lively to serena
Correct with spirit, eloquent with ease,
intent on reason and polite to please."

Pope

SUBS PLEASE!
"But now the sounds of population for,
No cheerful murmurs fluctuate.."

Goldsmith

P.T.B.TL,R
"I am silent in the Club..."
G.K.C.
ON DUTY
".. A weary time! A weary time."

Coleridge

APOLOGY
"Curs't be diverse, how well so'ere it flow.
That tends to make one worthy man my foe."

Pope

ooOoo

COOKING CONTEST

Enter your names now for the Grand Herring Toasting Competition: Prizes: 1 pocket knife (slightly damaged), 6 selected conkers and 1 stick of "Oh Boy" Chewing Gum. (Oh boy, oh boy!). Toasting fork provided. Bring your own Herring.

LOU'S DIARY

7:35 Mum called me to get up.
7:45 Mum shouted to me get up.
7:50 Mum screamed at me to get up.
8:00 I got up. had a cat's lick started brekker.
9:45 Arrived at school; had the cane for being late.
10:00 Felt ill, went home.
11:50 Visited Doctor, told I was in best of health.
12:45 Had dinner (standing up).
2:00 School again. Teacher told me to report at 4:30.
2:40 Arithmetic. Had four sums nearly right.
3:45 Six of-the-best for pelting inspector.
4:00 Cleaned all the inkwells.

4:30 Reported, had cane. Home to tea.
6:15 Went to play, found 10/-which I brought home to mum, who said I was a good boy for the first time in my life.
8:15 The policeman took my name for hanging behind the coal-cart.
9:00 Mum gave me a good hiding and sent me to bed. Slept soundly.

ooOoo

ST ANNE'S RADIO PROGRAMME - this evening

06:00	TIME. (roughly) NEWS (old) WEATHER FORECAST (wrong).
06:45	ST ANNE'S ORCHESTRA. (Comb and paper) with the celebrated conductor PETER MARTINELLI. M.D.
07:15.	CHOIR RECITAL conductor Wm. BOWLES.
08:00	I'M AN OLD COW HAND sung by horsemen BRETT (this takes half an hour as the singer stutters).
08:50	BELCHER & BUTLER the quick five comics (they ought to be shot!).
08:00	NEWS (as before).
09:10	TALK by Adolf Perla (alias Willie ever stop) on the strike of waiters etc.
10:00	BIG FIGHT BASHER BELCHER THE MASHER MACKAY running commentary by BATTLING BUTLER.

No offence gents

SECRETS OF SUCCESS

One of the secrets of success is to have a good figure. Your uncle Brett has a very good figure. Skinny people never get on in the world – it's only the plump people that become Company – Directors. (In these hard times perhaps only Company – Directors become plump people).

Let your uncle Brett (who as such a very good figure) teach you the sure way to fatness and success.

Right at once, enclosing a 15/-postal order (non-returnable). You will never look back, you'll always look round.

George Brett

ooOoo

FOOTBALL

Mike Plant - Summarises some incidents that occurred, during the Football seasons of 1945-46/47.

In 1945,, we lived in Herne Hill and my cousin Pat Thomas lived further up in Red Post Hill. I had started work at a Firm in Vauxhall Bridge Road, and Pat along with our other cousin John Macdermott, who lived in Vauxhall, was in a Secondary school in Kennington. At the time due to the Evacuation, all schools had closed, and it was the only school open in the vicinity. Pat was in his last year at school and was due to start work the end of the school year. In our spare time we played football on the cinder pitches in Ruskin Park. John Macdermott, informed Pat of St. Anne's Catholic Club in Vauxhall, who had two football teams and we should join them, to get a proper game of football. We did, and that is how we joined the Club. Pat left school and got a job in the headquarters of the London Transport at 2 Petty France in Victoria, where as an employee was granted a bus pass, all he had to say to a Conductor on a bus or tram was, 'Sticky'. With me sitting alongside him I got away without paying, although not permitted. Anyway at the Club we became members of the ''B'' team, regularly playing on a Saturday. We use to play against the Ragged School in Camberwell, in some cases, there were not enough 'Ragged players' that turned up for the game, and basically it became a scratch game. I became Captain of the 'B' team. Due to some of the senior players being conscripted into the Forces. In November 1945, I was selected to play in the 'A' Team, subsequently for the next three years, until I was called up in 1948. I played in the 'A' Team.

I remember that most of the games were played on Clapham Common and have a vague recollection of playing a couple of games on Tooting Bec. Common, where the running track was. Football training was held on a Tuesday night in the Hall, our coach then was the Millwall Left Back Bob Hardy who put us through our paces, then coached us on methods of football tactics and ball control. On Thursday it was pre match training running on the roads, then complete three circuits around the Oval Cricket ground.

Playing at Clapham Common St. Anne's V Corpus Christie. Opponent -?- Mike Plant,- Opponent?- Goalkeeper Mike Mulvey

On Clapham Common, during the Blitz a bomb had dropped on number 8 pitch, leaving a great crater. Obviously that had been filled in and to some extent made level. After it rained that particular area became a great lake, a hazard for all to avoid. If the ball happened to land in the water it stayed there, and it was the midfield players task to retrieve it, with two opposing players splashing about in the water trying to kick the ball out, they always finished up being soaking wet. Another Pitch number 14 was marked out next to the road crossing the common, with the Goal Line and Goal parallel with it.

On that Road the owner of a Mobile Tea Van used to park it almost level with the Goal area, possibly its owner wanted to watch the action on the pitch. It was when we were playing a game against Corpus Christie of Brixton, who had a giant of a Goalie and was a job and a half to score against him. So, as the first half remained goalless, when we changed ends, he was in the gaol with the Tea Van directly behind him. Les Green was our centre forward and after receiving a great pass from Lou Ager belted the ball past him to score a goal, in doing so the ball went whizzing past the Goalie and straight into the Tea Van, causing the Owner to duck hitting and knocking the Tea Urn on the floor causing much damage to it and the crockery, too the irate Owners annoyance. After the game which we won. As compensation we all had to pay one shilling each. What a laugh that was.

In one of the games played on Clapham Common. Bert Thomas suffered a broken leg and was carted off to the Lying -In –Hospital opposite Clapham South Tube station. He was in there for weeks on end and being out of work with 'No Pay'. The Team organised a concert in the Club to raise money to give to Bert. That night the Club was packed for the Concert that raised about £ 40 for Bert.

Dennis Lynch was the producer of a Play series.

And we all took Part in doing daft things.

Les Green sang two Frank Sinatra songs.

There was a Skit done on: '1066 And All That' In the Dock Sir Francis Drake was accused of Polluting the Air with Tobacco smoke?'

All he could say in his defence was 'Not Guilty M' Lord.'

Jock MacKay and his Girlfriend sang a Duet from the show of Oklahoma. Acting as Gordon Macrea and Shirley Jones they sang 'People will Say were In Love'

Lou Ager Bert MacAvoy and Peter Martinelli the only true musician who played Clarinet the other two were tuneless. in their own right? played a couple of tuneless melodies as illustrated by the photo.

Lou Ager- Bert MacAvoy-Peter Martinelli.

Paddy Mac, myself and Lou Ager, wearing lipstick powdered faces, dressed up in skirts and bras's, appeared as the "Andrew Sisters" and mimed the words to one of their records, called 'And she never took off her bathing suit.'

Sitting in the audience was my Mum and my Aunt Bridget Macdermott, who when we were doing the Andrew Sisters Act, I being the smallest of the trio, she recognised it was me. Aunt Bridget Nudging Mum retorted.

'Sarah that's your Michael dressed up in Girls clothes. If I were you I would put a stop to that malarcky ?' Later M um told me about this and we had a laugh at Aunt Bridget!

A bevy of girls dressed in Ball Gowns for the dance - all unknown - far right Kaye Plant in the white satin ball gown.

The match football was a 'sacro sanct' item in those days there were very few footballs available and after it had been pumped up ready for the following match fixture, it was given to someone to take home and bring to the match. One Thursday night after eleven o' clock the four of us Paddy McMonagle, Bert MacAvoy, Lou Ager and myself. Left the Club to walk home, on this occasion it was Paddy's turn with the Football. We had got as far as Fentiman Road where we would part company. Paddy and I would make our way down Fentiman Road, whilst Lou and Bert would carry on towards Stockwell. However, for some reason ? The ball was accidently dropped in the middle of Fentiman Road. So as you would do, we started kicking the ball about, carrying on all the way down Fentiman Road passing it to and fro across the road. In those days there was no traffic to worry about, but, our ball playing disturbed the Neighbours who called the Police. They arrived from both ends, it was a fair cop. 'Disturbing the Peace late at night?' Our names went into the 'BOOK' and we all had to report to our Local Police Station. In my case it was the Brixton Police Station at Gresham Road.

Next day Friday on my way to the Club, I caught a 34 tram towards Stockwell that stopped right beside the Police Station, and the stop for the Tram's change-over from overhead Electric pole to underground trolley in the middle of the road and visa versa. Getting off, I duly reported into the Station Desk Sergeant. When I stated why I was there and my name. 'Plant.' he asked.

'Any relation of Kaye Plant our Telephonist?' I replied.

'Yes Sir. That is my Sister!'

'Right. You have been warned. Off you go.'

I made a quick retreat out through the door and got back on the same tram outside, I even used the same ticket, and got away with that. I was lucky!

Pat Thomas and I visited Bert a few times whilst he was in the Lying-In-Hospital. It really was a women's maternity Hospital, later named the South London Women's Hospital. He was grateful for the money, but certainly not pleased about being the only man in the Hospital!

ooOoo

League Cup Winners 1946-1947 (Full team)

Back Row: Bernard Driver- Toni Maconi,- Mike Plant. –Mike Mulvey,- John Healey, Tom MacAvoy Rudy Perla.
Pat Butler
Front row: Jock Mckay,- Joe Connelly.- Les Green,- Lou Ager,- Paddy McMonagle

Supporters of the Football Team taken on Clapham Common after the Team won the final
Amongst the Girls are members of the Netball Team
At the rear is Ted Lock (Sponge man) Eddie Marcantonio
In the foreground four young supporters
Margaret Plant(kneeling)
Someone ?? Joe Plant & Kevin Lewis with football and cup.

Back Row: Jock McKay,- Toni Maconi,- John Healy(Capt),- Tom MacAvoy
Front Row: ? Mike Plant.- Mike Mulvey,- Lou Ager,- Les Green.
Missing players: Bert Thomas (Brocken Leg) Paddy McMonagle - Joe Connelly,-
Rudi Perla (Studying for Priesthood)

ooOoo

CUP PRESENTATION MADE
BY ANNE CRAWFORD.

Anne Crawford the Film star Actress of many films including Prison without bars (1938) They Flew Alone (1942) Millions like us & The Night Invader (1943) plus many more- in total 24 till she died in 1956. Was invited to present the Cup to the Winning Team St. Anne's

Anne being presented to ?? Mike Mulvey looking on -?- Fr. Bob Madden Ted Locke

Cup Presentation

Secretary of the League who was a Member of the Corpus Christie Team disputing St. Anne's Win, reluctantly holding on to the Cup - before Anne Crawford presents it to St. Anne's Captain John Healy

ooOoo

There was a party held at Langley Mansions the home of the Wilberhams to celebrate Des Lewis 's 21st. Birthday. All the football team and their respective Girlfriends were invited together with the Aunts, Uncles and Cousins.

The Below photographs shows, all past including then present and future members of St Anne's Club.

Rear: George Belcher Pat Thomas, June? Kaye Cyril- (Kayes Boyfreind.) June's Hubby
? Pat Butler Bert Mac Avoy. ? Pat Kowawski
Left: Toni Marconi Helen Cousin+ Irene McMonagle Kevan Lewis Pat Dixon. Des. Lewis Peter Martinelli Pat Locke Vera De Troia /
Joan Woodham Mike Plant
Fore: Les Green Tom MacAvoy Marie Caluori - Paddy McMonagle -Tom Lewis -Aunt Aggie -Barbara Spanswick.

Next Photo of the Cunningham Clan, taken at the same Party

Back Row: A: Bridie Dalton. -A: Julia Cunningham. -C: Tom Lewis. -U: Frank Lewis -C: Des Lewis. -Dad Plant: - June's Husband, -C: Mary McDermott. -C: Jack Plant. -U: Alec Humbey. - Kaye Plant. - C: Ray Batten?. -U: Tom Wilberham. – F: Cyril. F: June.?
Center A: Kitty Lewis F: Mrs. Brown. A: Nan Curtis
Below A: Agnes Humbey.- C: Pat Thomas. -Mum Plant.- C: Julia Wilberham. -A: Fan Wilberham. -C: John Mac Dermott.
Front: - C. Tommy Wilberham. -C. Kevan Lewis. - C: Mike Plant.
A = Aunts C = Cousin U = Uncle F= Family Friend.

No doubt there were other parties held at various venues to either celebrate Engagements Weddings, Birthdays or, going into the forces parties. Nevertheless the above two photos are the only evidence on hand, to illustrate a period of time when the previous overhead threats of the recent war had disappeared. IT WAS THEN A GREAT TIME TO ENJOY ONESELF.

ooOoo

1948/9

A post war memory by Phil Frost.

In late 1947 The London Federation of Boys Club s organised a trip to Germany, possibly as a part of a friendship program but that is something I am not sure about? But there was a big meeting between the heads of the four powers USA Great Britain, France and the USSR to agree the control of Germany. I was one of 12 Boys from London Boys Clubs chosen to go to Berlin. Initially we were interviewed by Field Marshall Auchinleck, who was the then President of the Federation. In Mid -February 1948 we set off catching the train from Liverpool Street Station bound for Harwick to catch the boat to the Hook of Holland, then by train to Munich through Germany onto Berlin. A city of devastation All that was standing of building was three walls their interiors gutted, when we arrived there women were still shovelling up ruble in the streets from the allied bombing raids. It made me think that Germany had been bombed into oblivion Phil relates that a few of them exchanged West German Marks for East German marks as it was not that hard to do as they had Spivs! There just like us back home. We crossed the border at the Brandeburg Gate into East Germany, By this time it's getting on and shops would be closing duet to the curfew. A couple of us ran into a gift shop I spot a lovely blue glass Schnapps Decanter and six cut glasses, for my sister who was getting married, we did not how easy it was to go from one zone to another. When one of our Tutors asked us where we had been to get the gifts We told him. He went a whiter shade of Pale I think we nearly caused a political incident. The two Foreign Office escorts were not amused. (Possibly they were the cause of the Berlin Airlift in April 1948??)

ooOoo

A comment on the following 1948/49 Magazine: There were no artistic images provided. Furthermore the Author adds many comments as to personal recollections of the time he was a Member of the Youth Club The following years Annal is something of a mixture of the Youth and Over Twenties activities.

1948
Youth Club
COMMITTEE MEMBERS
S. Talbut Hon. Sec   M.Bremer.
J. Denneny.   E. McMonagle.
M. White.   E. Belcher.
J. Healy.   V. Le, Grand.
K Walsh.

ooOoo

ST ANNE'S
OVER TWENTYS CLUB
CHRISTMAS MAGAZINE

THIS

HAS

UNIQUE

MEMOIR

PERCUSSION

1948/9

Price 1/-

INTERESTED SPECTATOR

Ad multos annos!

The "Over-Twenty Club" is one year old, and looks like a becoming a permanent part of the social life of Vauxhall. This first year has been largely experimental. As an interested spectator I have watched the committee trying to build up the Club with a distinctive personality: a Club that can claim the loyalty of its members: a strong, united, friendly Club. Has it succeeded? Not altogether. It will take a long time to develop such a Club. But it has had a reasonable measure of success. The success would be much greater if we all realized that there building and maintaining of a successful Club needs the co-operative effort of <u>all</u> the members. That committee alone cannot "make" any Club; it needs the enthusiastic support of each individual member.

And that support often means sinking one's likes and dislikes for that common good. Taking part in activities that make no personal appeal; doing the old jobs someone else has over-looked; or, very simply, exercising a high degree of charity.

Ad multos annos:

Father Madden

ooOoo

[Comment by the Author]

Upon reading this article about Fr. Robert (BOB) Madden thoughts on the newly formed Pella Club, is a true reflection on his continued beliefs that made St. Anne's Youth Club such a wonderful, successful and vibrant place, that many enjoyed its hospitality to create and cement friendship that lasted many years.

'BOB' did indeed create and maintain that stability within the Club. Enjoyed by so many, you cannot put a figure against the numbers, and it was not just a passing fancy of couple of weeks or months, once joined, it was years before members married other members or, moved away from the area. It was the vibrancy of life to be enjoyed whilst a member of THE CLUB and is revered by all those who were members. Sadly the Club as it was has long since gone. Nevertheless the success Bob refers to is the annual REUNION Mass held at St Anne's that bears testimony to his original thoughts:

Joe P. Plant.

ooOoo

CONTENTS

Dear members.

The event you have heard so much about, as at last materialised in the form of "Thump", the first magazine produced by the Over- Twenties Club. To all members who have subscribed to do its pages, we say a word of thanks, and hope all will enjoy it for the memories it may revive.

But above all we seek to foster the spirit of good Club membership by an interchange of thought, to share the joy of our Club, to give it active support, and add to its well-being for all concerned, that each and every one of us may seek goodwill in all that we do, to benefit all by giving off our best for the Club.

Yours sincerely.

Editor.

ooOoo

OVER TWENTY CLUB DIARY

8th.January. First meeting of Over-Twenty Club.
Election of Interim Committee.
17th March. Combined St Patrick's Day.
29th March. Easter Monday Ramble around Windsor and district.
8th.April. General meeting of Over-Twenty Club.
Results of past three months reviewed.
Carmel Denenny elected as Chairman of the Club for
ensuring year.
9th May. Opening cricket Match of season.

Report as Follows:-

CRICKET TAKES A BOW.
by J. Lynch.

The cricket team made a successful debut this summer, and if early promise is any indication, they should progress to higher honours in the season's to come.

The season began rather disastrously at Motspur Park when we lost by an innings and over a 100 runs to Torrington.C.C. This was a catastrophe in the first game, but undaunted, the team went to Carshalton only to meet with another reverse against a much weaker team, After this game a general meeting was held and the team was reorganized. Much hard work and many inquiries obtained us the use of Downside Boy's Club nets, this being the opportunity we most needed. Many enjoyable hours were spent there and everybody finished up at the "local" with a "pint" bread and cheese and pickles - it didn't need seaside or Swiss air to give the cricket as an appetite.

The first match after the general meeting was played against the Youth Club, and although we lost a number of players through the trip to Switzerland, we were reinforced by some new players who later proved their worth. We won this game by 10 wickets, the outstanding feature being with Vic Le Grande as 50. Other games were played and won, the first set-back being the draw with C.H. Coats Ltd. Who by the way played the role of fairy Godmother in providing us with a first Class pitch and pavilion Many enjoyable hours were spent there by supporters, players and opponents after the game. I think that Club as a whole owe Mr. Coates a deep debt of gratitude for his kindness and generosity.

The following week saw our first defeat since the reorganisation of the team and we were well and truly beaten by a better team the Ministry of Fuel and Power. We lost one more game during the season at Abbey Nomads and finished with the record reading: Wins 6, Losses 2, Draws 1, which is exceedingly good and a record of which I'm very proud

The whole team did well, all trying their utmost to pull off a win and all playing <u>as</u> a team which is one of the reasons we were so successful.

Before concluding I would like once again to say thank you on behalf of all the cricketers; to the Club for the financial help given; to Abbot Trafford for the next Downside; to Ealing Priory School for the loan of their ground; once again to Mr. Coates for his kindness, and last but not least to the faithful supporters who stood by two thick and thin even after the Lamberhurst Outing which proved so disappointing.

So St Anne's Cricketers, you can be justifiably proud of yourselves but remember next season we want to reach greater heights which means greater efforts so let's "go to it" for the love of the game and the will to win.

ooOoo

Diary Cont./-
17th May. Whit Monday outing to Climping with Youth Club.

Some unknown: Fr. Bob Madden Mike Macdermott- Mary Perla- John Kennedy-? Outing to Climping

29th May.   C.Y.C. Cross Country Run.
12th June.   C.Y.C. South-East Sports.
26th.June.   C.Y.C. South-West Sports.

Reports as Follows:-

ATHLETICS

Our first joint in this field was the Oval Inter- Club road race between Stance's and Christchurch Club on 14th. March over approximately 2 ½ miles, which resulted in a walk over for St. Anne's. Vic Le Grande, Ernie Morgan and John Kennedy ran for the youth Club.

Paddy McMonagle and Mike Plant

Next we had the C.Y.C. Cross Country run over 3 miles on Wimbledon Common, 29th. May, which was an all St. Anne's event. Members of the Over- Twenties Club who turned up and ran despite the heavy rain were Reg. Ball, Ernie Morgan and John Kennedy.

At the C.Y.C. Sports on the 12th. And 26th. June. The Over Twenties Club co-operated with the Youth Club and helped to win 3 cups for St. Anne's. John Greaves and Bill Gurr showed good form in the sprints while Ernie Morgan had a 'go' at the half mile.

If members can do a spot of regular training now, they should be in good condition for any future events.

ooOoo

Diary Cont./-

17th July. Organise visit to Guinness's Brewery.

Reports as Follows:-

OUTSIDE VISITS

Derby day
Guinness's Brewery
Borough council meeting

One sunny Saturday afternoon in June, we battled our way through millions of people in a vain attempt to catch a glimpse of the great race. We went successful but it was grand fun cheering with the crowds as invisible horses were by, even though we hadn't backed the winner.

But it we saw no horses at Epsom, we certainly had our fill of Guinness at the Brewery. There appears to be no limit to the half pint samples offered to visitors and I can't imagine how it pays him to take such thirsty parties as our crowd.

After the visit of three councillors to the Club, a group of us went to a very interesting meeting at Lambeth Town Hall and were thrilled to hear the mayor give a public welcome to the members of St Anne's Over-Twenties Club!

We are hoping to visit Mount Pleasant sorting office and a newspaper office sometimes in the future. Both outings will be in the evening.

Other suggestion will be welcomed K.D.

ooOoo

Diary Cont./-
18ᵗʰ July. Sunday hike to Tonbridge district.
1ˢᵗ.August. Outing to Bracklesham Bay with Youth Club.
Report as Follows:-

BRACKLESHAM BAY.

When an outing with our parents and friends was first suggested, it did not meet with whole hearted approval at the Club. Possibly 'parents' accounted for this, for many of them might be shocked at the 'goings-on 'of their offspring, and the attendance at Club might drop considerably.

As an experiment a combined outing was tried, and it proved a great success. Since then, it has become an annual affair, and nobody thinks with anything but pleasure (apart perhaps from Fr. Madden and the coach drivers) of the Parish Outing.

A wet day trip to Bracklesham Bay 1949

Back row: ??,-??,- Sadie - Kathy O'hearne Pat Thomas,- Eric Blackburn, -??- Joe Dixon,- Pat. MacDermott,-Pat Cooper, Pat Kirk,-Driver,- ??,-??
Front Row: ??,- ??,- ??, Jimmie Richardson, - Hilda Harris- Bill Tough, Sadie Brogan,- John MacDermott,-Adelina Perla,- Arthur Course,- Brian O'Sullivan- Tommy Wilberham,- ??,-??.

This year the outing was to Bracklesham Bay, and of course the weather was excellent, the trip to the coast was very enjoyably and was unmarked by anything exciting or adventurous. True, one Coach ran over a dog, but this is an every-day occurrence and it caused no excitement. Indeed it added a relish to the eating of our minced meat sandwiches. Possibly the poor animal was on someone's tea table next day as a sausage, so the accident was useful to the nation.

It is Father Madden's boast that he is one of the few people who know the correct road to Bracklesham Bay, for if a certain turning on the left some way out of Chichester, is missed one has missed Bracklesham Bay. It should be recorded, however, that Mrs Belcher and Brett of the youth Club discovered this route and arrived on bicycles at the same time as the coaches. Let no one discredit this performance, for although they took three days to find the place, they arrived hot but undaunted.

The first thing one notices about Bracklesham Bay is the huge amount of sea, the vast amount of sand, and the one native on an ice cream barrow. This is, of course, the best possible place in which to let loose "St Anne's Club", and very soon the sandy beach was dotted with figures that were eating, sleeping, running, swimming or moaning according to their ages and inclinations.

There is a great spirit of friendliness (incurred no doubt by a certain amount of spirit in boiled in route), and one small section of the party, of whose identity you shall remain ignorant, discovered some sailors and proceeded to play games with them!

The Over-Twenties conduct was of course irreproachable, and they conducted themselves with great sobriety and decorum. Isn't it strange what a difference parents make?

John Mcdermott-Kathy Anderton-?-Pat Thomas-Tom Mullen-Bert MacAvoy-? Bill Tough- /
Mike Plant / Kathy O' Hearne- Josie Course.

Father Madden was the first to find the tea shop, and he ate so much that the place had to close. The rest of the Club arrived just after this, and his reverence grinned superciliously through the window at them.

The journey home was uneventful, after all, the songs had been sung, and everyone was tired and heads began to nod and not a few to sleep a little, and we were pleased when the coaches arrived back home. Bed certainly feels good after a hectic Parish outing, and after good sleep we all feel refreshed and fit to start work on the Monday!

Footnote – liquor is banned on the coaches, but I often wonder what it is that Mr Bremer has in his little case which he will not let out of his sight all day. "First aid kit2 he says!

ooOoo

Diary Cont./-
1st.September. Opening games of Over- Twenty Football and Netball teams.
Reports as Follows:-

SOMETHING ABOUT FOOTBALL

After a very shaky start when it seemed difficult to find 11 players, I am pleased to say we are at last established as a team. We crashed into the football world with a magnificent win over George Payne's at Wadham, in my estimation we well deserved our win of 8-2, taking into account the fact that we were complete strangers on field of play. Our next game was a return match against Paynes, who seemed anxious to wipe off the defeat we had inflicted in our previous game.

They fielded a stronger team, but once again we were superior and claimed another victory winning 3-1. I would like to take this opportunity of thanking Ernie Morgan and the makers of Paynes Poppets for arranging these games, and the splendid reception we received at Waddon.

We then embarked on our league fixtures, a first game being against Valman Res. At Hackney. They proved very easy opponents for us and we recorded a victory of 5-1. We suffered a severe blow in this match as our skipper Harry Day had a re-occurrence of his cartilage trouble. He finished the game at left half and inspired of his injury he put up a very good show! He has been out of the game since, but hopes to be in the position to play around Christmas. His operation proved very successful, so here' s wishing him speedy recovery and return to the Club where I feel sure his absence is keenly felt.

1948-1949 Team

Back row: Bert MacAvoy- Eddie Marcantonio- Paddy McMonagle - Mike Mulvey -Toni Maconi –Peter Bone-- Lou Ager.
Kneeling: Jock MacKay- Vic Le Grande.- Bob Pettifer. - Tony Blackmore
Missing: Mike Plant Conscripted and replaced by Alan Ball
It was in the Summer time of 1948 that Mike Mulvey was killed on his motorbike in Ireland.

On October 3rd. We met Rosendale Res. At Brockwell Park, and they proved to be at strongest of oppositions to date, however, we are glad to say we won by 2-1. Next match we won against Wingers Res.11-2. The following week we suffered our first defeat against the colonial office 4-5 disaster overtook us in Gerry Lynch receiving an injury which turned out to be more serious than was forced thought, which necessitated an operation. He returned to his native Blackpool for treatment, and I have no news as to his progress to date. However, I wish him a speedy recovery.

The following week we defeated Lambeth 8-0. The next to date of going to press was against the Dolphins, which we drew 2-2. This game was played in thick fog.

Up to date we have only been able to accommodate the Youth Club once. They had the beating of us in the second half when their passing was very good and it seemed we were unable to stand the pace. It was a very enjoyable game although I think both teams were fielding reserves. It was a very clean game, and goes to show any animosity felt, was left behind at Vauxhall, and rightly so. Bert Thomas is a return game in mind when both teams will be at full strength, this should prove good entertainment and I feel sure we will give them a little more opposition.

We will endeavour to keep you informed of future results. I always give the necessary amount of praise have victory deserves should feel inclined to keep bad defeats a little quite. I feel sure the netball team will keep you well informed.

We are going on with our fixtures full of confidence and I hope the lads will show the same enthusiasm they have displayed so far.

Before I close I should like to thank all the Club members for their financial backing without which we should be unable to carry on. I can assure you the team appreciates all the help you have given to date.

Eileen McMonagle did a fine job of embroidery on their shirts with an effigy of a Saint. Flapper Thomas has done a magnificent job as secretary and has gone to a great deal of trouble and expense to keep the team going smoothly.

We are very grateful for the moral support we have received from a handful of enthusiastic supporters who always turn out when it is humanly possible. Their presence is a great help and gives us a great deal of encouragement. With a word of thanks to one and all concerned with football I will sign off for now.

J.G.

ooOoo

NETBALL
By E. Bremer.

Last July we played our first netball match with the team from West Norwood we then played several friendly's and joined the London Union League when the season officially opened in October

This is a small league and throughout the winter and only gave us eight games, but by playing other Clubs we are able to get to match every weekend.

Quite a few Girls belong to the team and all are very keen and if, any other Girls, interested in the game will come to the practices on a Saturday or Sunday, they will be more than welcome.

ooOoo

Diary Cont./-
29th.September. Organise party to Lambeth Council Meeting.
30th September. General open evening given by Over- Twenty Club.

[Authors note: whether this was part of the evening's entertainment I'm not sure but it did pop out of the wood-work as follows:-]

PROGRAMME

1   ALFRED..CYRIL DRIVER
    THE GOOD WIFE...THERESA DAILEY
    ETHELRED..CYRiL CONNEL
    THE MINSTREL ....RONNIE BELCHER
    Scene............................THE OLD WOMANS COTTAGE
2   IRISH DANCING ....MARY MACDERMOTT
3   THE PRINCESS AND THE SWINEHERD by Hans Anderson
    THE PRINCESS...MARA STOGDON
    THE EMPEROR..CYRIL CONNELL
    THE PRINCE..RONNIE BELCHER
    TH LADIES OF THE COURT.. PATRICIA MACDERMOTT
    KITTY WEAKNER
    MARITZA COLLINICOS
    LESLEY HUGHES
    SHEILA WEAKNER
    THE PAGE BOY..TOMMY WEAKNER
    Scene 1. The Emperors Palace
    Scene 2. Outside the Pig-sties
4   SCENE FROM UNCLE TOMS CABIN by HARRIET B. STONE.
    OPHELI...KATHLEEN AMER
    TOPSY...CYRIL DRIVER
    LITTLE EVA...LESLEY HUGHES
    Scene Miss Ophelia's Bedroom
5   COUNTRY HOLIIDAY by MABEL CONSTANDUROS
    EMMA..RONNIE BELCHER
    MARY...KATHLEEN AMER
    DOROTHY PERKINS..TERESA BAILEY
    ROSIE PERKINS...CYRIL CONNELL
    Scene A Platform of a Railway Station.

Diary Cont./-

3rd. October. Sunday hike to Woking district

Report as Follows:-

<u>HIKING</u>
'Who's coming hiking?'

My first reply to this is generally another question. 'How Far?' I start to 'hedge' a little but being like George Washington, I cannot tell a lie, and answer apologetically about 12 miles. Nobody can say that 12 miles is too long for one days walking, yet most people look a trifle crestfallen at this, before eventually replying. 'Alright, I'll come.'

Our previous hikes, or perhaps the rambles would be more appropriate, have I think being enjoyed by all as I am continually being asked for the date of the next one. And what could be better for one's health and spirits than to leave London's dirt and grime and saunter through country lanes, fields and woods.

Rambling is a thirsty business at any time, especially on a hot day, so I always try and arrange to have a picnic lunch near the local village, 'pub', which is appreciated by males and females alike. A nice cup of tea at the end of the Road is also an asset and can generally be managed.

A weary crowd of walkers start forth in true military style at the mention of first one word. 'Tea.'

So far the weather has been very kind to us, but now that winter is here, we cannot expect it to last. No one wants to get pneumonia through walking all day in the pouring rain, but a light shower, <u>if you are well clad</u> hurts no one, so I hope to continue rambles through the winter months and ask all enthusiast, in their own interests to come prepared for muddy walking, if not actual rain.

To come back to the question of mileage - we have only done one walk at 12 miles, the others were nine and winter hikes will be considerably shorter owing to the light failing earlier...

Well – here's to the next hike!!!

ooOoo

Diary Cont./-
<u>9th. October.</u> Week-end party to C.Y.C. Hostel at Ashtead 22 members of Over-Twenty Club made this visit.

<u>28th October</u>. Over-Twenty Club General meeting results of past six months reviewed

J.G.

COMMITTEE MEMBERS
Chairman - Carmel Denney
Secretary - Barbara Abrams
Treasurer – David Tuohey
Marie Perla
Alf Owens
George Belcher.

ooOoo

TABLE TENNIS.

Table tennis activities during our first year have been curtailed because of lack of time. With only one evening at our disposal very little table tennis can be played as the hall is usually required for dancing and other activities.

We have managed to run two knock out competitions. The first held early in the year was in three sections, boys, girls, and mixed doubles. Only the boys competition was completed and the winner was Tom Stock.

More recently a smaller competition was run and the winners were Anne Bremer for the girls and Tom Stock for the boys.

Now that we have a table erected in the oratory I am hoping to arrange more competitions during the winter months and I must ask your co-operation in making these a success.

So far the boys have had two matches. Home and away versus the Streatham branch of the British Legion. The away game was won 18-7, our scorers were Arthur Parsons 3 Vic Le Grande 5, Bill Harper 3, Bert Thomas 4 and Ernie Morgan 3.At home we won 18-7 and our scorers for this game were Arthur Parsons,4 Bert Thomas 4, Jerry Rance 4, Gerry Day 4, and Tom Lewis 2.

I intend arranging some more matches during the winter but these will be only occasionally while we have only one Club night. Regarding equipment, members have been very helpful in presenting us with bats, so we are no longer dependent on the Youth Club in this line.

The tables have not been treated very gently and I must appeal to all members to be careful when erecting than an playing, and to report any damage immediately to Committee members or table tennis Captains.

Thanking all members for their assistance in this at first very trying year

E. Morgan.

ooOoo

C.O.M.

We are glad to have this opportunity of advertising C. O. M. Since quite a few newcomers have joined the new section of the clubs the Over-Twenties.

Our extra show of devotion to our Lady entails very little really, attendance at the 9:30 a.m. Mass on the first Sunday and benediction at 8:30 p.m. on the first Monday of each month, also there is a short meeting held by Father Healey in the club library at 8:45 p.m every other Monday. There are definite rules of the solidity and every C.O.M. should make every effort to comply with them.

About 40 of us made our annual retreat at Grayshott again this year, and were sure that none of us regretted that weekend (and vocal cords certainly didn't).

Top Row unknown
Next down: Vi Bremer, ?-? Carmel Denneny. Next across: Maria Martinelli,- Olive O'Sullivan, -Marie Bremer.
Bottom row: ?- Paddy Daly -?' Elsie Bremer,- Joan Denneny.

We have heard that the parcels of clothes etc, collected for the Germans eventually reach Father Nilges in Frankfurt first July.

Our outing in September to Coombe Bank, a beautiful spot near Sevenoaks, was unfortunately hampered by the weather. We were very grateful to the nuns for making us so welcome.

The repository still exist at the back of the church, though customers are few and far between.

Annexed enrolment is at the beginning of December so we do hope that more of the club members will consider joining our ranks.

A.B.

ooOoo

GUILD OF THE BLESSED SACRAMENT

We hear on all sides now a call for Catholic action. I think every Catholic should take part. The first step is to join a Catholic Sodality.

I am now suggesting that G. B. S. For men over the age of 14 years. We all have a long way to go before we reach the kingdom of heaven. That G. B. S. Helps us on the road by sanctifying one's soul. And monthly obligation is to receive holy Communion at the Guild mass on the first Sunday of the month.

It is also a member's duty to take party in any processions of the blessing Sacrament whenever possible. Retreats are also arranged for the members.

Think this over and then get in touch with any of the clergy or member of the Guild.

Enrolments aisle periodically in the church.

G.B.
Member of the committee.

'SOUTH LONDON'

Have you ever explored South London or stop to consider the ancient history of your local territory? When sixpence was a princely fortune, my brother and I, loved to roam London in search of adventure, with the gangling chat nicknamed Wire Bones we would take up a penny ticket between two stations and then travel and network of the underground to reach our destination.

The greatest excitement of all was a trip "down south. On a Saturday morning we would walk all the way from Marylebone to Lewisham. Our pleasure was a cup of tea and a penny bun from the Lyon's next to the Gaumont.

The long hike would usually include a visit to St Mary's Clapham. A tedious and tiring walk, you may be thinking, and rather pointless if one is in search of adventure. Why not the City of London with its Tower, St. Paul's, Covent Garden and the like. But then, perhaps you have never really explored South London.

I shall never lose my fascination for the London which lies South of the river. Many of my North London friends know it only as a place to whiz through in luxury coaches, but beneath its grimy exterior I can still picture the undulating country which used to border the Thames. Though there is no Lavender left on Lavender hill, I haven't glimpsed the Meadows of the river wander from the buses which plunged down East hill towards the Town Hall. Further in East lie the mud-flats off Southwark with the ancient Borough Market, the George Inn and the old Elephant and Castle. Kings College and Guy's hospital can hold their own with such august establishments as St. Mary's and Charing Cross. And in the religious world, South London contains both the Palace of Canterbury and the most ancient Cathedral of the restored Catholic Church. Yet I suppose many American tourists hardly note of its existence.

But people are more important than monuments, and the cockneys of South London are a friendly race. More solid than the cousins of the North, they have customs and traditions of their own which rarely find space in the National Press. Someday I hope to see a separate council chamber, rise near New Cross. Then the people of the Old Kent Road, will at last be free of the dominion of the patricians of South Kensington, and the like, who possess most of the trolleybuses, theatres and concert halls and even the clean air of the parks.

D. O'Halloran

ooOoo

BERLIN

After many months of enjoyment on the coast of Belgium, at Blankenberge and Knocke, and aimless travelling about in Germany I found myself a member of the Occupation troops in the British Sector of Berlin, where I stayed for two years.

Berlin, a devastated and ransacked city full of starving Berliners and many other nationalities were proud of the fact that they spoke English and understood American. Notices were seen in shop windows to that effect. Before very long we were able to hear almost every Berliner speaking broken English in many dialects and with various accents.

Say a devastated Berlin because like many great cities in Europe it was nearly razed to the ground. I say ransacked because we were led to believe that the Russians had done all the looting there was to do before the other allies reached the city.

Life as a Soldier was very much the same, parades, work and guards. We had the famous Berlin Lakes on which to spend our free time in summer, also the famous Olympic Stadium was completely for the use of British troops.

The various cafes were frequent did during the winter months; one could spend a pleasant evening in any of those which were, "In Bounds" to British troops. It was in one of these cafes that one of our Sappers and three members of the R.A.M.C. gave their lives and many were injured rescuing scores of our late enemies, when it caught fire. There was a German fancy dress ball at the time. Eighty people lost their lives in all. They were mostly flimsy fancy dress, one minute they were scorching **inside** then came panic and the next minute they were frozen out in the night air.

Russians were the first troops to enter Berlin, called the Black spot of Europe, hence the British troops, a Black Spot encircled by a red ring. Used to say it resembled the Black Market surrounded by Russians, which in fact was true. Burling was the worst place for Black Market in any commodity and is surrounded by Russian Occupational territory.

The Black Market flourished evenings of one was persistently pestered by Germans – "Zigarettes Verkaufen?" "Have you any cigarettes for sale?" The price at that time was (15) fifteen marks for cigarettes. Consider the rate of exchange at that time, 40 marks equal to £1 pound – cigarettes cost the Soldier at 61/2. D for 10 in the canteen, we also had (50) fifty free edition.

The Russian Soldiers considered the working class of **Germany** as capitalists because of the wonderful living conditions in most of their houses. Very soon we, the British Soldier, was known also as capitalist by the Germans because of the fact that we were able to obtain the unobtainable notably cigarettes and tobacco and chocolate.

A tour was arranged for us to give us some idea of life in Berlin today. We learn about the democratic form of government in Berlin. I was there at the time of the elections and was pleased to see the Russian sponsored party voted out. Each Borough Council had a district officer from the corresponding occupying power in continual attendance.

We were shown a comparison in the rations. Unfortunately or unfairly, we were shown a comparison between German rations and British Army rations, which were, in essence, double the British Civilians Rations in Britain, but in reality were considered less – believe me. It all amounted to the fact that the lowest German ration (rations were graded to the amount of work done, i.e. A manual worker received a higher grade ration than an office worker) was 1,700 calories per day and the British Civilians Rations were equal to 2500 calories daily. Whereas the British worker could subsidise his meagre rations with un-rationed goods, ET c. the German worker had just the bare rations.

The state of some German houses was appalling, owing to bombed people who were living in cellars and ruins in overcrowded conditions, paying exorbitant rents, amounting to two-thirds of their income

The rate of disease in those dwellings was of course very high. Penicillin was not attainable in quantity for Germans; therefore there was a high death rate during the early stages of occupation.

As for clothing coupons there was no such thing for clothes or shoes. When anybody was in dire need an application had to be made to the Burgermeister for a permit which took a considerable amount of patients. With a permit one then had to have so many pounds of woollen rags, according to the article required and then pay for it! For instance a dress will cost £10 of woollen rags and the sum of 70 marks, which was half a man's income for a month. Shoes were practically unobtainable except through Black Market channels. Men's shoes cost about 1,000 marks.

So ration was very meagre, roughly about a quarter tablet of toilet soap per month.

We also visited schools where many statistics of family life are kept, such as percentages of children with no father or no parents at all, also percentages of children with no shoes. Many children went to School barefooted. At school the children received a bowl of soup as a midday meal price ½. Mark which was free from rations.

Our job as Engineers in Berlin was the maintenance of the British Garrison and at this corruption of wall potentials. It was during one of these destruction jobs that we had our second loss in the Squadron, our Major and two N.C.O's lost their lives.

During the time I was in Berlin the troops were allowed two privileged leaves home per year, but in between those leaves we were allowed short leaves to the various countries surrounding us. I went on such trips to Belgium and Denmark – but that's another story!

George P. Belcher,
ex-Sapper, R.E.
British Troops, Berlin.

ooOoo

DRESS MAKING CLASS

Another Dress

Short Skirts Sheila Mahoney, Kathy ? Kathy

THE PARABLE OF THE PINS.

By M. Day

Life and the way people live it is likened to two pins that a tin box with a lot of other pins. Penelope Pin was a little thing, full of the joys of living. She strove always to be on top of the box, eager to be out at work. Percy Pin, on the other hand, was an idle good-for- nothing. He had found a cosy corner at the bottom of the box on the date he was born, and he had stayed there, lazing through the days, laughing and sneering at Penelope for the zest for work.

"You'll wear yourself out my girl, you'll be old before your time, mark my words." He'd said. To which Penelope would reply.

"And that would be better than just rusting away which is what you are doing."

In the evenings she would return to the box full of the day's adventure. She would bring Percy a morsel of silk or satin or, a length of thread for his supper and relate her tales, trying to make Percy realize what he was missing and how dull his life was. But he was too comfortable at the bottom of the box and would refuse to be drawn out. One evening Penelope returned home very excited and said to Percy.

"I've had such a lovely day taste this." She offered him a piece of white satin. Percy tasted and smacked his lips. "Any more where that came from?" He queried.

"Plenty... replied Penelope... if you like to get it for yourself. Why don't you come out with me tomorrow? We're working on a wedding gown and the bride is so beautiful it's so romantic." Percy grunted.

"Why should I work myself to the pinhead for food when you're willing to bring me all I need?"

"You're a lazy stupid old pin... s

aid Penelope in a rage... I've finished with you. Find someone else to bring you your daily bread." Percy laughed; he'd heard all that before.

Tomorrow and the next a Penelope would still return with tasty titbits for him, so why should he worry.

Next morning Penelope awoke full of excitement at the prospect of another days work on the wedding dress. Percy, as usual, was still sounding asleep. Suddenly there was a terrific vibration and over went the pin box and the pins found themselves scattered in all directions on the floor. The Dressmakers cat frightened out of her fifth life was crouched under a chair. Percy, after the shock of being so rudely awakened, looked around him and saw for the first time in his life the outside world. He saw the white satin, the beautiful bride and the buzz of activity. He turned to Penelope who had fallen quite near him and said.

"Gosh you're right; Pen old thing life looks very interesting.

I think I'll start living it."

"Well it's never too late to begin. Said Penelope. But how wrong she was -the dressmaker gathering up the pins saw

Percy, dull and rusty, and cast him aside. He heard her soft voice say.

"How did that get in there?" As she dropped him into the wastepaper basket.

The sad thing is that although it's often quite enough to hear a pin drop, it's never quite enough to hear one speak, so poor Percy's loud protest were unheard as he went to his doom. Penelope wept awhile, but she soon recovered. After all, it had been very tedious trying to make Percy live.

See the point?

ooOoo

WHY A CATHOLIC CLUB.

by

Monica Day.

Remember the saying "atmosphere is everything?" We have, most of us, been in the midst of all sorts of atmospheres - the homely one, an electric (!) the cold one and a warm one, but surely our favourite atmosphere is a Catholic one. In it, we feel at ease and in our own element. Recall the war years, when the great majority of us were away from home, how comforting it was to go to Mass on Sundays and once more feel the arms of the church around us! For sometimes, service quarters, the factory benches and ARP huts, however friendly and sociable, possessed everything but a Catholic atmosphere. During those years, did you ever experience rather a lost and "out of it all" feeding when you came out of church and saw those little gatherings of people old parishioners - talking to each other? In church, you were part of the congregation gathered together for one purpose, but outside the church you were a stranger and you didn't know a soul. How you longed to join one of those groups - I know I did. I used to think of St. Anne's Club and the Saint Christopher's Cycling Club and experience a terrific longing for home and the Catholic Social Atmosphere. We're very fortunate in Vauxhall, we have a flourishing Social Club, and so people moving in from other parishes can soon join those little groups outside St. Anne's on a Sunday morning.

Do we in Vauxhall really realize how very lucky we are? What could be more refreshing to our minds and souls, after a long and tiring day in a world which is becoming more and more non-Christian (I mean generally, so please don't come to me and tell me that in your office the staff always say a grace before their "elevenses")todrop into the Club and feel in your own atmospheres? I don't think any of us who haven't left our parish realize how very important and necessary a Catholic Club is.

We may go to Mass every day of the week and find spiritual refreshment, but if we belonged to a parish without a Social Club, how long would it take us to get to know any member of the congregation socially? Those members of the Club-less parish would probably have to find their amusement elsewhere at a local dance-hall, at the cinema or public House, and really, what could be more soul destroying to anyone but an ardent Christian? And, sad to state,there are many Catholics who, no doubt they may never miss mess on a Sunday or Holyday, are far from ardent, simply because they find their relaxation in an un-Catholic atmosphere. They may think fervently on their religion one Sunday and don't come into contact with it until the next. Their companions and close friends are non-Catholics, and though these friends may be good and sincere, they would be that much better for a Catholic if they gave him a Catholic outlook on life.

Those of us who are living in good Catholic homes, maybe do not need a Club quite so much as a person who is away from home and living in "digs" or a hostel. For the latter a Club would give them the family life they were missing, for their spiritual father would be there, all hand to help and advice. Then there is the "Boy meets Girl and live happily ever after" aspect. What are the chances of a Catholic boy meeting the Catholic girl at the local dance-hall or similar place of amusement? Rather remote, and therefore lies the danger, don't you think? Or haven't you ever thought about it please do, it's important to our Catholic youth.

It is our happy task, being the members of good Club, to help to give that Club and all Catholic social

Atmosphere and a welcome to all strange faces. And while you are contemplating you will surely think with gratitude of those people who have worked and are still working to make St. Anne's Social Club one of the best youth Clubs in London.

ooOoo

AMBITIONS COMPILED:

This following entry must have been directed at some - then Club members?

by A. Parsons & R. Bail.

Obviously relating to someone's quotes.

Curiosity was surely be the darts and to my inquiries for the ambitions of those members. Their full names will not appear for the claimants with the object of desire as in their own words they offer scope for identity if you all like me curious.

1. Now who would want ......*"To run a Harem?"*
2. He said he wanted ....*"To find out where to get cigs."* Strange to say he smokes a pipe and rolls cigs.
3. This person wants to play Table Tennis like Ernie Morgan only without breaking his neck. This person more often than not plays snooker on Thursday evening. Ernie breaks his neck.
4. *"I want to own the Beehive."* Usually has a ghost story to tell, he must wish to be stung.
5. I wish......*"To be a school Teacher."*.... Jolly Good I say.
6. I *"would like to run for England"* If hard work has anything to do with it, you will.
7. I*" want to find a Red Barn."* It is not for me to say!
8. I want *"To add a few more decoration to Barnet Wood Cafe."* Well I do not think the Boys will object.
9. I wish *"To Qualify"*..........*???* DETERMINATION SHOULD WIN.
10. I want *"To travel in a caravan"* ....Who wouldn't? I'm all for a holiday in Ireland.
11. I want *"To look like Claudette Colbert."* .....I cannot dispute hairstyles.
12. I want *"To avoid the clutches of women"* ......You are no hermit.
13. I want *"To go into Brockwell Park at 9:45 am. To play Netball."*..... I will not say it, I am too well informed.
14. I want *"To reach the top."* ......

You have I am finished on this page.

ooOoo

ODD WISDOM.

By R. Bail.

A WOMAN'S THOUGHTS.

They sat in silence for some time
"Of what are you thinking" He finally asked.
She blushed and fidgeted uneasily in her chair?
"Never mind, she replied. It's your business? It's your business to propose not mine."

HERE AND THERE.

Definition of a kiss: A course of procedure designed to produce a stoppage of speech at a moment when words are superfluous.

HER OWN FAULT.:-

Mistress: "Mary, don't let me catch you kissing the grocer's boy again."
Mary: "Lor, mum, I don't mean to, but you do bob around so."

BUSY BODIES.

A master of a ship called out. "Who is down below?" a boy answered'
'Will Sir'
'What are you doing?'
'Nothing Sir.'
'Is Tom there?'
'Yes said Tom.

'What are you doing?'
'Helping Will Sir.'

ooOoo

MUCH FOOTING IN THE MARCH

By
E Bremner

The mighty eleven were out on the field.
The game had already begun.
When hot and dusty forms were seen trailing along.
We supporters turned up for the fun.

The brilliant red sweater which first court and eye.
Was worn by our goalkeeper Paddy.
The linesman was dashing by waving his flag.
Or was it the pants of his daddy?

The game was exciting, at least at one end.
Where one or two goals had been scored.
But down at the other, with nothing to do.
The poor dears sat feeling quiet bored.

Our goalie, so bored soon deserted his post.
And wandered away on his own.
His opposite number, hard pressed and hard kicked.
Was certainly not left alone.

Spurred on by the cheers, our St. Anne's won the day.
A fact which surprised everyone
They marched off the field and then to reap their reward.
But found only TEA and a BUN.

When the victors are invited us back in the coach
We thought that we sensed something phoney
Still they soon forgot encouraging cheers
And left us to take shank's pony.

ooOoo

A NETBALL CAPTAIN'S NIGHTMARE

(Apologies to Lord Macauley)

But Elsie's brow was sad
And Elsie's voice was low
And darkly looked she at the ball
And darkly at the flow

Their might will be upon us
Before we make a pass
And if they once should force a scrum
Their speed will make us gasp

Then out spake a sprightly centre
The leader of the pack
To every team upon this earth
Defeat cometh soon or late
But how can we play better
Then facing fearful odds
With confidence of each in all
Seven strong determined "Bods"

Then out spake bold Patricia
Of Gaelic blood was she.
Now who will play on either hand
And when this came with me
Then forward came proud Elsie
All of Anglo Saxon blood
So I will play on the right hand
And push them in the mud.

Then a great shout behind them
From all the team arose
Proclaiming we were ready girls
And ready on our toes
And that brave band without fear or fret
Bull swiftly on their opponents net
But Kathleen slipped down in the wet
Whilst poising for a throw

Team still stood still and silent
And looked upon the foe's
As a great shouts of laughter
From all the crowd arose
The gallant captain led them off
Looking forlorn and dejected
They were greeted with supporters cries
Of it's no more than we expected!!

ooOoo

CANTEEN CALLING
by R Bail

It is a Place for two. Boy,
A Girl, yes they make tea for you.
With or without does not matter,

For this duty brings about a little chatter.
There you are together, what could be better
Than the Canteen Calling?

ooOoo

A SUPPORTER.
By R. Bail.

In preparation for a season in a Netball League the Girls of the Over- Twenties have been playing in at various times in the past few months. On a certain Saturday I decided to support them I arrived at the station to find that I was the only male to travel with the team. However, I did not let this situation deter me from proceeding on what was to be an experience, for apparently one member of the team was to wear a slip which another member had been using. When the discovery was really made I cannot say, but as it happened dimensions varied necessitating immediate adjustment. I found myself witnessing a sewing Class and a chase for the cotton which seemingly kept finding its way on the floor of the compartment, coupled with a master plan with which it was intended to win the game. Frankly I wondered whether I had gotten myself mixed up in the wrong carriage, for the happenings sounded something like this.-

'When I say one you pass to me.'
'Where are the scissors?'
'Your number is three.'
'I did not think she was as small as that.'
'Your number four.'
'Have you nearly finished?'
'We are nearly there.'
'If the other side get wise, we will change it'
Results of the game, the whistle blew in time for the Over-Twenties to win by 12 goals 11.
The writer still suffers from the strain completing the afternoon peeling Orange for the team!

ooOoo

DODDERER'S DITTY

Old boys, young girls, at least we are told
Venture out first is in spite of the cold
In route for a dance, a nag, or a huddle
Risking a scandal but game for a cuddle.

Two join in amusement the need of all folk
When once they pass through the club for a joke
Eventually the evening begins –
Now, people walk about with their teas and things,
Then to the hall is the call
You will play a game with hand and ball.

Crackle and babble die down as they leave
Lovers creep off, sweet nothing to breathe,

Under their arms sheets of carols are crammed
Believe it or not, a few doorsteps to be manned.

J.G.

ooOoo

TONGUE TWISTERS

Swim, Sam Swim,
Show Them You're Some Swimmer,
Six Sharp Sharks Are To Take Your Liver,
So Swim, Sam Swim.

The Six Sick Sheik's,
Six Sheep's Sick,

Till Tom Taught Tact To Tim,
Tim Talked Tosh To Tots.

ooOoo

A CHRISTMAS THOUGHT

Christmas comes but once a year,
When it comes we are all of good cheer,
First think of God and of his birth,
Then you may come down to earth,
And enjoy yourselves. --- G.P.

Dear members.

A happy Christmas and a bright and Prosperous New Year to you all.

Our Over 20 Club has been running now for nearly a year and we all feel it has been a great success. We have a membership at present of about 100, but new members come along every week.

During the year and activities have been varied, anything from indoor cricket to a discussion on "Britain's trade."

The committee has from time to time been faced with immemorable problems, large and small. That policy has been to make as few rules as possible and only as the necessity arises, so that our present constitution has remained flexible and, as it were, "tailor-made" to the needs of the club.

We are at present planning the club's first Christmas Party, we hope it will be an enjoyable evening and will be if you all rally round and do your bit.

I should like to take this opportunity of thanking Father Madden for his help and advice and also for the way yesterday aside let us run the club ourselves. I should also like to thank the committee for their artwork and cooperation, also club members for the way they have helped to carry out the committee suggestions, et cetera. Last but no means least I should like to thank Mr Bailey for all the time and energy he has spent on the club, and for the crime way he has treated us.

Once again wishing you all a happy Christmas.

Carmel M. Denney Chairman.

ooOoo

– 281 –

Dear members.

It is fitting that I as Editor, should devote this corner to those members who have "Thumped" Home the joy to be found in the Club, for the free expression a greater degree of sincerity is born and with a sincerity of purpose for the good of all. So we look forward to the New Year with a high degree of enthusiasm for gradually the Club as climbed over its teething trouble, and is now you are a on the road bold endeavour purposefully intent on achieving greater success.

Finally a word of thanks to those who have worked, mainly the magazine committee in typing and formulating some into a magazine of interesting experience and Club humour. Thank you all.

Yours sincerely. Editor.

ooOoo

Brendan O' Dowde. Visited the Club in June 1948 when he was appearing at the London Palladium

Fr. ? Brenda O' Dowde- Fr. Healy

Brendan Singing in the common room recognised faces in crowd
Mike Plant (water damage) ? Bert MacAvoy ? Paddy McMonagle- Bernard ? - Tom O'Neil- Kathy Anderton-
Don Skinner- Roy Summersby – Pat Thomas - Eileen McMonagale - Angela Moran

ooOoo

FRANKIE HOWERD. OBE.

Comedian who after the war appeared on the Radio show Variety Bandbox and several other Radio shows, also appeared in a comic script of the Film Fun.

December 1950 Father Madden invited Frankie Howard to open a Jumble sale on a Saturday afternoon. There was a picture in the Local South London press of Frankie holding up a child's wooden tricycle that he was auctioning with a smiling Father Madden beside him. His appearance certainly drew in the Crowds to the Clubs This was his first appearance. He did it several times Later.

Frankie came all the way on his Trike

'Titter Ye Not' '

Oh well! Please yourself"

You can't have it. It's Mine

Three Little Fishes & the Momma Fishy too.

Any advance on Sixpence?   *Bob.; "You Hum it ". Frankie "I'll Play it!"*

[Authors Note]. Unfortunately, from 1947 onwards, the issues of the Youth Club Annals are no longer in existence. Whether they were produced or not I cannot say, as I never ever saw one during my time as a member. Therefore without their aid, it is difficult to follow the events of the Clubs activities, in a chronological sequence. Nevertheless, with the aid of many photographs from the Clubs Albums, those of visiting Artiste together with photos of outings and a few Holiday trips abroad submitted by old members, (without any comments or date). And relying on my own recollections of Club activities and the friends I became involved with, l will use with somewhat of a "Writers" licence to fit the photos into a suitable entitled passages of text, or events of the Clubs activities, as they occurred from the 50's onwards. My apologies for any that may deviate from the actual event.

ooOoo

YOUTH CLUB 1949- 1955. +
Youth Club
COMMITTEE MEMBERS 1949-1952

1949

S. Talbut Hon. Sec	E. Healy.
K. Anderton.	K. Daly.
B. Driver.	O' O'Sullivan
J. Healy	G. Belcher.
B Jeamonds	V. Le. Grande.
D. Rivers.	M. Martinelli
R. Walsh.	

1950.

D. Rivers Hon. Sec.	E. Healy.
K. Anderton.	P. Burton.
S. Mahoney.	A. White.
J. Healy.	G. Belcher.
B. Davies	P. Frost.
H. Spanswick.	

1951.

G. Belcher. Hon. Sec. E. Healy.
K. Anderton. N. Falco.
S. Mahoney. K. Weakner
J. Healy. E. Ford.
D. Rivers. D. Skinner.

1952.

G. Belcher. Hon Sec E. Healy.
K. Anderton. B. Jeamonds
S, Mahoney D, Rivers.
J. Healy. J. Dixon.
E. Ford. P. Frost.
K. Millet. W. Tough

CLUB MEMBERSHIP

What can be read in the previous passages, were basically related about the return of Old members to St. Anne's Club, yet for the younger new member, it was a period of time when they were trying to regain their purpose in life with the reopening of the schools in a devastated London. Wherever you went there were huge bomb sites and piles of rubble. With practically nowhere to go to play football but the streets where you lived, except the local Parks, on their enclosed Cinder pitch's, big enough for two and maybe three football pitches marked out and surrounded by high wire woven fences, a playground with swings etc., and a shallow paddling pond for the Kids to paddle around in. It was the era of mass followings of Professional Football teams. On a Saturday afternoon all grounds would be packed solid with thousands of football fans attending, amongst them young lads eager to see their team idols play football. The only other entertainment for them was the Saturday morning pictures and the Radio programmes Dick Barton and Children's Hour. Through various sources (Different Parishes) the word got around, that there was a Youth Club in Vauxhall, that had two football and Netball teams, and were open seven nights a week. It was like a magnet drawing young people from all over South London, school friends, relations; sometimes groups of friends joined the Club together.

Obviously many from St. Anne's school made up a bulk of the 1945/8 membership. The MacDermotts, Wilberhams, Greens, Blackburn, Smith; Richardson's - to mention a few. A group known as the 'Stockwell crowd' – hailed from St. Helen's Parish Stockwell. Margaret Furlong, Jane Titheridge, Sheila Monkton, Helen Hall, The McMonagles plus others? From St. Josephs School in Pitman Street in the Parish of the Sacred Heart Camberwell - The Bremers, Connelly's, Healey's, Pettifor's, Marconi's, Marcantonio's, Martinnellis plus others. From St Philips and James Larkhall Rise. The Ager Boys, Keith, Lou and Tony. - From St. Phillip and St James Herne Hill Parish. Jackie, Michael and Kaye, Plant, cousin Pat Thomas, Joe Connelly, Jimmie, Marie and Theresa Clinton. From St Joseph's Upper Norwood came Don Skinner, who caught a No 2 bus to Vauxhall. Another group joined from the Carshalton parish. No Doubt the most usual modes of transport was by Shank's Pony or, catch a local tram/bus or, whatever method of transport you had to get to the Club. Early In January 1949 my Brother Mike introduced me into the Club and I remained a member up to January 1955, when I was conscripted into the Army and returned back in 1957. To a different state of affairs as related later.

"There were many Girls who joined from the Notre Dame School at St. Georges."

The following are extracts of a few memoirs, submitted by old members, but there was one section of a memoir, which I thought was an excellent refection, on why young people were attracted to join the Youth Club. Submitted by Derek Rivers, its the first part of his memoirs. His other paragraphs are related elsewhere under their appropriate heading.

Derek Rivers Reflects:

The first reflection I have of anything to do with St. Anne's Parish. Was when my Mother told the tale of her forthcoming marriage to my Dad, who was a non -Catholic. That, entailed a meeting with Bishop Brown. My dad realising the problem asked the Bishop about converting to the faith. Whereas Bishop Brown questioned.

'Will it make you a better person?' To which Dad Replied.

'I don't think so.'

'Why. Bother?' Replied the 'Bish.'

During the years of the war my childhood was spent in Dagenham till 1945. When we moved to Clapham. I hated living in London and spent all the weekdays extremely miserable until Friday. Every weekend I would cycle from Clapham, on an old bike, via Stockwell, the Oval, Elephant & Castle, Borough, London Bridge, The City. Mile End Road, on my way to Dagenham. To my Gran's and spend two wonderful days with my friends, before returning on the Sunday by bike of course. Quite a round trip and not a recommended method of transport through the city even in those days. For two years I kept that up. I was so depressed, became extremely ill, was hospitalised and nearly died. The Doctor's told mum.

'If. Derek did not find a new life living in London. Then I'm afraid he would face the risk of yet another crisis.'

However my Aunt Louise, who lived in a flat above a Doctors surgery, in Harleyford Road opposite the St. Anne's Settlement, could see from one of her front windows, the antics of a young lad in the house on the opposite side of the road, who waved his arms about as he conducted an imaginary orchestra to the music of a gramophone record. That young lad was none other than Eric Blackburn. So amused by his antics, my Aunt told mum of the young lad opposite, who also used to go in and out of the Settlement with several other young lads from the school and found out that it was a youth Club they attended.

So suggested. 'Why don't you get Derek to join?'

Mum did decide and I was taken to the Settlement and was reluctantly sent through the door. And from that moment on my life change Dramatically.

Inside, I was met by Father Madden who introduced me to Harry Spanswick and Eric Blackburn. As one does I spoke to Eric about my Aunt Louise seeing him conducting his Orchestra?

'Heh Eric. My Aunt Louise who lives opposite you used to watch you waving your arms about conducting she thought you were very funny.'

'Does she. Well I like classical music?'

'Yes. She told my mum about you, That's how I joined the Club.'

'Good for her. Do you like that kind of music its classical?'

'Well Yes. I can play the piano as well.'

This was the start of a great friendship between the three of us. On one occasion we went to the Albert Hall to see a Classical Concert the Baritone singer was??????????????

I never dreamed of how much fun and happiness I was too enjoy in their company and the experiences that I would encounter throughout my eight years as a member of St. Anne's Club.

There was Snooker, Table Tennis, Football, Fencing, Rambles, and Coach Trips to the Coast, Holidays Abroad, and Dancing Classes. All readily available with a wonderful bunch of young people, nobody could imagine the contrast to my earlier way of life. So read on: The following are snippets of those experiences that I was too enjoy and relish. (see under appropriate heading).

ooOoo

Frank O'Sullivan (Canon) 7th. May 2010.

In 1937 my family moved from Battersea to a new LCC (London County Council) flat in New Park Road. Brixton where we enjoyed for the first time the luxury of a bathroom and a small kitchenette. Our flat overlooked a large House owned by the Southwark Catholic Children's Society; it Housed teenage Boys, a Housekeeper and her family and a resident Priest Fr. Barry. Later in the war the home was bombed and the Priest, the Housekeeper, and several of the Boys were killed.

I joined the Youth Club at Corpus Christie Church on Brixton Hill, because my cousins were members. On 3rd. September 1939, the day the Second World War broke out, I came out of the church to hear the announcement that war had been declared, almost immediately the sirens sounded, which we took to mean the Germans planes were coming. In the event no German Planes actually came until May 1940 when the Germans invaded Belgium, the Low Countries and France.

Early in 1940 we moved into a new council flat in Dorset Road and soon after this my cousin Tom introduced me to St. Anne's Youth Club. I was called up into the RAF in November 1941. Due to the ravages of age, my recollection of the Club is somewhat confused. I am not sure that some of my recollections refer to the time before I went into the RAF and the times I rejoined the Pella Club after the war.

In the early 1940's I remember learning to dance at the Streatham Locarno (Now Caesar's Palace)so that I could enjoy the Saturday night dances at the Club, until the Blitz put an end to them. I remember huddling together near the front door of the Club in the early days of the Blitz I remember coming out of the church on the 15th. September 1940 the most significant day in the Battle of Britain and travelling down Harleyford Road towards the Oval where a German Pilot had landed by parachute because his plane had been shot down *(it intended to bomb Buckingham Palace but crashed into Victoria station there are various stories about the Pilot being killed by local house wife's at the Oval)*. The sky was filled with vapour trails as scours of battles were fought in the sky. I went to work in Smithfield on the 30th. December 1940, the morning after the night in which much of the City of London was destroyed by fire and by bombs The building were left to burn because the fire hydrants had been bombed and there was no water.

As the war progressed members left to join the armed services or Land Army. They came back telling us of their experiences. I spent four and a half years in the RAF as a navigator hunting submarines, and despite some exciting moments we (fortunately) never found any. So far as I know only Peter Perla was killed. He died in the Battle of Kohima on the border of India and Burma. The Victory gained in this battle marked a turning point in the war in the Far East. 4,000 Allied Soldiers died in the battle – Indian British and African. And 5,700 Japanese. I remember them whenever I hear the Kohima Epitaph. On Armistice Day. 'When you go home tell them of us and say, for your tomorrow we gave our today.'

After I was demobbed in June 1946. I re-joined the Pella Club ; the new Name for the older members of the Youth Club the Club was open every night, which meant there was always somewhere to go. There were lots of activities: Football, Netball Club s, Table Tennis competitions, Debate and Drama Groups I remember taking Part in Paul Vincent Carroll's play 'Shadow and Substance'. Rudy Perla had one of the leading roles. He later joined the Silesian Order and eventually became Novice Master. Sadly he died in his mid-fifties. I joined the Church Choir, we were trained by Bill Hyde, the Choir Master of Westminster Cathedral, Bishop Brown always popped in on a Monday evenings to listen to us and say a few words. We sang at the Sunday Evening Services. Fr. Bob Madden. was Chaplain to the Catholic Stage Guild. I remember listening to a piano recital in the games room on \ Sunday afternoon it was given by Solomon, one of the top international pianists. We also had visits from Anne Shelton, whose popularity as a singer spanned the 40's –60's. We also had a visit from Danny Kaye, a comedian, popular for his part in the Pied Piper of Hamelin and of the song of the Ugly Duckling. *Out of the film: Hans Christen Andersen.*

After the war I planned to train as a Company Secretary but my plans were Dramatically changed on the 19th. March 1948 the Feast of St. Joseph. I went to Mass that morning and on the way to work the idea of becoming a Priest was planted in my head by the Holy Spirit. I'm sure the Holy Spirit planted it there because I was very busy looking for a wife among the members of the Club, having suffered a broken engagement during the war. Fr.

Madden sent me to see Archbishop Amigo, who sent me to St. Augustine's, a House attached to the Presbytery at the English Martyrs Church in Walworth., where eight of us continued working and studied Latin every night for two years prior to going to the Seminary. I went to Wonersh in 1950 and was ordained in 1956. I remember the Pella Club reunion in 1956 to celebrate the 21st anniversary of the setting up of the Club. It was held in a small hall in North Cray Road, near Bexley. There were fifty couples present most had met at the Youth Club.

I lost contact with Club members until I retired from the Parish Ministry in 1998 and was asked to celebrate the Mass at the Annual Reunion. On the death of Bob Madden I was asked to become the Club Chaplain.

In 2004 I visited a Priest Friend of mine, Fr. Michael Benjamin, who had served as an Assistant Priest in Camberwell in 1962. He was recuperating in the Nuffield Hospital in Ashtead after suffering a stroke. I went to the Presbytery in Ashtead in order to get a host to give him Holy Communion. I had a long Chat with the Parish Priest and discovered the Church, the hall and the Presbytery had been erected on the site on which a House had stood the House in which Club members enjoyed many happy weekends during and after the war.

Note for concluding para. See LEGACY @ end

<u>O</u>oOoo

Ernie Morgan reflects: **1942-1953. <u>YOUTH & PELLA CLUB</u>**

I was introduced to St. Anne's Youth Club by Bernard Driver in 1942.

Bernard & I had been close friends from a very young age when our families lived in a small street opposite the Catholic Church in Dockland, Bermondsey.

In 1937 the London County Council demolished most of the House in the street and the Driver family were re-Housed in Alverstone House Kennington Oval. In spite of this we still kept in touch and on the outbreak of World War II we were evacuated with our schools. Bernard to Lewes and I went to Brighton. Returning home in 1942 we met up again & started enjoying the facilities of a wonderful Club. Representing at football, cricket & Table Tennis. We were involved in many other activities including ballroom dancing, drama Class & the concert party with Mr. Hyde. Who can describe Mr. Hyde and the way he produced those plays?

The Pella Club - named after Bishop Brown who was the Bishop of Pella – was formed to accommodate those Club members who, when they reached the age of 21, still wanted to come to the Club, and any other people who were 21 and wanted to join in the activities of the Club. As far as I can remember the Pella Club met on Thursday evenings

Saturday 8th. May.

This date is very poignant to me.

On this day 62 years ago Bernard & I spent the day in the Oval Watching cricket between Surrey CCC and the Australian Touring side.

In the evening we went to the Club dance and it was there that I had my first dance with Mary Kennedy. We were married in October 1949 Mary Died in 2002.

ooOoo

Harry Spanswick. Reflects 2010.

My name is Harry Spanswick and I was born on 19. 07. 1931. In Lambeth in the parish of St. Anne's Vauxhall. This has been a major influence in my life and all the events of my life are rooted in this fact.

My Grandmother, Helen Susan Embleton, was also born in Lambeth in1886 and she was orphaned at eight years of age. When her father a Thames Waterman, died in 1894 and she was taken in by neighbours, possibly a local parishioner by the name of Aunt Kate Stack. My Grandmother attended the original Catholic School in Leopold Street when the school fee was 2 pence for each day attended, and was carefully watched by Father William Brown. She recalled being with the first twenty-five Girls taken to the new school building and walking over scaffold boards past the Presbytery, and how exciting they all were.

When she was twenty years old she married Henry Fredrick Spanswick, one of six children from a devout Anglican family and Father Brown was not too pleased about it. Their married produced twelve children, six Boys and six Girls, and my father was the oldest. He commenced school at St Anne's in 1911 and was followed by his siblings and many of their children followed on many a total of eleven uncles and aunts, fifteen grandchildren and ten great grandchildren: the last being my youngest daughter who finished in 1985, some ninety years from when my grandmother started there.

As a stranger to London, my sister took me along to St. Anne's Youth Club, then overseen by Fr. Bob Madden, and I had the opportunity to meet many other youngsters of my own age, to hear music, learn to dance, play football and cricket, engage in Athletics and gymnastics, as well as meet face to face with many famous stage stars and musicians from America and England. Most importantly, I met Josie Course who became my dance partner, my girlfriend, as well as my pen pal during the two years spell spent in the R.A.F. On National Service (1951-1953) and we were married at St. Anne's in 1954. We continued to live in the parish and our four daughters attended the school, sang in the Church Choir, joined the Brownies and Guides and made many good and loyal friends.

In the meantime most members of the Spanswick family had left Vauxhall: Josie had become a Teacher (Commencing her training in St. Anne's) and I had been working in engineering in the Fleet Street Printing industry, where I remained for thirty two years.

Note for concluding Para. See LEGASY @ end

ooOoo

Mike Plant reflects and collaborated by Mary McBride (nee Macdermott):

In 1944. Our family had returned back to reside in Herne Hill, an area where cousin Pat Thomas also lived. Pat was still at school in Kennington along with cousins Peter and John Macdermott. Mary Macdermott also had attended the school, and was already at work. Mary related the incident, about the three of them playing truant from the school. As the story goes, Mary was attending night-school at the same school, to be taught Short- hand and Typing. One evening she was stopped by a Teacher, who asked how her brothers, Peter and John were? Mary replied. 'Fine. Why?'

"Well we haven't seen them at school for several months!!'

When Mary questioned her brothers It transpired that the three of them had been going to the Pictures in Brixton and Camberwell Green. They got a thrashing from their mother and were marched back to the school by their father Peter, who told the teacher to give them another thrashing.

[Authors note: A slight repeat of Mikes previous entry but relating to a comment made by Mary Macdermott about her brothers Peter and John.

Josie Spanswick (nee Course) Reflects (1936-2010)

St. Anne's became part of my family's life when I was four years old and we moved from Bermondsey to live on the Duchy of Cornwall estate at Kennington. from then on St. Anne's Church, school and settlement were central to my formation, physically, socially, spiritually, intellectuality and emotionally. I am ever thankful for the wonderful foundation and nurturing that the community of St. Anne's gave me and for the presence of so many caring Priests, teachers, parishioners and friends that I encountered.

Whilst at secondary School I attended St. Anne's Church and joined various activities and groups (netball team, drama society, St. Anne's Guild, processions performances and choir.)

During the late teens I joined the youth Club and again participated in a range of activities including ballroom dancing and Old Tyme dancing, sports and activities, trips to the sea and countryside. Soon after the war ended a trip to Rome and Venice was organised- truly a unique experience at that time of austerity, rationing and recovery. Trips abroad were to continue some years after. Subsequently, many good friendships were made and have indeed become life long relationship. I met my husband Harry Spanswick (who also attended the school and was evacuated to Reading) at the youth Club and along with many other couples have been blessed with a lifelong commitment of 56 years to date. We were married in St, Anne's Church. Our Family of four daughters all attended the school and they retained many of their early friendships from this period. They were all baptised, received the sacraments whilst at St. Anne's and often share their fond memories of their time in the parish. Both My Parents had funeral Masses at the Church, as did my Grandmother and many other extended family Members.

ooOoo

Joining the Club. Eileen (nee McMonagle) – Married John Healy 1949.

I was invited to join the Club by Howard Saunders, a non-catholic member whom I met at the Tara Irish Club in Brixton. When I visited I was surprised by how many people I remembered from St Anne's School. The Club was a revelation. There was always something to do; many interesting activities and young people; it was within our limited price range; and available every evening and week-ends except for Thursdays (which was a boys only night, a condition required in order to affiliate to the National Federation of Boys Clubs). That was fine; after all, we had to wash our hair sometime. We were encouraged to assume responsibilities for other activities. At committee meetings, we could suggest other courses, air our grievances, ask for help and feel we were making a difference.

I joined in Drama, Netball, Dancing – Modern – Ballroom & Olde Tyme, outings to Bracklesham Bay and Camber Sands. Annual CYC Athletics,

Guild of St. Agnes Club etc. in fact, my mother offered to send my bed to Vauxhall..

John & I never joined the Pella Club as we remained involved in the youth club. We married in 1949 and had a small flat with my parents. We moved to Eltham in 1953 and continued for a while but the travelling was difficult and we wanted a family.

About 1956/7 Father Pierce contacted us and as we were available and had transport we returned to help with netball and football. We participated in club holidays and some social activities until we really did retire in 1961.

One of our last functions was to help Fr. Pierce when he invited Pella club members to bring their families to the Club on a Saturday for an indoor picnic.

I think it was by verbal invitation. They were asked to bring a plate of goodies, and we provided the basic tea, orange etc. What I found fascinating was as the children came in with the goodies (good club training, I expect) looking at them and guessing to whom they belonged. It was an enjoyable occasion and I think we may have repeated this just once more.

Looking back, at the many long term friendships we have maintained we were very fortunate. We were allowed to develop within the safe atmosphere of the Club surrounded by good humour and love. Many members married, and went on to be of service and help to their Parish Priests, as Lay Readers and Ministers of the Eucharistic. as well as giving other practical help probably because of our own experience with our renown club leaders. John and I always enjoyed friendship with the many priests in our parish over. the last 59 years and know that it started at Vauxhall.

ooOoo

Joe Plant reflects:

I joined the Club in September 1949. I had passed an Engineering entrance exam to the Borough Beaufoy in Black Prince Road. There I met Phil Darcy, Eddie Buchanan, Billy Lyons, we were all in the same Class in Bailey House, all Catholics and lived in Vauxhall. As we all played for the school football team. I invited them to join St. Anne's, that they did, and soon we were all playing for the Junior 'B' team of St. Anne's. At the Club I met Brian O'Sullivan, Arthur Course, Tom (Junior) O'Neill, Tom Marcantonio who introduced me to Derek Beamish, who went to St. Joseph's in Camberwell. Derek, was about nine months older than me and in the class above me at St. Joseph's. It was only through St Anne's, we met socially, which began a life-long friendship, soon to be joined by Kenny Richardson (Jimmy's younger Brother) and Brian Jenkins (Marian Sheean's cousin). We all lived within a few miles radius of the Club and when we were not riding bikes, to Brighton, Southend, Virginia Waters, long weekend trips to the Isle of

Wight and in the Summer the weekly evening cycling trip to the top of Reigate hill, a rest before turning to race back to the Clock Tower at Stockwell. We walked everywhere; a favourite hike on Sunday, after Mass at St. Anne's was a trip to the American Doughnut bakery, underneath Waterloo Bridge, on the South Bank, just to buy and gorge ourselves with fresh Ring Dough-nuts, then back home for dinner. Then the evening visit to the Club to Dance. Another venue, was the Battersea Fun Fair. The Club even organised trips to Southend for a day in the Kursal, just to spend your money on the fairground rides, watch the Wall Of Death Riders, eat Winkles, shrimps, candy floss and buy the usual, 'Kiss me Quick' hat, however without success!

All were employed in different types of work; I cannot remember any Club member that was unemployed. I started work as a Trainee Draughtsman earning £ 2-10/- per week out of which I gave my mother £1 for my bed and board, the rest was spent on paying for a bike and the odd drink or two in the Beehive (over 18 of course). I was the only one who did not smoke, the others, only affording to buy a packet of five Weights or Woodbines, and if flush, a packet of Spangles and Five Turf. The then new brand of cigarettes, nevertheless, as soon as they lit up, all began coughing their lungs up, it was pitiful to watch, as they with tears in their eyes spluttered. "It's gone down the wrong way."

The scene of social activity in London was changing fast., which provided us with a complete new lease on life. The West End was vibrant, big motion pictures to see, there was nightlife take your pick at dance halls dancing and jiving (Forbidden in the Club). Derek, Junior (Tom O'Neil) and I, with money, we had earned by the sweat of our brows in our pockets, were into the Jazz scene and used to frequent the Jazz Clubs of Soho, the Flamingo, 51 Club and the Star Club. It was a world of freedom that we lavished upon and enjoyed to the fullest. Nevertheless, within a short period of time that was to cease. The CALL-UP.

ooOoo

Pat Flynn Refects:
Main activity was ballroom dancing lessons, with a monthly dance on Saturday. When Jiving & the "Creep" arrived they were frowned upon. Also Johnny Ray's 'Oh What A Night It was'. Great deal of sporting interest, football Table Tennis,
Highlight of the year was a trip to Bracklesham Bay
Janet Kember married Patrick Flynn at St. Anne's on Easter Sunday (21st. April 1957) and wore the wedding dress that she made at St. Anne's sewing Classes & she also made her going away outfit. Father Pierce was going to announce this from the Pulpit but forgot!!
About that time most of the young men went off to do their National Service.
Lots of Stars visited. Anne Shelton, Max Bygraves, Billy Daniels, Danny Thomas.
At the end of the Club evening prayers were always said

Eileen Coburn - Joan Woodams - Maria Caluori

Joan Woodams married Pat Butler

Mike Plant -Bert MacAvoy- Peter Martinelli -Tony Maconi

Boys: Toni Maconi- John Healy
Girls: Helen - Peggy - Kathy

Group in Club Tom Lewis rest ?

Three of the Girls?

Tom Marcantonio   *John MacDermott- Bill Tough - Jimmy Richardson &?*   *Mary Chance Josie Course*
Ron Lovell - Gilda Marcantonio - Joe Plant.

There was a weekly fee to pay, cost can't remember? But! all members entered the Club through the main entrance. There to face a barrier. "A Table" at the end of the vestibule, adjacent to the door of the Canteen, with only sufficient access between it and the adjacent wall. Behind the Table sat the Keeper. "**George Belcher.**" Fortunately, If you were all paid up on your subs? Permission to enter was granted. Then you would squeeze your way through the access. If you had not paid your subs, you were Not permitted. SO. it was shell out time. George was a stickler for dues. Nevertheless, I only got away with it on one occasion. That was in February 1957? (explanation later).

In addition to the members, there were other people who were associated with the Club, Bill Bailey the caretaker, Mr. Hyde the M/C: Ted Locke with his cheeky face. Pat Locke's father: Ted was the 'medicine man' of the Football Team he used to run up and down the line, with a bucket of water and the magic sponge, ready to administer his wet sponge at any time.

Later in the early fifties a group from St. Georges Parish at North Kennington joined the Club. They were known as the St. George's Mob. They used to walk all the way from North Kennington. When I was attending night-school at the Borough Poly. I would catch a 77 bus from Waterloo to Vauxhall, and during the Smog's I would get a tube from Kennington North to the Oval them walk to the Club.

The only Club member that I remember owning a car was Arthur Course who purchased a 2nd. Hand Ford Zephyr? Circa 1953. Motorbikes Ron Lovell had a Triumph 500 and suffered a bad crash? Bill Tough bought a LANCHESTER then a Rolls Royce??

However the Clubs principle activity was to encourage youths, to take up sporting and indoor activities, such as Ballroom Dancing, Table-Tennis, Snooker, Darts Fencing, Keep-fit etc. Outside Sports: Netball, Football, Cricket, Athletics Hikes and Cycling, The Club was affiliated to the NFBC (National Federation of Boys Clubs) and their football league system, was based on those of the Football Association. Competing for Shields, Cups and medals.

The Time Table printed on the rear page of the 'Thump' Magazine provides a good guide to the Club's Weekly activity schedule as shown below:-

ST. ANNE'S CLUB
VAUXHALL

TIME TABLE
1948-1949

SUNDAY	MONDAY	TUESDAY	WEDNESDAY	THURSDAY	FRIDAY	SATURDAY
Football or Cricket. Netball.	5.50—7.15 Guild of St. Agnes (Girls, 11-14)	6.30—8 Junior Boys' (14-17) P.T., Boxing, Games, etc.	7—9 Keep Fit (for Girls)	6.30—8 Junior Boys' (14-17) P.T., Boxing, Games, etc.	7.30—9.30 Dramatics (Mixed)	2.30 Netball
7.45 p.m. Social Old Time Dancing, Discussion, Concert, Play, etc.	7-9 Choir (Mixed)	7.30—9.30 Coaching and Training for Football	7—9 Arts and Crafts (Mixed)	8—10.30 Over Twenties Club Only Special Programme	8—9 Irish Dancing (Mixed)	8—11 Dance Special Membership
	7.15—8.15 Ballroom Dancing Class (Mixed)	9.30—10 Billiards, etc.	9.15—10 Language Group Italian (Mixed)		9—10 Dancing, Table Tennis etc.	
	8.30—8.50 Benediction or C.O.M. Meeting		9—10 Dancing. etc.		9—10 (once a month) Discussion of Recent Films	
	9—10 Dancing, Billiards, Table Tennis, etc.					
	9.15—10 Scripture (Mixed)					

Also—Hiking, Swimming, Cycling, Running, Theatre Groups, Magazine, Week-end Holidays, Retreats, Holidays Abroad, Tennis, Outings, Parties, Etc.

ooOoo

THE NOTICE BOARD.

THE OLD NOTICE BOARD

OVER TWENTIES.

As the above Time Table shows. Most evenings there was always something going on at the Club. The Notice Board placed in the most convenient place informed all, of any Outing Ramble proposed Holiday trip abroad, The names of those selected for the Football & Netball teams. Meetings or anything that was associated with the Clubs Activities. were there for all to read and take note of, so, there was little need for information by word of Mouth. Any week day during a year, the Settlement Clinic was open Monday to Saturday, and the Club was open every night from seven till ten 'o'. clock. On Thursday night that was the night for the "Over-Twenties" members of the Pella Club. Many of the Classes were subsidised by the London County Council (LCC) as it was known then. There was a minimum number required to keep the Classes going, which was rarely obtained. Eileen Healy (nee McMonagle) a member of the Club's Committee remembers the occasions when the L.C.C. inspectors came round. They had to dash around, moving people from Class to Class, to make sure there were enough members present in each Class. It was quite funny really, as one night I and a few others were in the Foil Fencing Class, held in the School Hall when Eileen appeared and we were rustled out to join a Dancing Class with plimsolls on??? It was a must to all Males attending Dancing Classes, that they were to wear 'patent dance shoes'. and the girls suitable attire. On one occasion Maurice Green, who was always playing Table Tennis. (Maurice "did not" like dancing) But he was stopped playing by Eileen and ushered into the Dancing Class at the other end of the Hall. To be taught the steps in plimsolls, still holding a T/T bat in his upright hand.

Every night after a few prayers, the Club closed at ten o'clock. Everyone would walk down to the Oval tube station; too carry on talking, until gradually in pairs they drifted off home. Even during the pea soup fogs when you could not see your hand in front of your face. (I think we the boys, willingly, held more Girls hands. 'To Lead Us The Way.' As if we didn't know). It was a ritual, which for many years had occurred and continued. For whatever reason. I do not know?

ooOoo

THE DANCE HALL.

The Hall was quite big with plenty of space for many couples to dance around. At the top end for the Darts and Table Tennis area and storage for all the fold up tables and chairs, the stacks of chairs, were a source of annoyance when the T/T ball was lost behind them? The T/T Table was folded up and kept in the Leaders Room as was George Belchers Table. Access to the stage at the opposite end was by a free moving set of four steps, the stage was the place for a rather large radiogram, which frequently needed the needles to be changed, also home to an ancient wheelchair and an upright piano. Derek Rivers and Bill Tough somehow, would place some silver paper between the hammers and the wire strings, to make it sound like a Zither, (remember the Theme from the Third man Harry Lime?) Then the pair of them would bang out 'Chopsticks.' Much to the delight and applause from the onlookers.

I do not know what happened to the Wheelchair but it was a good prop for Plays.

Mike Plant Toni Maconi sat in Wheelchair & Bert MacAvoy

In the hall, a kind of segregation occurred with the Girls, standing on the left hand side, pensively waiting to be asked for a dance, whilst the Boys, would stand on the right. When the music started to play, there was a rush to take a fancied partner to dance.

It was used for Dancing Competitions, Plays, Visiting Celebrities, Jumble sales and any other function, that required a good area to accommodate a large audience. Nevertheless, for all members, it was necessary, to attend at least two Classes the Club provided.

Joe Plant reflects:

On a Tuesday Night in the Hall. Sessions of P.T. and Football training took place. First the P.T. (the coir mats, Box Horse, spring board etc. stored outside the Girls cloakroom, were carried out into the hall.) PT began with the usual physical jerks, running around the Hall, then the use of Box Horse, spring board and some mats. Our PT instructor was rather small in stature. I think an ex –Army PTI. Anyway he used to get everyone in turn to do the leaps over the Box Horse, and do what they called a Flying Angels. A fast run up to the spring board, bounce onto it, with outstretched arms soar over the box. On the other side he would stand waiting to catch you around the waist area. However, I being very small and agile, used to carry out this Flying Angel lark, until on one occasion I went too high. The PTI, misjudging me. Caught me around the ankles, bowling the pair of us over and crashed into the stage. Amid the mirth that followed, he declared there would be no more Flying Angels? He was more embarrassed than I was.

At the end of that session, a 'viscous' match of football was played, for twenty minutes with a Medicine Ball. One goal was the hole in the stage, whilst the goal at the far end, was a turned up Table. Two teams would be picked and the game would start. At some stage 'Buddy Higgins' would stand on the ball whilst someone would try to kick it from under his foot, he fending off anyone trying, very few succeeded! After that session it was to go running along the South Embankment as far as Westminster Bridge, cross over and back down the North side all the way back to Vauxhall Bridge then the Club. (That included running during a London Fog.) In Charge of that romp was Joe Dixon. 'he was tall' In his stocking feet he was six foot six. I think he was a trainee to become a Referee and was always eager to blow his whistle. No RED Cards in those days.

On one occasion we represented the Club, at a running event organised by the London Federation of Boys Clubs. We changed at Wellington Barracks, ran all the way down towards Whitehall, across the Horse Guards Parade, up the Mall, to Buckingham Palace, and were addressed by H.H. Prince Philip, stood on a Dias back at the end of the Mall. Then returned to change at Wellington Barracks.

ooOoo

DANCING CLASSES

With its existing facilities of a sizable dancehall, there was a period when the Club had different types of dancing classes each week e.g. Irish Step Dancing: Mary Macdermott, Jackie Plant, Eileen McMonagle, Patricia Macdermott plus a few others. There was Old Tyme Dancing and Modern Ballroom Dancing to the music of Victor Sylvester. Most popular was the - Modern Ballroom Classes. Beginning with the Bronze Medal, those keen enough graduated through to Silver Medal then Gold. 'Formation Dancing' teams were formed to compete in the London Ballroom Competitions. For those gaining proficiency medals in the three categories, Sunday morning Medal Classes were held in the Hall. The Club also was host to other Dancing Competitions on the London circuit, whilst others were held in other venues, one such place was the Warwick Club in Pimlico. Obviously members went to support the St. Anne's Dancing teams as per the photos below.

During the 46-49 period the teachers were Mr and Mrs. Hall until they emigrated to Canada then Mr and Mrs Moore. Through their skills, turned out very good Dancing teams.. Wearing of Patent dancing shoes was mandatory. Classes were split into two sections. Boys and Girls, to be taught the various steps of the Waltz, Quickstep, Foxtrot, by Mrs. Moore with the Girls and Mr Moore (seen in one of the Photos with John Gregson) He would become the woman partner, and place his hands on your shoulders dancing backwards to carry out the woman's steps. It was all very simple until you started dancing with a real girl to music. Then the fun began treading on each others feet. The Classes were held on a Monday evening beginning at seven fifteen, lasting an hour until, eight fifteen. Then it was time for Benediction. In St. Anne's Church. When everyone left the club and walked via the school to the Church.

Perhaps this is an appropriate time to add a comment that has been provided regarding. 'The Bish' Who could forget the figure of the 'Bish' walking up & down the centre aisle during Benediction, to the strains of. 'Lead Kindly Light' or 'Lord for to-morrow and its needs.'

Photos of some of the early dancing teams

Tom MacAvoy -John Healy - Paddy McMonagle -Mike Plant
Helen Hall -Eileen McMonagle -Kathy Anderton - Peggy

Looks Like Moira Stogdon and Mke Macdermott.

Mike Macdermott receiving Dancing award
From Ben Lyon & Bebe Daniels

Mr. Moore Dancing with Bebe Daniels. /

Charlie Dempsey. Bob Springall, Bill Tough. Derek Rivers
?? -- Sadie Thompson - Sheila Mahoney -Vera De Troia

Eddie Ford Kevan Miller -Arthur Course
??- Kathy Anderton ??

Derek Rivers reflects:

St. Anne's Club was my whole life – every night I would attend except Thursday. That was the Pella Club Night. Indoor games – football training, Dancing, Socials every other Sunday Old Tyme Dancing, Saturday night Dances. Table Tennis Matches, You name it was there But my real favourite was Ballroom Dancing. It all began when George Hall, to give us lessons in1949. After first getting hooked; I like others went through the grades up to

Gold Bar Standard. The Standard was so high that the St. Anne's Team of three (3) Couples, from 1953 won the annual LUMC and GC Competitions four years running. We also formed a formation team from 4 couples. We used to have dancing matches against other Youth Club s in London the nearest was over the water in Pimlico the Warwick Club. During that time George Hall and his wife immigrated to Canada and Bob Moore took over as Teacher to carry on the good work.

ooOoo

Still continuing. Following on after Mondays Benediction, with the exception of Tuesday and Thursday. After 9:00 it was dancing time for the next hour, to practice what you had learnt in the Classes but not to the music of Victor Sylvester, but to the popular music records of that day. Jack Jackson the BBC's Radio Disc Jockey, had a weekly hours programme, when he introduced all new recordings, by the American vocalists; Doris Day, Kay Starr, Frank Sinatra, Frankie Laine, Nat King Cole, Dean Martin, Guy Mitchell, Les and Mary Ford and a host of others, all were available on.78 r.p.m. Vinyl Records. For the young teenagers, it was a must to buy the records, to play them at home. First to purchase a record player on the never never, then take them to the Club to be played on the big gram by a member of the Committee. Usually either Bill Tough or Kathy Anderton. Nevertheless, there were a few rules to be observed (a) "NO JIVING" (b) the banning of certain unsuitable records?: 'Put Another Nickel In.' sung by Theresa Brewer, 'Come On to my House.' sung by Kay Starr and 'Blow Me A Kiss From Across The Room' sung by Kitty Kallen- 'Oh What A Night It wWas, sung by Jonnie Ray and- The Creep a new Dance that had formal no steps, but partners would cling close together and creep around the floor!

However, I must not forget the girls we danced with. Marion, Jane, Hilda Harris **(mentioned later), Eileen, Jean, Josie, Anne, Betty, Pat, Mary, Sheila, Nina, Sylvia, Helen, Maureen, Winnie, Joyce, Diane, Lily - plus many more. All good dancers and you always chose a favourite as a dancing partner. The records brought in provided an ongoing range of music for dancing for the years that followed. Nevertheless for those not dancing there was other entertainment on hand, Snooker on a full sized Table located in a Hut between the Club and the House. In the Old Oratory of the Settlement house, then out lived its use, that had been redecorated by members on Saturday afternoons. I was one such volunteer along with Harry Spanswick, Derek Rivers, Bill Tough, and a couple of others, who turned up to remove several thickness of wallpaper on the walls and ceiling, which was criss crossed with moulded timbers. (see photo on Page 14). It took weeks to complete and when it was finished. A Black and White TV was rented and installed in the room, to sit and watch those limited programmes available on a B&W screen. Due to the signal reception and screen contrast, necessitated the room lights to be switched off. Jean Lovell (nee Lyons) informed me that she and Ron Lovell, often watched TV programmes in there!

THE COMMON ROOM

The Common room almost a third of the size of the Dance hall, a place to relax in the armchair seats and tables to partake of tea, biscuits cakes or soft drinks served through the hatchway of the Kitchen (a Tiny Place fit for two people to make the tea etc.). Curtains adorned the windows a Piano was at the far end and on the right hand side was the door to the Gents Toilets including a shower. The Common room was also a place where conversing over refreshments with friends took place, or someone would play a tune on the piano.

Doris tinkling the ivories

I always found it an ordeal, opening the door of the Common Room to be met with a sea of faces, and you naturally gravitated to those of your friends. The more trendy people tended to gather at the far end near the fire and we used to call them the 'jazz crowd' *Possibly the Agers, McAvoys, Plants, McMonagles, Thomas etc, The era of Swing with*

Benny Goodman, 'Stomping at the Savoy, One 'o' clock Jump.' Glenn Miller- 'In the mood'. Harry James- 'Easter Parade.'
The other group collected near the kitchen and I have recently discovered (to my horror!) were referred to as the 'goodie goodies' – *Why?* Little did they know.

There was also the occasion when Artist did converse with Members and play music in the Common Room as per the photo of Steve Race: The Jazz Pianist. – Peter Brough The Ventriloquist of Archie, & Max Bygraves: Radio Star. Who was a member of the Cast of 'Educating Archie.'

Steve Race at the Piano with Father Madden- Eric Blackburn

Toni Maconi & Tom Galvin circa 1949

ooOoo

Mary Clinton reflects.

Father Madden tried his hardest to get me discovered as a singer. He had endless contacts in the theatre and the musical world. Father first heard me sing a solo in the play at St. Anne's called. 'The Constant Nymph.'(Circa 1945) I had to sing 'Only a Rose' (I still have the music and I still sing it party piece). He said he would take me along to the pianist SOLOMON to see what he thought of my voice. We went to some music studios in London and Father sat and listened while Solomon accompanied me in my songs. Nothing came of this audition except remarks from Solomon about "Have her voice trained. Keep Singing. Very Good' etc. etc.

The next thing Father did for me was to get me to take the place of JULIE ANDREWS in the Christmas broadcast of the "Educating Archie" show. Julie was going to be away on holiday over the Christmas and they were looking for a substitute.

I sang "Someday my heart will awake." By Ivor Novello- accompanied by the "Hedley Ward Trio."

Again nothing happened after the broadcast but I'm sure, Father would have gone on pushing me if I had not left St. Anne's when I went to Training College in 1946.

Teresa Wicker (nee Clinton) 2002-08-25. The following photos were taking in the Common Room circa December 1950:

Marion Sheean ? Teresa Clinton (5Gitrls unknown) Peter Brough, looks like Jim Kember Fr.Madden -? -Pat Macdermott Hilda -?- Joe. Plant. with Crew Cut. (2 Girls kneeling unknown)

Peter Brough applauding Teresa Clinton singing Jim Kember and a young Tom O'Neil

A visit by Peter Brough (Ventriloquist) the voice of Archie Andrews (dummy) the stars of the educating Archie radio programme that was broadcast on a Sunday that began on the 6th of June, 1950 and ran until 1958. Archie was the dummy of Peter Brough and the other starts that appeared in various acts throughout the series of programmes were Max Bygraves, Beryl Reid, Harry Secombe, Tony Hancock, Alfred Marks Bernard Myles, and 13 year old singer July Andrews. (see Theresa Clintons notes above,

Peter Brough & 'Archie's Autograph.

The programme was listened to by nearly 15,000,000, mainly young boys and girls who followed the stories of educating Archie. On one occasion in real life Archie was kidnapped and an anonymous letter was received that revealed Archie was to be found in King's Cross Station Lost Property Office.

Archie the dummy was put up for auction and sold in Taunton for approx. £34,000.

Max Bygraves in the Common Room with members of the Club.

Gilda Marcantonio - ?- Anne Hendry- Max Bygraves- ?- ?- Ron Lovell- Joe Plant - ? - Anne Hendy - Angela Moran

Circa 1952. A small Billiard table was purchased, and set up in the Common Room. The following photos illustrate its use and the type of furniture and curtains that were an integral part of the Club. The problems was the Table was constantly in use, and you could never get a game on it. One of the reason why we use to meet in the Beehive to play a game of Russian (Bar) Billiards.

Greg Sheppard - Trying out the Billiard Table

Joe Dixon - Roy Summersby- Greg Sheppard - ?

Usually on a Sunday night during an interval of the Dance or, another event the Common Room became crowded. Whilst waiting for refreshment Bernard Driver & Arthur Parsons tried to persuade everyone they were telepathic. Arthur would leave the room & Bernard would then go through the pantomime of stopping at several of the audiences, then passing his hands over each head he would repeat. 'The spirit moveth' - 'The spirit moveth' --- After a few of these intonations until finally, over the unsuspecting head he would pass his hands saying. 'The spirit resteth. The Spirit resteth.' Arthur would then be called back in and had to guess correctly. Who it was? Which he always did.

We all knew it was a scam, but never found out how they did it. I subsequently discovered that. As Arthur playing his part in sorting out the exact person within the enthralled audience, waiting to discover who it was. Bernard moved around the crowd until behind the person where- 'The chosen Spirit resteth.' Bernard would rattle the coins in his pocket. Arthur always guessed right.

THE CANTEEN.

I can't remember much about it except that when you were on duty, before the days of Coke, you had to prepare the bottles of drink, aerated water + one Tablet for a penny drink and 2 Tablets for a tuppenny drink; I can't think how anybody drank them – they were awful?

I remember ordering a cup of scalding hot tea and a Cheesecake (Why they were called Cheesecakes I'll never know as they were topped with icing and sprinkled with coconut strands?) All for three pence a bargain! JP.

ooOoo

New Year's Eve Fancy Dress Party

There was always a Fancy Dress party on New Year's Eve, with prizes for the Prettiest, the Funniest, and the Most original. Some of these events have already been recorded in previous Annals

1946

Keith Ager, who joined the Club in August remembers one year in 1946. His mother suggested he go in tattered clothes with a card on his back 'Sorry no coupons' He won first prize for the most original. "A lady's hair brush & mirror!" But as he was late arriving home? The time was about 10 'o clock. His father came down to the Club. He gave his mother his prize.

1950

A Spanish Senorita
Alias: **Nina Falco**

Rommel the Desert Fox with Iron Cross.
Alias: **Tommy Wilberham**

Joe Plant reflects:

That same year 1950. A film called the "Mudlarks" starring: Irene Dunn, Alec Guinness and Andrew Ray, was shown on the Silver Screen. Joe, enamoured by the thought of dirt behind his ears, entered the fancy dress as a "Mudlark". But it was Tommy that won First Prize, for the Original. Nina Falco for the prettiest. And all I received was a bar of soap. (Joke)

After the Club closed. Tommy and I went to pay a visit to Tommy Marcantonio, who was still confined to his bed. On the Bus Tommy got some rude remarks and Mrs Marcantonio almost had a fit when we knocked on their door.

C.O.M.

We had so much fun with the Children of Mary. The Christmas Party was always on a Sunday afternoon after Christmas and was one long laugh. The annual retreat was sometimes a day retreat and sometimes we went for the week-end to Grayshott, near Guildford. The retreats were run by the Cenacle Nuns, a rather austere order who would have been surprised at the frolics in the dormitories in the evening.

Provider unknown?

ooOoo

FENCING CLASS.

The Fencing Class was held in the Assembly hall of St. Anne's School. You were supplied with the appropriate attire: White fencing Jacket a Mask, issued with fencing Epee. Behind the mask you would take up the right stance say En -Guarde and try to kill your opponent. No blood was let, but I do remember that the strain of the stance on your left Ham strings was something else. I took this up because I thought I was "Error Flynn" (that's a laugh) he was one of the then Film *Idols* of the time, Robin Hood and all that?

Tommy Wilberham and Brian 'O' Sullivan were other attendees and really took it too heart At Brian's flat they practiced with real sword.

ooOoo

FOOTBALL

Throughout the war, the Saturday Professional Football matches was still an ongoing event and a welcome couple of hours enjoyment for the men, from their everyday concerns of the war, it would be silly to say that they attended in their thousands but many did. Towards the end of the war the Club was able to engage in football matches and play in the local South London League that was formed, but due to the prevailing circumstances the various open spaces throughout London had been used by the Army and Air Force, as sites for Gun Emplacements and Balloon unit, and large Communal Air Raid shelters were constructed for the civilian population. Clapham Common and Tooting Bec. Common were possibly the first Commons in South London to become available for matches to be played upon. Following on from those. The Parks and Commons previously requisitioned for Military purposes gradually began to be developed into grass Football pitches. Commons such as: Blackheath, Hackney Marshes, Mitcham, Plumstead, Wandsworth, Wormwood Scrubs and the furthest out Boston Manor. The Parks – Brockwell - Richmond – Norwood – Victoria, plus others? Some Parks such as Ruskin had cinder pitches that were available for more localised street kick a-bouts, and one can imagine, caused much damage to knees, with cinder burns.

The facilities available were crude: a water tap to get rid of the mud, a Hut or old House to change into football strip and visa versa. Goal Post had to be carried to and from the allotted pitch number, there were no nets! There was also some strange layouts of pitches for instance at Brockwell Park, for one fixture you could be playing on a totally flat pitch or, one of the up-hill pitches where the top Goal Post were only half visible, such was the variation of layout. At Wormwood Scrubs the pitches were overlooked by the Prison.

Club Football Leagues had also developed to embrace the increasing number of Boys Club's being opened. Within the Greater London area, League Tables and divisions were introduced based on a similar system as those of the Football Association. By the late 1940's. The League that St. Anne's had previously played in, was swallowed up and integrated into the new system. It was then that the St. Anne's team's, would find they playing on pitches across the width and breathe of London. The problem being transport. The mode of transport used was by bus, tram or tube. Nobody liked playing at Hackney Marshes, with its 100 pitches side-by-side, end-to-end, stretching for miles, you had to trek miles with the goal post to the allotted pitch. Many times a football from another game would land on your pitch, and much to the irate shouting of players that was swiftly kicked into another separate game, with the game over, caked in mud, soaking wet, and the goal post had to be carried back. With a quick splash of cold water, you changed and went home muddy. It was the same everywhere. On the way home the Star or, Evening Standard newspaper was bought to read the Saturday afternoon football results.

Whilst playing in one of the Charity Shield Competitions open to all Leagues, St. Anne's were picked to play against Chelsea Youths at Richmond Park, unfortunately we were soundly beaten the Centre Forward of that team, just happened to be no other than a young Jimmie Greaves! However we did become top of our League. Each player was awarded with a small Silver Shield. Nevertheless, regardless if it was Hail, Rain, Fog or, Snow we turned out. We relished playing football.

'A' Team Photo Circa 1950/51?

Back Row: Greg Sheppard Tubby Smith Mike Macdermott John Tierney, Don Skinner, -Jimmy Richardson
Front row ? - Roy Summersbee - Mike Higgins - Frank Flynne - Tommy Wilberham

Back Row: Derek Rivers- Bert Thomas – Eddie Ford- John Healy.-
Mike Macdermott-Eric Blackburn?- Ted Locke -Mike Higgins./
Front Row: Frank Flynne- Pat Thomas- Phil Frost- Don Skinner- Joe Dixon- Greg Sheppard.

VENUE: Looks like Brockwell Park??

Joe Plant reflects:

When I first joined the Club, I played football in the 'B' team for a few seasons. However some time passed by before Conscription took players away so, various positions in the team, became available and I was selected to play in the 'A' Team with some of the players mentioned below, that soon developed into a very good side. Unfortunately there is no Team Photograph of the Side, but I can remember the team's names: Eddie Buchanan - Goalkeeper ; Phil Darcy – Left Back. - Jimmy Rankin – Right Back; – Maurice Green. –Left Half. - Derek Rivers - Centre Half. - Brian Jenkins. - Right Half; – Pat Flynne. Left Wing - Frank Flynne. Inside Right. -Johnnie Manzie, -Centre Forward. - Derek Beamish. Inside Right. - Joe Plant – Right wing. Also John Docherty.

Where ever our Saturday or, Sunday fixture was, it was pinned up on the notice board Thursday evening with the venue time to meet etc. Plenty of time to get there for the kick-off usually at 2.30pm.The farthest I remember travelling was to Boston Manor, then, the last stop on the Piccadilly tube line.

As a point of interest. In Sept 19 55. I was posted to Ipoh North Malaya. I arrived on a Saturday, I was asked by another lad, who recognising my accent asked. "Where did I come from in London? I replied.

"Vauxhall"

"Oh yer. whereabouts?"

"Wandsworth Road.' I replied. He answered.

"I live in Old South Lambeth Road. Do you play football?'

'Yes.' What Position?' 'Right Wing.' 'Who did you play for?' 'St Anne's Vauxhall.'

'Blimey you must be good, fancy a game then? '

At that time I did not know I was talking to the Captain of the Units Football team, who incidentally lived two doors away from my Aunt Agnes. Behind the Albert Mansions. I played my first game of football on the following Tuesday evening, subsequently (when not on Convoys or, Kampong /Camp Guard Duties) played in the team throughout my time in Malaya. So you see the name and prowess of St. Anne's Club Football was known in Malaya.

ooOoo

NETBALL

Netball 1946-53, 1957-61 Eileen Healy.

I loved all sports and gladly joined the netball team, playing where I was needed. Uniform was basically the brown slips from Notre Dame ex-pupils passed on. We provided our own Aertex tops, I think. The rest of the team were good players and we were successful.

Top row Lily Coffey, Mary McDermott, Mary Hannon, Marie Bremer
Bottom row Barbara Driver, (Capt) Eileen McMonagle, Vera di Troia.

Barbara receiving Trophy Cup

I see we have two cups London Union of Girls Clubs and CYC Sunday League.

An umpire was imperative and we were fortunate to be provided with an L.C.C coach, a Mrs. Trickey, who umpired all our matches for many years. We played in the London Union Girls Club League on Saturdays and the C.Y.C Sunday League and were quite successful in both. Our Home pitch was in Vauxhall Park to start with, but due to the growing popularity of netball outside school, we had to go further afield to Kennington Park and Clapham Common.

The Club provided us with smart dark red wrap-round skirts which were all the games uniform and with our white aertex shirts we did look good. Team members moved on but we maintained our standards and were presented with our cups from Fr. Madden's celebrity friends. We were lucky enough to run two teams in some seasons entering other Leagues and gaining more experience in the business leagues. Lincoln's Inn Fields, rings a bell.

The younger generation from The Guild of St. Agnes, and of course, younger sisters, as well as Notre Dame friends, and ex-pupils from La Retraite were always warmly welcomed. John and I moved to Well Hall, Eltham in 1953 and travelling became difficult. So we retired.

Father Pierce contacted us and as we had transport we returned to the Club in 1and helped with netball and football. The Leagues has grown and we covered a wider area going as far as Mortlake, Streatham, Tooting Bec etc. Mrs. Trickey had retired to start a family, and so as well as providing transport, we had to have an umpire. We prevailed on John who took the exam and passed of course, if you can understand the off-side rule, you can do anything. By this time we had another motorist, Nina Falco so we could manage a team between us and travel longer distances.

Seasons started or finished with a knock-out tournament and my last season ended with a win in 1961, with a

much younger team. It's easy to see who is the old married lady – I am the one with the longer skirt.

I had never noticed that, before this picture was taken, It is quite a handsome trophy. They gave me a baby shower for my expected daughter but sadly, after fifty years, I recognise the faces but cannot remember their names...

I have some inch square photo's showing a practice match in Vauxhall Park being umpired by John and Fr.Madden. (the only time, I think)

Cup winner 1953-54 season

Captain of St. Anne's Youth Club (Vauxhall) netball team, 19-year-old Mara Stogdon, of Clapham, holds the London Union of Mixed and Girls' Clubs Division I netball cup for the 1953-54 season. The cup was presented at the Union's annual trophy night at Marylebone Youth Club, by the joint president, Baroness Ravensdale. St. Anne's also received the ballroom dancing cup.

THE GIRLS IN ACTION

'Got It'   *'High Ball'*

'Hands Off'   *'That's mine'*

Fr. Koch training the Netball Team struggling in the Tug 'o' war

Unknown, Kitty Weakner, Unknown,/
Mary Hannon,
Unknown, Betty Jeamond, Marie Stogdon.

ooOoo

ATHLETICS.

Annual Athletics CYC Challenge. Eileen Healey

A young Jean Lyons competing @Battersea Park

I remember this arriving towards the end of our netball season. We had to find someone for each race. We all travelled to Tooting Bec where there was an open track and we duly dressed and put on our plimsolls and joined in after watching everyone else on the track. London had the Olympics in 1948, so we had some idea. The only time we saw anything would be in the cinema on a newsreel. The track was the obvious placed to start. I joined my brother, Paddy, John Kennedy, and John Healy and followed them round the track. I kept up with them, until they noticed, then they exerted themselves. and left me behind. I tried out the Long Jump, I could do that, then the High Jump, bystanders were quite helpful offering advice. And I quite enjoyed that. We continued practising especially the starts. We travelled home quite tired. Next day I could hardly walk, I was so stiff.

Obviously we needed more volunteers and help. Advice we had plenty. It was bodies we needed.

Fr. Madden was very encouraging and we had more volunteers and managed to cover most events. I do not remember the results. But John Kennedy was a. winner and a few of the older club members joined him running regularly. Over the years, I know we grew quite competitive, and were quite successful. But I don't remember ever receiving a certificate, medal or cup. The taking part more important?

CLUB HIKES/RAMBLES.

These normally took place on Bank Holidays and involved taking a train to 'far distant places' like Purley Downs, Epsom Downs. Box Hill, Richmond, Marlow plus other places.

Below photos taken at different venues

Ernie Morgan

Bernard Driver

Tommy Galvin & Bill Tough Camping.

One swimming +

Two Bathers by the Thames?

Greg Shepard - Derek Rivers -?

Tie it there Shipmate.

Swabbing is the Game??

Four men in a boat

ooOoo

Richmond 1949.

In the summer trips outings, to the above stated place would be arranged the Girls would go by train taking with them a wind up gramophone and records some groups The boys would cycle there. Both groups would meet up in the Meadow at Richmond. To spent the afternoon swimming and dancing kicking a ball about and with a lot of swerving to miss the cow pats lying around. (Some were not that good and finished up in a cow pat)?? Leaving there in good time to get back to the Club for the evening Social They didn't go for the Old Tyme Dancing but there was a always a jazz session in the interval .... *Well that reflects the swing era does it not???* where did they find the energy? *Harry & Josie did a unique spot of jiving. That eventually got them banned from the Club for a period of time.*

Boys:Phil Frost -John Macdermott - Harry Spanswick //
Jimmy Richardson - Frank Flynne – Derek Rivers –
Pat Oliver –Pat Thomas

Kathy Anderton- Derek Rivers- Josie Course- /
Mike Macdermott.

ooOoo

POSSIBLY TAKEN AT BOX HILL

Mara Stogdon - Audrey Jones.- Angela Moran – ? -Margaret Furlong - Joyce Brady (Mother of Jo Brandt)

BIKE TRIPS

Joe Plant reflects:

Greg Sheppard- Eric Blackburn- Pat Thomas- Derek Rivers./
Vic Le Grand. ?- [Note the Girls bike frame] Venue unknown.

I remember the first trip I went on one of these outings was to MARLOW on the Thames. I did not have a bike and did not know anyone who had one to borrow from. We all met outside the Club, I was the only one that would travel by train out to Marlow. So whilst the Cycling party departed by bike. I headed for Vauxhall Station en-route by train to Marlow. The plan was I would meet the cycle party on Marlow Bridge. It had started off a nice day and was quite sunny however, whilst on the train, the heavens opened, it chucked down with rain, it became a filthy day. When I arrived at Marlow. I sheltered under the Bridge, from there I had a good view of the Weir and the swirling waters of the Thames, being splattered with rain drops. I waited and every now and then, ventured out up onto the Bridge, to see if they had arrived. No such luck. Disgruntled I ate my sandwiches and about 4'o'clock, gave up waiting, caught the train back to Vauxhall. As it happens the cyclist, never made it. In the pouring they gave up about 11'o'clock. Did an about turn back home.

Oh to own a Mobile phone back in those days?

My first real cycling trip was possibly at Whitsun in 1950. When a mixed Club cycle outing was arranged to Sevenoaks in Kent. I had to borrow a bike from David another Lad in the Flats. Meeting outside the Club with a variety of cycles, mostly borrowed and armed with our usual Paste sandwich's in a paper bag, and drink, slung over shoulders in a rucksack. With eagerness we set off down Harleyford Road around the Oval, along Camberwell New Rd. Onwards through Camberwell Green, Peckham Rye, New Cross where all the cobbles were, trying to avoid the tramlines that were a hazard to bike riders, if your front wheel just happened to get stuck in the tram rail, over you would go, and were lucky not to be killed by a car. Up Blackheath Hill and out towards Sevenoaks. However we never made it!! Some bright spark took the wrong turning, instead we finished up in Chiddingstone, about 4 miles past and West of Sevenoaks. However the Girls were very tired and we decided to stay there. Sitting on top and around a very large round stone! There to eat our Paste sandwiches. Someone went and viewed the Local church and came back full of information about the large stone, was the 'Chiddingstone' As folk lore had spake. It was supposed to be rated as a bridal chair for prospective young lovers?? There was some rapid descents by couples sat on the top. We left the bridal stone in good time to get back to the Club. I think that was the last time the Girls went on a long cycling trips?

As the football season had finished. During the months of summer time, Cricket and Athletics were taken on by those inclined to participate, whereas, there were quite a few cycle trips arranged. I invested in purchasing one, as a few others did. There were trips down to Brighton and to Bath (a very long run. A couple of members I can remember doing that run was Arthur Course, Kevan Delaney, Tom O'Neil and Joe Dixon.) On a Tuesday night, our normal night for Football training, instead a party of about eight. Headed by Joe Dixon, Arthur, Keven, Junior O'Neil, Derek, Kenny, Brian and myself. Would cycle to the top of Reigate Hill, there to stop and have a cup of tea at the Bridge House. On my first trip I missed the turning & carried on down the hill, over the railway crossing almost into Reigate, before Kevan Delaney caught up with me and advised me of my error. It was a hell of a climb back up! I never did it again. At the top the others having drunk their tea were ready to race back to the Stockwell Clock Tower. Oh happy Days!!!

Joe Plant- Brian Jenkins - Derek Beamish-
photo taken by a 'Shaky' Kenny Richardson.

Richmond Park was another venue that the four of us mates - Derek, Brian & Kenny and I would cycle too. One Saturday accompanied by three girls: Joyce, Maureen & Diane. We made a trip out there. It took us ages to get there, the Girls were constantly stopping for a rest. We left them inside the park entrance, so that we could carry on our fast cycling around the park. And it took us ages to get back home.

Other trips made by the four of us, were to the Isle of Wight. We would meet at the Club on a Friday night about 7. p.m. Loaded up with borrowed camping equipment. Then cycle down for a weekend on the Isle of Wight. Catch the early morning I.O W. Ferry and stay overnight at Sandown. Early Sunday ride back in time for the Club Dance! Absolutely crazy but we were young with bags of energy.

ooOoo

WOODROW HIGH HOUSE AMERSHAM

Memories Of Week-Ends There By Joe Plant & Others.

The NFBC, (National Federation of Boys Club's) held weekend breaks, at Woodrow High House an old Manor House located at Amersham Buckinghamshire. Where young lads from Youth Clubs all over London would learn about simple D.I.Y. or other social and Club activities, such as acting plays, making films or, even assault courses. As the Club was affiliated to the NFBC. I like a few other members were fortunate enough to attend a few of these week-end jaunts therefore can put some words together to relate the passage of time spent on a week-end staying at the House..

Joe Plant reflects:

Father Madden approached me and Phil Darcy and asked if we would like to go on a week-end trip the following week to Amersham and stay at Woodrow High House. He advised us what it was all about giving details of what clothes to take, for a couple of nights overstay (Friday & Saturday) and to ensure we had torches. How to get there etc. It seemed Okay to me and to Phil so we agreed. Both Phil and I were in the same class at the Beaufoy and used to walk to school together, so we agreed to meet up together outside Stockwell tube station and catch the tube to Baker Street then change onto the Metropolitan Line that went all the way to Amersham.

Photo of Green Lady by kind permission of Woodrow High House

When we arrived there on the Friday evening, there were a few other boys going our way. We all had instructions how to get there by walking up a hill towards the House. It was quite a walk before we got to the entrance gateway. With torches flashing this way and that, we arrived at the house. Greeted by the housekeeper, with our names taken we were shown upstairs to dormitories to leave our possessions, then return downstairs for supper. Very basic but sufficient. A gentleman came in and told us that we all had to assemble in the "Green Room" for a talk on the House and what the week-end was all about.

Entering the "Green Room" the warmth and smell of burning wood filled the room. The light from the chandelier, presented us all with the sight of plush green leather armchairs and seats, there was a grand piano with a single candle stick placed on the top, a log fire was blazing away in the rather big and grand fireplace, Above the fireplace was a large picture of a woman dressed in green.

The Gentleman dressed in a sort of country attire three piece large beige checked suit with leather patches on both elbows, entered the room and strode purposely towards the fireplace where he turned a welcomed us to the House and explained what we were going to do during our week end stay basically learn about DIY. Mending fuses and broken windows etc. then went on to tell us a little about the house, before he mentioned the picture of the lady. It was then he moved towards the Grand piano and taking a box of matches from his pocket lit the solitary candle and sat down on the piano stool. Suddenly the lights went out plunging the room into darkness and only the pleasant flickering light from the crackling wood fire lit the darkened room. Some murmurings could be heard from some of the boys. The Gentleman spoke in a clear yet theatrical voice and said he was going to relate the story of the Green Lady.

"She still haunts this very house." Slowly raising his arm pointed an extended finger to her picture above the fireplace, his remark had all faces turn to see it shrouding in darkness.

"The women in the picture is that of Lady Helena Stanhope, who was betrothed to Sir Peter Bostock and dates back to 1685 during the Monmouth Rebellion. During the final battle at Sedgemoor, where the supporters of the Duke of Monmouth, were routed by the army of James the second. Many of the aristocracy fled the scene, and in Sir Peter's case he made his way to his fiancé's house right here at Amersham. As the story goes the search was on for those who had escaped capture and James Troops began scouring the country to apprehend the escapees. As you will understand Lady Helena gave him shelter and hid him in a Grotto on the estate, each day she gave him food and water, until one day she was seen. The very next day upon her return to the Grotto, she discovered it was empty. She searched the grounds and eventually found his slaughtered body. Distraught with her loss she returned to the house. Stricken with a broken heart, she drank poison and killed herself."

"Now! The tale of Lady Helena's Ghost that has appeared on several occasions and been witnessed by boys, similar to yourselves upon week-end visits. (At his last remark above the crackle of the wood from the fire, you could hear the shifting of bums on the green leather of the furniture. No doubt the hairs on the back of heads were also bristling! As he continued.)...

"However, the very first sighting was in January 1946 shortly after the Federation took over the House, which was being refurbished by workmen. It was Terry Lawson the Secretary of the Federation, who was staying in the house alone when one Friday night, such as this one! Before retiring he lighted a candle to light his way up to one of the rooms. then turned off the lights downstairs. In his room he soon fell asleep suddenly he was awakened by something. As he lay there in the darkness listening. All was silent until in the passage outside he heard the sound of light footsteps and a sound of swishing, like material being dragged over the floorboards. It came to a stop just outside his room, then carried on. Disturbed by this he lit the candle noted the time of his watch, that showed just after midnight. Once again he got out of bed cross over to the door slowly opened it, looked up and down the passageway but there was nothing there!

Puzzled, he returned to his bed and was just dropping off to sleep again, when the grandfather clock downstairs struck the hour of three. Strange as a few minutes before his watch had shown just after midnight. A few seconds later he heard the same footsteps coming up the stairs and along the passageway, with the same swishing sound of material, maybe a long dress being dragged over the floorboards. It briefly paused outside his door, before moving on towards the next room known as the Cromwell Room then silence. This time he did not move and gradually he fell asleep.

The next morning when other group of young people arrived, he related his concern of his nights experience. This developed into a rather excited search of the house looking for secret panels or underground passages, which they felt existed in the Old House. All to no avail nothing was found. After a hard days work, come night time everyone retired to bed, except one boy who thought he might have better success when the house was quiet. Leaving his room he crept quietly down the corridor to the top of the stairs, when he heard footsteps behind him. Turning round he saw the spectre of a woman dressed in a long green gown gliding towards him. As you can imagine this was a ghostly figure and the hairs on the back of his head bristled, he froze staring at her ghostly face with a look of urgency on her young face, as she hurried past him without a glance, as she quickly carried on down the stairs. Controlling his fear he decided to follow her down the stairs, then to see the back of her disappear through the open doorway of the dining room. Just as he arrived at the doorway he saw her ghostly figure disappear through the centre window (which was where the front door used to be). Quickly he moved to the front door, upon opening it saw in the partial moonlight her spectral figure moving across the field, and continued to follow her over the field towards a spiny, where she disappeared from his sight. He continued on to the spiny where in the dim light he made out the shape of grotto. But no sign of the spectral lady in green.

Disillusioned, but with morbid interest, he retraced his step back to the house. Where again he was confronted by the figure of the spectral Green Lady, about to enter back through the window she briefly turned looking back, and he noticed a look of anguish on her young and beautiful face with tears streaming down her ghostly cheeks, she was crying. Gone was his fear, the hunt was on, he re-entered through the front door to see her carry on in a staggered motion towards the stairway, just as the grandfather clock chimed three. He followed the spectral figure up the stairs along the passageway, where she paused then carried on to the Cromwell Room where she disappeared through the closed door. Following behind he opened the door and saw her take what seemed to be a bottle from an imaginary cupboard, moving it quickly to her lips, drank deeply of its full contents, before falling to the floor, her body splayed out in her green gown, her face tortured and twisted in agony before vanishing from his sight.....

Just then the grandfather clock outside struck the hour of nine! Had everyone in the room transfixed in horror.

Fit to scare even the toughest of all, then it was off to dormitories, and lights out. In the pitch-blackness, from under bedclothes, someone trying to scare the hell out of everyone, would emit ghostly noises. The weekend was somewhat regimented, strict meal times, making our beds and keeping the place clean, and engaged in the purpose of the objective for that week-end- DI Y. Not a weekend holiday as one would seem. We returned to the Club in time for the Sunday Social.

I remember one week-end in particularly Bill Tough, Kevan Delaney, Brian Jenkins and I, met at the Club bound for Amersham. After arriving there and listening to The Story of the Green Lady On that occasion, the object of the week-end. for the four Members from each Youth Club:. Was to produce a Black and White 8mm film called. The "Vagabonds." Each team were provided with a small Cine camera and film, with the purpose of writing the script, make props, act and film it. Our production team were Bill as Director/ Cameraman; Brian was the Continuity man, Kevan and I, the Vagabond actors. Sneaking out after the Green Lady Story, by lighting our way with hand torches, we went across the fields to the local pub, where over a couple of beers, we wrote the script. Returning, got back in undetected. That week-end was hilarious fun and after many rehearsals (yes, we did have words to speak, although it was a silent film) We eventually took the camera outside to make the film.. Our results plus the other clubs efforts, were later shown at the National Film Theatre. The results of ours and other films. I believe are still in their achieves? J.Plant.

Derek River eflects:
Derek Rivers and Harry Spanswick also spent week-ends there. He remembers Woodrow High House. Amersham Bucks as follows:

Harry and I spent a couple of weekends there on. 'How to Run a Youth Club'. I remember the first Friday night getting off a bus, in the middle of nowhere, in pitch blackness we tried to find the place. But we had a lot of fun and games in the House. And after the ghost story about the Green Lady were billeted in the Dorms. And spent many times enjoying Wrestling with Harry.

ooOoo

1951.

On the 16th. dec. 1951. His Lordship William Francis Brown. Bishop of Pella died.
A GREAT LOSS TO ST. ANNE'S AND TO VAUXHALL.

A tribute was published in the St Peter's Anglican church
kennington lane - monthly leaflet Dated jan. 1952.

THE LATE RIGHT REVEREND MGR. WILLIAM F. BROWN, BISHOP OF PELLA

Nearly 60 years ago—in fact, two years before the late Fr. Herbert died—a Roman Catholic priest arrived in Vauxhall to found a Mission in the area. He was young, had been brought up in the Scottish Episcopal Church, and had left it to join the Roman Communion. He was ordained priest and sent as curate to the Church of the Sacred Heart, Camberwell, from whence, after a few years, he was sent to Vauxhall. His first church was a small school in Vauxhall Walk, and the daily Mass had to be said in the priest's house.

From those small beginnings in 1892, and bridging a period of 60 years, we now see the dignified Church of S. Anne, with its Rectory, its Schools, Settlement, and Parish Hall. The leader and inspirer of it all was Father Brown, as he was always affectionately called, in spite of the fact that later on he was Monsignor, and from 1924, a Bishop of the Roman Communion.

His ministry to his flock in Vauxhall always had the first claim on him during these long years, but he found time and energy for very wide public work, and was a powerful leader in Social and Educational Problems, not only in London, but even as far as his native Scotland, where his name is especially revered for the great work he achieved for the Schools' Settlement. I cannot attempt, nor would it be fitting on my part, to write more about him, but there are two matters concerning him which relate to his dealings with us. The first is his real personal kindness to the clergy and people of S. Peter's, and the happy atmosphere of friendliness and mutual respect which we were able to maintain, in spite of the fundamental difference which separated us.

The second is a most remarkable fact. When our church was in dire straits owing to the destruction wrought by the flying-bomb in July 1944, Bishop Brown used his influence, and visited a highly-placed person of the War Damage Commission to lay our case before him. We were the first Church to be restored in the Diocese, and Bishop Brown was one who, with others, helped to save our glorious Pearson church.

All kinds of Vauxhall people, not of his flock, were his friends. We shall all miss him, because he was, in the most real sense, part of the life of Vauxhall, and a friend to all. It is most fitting that this distinguished priest, who by his own desire chose to spend his life in our humble neighbourhood, should be laid to rest within the walls of the Church he built.

May an "Anglican Vicar" breathe an affectionate prayer? "God rest his soul, and reward him for his labours faithfully done in the Name of Our Blessed Lord."

CLUB OUTINGS.

Every year after the war, Father Madden organised trips to the seaside, either to Camber Sands, Bracklesham Bay, or Climping. Depending on the number going, a number of Charabancs, were **hired** from the Orange Coach Company in Brixton, to transport Club members and their families, for a day's outing to the chosen venue by the sea. Bearing in mind in those days these seaside beaches were void of shops, fun fairs, Café's or Public Houses. Maybe the reason for them being chosen???

Early morning on the specified day. All participants would arrive at the Club, loaded up with shopping baskets, one filled with swimming outfits and towels, in the other packed lunches of sandwiches. With rationing still ongoing, the sandwiches were filled with a variety of the well-known 'Shipham's' Paste, either fish, meat or, chicken; hard boiled eggs, then there was cheese with tomatoes, cucumber, maybe a few salad leaves with beetroot, which by the time they were ready to eat, would be rather soggy. For afters, usually oranges, a packet of Smith Crisps. For drinks; bottles of R. Whites Lemonade, Cream Soda or, Tizer. If it was a boiling hot day these drinks would be consumed Luke warm." However, 'other' concealed refreshments were taken!!

The Charabancs would soon fill up and set off in convoys, heading for the sea. A half way stop would be made. If bound for: Bracklesham, Climping it was at Hindhead at the Devils Punchbowl. To Camber Sands possible Sevenoaks.

RAMSGATE 1947/8.

I understand that this trip was organised by the football team. So it seems that it was a 'boys only' adventure to that popular Cockney seaside venue where: Beer, winkles, cockles and muscles. 'Alive Alive Ho ' were to be enjoyed. As it appears from these Photo's'

Bert MacAvoy - Dennis Lynch -Lou Ager –/
- Eddie Marcantonio Keith Ager

Lou - Paddy McMonagle　　*Les Green - Paddy & Lou*

Possibly another outing also to Margate

Eddie Ford sweeping a girl ? of her feet　　*Tom Marcantonio & Girls ???*

CAMBER SANDS 1947.

Camber Sands on the East Sussex coast, has 'Sand Dunes' with small hillocks and dips, before one reaches the sandy beach to the sea. It is a place when its very suuny and with slight breeze, one can become very rosy by the end of the day, romping about in the Dunes. Alternatively if it is overcast and windy, that is the place you do not want to be at. Sand whipped up by the wind gets eveywhere, and you just have to sit there and bear it. As shown below during the outing of 1948.

There is a story behind the 1947 trip to Camber Sands as related by Marie Martinelli as follows:

In the summer of 1947 Father Madden placed a notice on the Notice Board stating that 2 Coaches would be available for an outing to the sea. Everyone became excited about the forthcoming trip. However, two days later another notices appeared Stating that: Seats for the 2 Coaches will be allotted You cannot pick your seat.

Well ! I had started to go out with Peter Martinelli and there was no way he was going to the seaside without sitting next to me!

So he put his own notice up own notice up on the Board. Stating to the effect: That we could all pick our own coach and seats.

Father Madden was incandescent. To put it mildly ! He Banned Peter for 3 months so we are not in the group photo below. The girl in the Bikini Bathing suit Father Madden did not like that. But seemed to step aside of this one.

Back Row: ?-?-? Eileen Caluori- Vera De Troia Margaret Daly
Next Row Elsie Bremer - Bert MacAvoy –Pat Butler- ??- Pat Locke -?
Seated: Phillis Cullen- ? - Les Green - Tom MacAvoy – Peter Perla.

ooOoo

ANOTHER TRIP IN 1948

John Healey- ?-? Fr. Madden - Eileen McMonagle - Windswept. Greg Sheppard-? *Horseplay in the dunes*
Anne Hendry -Nina Falco -? *Ron Lovell- Tom Marcantonio-? -Pat Kirk.*

SEVENOAKS - STOP OVER

?- Tom Marcantonio *Rear: Charlie Dempsey - ?-Phil Darcy -Frank Flynn/*
Middle: Tommy Marcantonio- Kevan Delaney- Pat Flynn Jimmy Kember-
Kneeling; Tommy Wilberham (going Mexican Style)

CLIMPING.

Another beach resort in West Sussex. Unlike Camber Sands, it has small sand dunes, a pebble beach, with a very shallow sandy shoreline. Ideal for paddling or going further out for a deeper swim.

Fr. Madden – *?-?- Jimmy Richardson- Pat Thomas-/* *Kenny Millett – Don Skinner- Eddie Ford.-/*
Phil Cullen *Phil Frost- -Derek Rivers-/* *Roy Summersby – Ken Miller*
Harry Spanswick- John Macdermott.

Buddy Higgings- Joe. Dixon- /
Roy Summersby

Billy Tough Sheila Mahoney- Derek Rivers.

ooOoo

1952. OUTING
TO CLIMPING

Rear Top: Derek Beamish.- Joe. Dixon.- Joe Plant.- Phil Frost.
Standing: Maureen - Kenny Richardson.- Pat Kibble,- Boy?,- Sylvia Sheean,- Fr. Byrne –/
Maurice Green,- Gilda Marcantonio,- ??- Brian Jenkins – Eileen Bragg.- ??-Mary. -Boy??
Front Row.: Maria? - Joyce, - Winnie Dwyer - Diane, - Mary Haggerty,- Marion Sheean – Helen./
Posing: Hilda Harris.**

ooOoo

BRACKLESHAM BAY.

6th. June 1947.

Girls: Joan Denneny- Marie Bremer- Sheila Talbot-Mary Martinelli - ?/
Fr. Madden - Kevan Lewis -?
Mike Mulvey - Tubby Smith - John McDermott - ?-Bert McEvoy?

Eric Blackburn –Pat Thomas

1952:HINDHEAD - THE DEVILS PUNCHBOWL

A stop for the usual stretching of legs, visits to the conveniences, a cup of tea and Eccles cake, before Father Madden would herd everyone back on board, for the last leg of the journey, onward down the winding leafy lanes of West Sussex, bumping and jostled by the motion of the coach to arrive at Chichester then, on to sun soaked Bracklesham. Out of the three venues, I think Bracklesham was the favourite?

Bill Tough-Pat Flynn- ?- Derek Rivers - Sheila Mahoney/
Fr. Pearce-Tom Marcantonio -? -Mike Higgins.

Ken Miller- Tom Marcantonio- Mike Higgins -/
Phil Frost - Jimmy Rankin-
[Pity about the water damage.]

ONE COACH LOAD

In doorway: Tommy Marcantonio- Jimmy Rankin.
Rear Row: Pat Flynn - Derek Rivers- Fr. Pearce -?- Mike Higgins,- Maurice Green,- Phil Frost -/
Brian Jenkins,-/ Jimmy Kember?- ??,-?-Bernard Moran.- Frank Flynn,-/
Kevin Delaney,-Pat Kibble..
Center Row: Bill Tough,- ?- Sheila Mahoney,- Hazel - George Belcher - Helen,- Mary Haggerty,-/
Maria?./ Kenny Richardson.
Front Row: Janet Kember,- Joyce,- Maureen, - Diane,- Joe Dixon- Derek Beamish,- Joe. Plant.

Usually upon arrival about mid-day. With the sun blazing down, all would spill out of the Charabancs. Then in groups, spread themselves along the top of the coarse windswept grass... Towels were laid down, followed by unloading the picnics and goodies. As they sat in the tranquillity of a peaceful sunny setting. Gazing out across the vast expanse of blue sea towards the horizon, the quite chatter and munching of sandwiches carried on, to the background sound of the pebbles along the beach, being gently washed and rolled about, by the ebbing sea as if, beckoning all to come on in! Knowing that the members of St. Anne's were about to invade its flat sands in their hundreds. With outstretched towels, some of the girls would cluster around 'brave Girls' as they changed into their costumes, before venturing down onto the pebbles, spread out their towels, ready for a sun bathe session. Whilst the Boys, with a towel wrapped around their middle, would wriggled their way into a cossie, then run to the edge of the pebbles. Halt, before gently tread their way across the hardy pebbles, then race across the flat sands into the freezing cold sea. Soon to emerge gasping for breath, excitedly shouting ; "Come on in. It's lovely and warm"!!!

Lunch Time- Soggie Sandiches.   *2 windswept girls?*   *Tom Marcantonio with Another Girl*

After the quick dip, and a towel down, all made their way back carefully over the pebbles onto the flat sandy beach of Bracklesham Bay, with its expanse of open sandy shore, the ideal place for teams, Boys against Girls. To play Cricket, Football, or Rounder's, usually Girlie stuff. "Rounder's"

Where's the Ball? A Game of Rounder's on the flat beaches'
Note: White Pebbles behind'

As the afternoon wore on, with the rounder's finished the Boys would either play tag cricket, or kick a football about As the sun beat down, some went for a swim, whilst others sunbathed on the sand or, lay out towels on the pebbles, to get burnt in the hot sun, then possibly finish off some rather soggy left over sandwiches, and a swig of warm Lemonade?

Kevan Delaney Ron Lovell Frank Flynn   *Frank Flynn & Pam*   *Is it Frank again?*

Hilda- Helen- Marion- *Eileen / Helen - Hilda - Joe Plant - Marion Sheean*   *Brian / Kenny -? -/*
Sylvia   *Joe / Derek.*

Round about six o' clock. It was time for the homeward journey. With glowing bodies, the packing up began; all debris was carefully picked up and packed away for the return journey. **B**ack on the coach, the usual pairing up occurred, then the sing song, with a half way stop at Hindhead. By the time the coaches arrived outside St. Anne's, there was a lot of hot sun burnt bodies, all having had a wonderful time, about to de-bus. A good days outing over until Next year?

The following night at the Dance, there were quite a few rosy faces, burnt arms sore backs. Having a dance was a bit of an agony. The Ow-ing & ooh-ing don't touch keep away! That went on was no-bodies business?

However, there were more adventurous outings arranged, for those that could afford the monies to pay for the more exotic trips to Europe. Several of these are recorded by those who went on these two-week holidays, under the following headings. Some of the photographs might not be applicable to the actual venue, as none in the photos in the Clubs Albums were notated. But please excuse my mistakes if found incorrect.

HOLIDAYS ABROAD

The first 'overseas holiday' was in 1948. When Father Madden took a group to Lake Lugarno the Italian lakeside. There is no write up on this Holiday but a few photos supplied by Ernie Morgan with notations of who is in the photos were a great help these are a selection below. Their trip I imagine would take them by train from Victoria to Dover, Cross Channel Ferry – then train to Paris - change again down to Basle change again- then finally Lugarno Italy. Possibly taking two days there and two days back. Members of that party are as follows:

Father Madden. His Brother Vincent- Ernie Morgan- Bernard Driver – Richard Welsh –Mike Macdermott -John Le Gray- Frank O'Sullivan.---Girls: Anne Bremer- Paddy Daly -Elsie Bremer – Olive O'Sullivan- Barbara Driver-Doreen Macdermott- Carmel Denenny- Marie O' Sullivan - Marie Martinelli- Lily Coffey- Sheila Talbot. Marie Perla. (Christian names only in photos).

Richard- John- Paddy-Mike-Elsie-Frank/   *Vincent – Carmel - Doreen*
Lily-Olive-Barbara-Bernard-Marie P.

Bernard- Mike- Marie

Barbara-Marie M-Sheila- Ernie- Olive-Lily.

Fr. Madden-Mary-Carmel-/
Marie M. –Barbara-Anne-?-Lily.
Catching the Bus to Milan

Vincent –John.
At the Glacier.

Barbara-Lily- Maria M- Mary O.-
Absolutely freezing

Top Row: John- Maria P- Carmel- Doreen-Mary M-/
2ⁿᵈ. Row: Paddy-Elsie –Maris O.- Anne-Olive-Barbra/
Seated: Frank- Bernard –Vincent-Richard-Mike
About to return home.

TRIP TO ROME AND VENICE

1949 Rome & Venice Josie Course
Few out in an old converted Military plane Doesn't remember anything apart from going on a coach to a RAF airfield to catch a converted RAF plane.

Anyway researching into the matter, have found out the following that might explain the circumstances regarding the Converted RAF Plane:

The Berlin Air-Lift of 1948-49 finished in May 49. Its aftermath created a considerable number of aircraft and Pilots laying idol with nothing to do. Some entrepreneur had the idea that some of the planes could be used to hire out for trips, and for the first time, it was possible for the working class people, the opportunity to take part in oversea holidays by air. The cost of hiring a Dakota Aircraft, carrying 32 passengers cost 2/6p per mile. Bearing in mind that St. Anne's was in Vauxhall, and the RAF airfields surrounding London, were RAF Northolt and RAF Croydon. Northolt was under re-construction for the new Heathrow Airport. Its only accommodation was tents for the construction company. The other RAF Croydon that was being used as a RAF transport unit. It being the old London Airport had Customs facilities in situ. There was also another clue to consider that of a report in the 1946 Annals, written by Olive O'Sullivan entitled. 'To Eire - By Air'. Their plane took off from Croydon. With Fr. Maddens connections in the Variety Club. He could have been aware of the opportunity to fly to Rome; also he might have had sponsorship, for two of the Members as indicated by Eileen Healy in the next report on a trip.

Out of the two old RAF Fighter airfields, Croydon being the nearest with the appropriate Customs House. I would say that was the one they flew from. The aircraft could well have been a Dakota. Possibly the following three photos were taken in Rome?

Josie Course- ?- ? -?

ooOoo

TRIP TO VENICE.

Eileen Healy comments.

In 1950, Father Madden took a party abroad and for the first time raised sponsorship for two club members' costs. All members could vote for whom they thought were contributing to the Club, the most. In 1950 we voted for Bernard Driver and Kathleen Anderton.

Derek Revers reflects on Venice:

Venice: Before the trip George Belcher and I sent away for a pair each of White swimming trunks. They looked quite sharp and smart in the catalogue. Duly they arrived in the post, duly packed away ready for a swim. The first day we all went for a swim in the lake? George very eager to try out his new trunks, dashed into the cold water, did a few strokes swimming about then began to wade out. Much to my horror! George's trunks had become transparent. A sight to behold. Gasps from the Girls, titters from the Boys and poor old George, unaware of his see through trunks, kept on wading out. I never did go for a swim.

On the ferry boat en-route
Only girl recognised Nina Falco (with hat)

?- Eddie Macantonio - ?- ?/

ooOoo

TRIP TO SITGES.

Eileen Healy reflects on Sitges

In 1951, I was the lucky girl to get a sponsorship and I cannot now remember the lad. It was my first time abroad and so we saved hard so that we both could enjoy it. We caught the boat train from Victoria Station, another train to Paris, a new train to Barcelona (this one had couchettes, bunk beds – an extra) and then a coach to Sitges. The journey had taken about thirty-odd hours.

The Terramar Palace was a lovely hotel, with its own jetty and beach, tennis courts, etc., John and I had strapped our racquets to our case and were looking forward to playing. The weather was fantastic, I like the sun, the swimming was great, and there was a promenade along the front all the way to the little town.

We were dismayed when out walking we were suddenly caught in a thunderstorm. We found shelter in the shops. We thought we had left that kind of weather at home and were agreeably surprised at how quickly all the puddles disappeared. The food was delicious, and the fruit especially the cherries were nectar. The swimming was wonderful – and some of the group wanted a midnight swim. Father gave permission but privately provided a large torch for me – as duenna – to keep a lookout in case anyone got into difficulties. They all entered the sea enthusiastically but there was quite a difference in temperature; much shrieking and laughing as they splashed around. I was well wrapped up and fortunately was not required to come to anyone's assistance.

We travelled to a bullfight which was quite a spectacle and left us with very mixed feelings. The crowd got very involved with the matadors, passing quite severe criticism on their dexterity with the cloak.

To me, the matadors looked very young men, and after seeing six bulls dispatched I think we all were ready to go. I have a lot of photos, but they are quite small.

On the way up to Monserrat

We visited a large Temple dedicated to Jesus which had been ongoing since 1933, I really cannot remember much more about it except that it was high up in the mountains..

We travelled up to Monserrat, very high in the mountains again. This I think had the black Madonna. The scenery was spectacular and rugged. It was my first time in foreign climes. I found it all amazing.

In the centre of Monserrat.

Derek Rivers Sheila Mahoney Betty Jeamond
Winnie Dwyer Vera De Troia Anne Hendry

A motley gathering.

One morning we awoke to the sounds of bells and wandering into the town found the streets covered in patterns, like long carpets of coloured flower heads.

In other areas there were patterns also, of egg-shaped metal containers.

Later we were told that these were firework bangers that kept going off during the day as part of the celebration. Of what, I cannot remember, but it was definitely noises. I think we had a special celebration in the evening and watched fireworks from our hotel. We had a marvellous time playing tennis and didn't realize how tanned we had become. In fact when we reached home my mother didn't immediately recognise us.

Fortunately I suffered no ill effects from the sun and neither did John because he had served in India and Burma during his National Service.

Betty Jeamonds -Anne Hendry -/
Winnie Dwyer

Tom Marcantonio
Adeline Perla- Margaret Furlong- Marie Perla

Adeline Perla – Marie Perla - /
Anne Hendy - Nina Falco

Group Photo

Pyramids

Mike McDermott
& Adeline Perla.

Mike Macdermot
& Margaret Furlong

? - Eileen McMonagle –John Healey -
Sheila Mahoney -Derek Rivers -/
George Belcher - Tom Marcantonio

Daly sisters & Doreen Macdermott.

Armed Spanish Policia
being taken into custody
By Eileen McMonagle & Nina Falco.

Kathy Anderton Sheila Mahoney??

Arthur Course -Ron Lovell/
Marcantonio - Kevan Moran

?- Anne Hendry- ?-?-Winnie Dwyer- George Belcher-?

Andy (Waiter) --Nina Falco -Ron Lovell
Amelio (waiter) - Arthur Course.

Sheila Mahoney with 3 Caballeros
Phil Frost -George Belcher- Jack Greer

ooOoo

RAPELLO ITALY.

On the Boat leaving England Date en-route to Rapello Italy1952

Vera De Troia- ?- Tom Marcantonion.- ? -Nina Falco

Derek Rivers refects: Rapello Italy 1952

Was the place where George Belcher advised me? 'Derek. With your fair skin and hair colour. How would you to have a nice tan and turn brown?' That I would like! As I always went pink then red like a Lobster. 'Yes. George. What do you advise then?'

'Derek. The best way. Is to apply vinegar all over yourself, I can assure you it does work. You will stand out in a crowd.' I purchased some vinegar and rubbed it into my skin; it smelt a bit and thought it would wear off in the sunlight. I remember standing in a queue in the Italian Post Office, buying some stamps for the postcards. When I noticed the local Italians were moving away from my presence. I thought it was odd? But must have smelt like a fish and chip shop? Never did get that lovely tan as promised. Nevertheless, did stand out in a crowd?? Well they did move.

Every one of those trips were memorable for the enjoyment and interest, on one occasion, I remember an incident in Paris, which could have been much nastier than it ended. The boat train we were on arrived in Gare de Nord. Where we had to get off and travel across Paris by the Metro to catch another train at the Gare de Lyon en-route to Italy. The boat train had been delayed and we had little time to get to the other side. Father Madden told us. 'Look to save time most of you get out, whilst George and Mike throw out the cases through the windows.'

This seemed a great idea, so all got down onto the platform to receive the out-coming missiles, some cases were hurled through an open window, whilst George Belcher, decided it was quicker through a closed one. Crash! Out came the window with the cases. Panic! Father Madden immediately fell to his knees in a state of prayer, exclaimed. 'Holy Mary Mother of God. George! At least open the window first.'

The irate Guard came charging up. Gastrulating in his best French, to make us Angelis feel Inferior. He ranted and raved at the destruction to His Train. More French Gendarmes arrived and, we were all frog marched off to the Station Masters Office. A rather heated discussion took place. Until EntalIe Cordiale took over? I do not know how it was resolved. But the dash across Paris was one of the most hair-raising experiences I can ever remember.

Mike Macdermott reflects. Phil Frost & I, were with Father Madden's Group spending a holiday in Rapallo (Phil and I were asked by Father Madden to look after Tommy Marcantonio as he was recovering from TB) we all had a wonderful time. Father M. had instructed that everyone had to return to the hotel at night at a reasonable time when all the doors would be locked. As far as Father M. was concerned everyone behaved and adhered to his rules.

HOWEVER. Phil's and my room was on the ground floor and our window was left open for all those 'Dreadful Youngsters. 'To creep back into the hotel at all hours of the morning. Of course Phil and I never did such a thing???

Group relaxing by the harbour.

? -Tom Marcantonio- Anne Hendry /
George Belcher- Sheila Mahoney- /
Derek Rivers -John Healey

Nina Falco - Tom Marcantonio-?

Sheila Mahoney–Tom Marcantonio

Postcard from Italy

Two wanderers

On the scrounge shopping
Nina Falco pointing -Sheila Mahoney -/
Eileen Healey - Mike Macdermot & Derek Rivers

Three sunbathing beauties

Adrift on a raft

Table Tennis
Maybe: Mike Macdermott & Derek Rivers

Rear: Vincent Madden Fr. Madden - George Belcher /
Nina Falco - Tom Marcantonio/
Center: ?- Anne Hendry-Eileen Healey -Anne Hendy.
Seated. Winnie Dwyer- Betty Jeamonds.

Tom Marcantonio ? - Adelina Perla-/
Anne Hendry -Betty Jeamonds

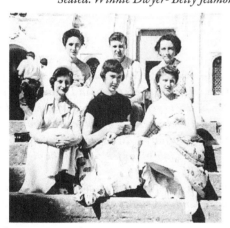
Back Row: Nina Falco- Tom Marcantonio - Anne Hendy /
Sitting: Winnie Dwyer - Anne Hendry- ?.

Nina Falco -Tom Marcantonio - Anne Hendy

Photos taken at Pissa

Tom O'Neil

Arthur Course and Tom O'Neil Trying to get to England

*Arthur Course/
Tom O'Neil*

*Tom / Brian O'Sullivan -/
Tom Marcantonio*

*Arthur Course -Tom O'Neil-/
Tom Marcantonio*

TRIP TO ROME.

Eileen Healy reflects Rome.
Italian Olympics – 25th August – 11th September 1960.

Father Gary Pierce organised a trip to Rome where we were able to see Pope John Paul 1, Vatican City – St Peter's and some Olympics. We were all quite excited and for many club members it would be their first trip abroad. We were travelling by coach and ferry and it was an opportunity to get to know the youngsters. All the lads were smartly dressed with the shoes and the hair and one was really being teased, he was called Jimmy. The Italian pointed shoe was the height of fashion and Jimmy had these long Italian pointed shoes on his English size feet. Farther Pierce came along and suggested he had better keep to the middle of the ferry in case he pierced the sides of the boat and caused us a problem.

We continued our journey and arrived at the convent where we were sleeping, but we would be catered for in the restaurant around the corner. The Nuns were of a closed order and although our rooms were tidied and beds made, I never saw one. Most of our arrangements were made in the restaurant where we occupied a very long table seating about 33-34 in the centre of the room. We had continental breakfast, pasta lunch, or packed lunch if we were out visiting and a special evening meal. The restaurant also dealt with their local customers. So we did have to arrive quite promptly. Father Pierce dealt out our Olympic tickets and suggested that we swap around amongst ourselves and make our own arrangements. We were given quite a large map of Rome supplied by B.P. which I still have. On my group visit to the Athletics Stadium, there seemed to be many seats available and having found ours, we made ourselves comfortable and looked around. Looking back now I can understand our confusion. The contestants lined up, the gun went off, they went off and suddenly there was a deep rumble of IT – AL – Y – IT – AL – Y and it sounded threatening. I nervously looked around the arena and heard other groups joining in with their chants. Nowadays, with all the publicity and knowledge about events and contestants in all the variety of sports, we would have recognised the contestants and perhaps the colours of each nation and felt comfortable supporting them. Not being a regular visitor at football matches or rival games I was unprepared for the amount of support given to the home nation. We did try to support Britain but we really didn't know who was running and thus cheered everyone.

We visited Ostia for swimming and sunbathing.

We went to Castel Gandolfo where we had an audience with Pope John Paul.

We were extremely lucky being the only English visitors in the English section and were within touching distance when he was carried through to his chair. We went to Vatican City and saw St. Peter's Basilica in all its splendour.

We visited the catacombs – did we have a mass? I have heard mass there.

The more I think about it I'm sure we did. I remember standing around a stone altar with some of the group, very involved. It was the closest I had ever been to the presence of our Blessed Lord. Pre-Vatican 2.

We visited many of their ancient monuments conveniently in the centre of Rome.

And Margaret and John Kavanagh and John and I caught a train to Naples to see the Bay and yachts, but that was another adventure.

We were expecting a great treat for an evening meal. The younger members were getting a bit homesick for an English dinner and obviously asked what was on the menu. Sitting down for dinner that evening there was a buzz, the plates started their long trip journey from the top and round the table that was seating about thirty-six of us. We were all busy discussing our day, and didn't notice anything amiss until a plate arrived with a roast chicken complete with feathered head. It was quickly passed on and on and on until it arrived back to Father Pierce and the head waiter. Father obviously, had a plate with a headless chicken, and of course, there were several others of our company too. A halved chicken – two portions. Consternation. The waiter was confused. Why were we refusing to eat our favourite dish? Apparently, chickens in Rome are a good bit smaller than our country ones and as a mark of good faith, so that they could not be confused with any other type of bird, were served with the head. I can often see that long table, with its entire diners ready for dinner; perform the quickest sleight of hand, in order to get a headless chicken. It was really a case of 'I'm alright. Jack'. Needless to say, the chicken was taken back to be decapitated and freshly served again, it was much enjoyed. And whenever we had chicken again there was much hilarity. On our return journey we were due to sleep overnight in dormitories in a Y.H.A house in the Swiss mountains. The weather was extremely hot and our arrival found it had a large open air swimming pool. The youngsters rushed to claim their bunks as they wanted a quick swim. I waited down in the garden for their return as George Belcher and John and I were in loco parentis. Jimmy was the first one down. He made a running dive straight across the pool and up out the other side, quickly followed by several more – they were like penguins. But of course, the water was ice cold from the mountains and not the warm seas of Italy. I don't think I've ever laughed so much – even now, fifty years later. What a great time we were able to enjoy.

We had thrown some coins in the Trevi Fountain and I'm happy to say John and I were able to return to Rome two/three more times. Our two children have children and are happy and healthy. We almost completed 48 years of marriage. Thank you God.

He's mine ! Someone ?
claiming a Swiss Guard in Rome?

Eileen & John Healy /
Sheila Mahoney -George Belcher ?/?

Bernard Moran and Bill Tough
in Paris

ooOoo

THE CLUBS WATERING HOLE THE 'BEEHIVE'

Tom-Eddie-Lou –Helen- Mike -/
Paddy –Bert- Pat -

Beehive Circa 1950 /-2014

Modern change

Derek Rivers. Reflects: Dec. 2011

Many good marriage matches amongst Club members took place and in the early fifties. I was fortunate enough to have met Sheila Mahoney. In order to afford an engagement ring and as I was a "Liberace" at the piano keyboard?? I ventured to ask the Landlord of the Club s local watering hole "The Beehive". If. He would allow me to play at the weekends. To which he agreed. I played the piano in the Saloon bar for nearly two years and witnessed only one punch-up in all that time. As I tinkled the ivories, I heard a bit of an argument going on, but still played on. The next thing some bloke, was being hurled across the room. That is when I stood up. Ready to make an exit into the Gents, conveniently in the corner next to the Piano. Still tinkling the ivories, banging on the keys to the tune of Max Bygraves fame. "When you've Got Friends and Neighbours". A rather apt tune for that specific incident. I got an extra pint for bravery?

I am still in touch with various members of St. Anne's Club and its activities, members and memories are all golden to me. But my most precious gift from St. Anne's was Sheila Mahoney.

ooOoo

Joe Plant reflects:

Every Christmas Eve, the Club held a dance. We would leave, to visit the Beehive before attending Midnight Mass, then back home to my Brother Mikes Birthday Party. The same happened on New Year's Eve the Club dance, then the Beehive, if you could not get through the doors. Great times had by all. However, on varying Saturday nights, we would meet at the Beehive. Before making our way to those dance halls with "LIVE" bands playing. At Lambeth- the London School of Dancing (LSD), the Peckham CO-OP, at Streatham the Locarno not forgetting the Lyceum in the Strand.

The Beehive was the venue where the five of us met, to have a game of Bar Billiards or **Darts.** Out of the five of us for Call up, Derek was the first to receive his Brown Envelope. He had to report to a Medical Centre on Blackheath, in a fortnights time, Because of flat feet and the state of his lungs, thought, he would fail it and he decided to cultivate his cough and for two weeks he chain-smoked until, as he lit up his fag, he was retching at will with the first drag, coughing like mad, his eyes streaming with tears. I thought "Damn silly". Still I could not fall back on any ailments or deformities. We arranged to meet in the.' Beehive' after his M.E. To talk about, his experience at his medical.

Two weeks later in the Beehive. Derek had us in fits of laughter, with particular emphasis on his cough. According to him he did it so well, he nearly died; they had to administer oxygen to bring him back to life. He even asked the Doctor had he failed, to which he got the curt reply.

'Your results will be posted to you within two weeks. Until then wait.' Brian exclaimed.

'Blimey another two weeks before they declare you dead.' To which Derek retorted.

Hoi! I'm not bleedin' dead; I'm only trying to get out of the Kate, wait until it's your turn.'

Derek promised, when he received his results he would delay opening the Brown Envelope, until we met in the Beehive, there to rejoice in his failure. Subject closed, back to darts.

'C'mon Brian. It's your turn for another drink' Derek obviously wanted to drown his sorrow. Brian retaliated.

'Don't 'ave no dosh. I'm broke.'

'You're always broke when it's your turn.' Kenny joined in.

'Bet yer ain't got any fags Iver?' I suggested...

'Right Jews match past' How much change yer got?' Out came the shrapnel. Halfpennies, pennies, three-penny bits, tanners, and a couple of shillings. Junior began a fit of coughing, whilst Derek counted it all out exclaimed.

'Enough for half each. Get em in. Who's chalking then? Nearest Bull.' Five separate darts were thrown, Brian was chalking.

Within two weeks, Derek did receive his results. We met in the Beehive. Brian and I were just finishing off playing a game of bar billiards, Junior was at the bar ordering a round, when Derek arrived followed in by Kenny. Junior had a moan at buying more beers, before we sat around one of the Tables, all eagerly awaiting his announcement. Derek, smirking, with a fag stuck out of his mouth, waved the Brown envelope in our faces. Now was the time, merrily coughing away he stood up and through a haze of smoke, he slowly opened up the Brown Envelope, taking out the sheet of paper, quickly scanned the wording, gradually his face turned pale the same colour as the froth on his beer, his jaw dropped, his fag fell onto the floor he uttered a strangled cry. 'I don't believe it I've been Passed A1.' Picking up his fag took a drag causing another fit of coughing, physically shattered he sat down in the nearest chair before taking a quick swig of beer. Placing my hand on his shoulder with compassion asked.

'Anything else in the letter, about when you gotta go in?' Shaking his head mournfully replied.

'Nah. Just wait for further information. Aw bleedin' ell.'

The four of us stood there watching his dejected form, hunched shoulders arms resting on his knees his fag lightly held between his fingers as he mournfully looked into his half full glass of beer in front of him. The inevitable had happened the beginning of our immediate involvement with National Service. I looked at Junior, he rolled his eyes upwards, and I knew what he meant. Junior and I were the next two, due to receive our Brown envelopes. So began a night for commiseration and reflection. Derek, picked up his fag, drawing deeply, caused another fit of coughing before taking a quick swig of beer, he sat down physically shattered. Brian changing the subject exclaimed.

'Anyone for a game of Bar Billiards? 'Kenny replied.

'Yer alright I play yer.'

Unconcerned those two twerps set up the Bar Billiards game; they still had a couple of years to wait!

Within a month of that night. Derek received his call up papers. He had to report to The Royal Signals Training Camp in Catterick. Six weeks later he arrived home on a week-end pass, having completed his basic training, looked very smart in his uniform, his face glowing from outside exposure, he wasn't coughing. Drinking beer in the Beehive, he related his experience of his past six weeks. 'Our Bleedin' feet didn't touch the floor, double here; double there, everything done at the double.' He was training as a wireless operator. By trade Derek, since he left school, was a Tailor's Cutter at the John Lewis Stores, Give him a piece of cloth and he could tell you who wove it and where it was woven. Nevertheless, sparks forget it; absolutely *no knowledge of electrics whatsoever. How the Army ever sorted out service trades, with similar careers, was beyond everybody's comprehension. He came home on leave a couple of times during his Trade Training and during those times with us, he would be trying to remember the Morse code. All we ever got out of him was 'Da Dit Dit Da Dit Da.' whatever that meant, he was hooked on it, I think he was trying to take part, in the Goon show, at that time nearly everyone were trying to imitate the characters broadcast by Spike Milligan, Harry Secombe, Peter Sellers, etc. Derek also had tales to relate with a knowing look at me. 'Just you wait mate, your turn next.' However, his call-up had happened about six months earlier. Then it was juniors turn, he got his Brown Envelope a month before me, but he had a Doctors Chit. Anyway, we met down the Beehive for the opening of his results. He was Cock 'o' hoop, he was unfit for National Service, something to do with his ulcers, but he still carried on smoking. Such were our days of a carefree life of abandonment.*

Joe & Derek - National Service Days - Rare Week-end Leave.
The only week-end- *Get together. Circa June 17th.1955*

I had my medical on the 3rd. June 1954. However for some reason (I found out two years later) I had been deferred until I was eventually called up on the 3rd. February 1955. After having completed my Basic and Trade Training I was posted on Active Service to Malaya. A hot bed of war against the Malayan Communist Terrorist that had begun in 1948 and finally ended in 1960.

In January 1957 I was flown back to Blighty and in late January. After being demobbed in excess of my two year mandatory term as a National Serviceman, returned back to my roots at St. Anne's Club. There to be confronted by no other than Mr. George Belcher this episode stated later.

A point of interest. On Friday 28th June 1957 Derek Beamish immigrated to New Zealand. A host of Club members went to Paddington to say Bon Voyage, little did they know at the time that another Club member was also emigrating to NZ, the person in question was Hilda. Harris** Sailing on the same boat she was being waved goodbye by her friends etc. so it was a double goodbye.

ooOoo

1952.
CLUB PHOTOS AND PARTIES

Saw the Arrival of Fr. Byrne and the departure of Fr. Bob Madden although he appeared from time to time after that. A Collection was made by the Club members to buy Father Madden a 'Particularly Treasured' present:-

AFTER MANY SUGGESTIONS IT WAS DECIDED TO BUY HIM 'A SET OF SILVER BACKED HAIR BRUSHES'!!!

Rear: Roy Summersby- Ken Miller - Buddy Higgins -Maria?- ? -Tom Lewis- Tom O'Neil -Marion Sheean- Ginger (Snooker player)- Bill Tough- Joe Dixon- Helen -Phil Frost – Greg Sheppard - ?- Kenny Millett.
Central: Brian O'Sullivan -Tom Marcantonio- Eileen Healy – Betty Jeamond- Nina Falco- Joe Plant - Kevan Moran –/ Eddie Buchanan - Phil Darcy (Behind George Belcher)
Front: Kevan Lewis- Tommy Wilberham- Anne Hendry-Fr. Madden -Fr. Byrne –Jim Kember -Janet Kember -/ George Belcher- / - ?- ? -?

Note the style of dress worn always smartly dressed when attending the Club.

Back: Tom Lewis- Brian O'Sullivan- Joe Dixon and Helen
Rear row: Tom O'Neil - Bill Tough – Joe Plant- Ginger? (the Snooker Player)
Front: Anne Hendry- Eileen Healey - Nina Falco - Bernard Moran - Eddie Buchanan

This photo Taken at the *Little Sisters of the Poor at St Joseph's Convent just off Meadow Road.* When they had the August procession. *Circa 1956*

Rear:Brian Jenkins ? Derek Beamish- Someone smoking behind could be Tom O'Neil
Front: Diane - Joyce – Jean Lyons - Tommy Marcantonio- Brian O'Sullivan

PARTIES.

There was always a reason for a party inevitably an 18th. Or 21st or, maybe just a get together, whatever, during the 55-57 period I missed quite a few of them, as can be seen by the following.

Kevan Lewis reflects.

On a Saturday circa 25th May 1956 Kevan Lewis had his 21st Birthday party held in the Club His Aunt Julie arranged the party and his Aunt Bridget supplied the Cakes etc. Somewhat of a surprise event Father Bob Madden was invited and during the proceeding. Aunt Julia had all the Girls lined up and had to kiss Kevan, Wow! What a lucky boy. But was his face bright red??

Tommy Wilberhams birthday 31st December

Bill Tough –Gilda Marcantonio - George Belcher- Uncle Tom. -Ron Lovell Kissing Jean.- Tom. O'Neil-Tommy- ? – /
Tommy Marcantonio
Pat Mc Dermott - Julia Wilberham - Aunt Fan - Arthur Course.
by the state he's in?? Possibly Tommy Wilberhams Birthday.

Another Party at Brian O' Sullivan's circa. 1956

Jean Lyons and Ron

Derek Maureen - ? ?- Brian O'Sullivan.

Arthur Course Tom O'Neil –/
Maureen- Derek-?

Possibly another party??

? Arthur Course - Brian O' Sullivan -/
Anne- Tom O'Neil

Derek Beamish-Joyce - Anne- /
Tommy Wilberham

Jean Lyons – /
Brian O'Sullivan

Jean - Arthur

Tom - Jean

Sleepy Tom - Arthur – Jean

Tom Marco -Jean Lyons- Anne- Junior

Gilda Marcantonio - Jean - Junior

Derek - Joyce -Arthur   *Tom Marco - Jean*

Obviously within the Club, friendships did develop into groups, and tended to go out as a group to different venues. As I have already stated the entertainment available in the West –end was widespread, and to see one of the Singing Stars of that period, whenever they did come over from the U.S. You would have to go to a West-end Theatre or Large Dance Hall:- the London Palladium, Hammersmith Palaise, the Strand Lyceum, the Royal Festival Hall plus others. Usually in the Club's Common Room, those groups would discuss plans to book up as a group, to see the Stars perform. In opposition to the big bands, that played at the West-end Dance Halls, where you would go to dance to the live music of the big bands of Ted Heath, Jonnie Dankworth, Eric Delaney etc., there were also Jazz Clubs established within the West-end area of Soho. Such as the 100 Club, the Flamingo, 51 Club, the Star Club, plus others. They were the venues of the Traditional and Modern Jazz music. 'Trad, Jazz' bands; of Humphrey Lytlleton, Chris Barber, Acker Bilk: and the 'Modern Jazz'; Ronnie Scott, Tubby Hayes, Tommy Whittle, Alan Ganley. The first annual Soho Fair started in the Summer of 1955. It was the beginning of the transformation of the music scene in London. What followed was the beginning of the Skiffle, Rock and Roll groups and other musical groups that transformed the way Teenagers listened to music. As illustrated by the Disc Jockey article in the 1963 Clubs Magazine.

A few Members of St. Anne's Club did attend the very first SOHO FAIR. An all-day affair, as illustrated by the photo below one taken at night-time.

The first Notting Hill Carnival 1955

Photo taken at Tom Marco's Aunt Meme somewhere in Soho   *Tom Marcantonio strutting his Stuff*
Before the night time bash.---   *onlookers Arthur Course Kevan Lewis.*

By Wall Tom Marc ??
Seated Tom Wilberham. -Tom Marco's Aunt - Jean Lyons - Derek Beamish- A cousin?- Arthur Course -/
Ron Lovell - Joyce/ Backs to viewer - Diane - ? - Pat Kibble-?- ? -

ooOoo

Joe Plant reflects:
During that period of time, I was not available for any of these shenanigans that went on. And was only informed of them upon my return to the Club in 1957. Only too pleased to be back amongst my friends at the Club. However things did not work out the way I expected. So, the following is an extract from the Last Chapter

of my book on my National Service Days, after I had returned from Malaya 18 months later. Dressed in civvies I went looking for Derek. Knocking on his door to find him not in. his mother said he might be down the Club?

From Derek's House I caught a bus back to the Club, upon entering through the door, there in the little hall-way sat the guardian of the Club -GEORGE, BELCHER, - his small table still barring the entrance and still controlling who was allowed in. Looking up, recognised me.

'Hello stranger long time no see. Your nice and brown, been on your holidays?'

'No. Not been on my holidays, but its freezing back here.'

'Yes I suppose so; I heard you were out in Hong Kong. Must have been hot out there? Did you like it?'

'No and I wasn't in Hong Kong. Ain't paid my subs, can I get in?' George replied.

'Well all right! Seeing that I know you.....asked...You seen Derek lately?'

'Not really, ain't seen him for twenty months, I'm looking for him now. I gather he's not here then?'

'No, I wouldn't be asking you, if he was here.' Someone else came in behind me, distracting his attention and not wanting to continue with this mundane conversation, squeezed through the gap, and preceded through the door into the hall. As usual a couple of lads were playing Table Tennis; the record player was on and a few pairs of Girls were dancing together. Did not see many faces that I knew, apart from Bill Tough who was dancing with a girl, I did not recognise. At the far end standing by the stage, I spotted Kevan Delaney. Making my way down the hall he greeted me.

'Hello stranger. Home on leave are you?' Followed by a favourite...'When yer going back?' Ha Ha.'

'No I've just got demobbed. I'm a free man, done my bit that's for sure.'

'You're looking very brown. Where yer been then. Cyprus on your hols? Heard there's a bit of problem out there. Did yer do any fighting?'

'I was out in Malaya. Not Cyprus.' I retorted, getting rather annoyed. First it was Hong Kong now Cyprus. Kevan now getting interested in geography asked.

'Where's Malaya?'

'Wot dyer mean. Where's Malaya? It's out Far East, there's a war going on out there.' Keven showing interest asked. 'War! What war?' I gave up and asked.

'Is Brian and Kenny here?'

'Nope their both in the Kate! Ain't seen them for some time. Tell a lie. Brian was in here the other weekend with his girl-friend Sylvia.' Just then Joyce walked in, came straight over to me kissed me.

'Hello stranger, nice to see you back, Derek said you were out in Singapore. Have a good time? ...she giggled... You're looking browned off.'

I was browned off; nobody had missed me, but there again, out of sight -out of mind. I had a few dances with Joyce, and as there was not much going on, invited her out for a drink over the Beehive. There Joyce related to me all about the parties etc-----

THE FIVE REMNANTS OF THE FIFTIES

Derek Beamish - Joe Plant - Tom Wilberham - Anne O' Neil - Jean Lovell
St. Anne's Reunion 2014.

THE STARS /ARTISTES
THAT APPEARED AT THE CLUB.
<u>Sunday night Social – Visits from Celebrities</u>

Father Madden, was Chaplain to the Variety Club of Great Britain. With his connections in the world of Variety, In aid of charity, on various occasions, he invited famous Variety Act Celebrities, who were performing at the London Palladium or on the Radio. To open a Club event e.g. like a Jumble sale, present awards, and later to sing or perform their act. either on a Saturday or Sunday evening Club social. Names of English performers were Anne Shelton, Sir Alec Guinness, Max Bygraves, Frankie Howerd plus many more. Canadians: Bebe Daniels & Ben Lyon. Americans: Danny Kaye, Billy Daniels, Vic Hyde, Danny Thomas, Frank Cook to name just a few. Already the name of the English film star Anne Crawford has been mentioned presenting the Football Cup to John Healy. Including Frankie Howerd opening a Bazaar.

There is a mention of Danny Kaye visiting the Club (Ref Cannon Frank O'Sullivan and Ernie Morgan verbal) But I cannot find any photos to clarify his visit possibly 1948/9? However I did find the Club's Autograph Book that revealed; the list of the following Celebrities that visited the Club, in the early 50's. Unfortunately photos of their visits are not available except those listed below.

Bernie & Olive Payne –
Bernie Fenton - Bert Ross-

Brendan O' Dowde	David Reid
Dennis Connor	Dennis Day
Eric Sykes	Ernie Gilda
Frank Cook	Joel Mathews
John L. Carter.	Majorie and Judd Mcmichael
Paul Duke	Peggy Ashby
Victor Rasputin	William Rockwell

Including a few others not noted.

Jimmy Durante & Fr. Madden

Max Bygraves Being greeted by Bishop Brown:
President of the Club. & Fr. Madden

SIR ALEC GUINNESS CH. CBE.
PRESIDENT OF THE CLUB

Famous for his various acting skills and ability to act out different parts:

The Ladykillers and Kind Hearts and Coronets, in which he played eight different characters. Herbert Pocket in Great Expectations - Fagin in Oliver Twist - Col. Nicholson in The Bridge on the River Kwai.- Prince Faisal in Lawrence of Arabia- Yevgraf in Doctor Zhivago and Professor Godbole in A Passage to India. He is also known for his portrayal of Obi-Wan Kenobi in George Lucas's original Star Wars trilogy. Alec Guinness was one of three major British actors, along with Laurence Olivier and John Gielgud.

Sir Alec Trying out the Dance floor with ?

Telegraph received 30 Aug 63.

ooOoo

ANN SHELTON OBE. VICE PRESIDENT
(The Lilli Marlene Girl)

A regular visitor to the Club on several occasions

Born in Dulwich sung with Ambrose, Glenn Miller, Bing Crosby plus others favourite of the Troops

Shelton performed at military bases in Britain during World War II. Her radio programme, Calling Malta, was broadcast from 1942 to 1947. In 1944 Anne was invited by Glenn Miller to sing in France with him and his orchestra. She declined because of prior commitments. Miller died during this tour when his plane crashed. Shelton appeared with Bing Crosby on the Variety Bandbox radio programme. In 1948 she recorded "Galway Bay" and "Be Mine" was popular in the United States she toured there in 1951.

Fr. Bob Madden arriving with Anne Shelton

Anne Posing with her sister Jo.
Jim Kember- Joe Dixon -? -? - Anne -? - Winnie Dwyer /
-Jo-Gilda & Tom Marcantonio - Joe Plant -Vera de Troia

Phil Darcy greeting Anne

An Old Lady Fan
Faces Pat Kirk -?- George Belcher /
Tom Marcantonio

Anne Hendy give another Bouquet

Anne sings Lili Marlene

Another visit by Anne

Anne Admired by the Clergy
Fr. Madden- George Belcher- Anne- Fr. Byrne-? - Fr.?- Jo. Shelton- Fr. Healy

"Anne Can you sing Galway Bay Please?"

George receives a briefcase

Phil Darcy a Silver Dance medal

ooOoo

JOHN GREGSON VICE PRESIDENT

Was a regular visitor to present cups or medals etc. Visited the Club four times
(Different suits and tie)

John's best known role was in the comedy Genevieve starring Kenneth More, Dinah Sheridan and Kay Kendall. He also appeared in the Ealing comedies Whisky Galore!, The Lavender Hill Mob, and The Titfield Thunderbolt. His best known drama films include The Battle of the River Plate, Angels One Five and Above Us the Waves.

John Surrounded by the Girls
Girls -? -Marie Stogdon- Nina Falco - Betty Jeamond - Anne Hendry- John - Lily Coffe?-?-? Angela Moran

John giving out awards to the following.

Mike (Buddy) Higgings   *Hilda Harris & Mr. Hall*   *Unknown*

VIC HYDE Vice President
Mayor of Niles Mich. U. S. A. Multi Instrumentalist.

Known as the "Modern-day Pied Piper," "multitrumpeteer," and "international musical phenomenon," traveled the world with his one-man band comedy show. Some 65 instruments were part of his act, and he played some at the same time.

Jean Lyons presenting a Bouquet of flowers to Gaynor   *Vic & Gaynor's Autographs*

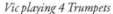

Vic playing 4 Trumpets   *Vic and combo playing Jazz*   *Young Girl unknown*

Vic wowing all after blasting off the roof   *Signing Autographs*
Faces in crowd: *Kevan & Tom Lewis ????*
Joe Plant-Eddie Ford - John Macdermott- Vera De Troia -Ron Lovell -Tom & Gilda Marcantonio /
Angela Moran-Vic -? – Kenny Millett- ?- Pat Kibble.

Vic & Gaynor give a Hot Dog Buffet in the Club.

Vic, Gaynor & Fr. Madden   *Enjoying a Tipple in the Common Room*   *A made up Tuba?*

Doris "Whose for a hot dog?"   *Gaynor cannot keep up '/*   *Don't you Brit's know*
    with the demand!   *anything about Rationing?*

Gaynor talking with /
Teresa Clinton

Not you again? Vic serving to
Tom Lewis- ? -Marion Sheean -? –
Derek Rivers - ? - Joe Plant.

The Mayoress of Lambeth gets into the Act.

ooOoo

BEBE DANIELS & BEN LYON

Film and Radio Artiste famous for their Radio programmes 'HI GANG' with Vic Oliver and later in 'Life with the Lyons' with their Daughter Barbara and Son Richard.

A bouquet presented by Angela Moran to Bebe Daniels

Josie Course gets a hug from Ben

Not to be left out! Bebe cuddles up to Harry Spanswick

ooOoo

TOMMY MCGOVERN BOXER

British lightweight Boxing Champion: Lambeth Born fights out of Bermondsey.
Won 46 fights lost 17 draws 4. Fought from 1946 till 1953. A great fighter of the era.

Fr. Bob Madden greeting Tommy.

Tommy discussing Boxing with the Mayoress of Lambeth

ooOoo

BILLY DANIELS

Married 1951 to Martha Braun Boston Socialite
Took Vauxhall by storm.

He toured the UK's Moss Theatre circuit in the 1950s as "America's most exciting singer". His forte was as a night-club entertainer, and he was the biggest cabaret draw in New York throughout the 1950s, appearing alongside the comedian Jimmy Durante. His vocal styling's and trademark dance movements were widely imitated by the impressionists of the era. He was popular in Europe after he headlined the London Palladium in 1952, having broken the house records.

Fr. Bob Madden being mobbed by Billy Daniel's Fans /   *Police Escort for Arthur Course*

Eddie Ford-- Arthur Course - Billy Daniel's

Billy & Martha at the entrance　　　*Bouquet to Matha by (?) & Winnie Dwyer*　　*Billy*

Billy signing autographs

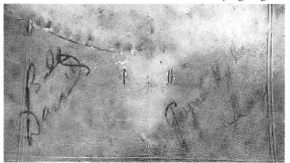

This is a copy of Billy Daniels Autograph

Billy surrounded by Autograph Hunters
Tom Lewis ??. Lily Towner. Margaret Plant – Billy-/
Joe Plant - Pat Thomas - Kathy Anderton -Buddy Higgins

Billy singing That Ole Black Magic
From the rear Arthur Course? Possibly Bill Tough? Kathy Anderton, Mike Higgins

Gilda Marcantonio (Star Struck) Tubby Smith /
Daniels.

ooOoo

MAX BYGRAVES OBE.

In the 1950s and 60s, Bygraves appeared as a guest on several television variety programme's both in the UK and United States. These included Ed Sullivan, Jack Benny, and Jackie Gleason, in America, but his place as a broadcasting icon was founded, along with several fellow artists, by appearing as guest 'tutor', to Peter Brough's ventriloquist dummy, Archie Andrews, in the long running BBC radio show Educating Archie.

Universe Newspaper Cutting/
dated May 1951

Welcome Back Max

Whose a WIDE Boy?

'YOU NEED HANDS'

?- Teresa Clinton - Max
Marion Sheean - Anne Hendry -Kathy Anderton - Max - Joe Plant-

Signing Autographs Faces in Crowd

ooOoo

DINAH SHORE

Dinah Shore became the first singer of her era to achieve huge solo success. She had a string of 80 charted popular hits, lasting from 1940 into the late 1950s, and after appearing in a handful of films went on to a four-decade career in American television Dinah was ranked number 16 as top fifty television stars of all time. Stylistically, Shore was compared to two singers who followed her in the mid-to-late 1940s and early 1950s, Doris Day and Patti Page.

A Bouquet for me ? Fr. Bob Madden Greeting Dinah Shore and party.
That looks like Vic Hyde also????

ooOoo

DANNY THOMAS

Danny Thomas starred in 1952 film version of 'The Jazz Singer' opposite the popular contemporary vocalist Peggy Lee. It was a remake of the original first talking movie of the 1927 Film starring Al Jolson. He also and played the songwriter Gus Kahn opposite Doris Day in the 1951 film biography. 'I'll See You in My Dreams.'

Danny being greeted by the Clergy.
Fr. Madden and Arthur Course

'Don't Forget Girls Smile'
Danny surrounded by the Girls Netball team.
Lily Coffe - Eileen McMonagle - Betty Driver - Danny-?? ?-? -Vera De Troia.

Joyce - Danny - Nina Falco ??

' Hello Blue eyes'
Arthur Course- Bill Baily- Danny - ?

ooOoo

VERA LYNNE DBE

Anne is best known for her 1939 recording of the popular song "We'll Meet Again", the nostalgic lyrics ("We'll meet again, don't know where, don't know when, but I know we'll meet again some sunny day") Were very popular during the war and made the song one of its emblematic hits. During the Phoney War, the Daily Express asked British servicemen to name their favorite musical performers: Vera Lynn came out on top and as a result became known as "the Forces' Sweetheart". In 1941, during the darkest days of the Second World War, Lynn began her own radio programme, *Sincerely Yours*, sending messages to British troops serving abroad. During the war years she joined ENSA and toured Egypt, India and Burma, giving outdoor concerts for the troops. In March 1944 she went to Shamsheernugger airfield to entertain the troops before the Battle of Kohima. Anne was awarded the Burma Star for entertaining British guerrilla units in Japanese-occupied Burma.

Selling it Cheep!   *Vera Chatting to Tommy MacGovern Fr, Madden*

ooOoo

AMERICAN ENTERTAINERS

NOT RECOGNISED

Others Unknown Far Right Peggy Ager?

Pat Macdermott- Marion Sheean - Janette Kember ? Not Sure Could be Frank Cook - Ron Lovell/
?-? - Anne Hendy- ? - Tom Marcantonio -?-?-?

ooOoo

Fr. Madden welcoming ?   *Phil Frost receiving award ?*   *Unknown*

ooOoo

FRANKIE LAINE.

A clarion-voiced singer with lots of style, able to fill halls without a microphone, and one of the biggest hit-makers of late 1940s/early 1950s, Originally a rhythm and blues influenced jazz singer, Laine excelled at virtually every music style. He was also known as **Mr. Rhythm** for his driving jazzy style. Laine was the first and biggest of a new breed of singers who rose to prominence in the post–World War II.

ooOoo

Youth Club Magazine

[AUTHORS NOTE] Eileen Healy kindly provided four copies of the CLUBS MAGAZINE, three of 1963, and one of 1964. The first, published in April 1963. Vol 1. No. 1. Having compared them with those that with the CLUBS ANNALS of 1941-1946 /1948/9 issues, it is no surprise that they had somewhat changed. The size changed from an A5 to an A4 size. The variety of the contents had also been reduced, the exclusion of The Club Diary in its previous format, little or no stories, and from what the Author has understood from the entries, they were directed more on the current issues of those days associated to the Teenage Youth. Netball and Football, Table Tennis, Snooker plus entries on Fashion, Current Pop records, and <u>primarily giving dates of a seasons future fixtures dates</u>. And with the absents of any photographs available, plus any input by any members who actually had experience of those years, it is very difficult to establish a flow of text to interest a reader. Therefore, only the first issue has been fully transcribed followed by abridged entries of the three other copies available. Certainly In no way am I taking away the effort of the Production of the Club's Magazine, as times had changed and so had the thinking, as the Magazine became a forward Diary in itself. When they finished publication is a mystery.

ST ANNE'S CLUB
ST ANNE'S SETTLEMENT
HARLEYFORD ROAD., VAUXHALL, S.E.11
<u>PRESIDENT</u>
Sir Alec Guinness, C.B.E.
<u>VICE –PRESIDENTS</u>
Miss Anne Shelton
Mr. John Gregson
<u>CHAIRMAN</u>
Rev. C. J. Byrne., M.A.
<u>CLUB LEADER</u>
Rev. P. G. Pierce, B. A.
<u>ASST. CLUB LEADER</u>
Miss Pat Cassidy.
<u>EDITORIAL STAFF</u>

EDITOR:	Tony Belcher
FASHION:	Pat O' Connor & Wendy Clark
SPORT:	Micky Powell & Jonny Burkhard
RECORDS:	Jimmy Brack
ART WORK:	Roger Kennedy

The editor would like to express his gratitude for the help and advice received from Brian Gosnell

<u>CLUB COMMITTEE 1962/63</u>
Secretary: Tony Belcher

Helen Hellewell	John Maguire
Margaret Egan	John Newman
Anne Stock	Roger Kennedy
Pat Colliver	Paul Leggett
Gloria Pook	John Burkhard
Pat O' Connor	Mick Powell

ooOoo

A MESSAGE FROM THE CHAIRMAN

It is with great pleasure that I write this short forward to the Club magazine and congratulate those responsible for the venture.

There is no doubt that it will be of benefit to the Club and all its members. Others, too, in the parish and neighbouring parishes, will be interested to know what St Anne's Club is doing and there is no better way than the regular publication.

Regular is important word here and the best wish I can extend to the editor and his helpers is that they do not weary in well – doing. To keep going year after year is not easy as they are bound to find out, but I am sure we have the material in the Club to make a grand success of this venture, as I called it above.

We are sure, too, that many of our older parishioners will be interested in the Club's magazine – more and more, as they get to know about the Club's activities – and perhaps, as the magazine appears each two months some of them may even buy a copy if by chance any copies are left.

Once again, congratulations and God speed.

ooOoo

A LETTER from Alec Guinness.
Transcript as follows.

Dear Editor.
You have asked me to send you a letter for inclusion in the magazine, but I don't think this will be much more than a note in the wave of the hand from (temporarily) us sunny Spain, where I have been living and working since last November. I regret that work and various chores, to say nothing of a fabulous holiday on a yacht (not mine) in the Greek islands as kept us out of England in nearly a year, and consequently prevented me from visiting the Club.
Although I turn up so seldom, and am so useless to you, I would like to assure you all that I think of you often and with great affection, and take great delight in hearing of your enterprises, sounds to me and admirable idea and I wish you great success and that it will be well and truly supported by all.
A happy Easter. God bless you all
Yours sincerely
Alec Guinness.

ooOoo

THE LEADER'S PAGE.

September 1954. That was the month and the year when I came to St Anne's Club. The oldest amongst you had just about reached teenagery then and the youngest had not yet started at the infant school. More than eight years have passed and not until now as a Club magazine been produced. I must strike my breast and say 'through my fault'.

At last I start has been made through the enthusiasm of Tony Belcher and his editorial assistance and I hope this magazine will prove to be a regular and lasting expression of the Club's vitality, and a means by which both members and others will come to a fuller appreciation of what the Club is and what it is trying to do.

There has been a great deal of discussion at national level as to what is a Catholic Club this is a subject I can recommend to the editor for a further article. We can say here that a Catholic Club must be one where the great majority of the members of Catholic and where they find the support and encouragement they used to lead their life in the conscious practice of their faith. Through the Club they should be helped in being faithful to God and his church, to the mass and to the sacraments. One great source of encouragement and joy has been to have so many good Catholics in the Club and to have seen others, in spite of difficulties, come back to the maintain their religious duties. We do not set out to be a marriage bureau but not the least of the achievements of the Club as being the number of happy Catholic marriages. We do, of course, allow the percentage of non-Catholics to be members: and it has been my experience that from them comes most loyal and active support.

Had the editor allowed me more than one page I would have taken the opportunity of thanking by name the many people who have felt the Club and me during my years with you. He tells me that future issues will relate the history of the Club and then I shall be able to pay my tribute to former members such as George Belcher, Eddie Ford, Kevan Delaney and others. I shall not mention the names of present members, but those who worked so hard may be sure I am aware what they do and am grateful for it. With the first number of the magazine we welcome Pat Cassidy to the Club. She comes as a full-time assistant leader, and she will have a special responsibility for the girls side of the Club. Her coming, as well as his publishing event, gives extra promise for the Club's future.

Holy week is now upon us make it a week that is really only to you. Try and receive our Lord in holy Communion on Maundy Thursday when He gave the apostles their first communion; on Good Friday when He gave himself on the cross in sacrifice for you; and on Easter Sunday, the greatest day of the year, when He rises from the dead He was your God. Do all that and we know that our wish for happy Easter for you all will be granted.

ooOoo

CLUB CLASSES

DATE TIME.	ACTIVITY	TUTOR
MONDAY 7.30 – 9.30	DRAMA	Mr. K. Walsh.
TUESDAY 7.00 – 9.30	TABLE TENNIS	Mr. Ebsworth
WEDNESDAY 7.00 – 9.00	TABLE TENNIS	Mr. Ebsworth.
7.00 – 9.30.	DRESSMAKING	Mrs Brilley.
7.00 – 9.30	PHYSICAL TRAINING	Mr. Brilley

Committee meetings are held every fortnight. If you have anything you would like discussed at meetings please let committee members know.

ooOoo

TABLE TENNIS

This season the Club entered into two table tennis competitions with five different teams.

The Lambeth league has an under-17 and over-17 league together with the smaller league for the so-called weaker sex. Although we usually manage to finish the season at least the winner of one of the leagues I don't think our chances of success this year can be rated very high. The senior and junior boys have so far won only half of their games but I hope, however, before the end of the season the results will be more promising.

Our young ladies, for the want of a better word, I having a dingdong battle with their old rivals the "Duke of Clarence." Last year the honours were shared between the "Duke" and ourselves. The one defeat suffered by us so far this season is to the unbeaten "Duke" but I am certain that in the return match victory will be ours.

Turning to the other competition, which is the C. Y. C., We have had success after success. So far the boys have won 10 matches on the trot with "Old Man Gosnell" shown is why Johnny Leach turned white plain against him. He could be better if he wasn't so old. The other members of the team have interchanged between snooker and table tennis so, therefore, a cross-section of boys have played.

Walworth, last year's winners, come down to the Club with an unbeaten record but were stopped in their tracks by the tenacious hard-hitting of Johnny Burkhard, the consistency and accuracy of Johnny Maguire and last, but not least, the KG and subtle play of the "Old Man".

If the remainder of the season continues in the same trend then the "Saints" will be champions.

What has been said for the boys can also be set for the girls who have played half the number of matches without defeat. I confidently ticked that out lasses will win their league so the drinks are on them if they do.

The season so far has had a mixture of good and bad but overall the results have been most promising. One of the complaints is the unwillingness of a majority of boys (NOT GIRLS) to travel and play away. Club spirit and success can only be gained by the players being prepared to give as well as to take.

A Club individual table tennis competition will be starting within the next few weeks, so hurry along and get some practice in with Mr Ebsworth. Who knows, you may be the next champion.'

ooOoo

SNOOKER

Because of the popularity of snooker in the Club it was decided that we should enter into the C. Y. C. Snooker league. Next year we hope to enter two teams in the game continues to be the main attraction for the boys.

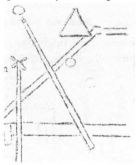

To date we have won four matches out of seven which is very encouraging for the future. Peter Wood, with his trusty cue, and Johnny Burkhard are at the moment the Club's stars but who knows after our own tournament we may have budding Joe Davis in our midst.

Two memorable victories were the slamming of last year's winners, Peckham, and this season's league leaders,

Walworth. Both matches were won by the odd game in three with tense and exciting struggles prevailing.

Although it is not expected that we shall win the league this year the atmosphere of league matches, as opposed to the usual friendly games, has brought about the concentration needed. Next year will, I hope, bring St Anne's into the limelight of the snooker world.

The snooker table should be clean and smooth, therefore, it is hoped that everybody who uses it will at some time both brush and iron the table. This will not take up more than 15 minutes of your time but it will provide hours of enjoyment for others.

ooOoo

FASHION

APRIL- MAY. The weather is here last weekend cast aside those coats, hats, scarves and gloves donning down brighter, lighter clothes. It seems that the fashions this season won't be as fussy as last year's frills and flounces, the latest shift dress should be a cert and I am sure a blessing to those who endeavour to make a few of their own clothes.

"The Shift" can be made and worn in many different ways to suit individual tastes. It is made of two completely straight pieces of material with no darts. There are many different ways of varying the style:-

i.e. Buttons can be placed on either side of the dress or centrally.

The belt can be worn on the hips or under the bust or in the most common of all places THE WAIST!!!If made up in a striped material piece can be inserted in the yoke of the dress with the stripes running horizontally in contrast with the vertical ones.

These dresses are so easy to make as you can tell from ad description, 2 yards of material is all that is needed, and Mrs Briley who takes needlework classes at the Club would only be too pleased to help anyone wishing to try their hand at making a few for their own summer wardrobe.

THE SUIT SEASONS UNDERWAY

Suits are once again very much the trend with jackets worn at any length desirable. Military styles lead the way, with brass buttons, badges and pockets. The newest colours of the sea-going shapes, oceans of blue, green and once again navy blue is very much the colour. Not forgetting those eye-catching colours, pale pink which is very flattering to the complexion, lemon which shows up that lovely tan (in anticipation of a hot summer, OF COURSE,) and also orange which is a trend setter every time. Skirts are optional, straight, flared or easy pleated.

SHOES

Step out of those winter boots into new spring shoes, and step out in style:-

The favourite toe is gently rounded off (which will be a blessing for our poor buckled feet) the heels are small and chubby but elegantly slim at the tip. Sling backs seem still to be very much in the swing of things. For one of those romantic trudges through the deep mud of the country lanes and fields PLEASE don't wear your best shoes but a pair of real call on casual fatties.

MAKE UP

I very heavily made up and a pale (but not too pale) powder should be worn to complement them. Bright lipsticks are also being worn and that insipid complexion is no more. Make the most of yourself – drywall colourful, refreshing and dewy look.

ooOoo

RECORDS

Hi there.

This is your D.J. – J.B.

we start off the column this month with L.P.'s, the first record being Duane Eddy's 'DANCE WITH THE GUITAR MAN'. This is a good twist and limbo record. He is backed on most tracks by the Rebellettes -, who are also on the single of the same name.

****

Little Eva is my next star and her latest L.P. 'LLLLLOCOMOTION'. This young American recording star whose tour of Britain was such a success, follows that great hit single of the same name with this wonderful L.P. if you liked her previous singles you will rave over this.

****

and now my record of the month is that great young songstress Brenda Lee's latest L.P. 'BRENDA THAT ALL.' It has been in the US charts for 15 weeks. Brenda is now touring this country and we should like to take this opportunity to extend our sympathy that her house in Nashville was recently burnt to the ground. Altogether there are 12 tracks on this L.P. including I'm Sitting On TOP OF THE WORLD and 'VALLEY OF TEARS' also 'SOMEDAY YOU'LL WANT ME TO WANT YOU.'

****

my next record is Chet Atkins. 'CARIBBEAN GUITAR'. This is a very relaxing record if you like good guitar music. It's great to dance to.

****

the tornadoes have a new LP called 'THE BEST OF THE TORNADOES'. But you will be surprised to hear that it will only be released in America but later on it should be released in this country – I hope!

****

SINGLES OF THE MONTH.....

Neil Sedaka, this great singer who brought you 'BREAKING UP IS HARD TO DO' should follow up that success with his latest is called 'ALICE IN WONDERLAND'. Neil is on his usual sure – fire style on this disc – it was written by Neil himself – and this record is a BT number with unusual lyrics. This record is climbing the top 100 in America, its place so far is number 40 and the flipside is 'CIRCULATE', a big band ballad.

****

RECORDS - ROLL ON-----

Roy Orbison, the man who sang 'DREAM BABY', comes to life with his new disc affectionately called 'IN DREAMS', since his smash hit 'DREAM BABY' he has reverted to his slow mournful style which are a great success in the States. His last two discs 'THE CROWD' and 'WORKING FOR THE MAN' were in this idiom, now 'IN DREAMS' Ray returns to his hit making style. This disc should take over where 'DREAM BABY' left off and should be in the top 10 very soon.

****

Bobby Darin has a new EP which is called 'THINGS' and this is a real humdinger with four good rock tunes to dance to. 'LAZY RIVER' and 'MACK THE KNIFE' were the greatest hits of Bobby's career so, therefore, this EP could well register in the top sellers. The four titles on this EP are 1) THINGS 2) JAILER BRING ME WATER 3) BABY FACE 4) LOOK FOR MY TRUE LOVE

So if you want a good record to dance to this is the one for you

****

 NETBALL

as a Club activity netball has, over the years, dropped from one of great interest and is now supported by the very few. One reason for this has been the fact that a few years ago the rules were completely changed and those then interested were not eager to start afresh. This changing of rules also led to the closing down of both the Saturday and Sunday leagues in which we played regularly and which we also used to win with a certain amount of regularity.

Last year we entered in the floodlit netball league run by the Lambeth Council of youth and managed come equal top with Cowley. This year it looked as if we would not be able to get even seven players from the Club members. But an influx of good netball is from Notre Dame, Battersea added to Margaret and Angela Donaldson has carried us success-fully through. There was one terrible evening when only five players were able to turn up and Cowley gave us our worst beating in years. But the full team managed to beat Cowley 28 – 22 in the return. So it looks as if we shall share the championship with Cowley again this year.

The London union of youth Clubs is running a summer league on Saturday afternoons and this may prove the chance to re-establish netball as a major Club activity. It should be mentioned that the team of older girls plays under the Club's name and with much success in the second division of the Surrey County league.

Asked to comment on netball one of the boys wrote:-

'Last year the gym at the Sacred Heart School was available to us for netball training. Needless to say after a few weeks it was obvious our girls on not prone to anything energetic. From what I have seen exercise is greatly needed by the Club girls. By the way, a round ball is used for netball and the object of the game is for the team to throw the ball to one another and to put it through a metal ring which lies vertically with the ground at the top of a pole. He knows! And if you can work out what vertical with the ground means so will you.

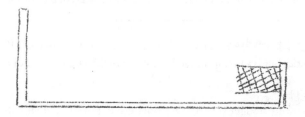

ooOoo

FOOTBALL U16

Meet our stars of tomorrow (or the next day) the St Anne's U.16 side, goes Wills red Devils, beaten in only one league game they are also in the quarter-finals of the sea. Why. See. Under 18 cup.

In goal we have Alf "Stonewall" Chapman - a fearless last line of defence. Backs are Noel "Tearaway" O'Connor - the give and take specialist: Noel could develop into quite a good wrestler also a lot of opposing wingers think, and Jack "Icecool" Killough - slight in stature: Jack has fantastic anticipation, keeps call under all pressures and "the Rock to play a bank game. Charlie" the Juggler" Forbes-a great ball – playing halfback: Charlie, I think, could play all day at full pace without getting too tired. At centre – half we have Vic "the Rock" Clark - a very uncompromising player and renowned rough and tumble specialist: Vic as the ability to dominate the "middle" especially in the air. Left half and captain is Tom "Perpetual Motion" Duffy- an inspiration to the team, hard tackling Tom covers more ground during a game than any two players I've seen without seeming to hurry unduly.

The Forwards:-

Brian "the Fox" Dyer – a skilful ballplayer: although he's probably the smallest player in the league he has as much heart and guts as the largest. John "Cannonball" combines speed with a natural ability of taking hard chances and making them look easy. John "Slippery" Salmon probably the brightest 'star' in the side of 'stars', John was picked as reserve for the south of England. Fishermen will tell you how difficult salmon are to catch and this one is no exception, the complete footballer in every sense of the word. John really looks like a professional prospect. Richard "the Rocket" Langford – a big strong player, is capable of turning the match our way with one of his rocket shots. Kevin "the elusive" Holohan-and natural player who has shown this season that he can also score goals. Ian "the red Flash" Treacy – fast hard winger with a great left-footed shot.

STOP PRESS!

Our lads have reached the final of the Catholic youth Confederation under 18 cup competition. They will meet Streatham Catholic in the final. The date and venue of the match are yet to be announced.

Psssst-we have our spies out to see what the opposition are like.

ooOoo

FOOTBALL 1ˢᵀ. XI

Goalkeeper- Not much can be said about Brian but if he forgot to tell you he was Like, fearless with on canny positioning, it probably because he was telling someone else.

Backs- Mick Powell is undoubtedly a good snooker player but the cue tended to get in the way when running(running?)

"Mr Football" Martin Mulvey, the less said the better

Half Back - Judging by Mick "Sprint" McLaughlin's performances this season, some more bitter drinkers in the team will be most welcome as would training sessions in the Beehive.

Capt. John "Hippo" O'Brien who is never slow to tell us about the great goals he scored, but slow to mention the chances he missed, had an up and down season. Mostly down.

Frank Burkhard once again made the C.H. position is own, to beat him in the air a centre forward would surely need wings.

Jim Turner is a strongman of the line and one wonders if he practices dribbling with his two young children.

John "Back Chat" Maguire tried throughout the season. Why must he always argued with the ref, is it because he can't win with H.H.

Roger "Cheyenne" Kennedy greatly improved from last season, let's be fair, he could have got worse.

Donny O'Keefe the smiling Irishman with a twinkle in his eyes and toes.

John "Tantrums" Burkhard swapping from goalkeeper to winger, hel, ped the Club to have its leanest season for some time.

We also had Don Pappas cousins played for us. John and George Bishop who played very well and were a great asset to the team. Mick O'Brien, Sean Gavigan, Pat Kilbane, John Newman, Ted Clift and Eric Young also turned out for the team. To strike a more serious note the team never quite lived up to expectations. They were knocked out of the C.Y.C. Cup by a 2nd. Div. Team who only had ten men. This game should never have been lost, what was due to overconfidence and lack of fight.

In the other cup, the L. F. A., They were knocked out after having three quarters of the play. This game can't under a lot of criticism because of the team selection, many regular players were dropped and guest players stepped in. In the lead the team had a poor start losing the first three matches, but picked up well and had a run of five wins and that is all the games played so far owing to conditions. Special mention must be made of certain players – Mick Powell, Roger Kennedy, and Jim Turner who all played their best season for the Club. Summing up this hasn't been one of the Club's better seasons.

ooOoo

THE FIGHTING MAN

by K.C. Walsh

Tim Healy, driving his battered Ford along the bog road, came upon the Tinker suddenly. He was an old man and he was muttering strange curses at is poor dilapidated old horse, struggling to pull cart out of the muddy ditch.

Tim rattled his car to a stop for he had a kind heart. "Faith" he said, "and the baste will drop dead on ye if you keep it straining like that. Sure it's not moving the oul'car an inch. He'll burst his heart."

Willie now! Said the Tinker in a slow melodious voice. And he might as well burst his heart for hasn't he almost broke and mine!

"Ah" smiled Tim, since her horse is always good for something to these dead you might as well give him a chance to die naturally. Wait now! Get him out of the harness and I'll give ye a pull with me oul'car. That should shift it."

"Your very kind!" Drawled the Tinker and the removed the horse accordingly.

Tim took some rope from the back of the Ford and tied it to the rear bumper. The other end he fastened to the axle of the cart. "There now" the said. "We'll have it out again in the road in a minute."

The Tinker spat and ask, "Will the road hold."

"The back of the car will come first." Cried Tim and jumped into the front seat. He rubbed his hands together, revved up and took the strain. The Tinker stuck an empty pipe in his mouth and watched silently – and there was no expression on his face at all.

A few seconds passed with the noise of straining machinery screaming in protest. Then, with a snap, the Ford shot forward, it bonnet buried in the opposite ditch. The rear bumper lay on the road with a piece of rope still tied to it.

Tim tried to reverse but his front wheels were firmly stuck. He sighed philosophically and climbed out. "And now both in it. Old man!

The Tinker gazed at him with an expressionless face. "Tis going to rain." He said.

The sky was darkening. The mountains in the distance were dark and forbidding. A chill wind began to whisper down them and across the bogs. Tim shivered but such being his nature he made no complaint.

I'm hungry said the Tinker simply. Tim glanced at him then went over to his car. From the pocket in the door he brought out the package and a flask of tea. He unwrapped the paper and handed one of the two sandwiches to his companion. "They're ham" he said, by way of explanation. The Tinker took it silently and munched but not in the way that a hungry man would. Tim poured some tea from the flask into a plastic cup and was about to sip it when he felt the eyes of the other upon him. He paused then offered the cup silently. The Tinker took it, drank deeply and handed the cup back.

Tim tried to make conversation. "Sure maybe some fella with the lorry will come by and get us both out."

The Tinker answered slowly. "They won't. I've been here for three hours and some passed by but they were not interested in helping a Tinker. Besides, at night this road is seldom used – and will soon be dark." As he spoke first drops of rain splattered around them.

Tim shivered again. "Ah well ye never know." He couldn't think of anything else to say.

They sat there be talking for 15 minutes then the Tinker suddenly rose. "I'm satisfied." Was what he said.

Tim, feeling the chill creep into his body, nodded. He had no idea what the other meant but it seemed of no importance anyway. In a disinterested fashion he watched the Tinker cross to his cart and faced the empty shafts. Extended an arm he grasped one of them, then stepping back, he drew the cart out of the ditch as if it was a toy. Without speaking he crossed to the Ford and did likewise. He whistled and his horse trudged forward to be eased between the shafts. Only then did he turned and faced Tim.

"You've been very kind when you needn't have been. Such people as you are rare and I'm permitted to help them towards their ambitions once they've proven himself. But only one every year."

Tim was stunned. He had watched the performance of an old man paralysed with all, respect and fear that was not natural.

The Tinker continued. "There have been years when I've met no-one and there have been of the times when men have asked for things that I knew would not bring them fortune. I help them just the same. What would your wish be Timothy Healy?"

Tim finally started, "Tis - tis a powerful strong man you are- though faith ye don't look it."

"My strength," murmured the Tinker. "Is not of this world. What is your wish now?"

"Anything at all?" Gasped Tim.

"Anything- except a pot of gold. We don't provide them any more. But maybe you have an ambition other than farming?"

"I have" said Tim I and the other warily, "but tis a silly one. I would like to be a champion fightin' man."

"Boxing or wrestling?" Asked the Tinker quietly.

"Oh-at the boxin!" Said Tim.

"Good for you!" Said the Tinker, "well – sleep deep tonight in the morning will see you a new man."

The rain had ceased but the chill, damp wind still blew down from the mountains. Everything was silent as only the bog country at night can be silent. Tim was filled with the sense of unreality. But there was the broken bumper with the rope tied to it, lying in the road. There were the wheel marks in the ditch and the mud still clung to the Fords radiator. He shivered suddenly but this time not entirely with the cold.

He gathered his belongings into the car and drove away. Back in his cottage, by the term fire, he wondered again about the strange encounter. But sleep takes away all feeling when it's strong enough in a man. And Tim slept well.

....

There are many, no doubt, who remember the meteoric rise to ring fame, of the young countrymen with the uncanny skill, the beautiful muscled body and the knockout punch. You may have read in the papers yourself how he came apparently out of nowhere, levelled the best men in the booth's and after them, the best in the country, North and South. Then didn't he come to England and there was no one, it seemed who could stand against him, at all. He had to meet the champion and it was a fight everyone wanted to see.

Gunnar Ross was proud of his title. He had defended it successfully on four occasions and he had his eye on a trip to America with the championship of the world at the end of it. He was determined that no country bumpkin was going to end is aspirations. He told himself that he was the best – and he really believed it. He was a tall, powerful men, dour of visage with the speed and ferocity of a tiger. He had the knack of intimidating some of his opponents before a glove was raised, just by the way he glared at them.

Tim climb between the ropes with the memories of his previous victories strong within him. He had been granted the gift – a great gift – of invincibility. The stairs of the champion meant nothing.

Before the fight was half over he realised that this was the hardest opponent he had ever met. He had a terribly heavy punch and only his fantastic speed had saved him on a few occasions from the vicious hooks and swings of the champion.

Three times Ross sprawled on the canvas – and three times he rose but each time a little more wearily.

In the 14th round, Tim drove his man to the ropes. It looked as if the fight was all but finished. Out of nowhere a vicious right landed under Tim's heart and the following lift up smashed into his chin. Sick with pain and shock, with the roars of the digital crowd in his ears, Tim sank to his knees, clutching the rope. Dimly heard the count begin. Halfway through he heard it clearly. He refused to believe that he was actually down and he gazed in wonderment at the menacing form of the man who had just put in there.

The referee said "Ten"

slowly Tim Rose. He felt in excellent shape but he had actually been down – counted out. He couldn't believe it. Ross patted his back in the usual fashion and muttered something about it being his hardest contest. His second is said he was unlucky. Many people said many things. But they all meant nothing to Tim for didn't he know that he had been gifted with greater skill than any man. Or was it all a lie?

It was a minor sensation when Tim Healy retired from the ring. Yet it soon died as those things do. "After all." Tim thought to himself, haven't I enough money now to purchase the best farm on the market and haven't I a fine girl soon to be me wife. I'll be content with that."

So it happened that some weeks later he had a strange desire to visit the same bog road where he had first met the Tinker. He drove slowly along in his brand-new car, musing on many things. He felt no surprise when he noticed at the same point on the road, the old car, the same old ageless horse between the shafts and the Tinker on the seat puffing his pipe.

Tim drew up. "Well now – and isn't this a peculiar meeting." He said. "Would it be by accident I wonder?"

"You never know – it might." Said the Tinker, complacently.

Momentarily at a loss for words, Tim said. "I see you're not in the ditch this time."

"I'm not, since you mention it." Replied the Tinker.

Tim, feeling nervous and a little foolish, decided to ask the thing that had been bothering him. "I can't help feeling curious about me last fight."

"Indeed?" Said the Tinker politely.

"Aye." continued Tim licking his lips. "You said I had the skill and the strength to be champion, for you'd give it to me."

"I did of course." Said the Tinker blowing a puff of smoke towards the distant mountains.

"Then how the hell," blurted Tim, becoming irritable, "did I lose me last fight."

The Tinker removed his pipe and looked at him solemnly. At that moment he seemed to be very old and very wise.

"Me boy" he began, "You could have won that fight easily enough. You had the strength and the skill. If you hadn't remained on your knees for so long, wondering how you got there, the fight was yours. Wasn't your opponent down three times and didn't he get up and fight back. Ah me Boyo, I give you all the skills needed and the strength and speed but it was enough."

"What did you miss out so?" Asked him, not comprehending.

"Nothing." said the Tinker simply. "I gave you all I could. What was missing was the heart – the heart to rise when you're down. No-one can give a man that. He has to find that for himself." He relit his pipe. Still – you learn something and that never does a man any harm. You did the right thing boy. Go back to your farm and the fine girl ye have to be your wife. God bless you and good luck to you both. May you have five children and may die in Ireland. With that, the man of the road, touch the horses hindquarters lightly with his whip and he moved off. He never looked back.

Tim stared at the mountains now slowly turning blue. He took a deep breath of the perfumed air. He sat still in his seat for a few minutes, thinking. "Be the hokey! Your man was right!" He said at length. He drove off and there was nothing on the road.

ooOoo

19 SPANISH HOLIDAY 61
by Keith Piggott

We left Victoria station at about 10:30 a.m. Saturday 19th of August and arrived in Paris that evening. After a couple of our stay, which seemed enough time for one or two persons to get lost, we continued our journey to Spain. Eventually we arrived at Castelldelfels having changed trains at Barcelona – it was early Sunday evening.

When everybody had unpacked, settled in their rooms and had had a rest we made our way to the village church where Father celebrated Mass.

The hostel Del Mar which was our new abode, was two stories high with the dining room and bar adjoining the south wing nearest the sea. First night there, nearly everybody went to "Uncle Ned" early, one or two though, ventured out into the new surroundings.

First impression given, was that the locals had never seen the immaculate British race in such vast numbers and were therefore, a little curious. We later found them to be very friendly and helpful at times. It didn't take us long to fall into the Spanish easy – going way of life and after a few days we began to wonder why everybody back home rushes around so. Although this is true we couldn't afford to stay in bed too long for a morning, firstly because you would discover that when you wanted to wash there wasn't any water, secondly because brekkies wasn't served later than 10 or 10:30 a.m. Some got over one of the water problems by washing their teeth in the "vino" instead of "aqua" which was very refreshing.

Lunch was served about 2 p.m. and dinner about 9 p.m. so in between meals we either rested or went for a stroll instead of having a "milkyway".

On the corner of the crossroads opposite the hotel was "EL Pinar" a small restaurant/bar which we frequented. The gov'nor there was quite a friendly chap and one day when we strolled in for an "lemonade" we were greeted by his two new assistants behind the bar, who spoke almost perfect English. On close observations, to our surprise, we discovered that they were, in fact, two of our own lads.

Siesta in Spain is about 3:30 p.m. and it's a time when most of the shops close for hour; owing to the heat.

As is normal the word soon gets around about a new place to visit and we went to a Club called "El Parata". This had a small circular dance floor amongst a sub-tropical undergrowth with coloured lights in the trees and alcoves dotted here and there.

About 20 yards from the hotel grounds was the sea and the enormous beach of fine Zirconium sand. At certain times of the day the sun in Spain can be very vicious as one or two of the Club members can tell you from their experiences of looking and feeling like a roast potatoe. Near to the beach was another "cantina" which was very handy after having a swim.

"John's Cantina" I believe was popular with most people having got a "Juke – Box" with good records. It is situated opposite the entrance to the railway station and near all the shops. Cigarettes are cheap once you acquire the taste for the local brew, otherwise Americano "fags" are in "mucho" abundance.

We visited Barcelona a couple of times once to see a bullfight and tour the town. Some of the group went in a party to the bullfight then went to some night spots. We visited Monserratt, a monastery which is situated high in the mountains and besides it being beautifully itself the surrounding view was marvellous.

During our stay we had two parties at the hotel. One for the birthdays of three of the group. The other a farewell party – both were terrific. The Spaniards enjoyed themselves also, by watching us dance. The last few days of the holiday go so quickly and everybody makes this most of them, we were no exception and as taxis were cheap to hire we got around quite a bit.

ooOoo

WHAT ABOUT THE WORKERS

Just a few words to express our thanks to members were worked on decorations and generally mending the old Club.

How many of you remember when Table Tennis used to be played in the common room? It wasn't long ago, but the great transformation has taken place in that room. Jimmy Redbridge, Chris Braak and Derek Merrales were to the fore with brushes in one hand and paint pots in the other. Martin Flynn, Noel O'Connor, Brian Dyer, Billy Clements and Malcolm Hyde turned up to paint and give a face – lift to the toilets. Patsy Culliver, Wendy Clark and Pat O'Connor sewed everything up by – recovering the settee and making curtains. Mickey Reid ably assisted by Bill O'Mahoney at times, did a great job on the lighting. After finishing in the common room, Jimmy, Chris and Derek started painting in the hall, they spent a lot of time getting it ready before the Christmas festivities were due to start.

Johnny Newman, helped by many of the young lads, arranged the paper decorations which we know were appreciated by other parish groups as well as the Club.

Working together in the Club can be enjoyable and gives enjoyment to others for a long time after.

ooOoo

TOP TEN WITH A TWIST

It might as well rain until September – it will probably slow.

Gossip Calypso – very popular on as wives Joyce.

What now my love – I've washed up, swept up and taking the dog out – well?

Dance on – not me toes, you fall!

Will I walked?...... Well, if that's a you feel, write your own magazine.

Sherry – I don't mind why do, sir.

Loop de loop – the French merry-go-round.

Coming home baby – about time too.

He's a Rebel – and him, and him, and in...

Return to sender – GPO's speciality...

***

A twist in time keeps the figure fine.

***

COMING EVENTS

APRIL 15TH. EASTER MONDAY. The Club ramble – a coach will take us from the Club to Newlands Corner – then the big track through the countryside of Surrey. Johnny Newman has supplied us with a map of the area, hope you can read it.

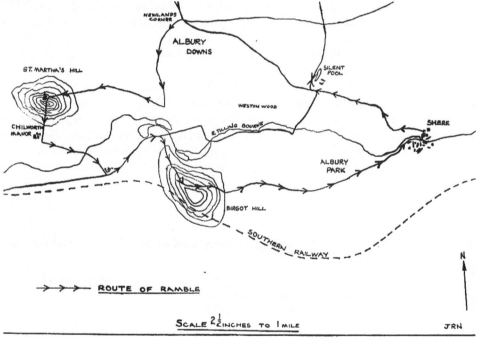

ROVING REPORT.

By Ann O'Nymus.

Easter Monday arrived oh yes the ramble. Hurry up – don't want to miss the coach. On arrival at the Club I found that all the best seats in the coach had been taken as usual – have to get up earlier in future.

The coach set off at about 1020 a.m. and the start of the journey was unusually subdued especially for the St Anne's Mob. There were a few mumblings about the weather being slightly over-cast and then the sweets and cigarettes began to flow. The first hour or so flew by and we arrived at the car park at Newlands Corner. Everybody out was the general order. I've never seen a more assorted lot out of so few, about thirty-eight to be more precise. A quick look around saw jeans, boots, big belts, small belts, holdalls, rucksacks, berets, bonnets, coats, jumpers, sandals and fluorescent socks – coloured blue, red, brown and black. If the day wasn't going to be bright we were.

"Head and up move out" shouted 'Gil' father Pearce and the long thin line started out with 'Rowdy' Newman fetching up the drag. Father certainly set a speedy pace to start, we all thought he wanted to make the round trip by lunchtime. Some did take in the countryside though and began to trail behind, transistor radio and all. After trudging across Albury Downs and through some winding lanes we came to the "Sandpit". Sorry we forgot to fetch out buckets and spades. Anyway, a good stopping place to regroup the herd. I heard that the tail end of the party had played a great 45 minutes of football on the way across the Downs and through the lanes. Had to get our ball back from a couple of gardens too.

Out came the bottles of pop and fruit during our short stop. Some tongues began to hang at half-mast. Pick yourself up, must keep rolling, rolling, rolling.

Pressing on through the lovely countryside we came to the foot of St Martha's Hill. "We've not got to walk up there?" and "Let's go around" were some of the retorts on the sight before them. Finally on reaching the top everybody gave a sigh of relief, fell down, and the outstanding sound was a rustle of sandwich packs and suction on vacuum flasks. "They're game lads you know", yes that's the boys who no sooner than finishing their lunches began to play football. Not for Jimmy Bremridge who had taken his big boots off just to give them a rest.

After slipping and sliding down St Martha's Hill we came to Chilworth Manor. The people at the head of the snaky column saw the Percy Arms, the sight in itself being an excuse for a drink. At the Percy Arms it was decided upon to take a different route into Shere. Catastrophe. We seem to walk in circles and up and down the Birgot Hill trying to find a way out but we were it seemed surrounded by private land and fences. In the end we came back to civilisation and hard roads at Albury.

We decided not to go to Shere as time was getting on so we went direct to the Silent pool. At least some of the party did, in the process of getting lost at Birgots Hill, we were split up into two or three small groups. The Silent Pool was not at its best, the entrance been very muddy and round at the pool it seemed very dark.

The last mile, as we were told, up the hill to Newlands Corner seemed like a dozen miles. At the top we made our way to The Barn Cafe for much-needed refreshments and then re-joined the coach at the car park. One small group were lucky because they waited at the Silent Pool for the coach. The last part of the fun and games came when Jim Brack was left at the top of the hill and then thumbed a lift to the Silent Pool thinking he would miss the coach. A great day enjoyed by all. Thanks to Father Pearce for organising another wonderful addition to the memories of the St Anne's Club members.

ooOoo

MR WALSH'S FABULOUS REVUE singing, miming, and dramatics – not much to put up with for 1/6p
JULY 14TH. ANNUAL CRICKET MATCH at Beaumont College, Windsor. Coaches will take players and spectators down to Windsor, stopping on the way, at Runnymede, for lunch.
JULY 20TH. WERE ALL GOING ON A SPANISH HOLIDAY. (No report available)

GOSSIP COLUMN

Pin your ears back everybody here comes the latest gossip....

.... Molly (Lee McLaren) and Frank Burkhard who were married in early 1962 announced the arrival of St Anne's future football captain (Philip Anthony) born on 1 January 1963....

.... Peter McLaren, Molly's brother, is now ranked number six in the welterweight division of the British boxing board of control for... Oxon Pete.....

..... ATTENTION – STANDARD AT EASE – have you heard Jack Frost has signed on for five years in the Army.

Who knows we may have a future parliamentarian candidate..

.... Congratulations to the latest engaged couple – Margaret Egon and Johnny Newman. We wonder who will be next HH and JM perhaps, (not mentioning any names of course)...

..... October will be the month for the wedding of Christine and Roy. May we take this opportunity in wishing them every success and happiness for the future.

A late welcome goes out to new members were joined the Club since Christmas

Frederick Webb	Marian Scott
Noel Roche	John Helen
Maureen Quinn	Lawrence Brady
Elizabeth O'Sullivan	Jim Whitehead
Peter Fourniss	Dennis Good
John Day	Tom Ely
Denise Donovan	Raymond Butcher
Elizabeth Carroll	Noel Moran
Brian Brady	Terry Smyth
Robert Beckley	Lynn Dawson

We hope your stay at St Anne's will be a pleasant one.

Who knows you may be in the next issue of the gossip columns.

"Opera?"

"Oh yes, that's where used dapper guy and instead of dying he sings."

GUINNESS IS GOOD. Especially in LAWRENCE OF ARABIA.

LETTERS TO THE EDITOR

None received as yet, but will be pleased to hear from you about grumbles, moans, queries, ideas et cetera.

The following is an extract from the ST.ANNE'S ANNAL'S JULY 1943 issue

A GRUMBLE.

Having been a member of the Club for some years now I think I can speak with more than a little authority regarding the atmosphere of the Club. For some time now there seems to have been a lack of spirit and sociability which although it may pass unnoticed by members, must be very apparent to newcomers. How many can honestly say that they know everybody in the Club? It is obvious that you cannot be everybody's bosom pal but it is the duty of all members to be good mixers and not split up into small groups as though the rest of the Club was beneath one's dignity.

It is extremely hard to be chatty and at ease with a complete stranger but even a few words will help to make a person feel at home. The number of would-be members who have been literarily frozen out of the Club must be enormous.

With just a little thought for others and very much less egoism St Anne's can once again become a model Club. So what about it fellow members?

ooOoo

HAPPY EASTER TO ALL.

ooOoo

LEADER'S PAGE

A Club is fortunate if it has good traditions. You may remember from your catechism that a tradition is to handing on or the handing down of an opinion, belief or custom from one generation to another. One opinion or belief that has been handed on to us by successive generations of Club members is at St Anne's is a good Club they have also handed down to us the customs that helped to make it so – the practice of members behaving in an orderly manner, of there being respectably dressed, of the Club having a friendly and homely atmosphere. Members come and go. Club activities change. Yet, because of the traditional spirit which animates the Club, St Anne's Club is always essentially the same.

I was talking to a number of former members one Saturday night in early May when the Old Member's Association was having a reunion. They were saying how they still felt at home coming into the Club and I reflected that but for their age and the fact that they were now fathers and mothers of families they would still find it easy to fit into our Club life. They were still proud of the Club and it is a good thing to be able to take a rightful pride in something that is worthwhile. As long as that sense of pride remains in the Club there will always be both the consciousness that membership is itself worthwhile and the desire to do something worthwhile for the Club in return.

To do something worthwhile for the Club does not mean you have to be good at games. Serving at Club benediction; helping in the canteen; making curtains; decorating one of the rooms; supporting any Club event; saying Club prayers devoutly and with meaning – these are the few of the ways in which you can help the Club and yourselves. Of course, those who are good at games and turn out so regularly for the Club at football, Netball, Table Tennis or Snooker are using their talents to the benefit of the Club. They help also to keep the Club's name to the forefront in the world of competition with other Clubs. They have had some reward this year in the number of cups and medals they have one.

I would like to mention to names of those who have helped to foster and encourage the Club spirit by their enthusiasm and support. One is Brian Gosnell whose keen management has brought such success to the under 16 football team. The other is Mr Don Papa Who has been at an unfailing supporter of all that the Club has tried to do.

Tradition and spirit are not enough of themselves to keep the Club going. In this world where little is given away free a Club must be able to pay its way in order to survive. Sometimes it seems that we are surviving by the skin of our teeth. In the next issue I shall try to give you some idea what the expenses of the Club are and where we get the income in order to meet those expenses. All I need say here is that your subscription play a great part in helping to make ends meet and a prompt they are paid the happier we feel.

ooOoo

CRICKET.

For the Club to have a game of Cricket is quite an occasion and the challenge by St Dominic Savio therefore was taken up with great interest among Club members. On Sunday 19th of May, a rather chilly afternoon 11 players turned out on Clapham common looking like supporters of 'Alice Nunns', rather than Cricket, by wearing a collection of coloured pullovers, shorts and trousers.

On winning the toss elected to bat and 'Dusty' Miller and Brian Dyer open the innings. 'Dusty' got off to a good start by hitting two two's off the first over. The next five overs produced only four more runs plus a let off for Brian who was bowled for one and the same fate struck Sean Gavigan who was dismissed for a Duck. At fifteen the third wicket fell when the plodding 'Dusty' was brilliantly caught and bowled for six. The situation look very bad for us until John Maguire joined John O'Brien, this peer attacked the bowling and soon the fielders were spread out around the boundary. The fielding was not as good as it should have been and many catches were dropped. John O'Brien was dismissed for sixteen much to the joy of our opponents, this joy was short lived when John Burkhard reached the crease, he and

John Maguire added a quick fourty runs before John Burkhard was caught in the deep.

In his first over John Busby took a neat return catch to dismiss that opening bat. A fine piece of fielding and a hard return which knocked down the wicket by Noel O'Connor ran out a dithering batsmen. The wickets began to fall steadily until the fifth wicket stand pushed the score into the thirty's. It was then that Sean Gavigan keeping wicket was struck in the eye by a ball which flew off the edge of a flashing bat. After attention he was helped off the field. John Maguire took two wickets quick wickets and although the remaining back and defended stoutly John O'Brien and brother Mick finished off the tail.

Our opponents scored 65 and this low score can be credited not only to the bowlers but also the keen fielding of all the team.

A great match was enjoyed by all involved. Our thanks go out to St Dominic Savio team for their challenge which ended in an afternoon of friendly rivalry.

ooOoo

OPPORTUNITY

By K.C.WALSH.

Grayson lay motionless, listening. He was glad his wife was a heavy sleeper. He was glad, too, that she was a nervous woman, and insisted upon sleeping only behind a locked bedroom door. And then, suddenly, her voice pierced the darkness in a hoarse whisper.

"George! Are you asleep, George? I – I'm sure there's someone breaking in!"

The fast beating of his heart almost choked him. It seemed to be pumping all the strength out of him. He could feel the perspiration on his forehead turned shudderingly cold. Oh why did Kit have to wake. The inevitable sequel made him feel faint with fear. But he made no movement. There was just a chance that if he feigned sleep, and there was no more sounds...

"George!" Kits voice came more urgently, more hoarsely, as a shuffling noise under the window was repeated. "Wake up-- at once!" As she began to shake him frantically.

It was no good. He pretended to wait with a start.

"What-- what is it?" He demanded loudly thinking that the sound of his voice might scare away any intruder.

"There's a burglar-- trying to get in downstairs. You'd better see what-- what's going on!"

He tried to keep his voice steady." Don't be silly Kit. If you've heard anything it'll be Jones. That's the worst of sharing a house-- you can never call play short own. He'll have had one of his indigestion bouts and gone down for his white medicine."

"No, it isn't our Landlord!" Kit always annoyed George by calling Mr Jones 'our landlord'. "When he goes down at night he always switches on the landing light. It makes a yellow glow under our bedroom door. But there isn't one now. George, you must go down and set my mind at rest. I'll not sleep another week until you do."

George swung his legs over the side of the bed and groped his way to the door. If he lived until tomorrow he'd have a dog-- an Alsatian, too. Then, uttering a quick prayer that there might be no intruder in the house, he crossed the room, turned the key silently, and slid the door open....

Tuber stood by the thick bushes in the front garden and looked at the house raring up in front of him. He'd cased it for a week. Two middle- aged men and a timid-looking woman.

"A piece of cake!" He told himself jauntily tried to stop his knees from trembling by bracing back is legs.

He was sick and tired of being on the fringe of Clappers gang. He wore the same outlandish clothes as they did, and swaggered out in the approved Teddy boy style. He chewed gum and carried a knuckle-duster. But the others still wouldn't accept.

"Sixteen, and not done a thing yet!" Clapper had jeered at him last week outside Sammy's milk bar. "Why, but got I even take in your name yet. Cracker group-use a bicycle chain on someone-- anything to show you got guts, and I'll take you one. It doesn't matter that you're a shrimp and look as if you wouldn't know what to do with a good dinner. So long as you can flick a knife quickest, you an' me'll get on fine".

As it had done for a long time now, the urge for recognition deadened his natural fear. All he had to do was to pinch a gold watch or some other valuable article, and Clapper would have to admit he was a somebody-- a terror away who knew the ropes and did things.

He looked up and down the road then tiptoe gingerly to the front window. He could see something faintly gleaming on what looked like a sideboard. A piece of silver plate, no doubt. That will be the very thing.

Elation bold up inside of him. Only a piece of glass separated him from his spoils. This was his opportunity. He smiled to himself as imagination ran away with him."Hey, Clapper, how about this?" He could picture himself saying." Why not this silver dish of last night". Clappers approve impact on the shoulder was a foregone conclusion.

He turned to open the window of the house but it would not budge. His hands were clumsy. At the end of the road car passed by. He paused. The second car turned up the road, its headlights glaring like beacons.

Tuber froze in panic his belly turned to water. The car went by, however. He had not been seen.

Five minutes later his thudding heart had quietened down sufficiently to let him move again. He crept to the back. It was safer there. Less chance of being spotted. Two windows he saw, looked out onto the back garden. The smaller one, he reckoned, will be the scullery. That would do fine. To his amazement, the window was locked. It opened with only the faintest of creeks. He flashed his torch around and saw a sink directly beneath. This is too easy. He was in. But more important still if all went well, a few minutes and he will be out!

Scarcely daring to breathe, he slipped forward. He was unaware of the four inch high step until he tripped over it. He went down with his hand bent under him. When he got up his wrist was soggy and useless. He could have screamed with pain. He retrieved his torch and snapped it off. He waited a long time, or so it seemed to him, but – no one seemed aware of his presence. There was not a sound in the house. He moved forward at last. He felt sick. His wrist hurt abominably. He wanted only to get away from this house -- reached the safety of his own bedroom at home again.

George stood on the top landing. He knew for certain there was someone in the house now. That dull thud had come either from the kitchen or the scullery. He thought. "If he's armed he'll shoot. Or maybe he has a knife". He felt the perspiration begin to trickle down the side of his face. Should he call Jones? No, Jones would panic and switch on a light and thereby give away their position. And then he stiffened. Supposing there was more than one intruder? What would he do about that? Although why should he do anything at all, provide the burglar or burglars, didn't come upstairs. The ground floor was no concern of his. Jones occupied the whole of the ground floor. The fact that he chose to sleep in the attic at the top of the house was his own affair....

Suddenly Kits whisper broke through the heavy silence." George? Are you still there George?"

He could see her framed in the bedroom doorway. In a long white nightdress she looked like a ghost. Grayson motioned her back viciously, although he doubted she would see his action. He couldn't talk- not even whisper. His throat was too dry. If only Kit will go back to bed and not stand there watching him. After all these years he mustn't let her find out what a coward he really was. He edged to the bottom of the first flight. All was silent.

Tuber had to force himself forward. He wasn't cut out for this lark. He will grab the first fairly valuable article the beam of his torch settled on, and scram! All he wanted was something to show Clapper and the boys-- and then no more of this nonsense.

Two doors came into focus. He turned the knob of the nearest one. It opened. Simultaneously, he let out a vile curse as his torch light ran along rows of cups and saucers, plates, bowls, and oddments. Hell! A blasted cupboard. And then he drew in a breath through his decayed front teeth. What was that in the far corner of the third shelf? A cash box. He'd heard some people put their valuables in the place burglars were likely to search.

He touched the box as if it was hot. It was unlocked. The lid lifted under his fingers which fastened on a bunch of notes. Fifty of them if there was one, he guessed.

Hell, if only his wrist didn't hurt so much. It wouldn't hold the torch any longer. He put it between his teeth. As he did so his elbow knocked over a plastic egg cup it hit the floor with a loud, hollow plop. He sweated and held his breath. He mustn't be caught now - not with fifty quid in his paws.

Nothing happened. He caressed the note once again. Gosh, what a break...

George Grayson had a sudden idea. If he were to creep into the toilet and pull the flush chain, that would surely frighten any intruder away. He could then say the burglar had beaten it when he burst in on him. But there was his wife, blast her. The lavatory was on the same floor as their bedroom. She would see him go inside.

He paused and listened intently. There seemed to be no further sound from below. He braced himself. He was a fool. Who would want to break into the house. There was nothing of value to steal. Nevertheless, he would have a dog tomorrow...

He stared into the black wall of the hall and continued slowly down the stairs. Almost before he realised it, he was outside the door of the kitchen. Then he heard the hollow, plopping sound near at hand the receding tide of his fear came rushing back in a gigantic wave. It envelopes him completely and left him leaning helplessly against the door. He put his two hands on the lintel to prevent himself from falling.

Tuber had never been so excited in his life. Fifty quid what a haul. All he needed now was some object of reasonable value to take along to clatter. The money was his. There would be no splitting of that. He clutched it tightly in his left hand, along with the torch. He sent the thin beam scanning towards the other door. There was that shining object he had seen in the front room. He would get that and then.....

He let out a yell of terror as the light came to rest on Grayson's face, slack and open-mouth. In the torch's light it appeared grey and the globules of sweat gleamed like glass crystals.

He recalled and with another shriek he dropped the notes and the torch, blundering through to the scullery, forced wobbling legs onto the sink, and fell through the window to the garden below. He was over the fence and down the deserted road in a matter of seconds.

With the realisation that the intruder had vanished, a surge of exaltation smothered the black panic in George's heart. He noticed the open window, but clumsily unbolted the door and almost fell out. His groping hand crashed itself on the pebble-dashed wall.

Ten minutes later, Kit was bathing his knuckles tenderly while a wide eyed Jones was retrieving his scattered notes with a shaking hand.

"You certainly have guts," Kit was saying." To tackle the man single-handed. A burly six footer, you said-- and you so small."

ooOoo

<u>1963 Vol 1 Issue 3</u>

LEADER'S PAGE.

CHRISTMAS. What thoughts come into your mind when you read that word. It may be a picture of yourself buying Christmas presents, or receiving presents, to whom to send your Christmas cards. You may think of Christmas parties or of your Christmas dinner. It may be the memory of the last celebrations at the office when you made a full of yourself or it may be looking forward to the school holidays. Or would you think of what the word Christmas really means? The Christ Mass. A picture of Midnight Mass – the priest at the alter – Christ, the Son of God, who came into the world in the stable at Bethlehem, coming on to the alter at the words of the priest, 'This is my body'. Christ coming to you in a holy Communion as you kneel at the alter rails.

It is the thought of Christ which really matters at Christmas. Without him all the rest has no meaning – presents, cards, celebrations. Christmas Day is Christ's Day, His birthday. Because He was born we have become by baptism not just creatures but children of God and brothers of Christ. We celebrate a birthday in the family–the most important birthday in all history.

Not everybody thinks of Christmas like this. Many people know or care nothing about Christ. They are indeed pagans and many of the ways they celebrate are pagan – a throwback to the time before Christ when the winter festivals were celebrated in a mood of complete irresponsibility leading to all kinds of degrading scenes. Young people today, Christmas included, often get affected by this spirit of irresponsibility at Christmas time. It is a Christian act for a fellow to go to the office party or to a friend party or into a pub at this season just to drink and drink and then to become very, very childish or very, very objectionable? Do you act like that? If so, why? To honour the birth of Christ, it is rather an insult to Him. To make yourself one of the boys? They do not think better of you for it.

Of course, it is not only boys act like this. Sometimes girls or even sillier. One should give a word of warning to girls were just started work. If there is a party at the place where you work just remember that people will not think less of you because you insist on sticking to soft drinks. Everybody knows that girls of your age are not used to alcohol. If anyone sees you drinking he will not only know that you are weak – will but also that in a short time you will not be fully conscious of what you are doing an advantage can easily be taken of you. Older girls may think they are aware of the dangers and can cope with them, but they may well be proved wrong as others have learnt to their cost in the past. If you want to celebrate Christmas with a drink, do it at home with the family – if your parents let you! But don't that the celebration of Christ's birthday become a mockery of what it should be.

I hope all that does not sound too depressing when we should be speaking about the happiness of Christmas, but I feel I should say these things in order that this Christmas may be a truly happy time for you and not marred by any regrets.

In the Club we shall try to make our contributions to the festivities with the party on the Sunday before Christmas – and this year we hope the decorations will be up to the traditional standards.

As usual some rows of seats on the right – hand side of the church will be reserved for Club members going to midnight mass. Remember, if you are receiving Holy Communion, not to eat anything or drink any alcohol after 9:40 p.m. but you can have a cup of tea or coffee or soft drink up until 11.40.

For you all made this be a Christmas full of blessings and the happiest of your lives.

ooOoo

THE 2 'C'S

At one of their meetings the 2 'Cs (canteen committee) made a list of the advantages of working hard to build up an efficient canteen, and decided that it would help to develop the following dazzling list of talents!

1. How to cater
2. How to be observant for bargains
3. How to keep accounts
4. How to make a kitchen bright and easy to work in.
5. How to cook
6. How to make food look attractive
7. How to entertain guests
8. How to give service to the Club and pleasure to the Club members.

The following are members of 2 'C's

Penny Bizzell	Maureen Delanhunty
Mary Basser	Susan Green
Margaret Callan	Pamela Hudd
Betty Carole	Pat O'Connor
Wendy Clark	Susan Tutt
Denise Donovan	Gloria Pook
Lynne Dawson	Margaret Kavanagh

and several other members have offered their services if needed.

On behalf of all Club members thank you to seize for the enthusiastic service that has been given so far.

[Authors note: It appears that the canteen facilities had radically changed from what it used to be back in the 'Old Club' days. Possibly due to planned changes to the Clubs Premises caused various major changes in the Clubs Layout??].

ooOoo

IN OUR VIEW

BY. Sheila Lodwig & Moira Sullivan.

Our first impression upon arriving at the Club was how fortunate the members are in having the own building, whereas other Clubs have to use either school or church walls. This, of course, enables you to carry on various activities at the same time.

On entering the Club, we noticed the friendly atmosphere and we have found this every time we come. When we first came we were shown around the Club by Pat and Tony. On this tour we were especially struck by the canteen (run very efficiently by the members) and the room in which it is. The Club is fortunate in having its own games room, which is obviously put to good use, judging by the array of cups. Having seen the needlework room we were surprised by the size of the room used for cookery classes, but we are assured that the class achieves good results, and the girls attending these classes seem to enjoy them.

We think that it is unusual to find a common room in a Club instead of the usual run-of-the-mill dancehall. This contributes to the informal atmosphere of the Club, and seems to provide a friendly meeting place for the members.

Before we came we were very pretty apprehensive because we did not know what to expect, but the welcome you gave us soon set as at ease.

ooOoo

OUR WEEK-END AT WAXWELL

A few weeks ago a group of boys and girls, all mainly Club members, spent the weekend at the home of the Grail Organisation Waxwell Farm Pinner.

On arrival we were warmly greeted by the Grail members and a hot supper had been prepared for us. This was followed by the first discussion which was "How Many Children and when", the speakers were Mrs Howard and Mr Rigg (with a total of 9 ½ children between them, we all agreed that they were very able speakers on the subject.) After a short talk, the rest of the evening was spent in discussion, not only with the speakers, but also between ourselves.

The next morning came too soon for some of the boys, who arrived at breakfast late and sleepy – card schools must be very tiring –!! However, after breakfast a morning walk in the spacious grounds soon brought everyone back to their senses again.

The morning's first discussion was led by Miss Adams, "On Boy and Girl Relationships Leading to Marriage, this proved to be one of the most argumentative discussions of the weekend and everyone's views were expressed quite openly on this subject. Before Mass Canon Arbuthnott talk to us about "The Churches Law on Marriage" although most of us were taught a great deal at school, it was good to have our minds refreshed on this subject.

The afternoons discussion, unanimously agreed by all as the most interesting and worthwhile, was given by Father Casey of the Catholic Housing Society on the question of buying a home. This dynamic Priest and his helpers have lessened the problem of housing considerably since the Society was formed a few years ago. We are sure that when the time comes all of us will endeavour to purchase a house with help of the Society.

A social was arranged for the evening, but unfortunately the record player broke down, but Radio Luxembourg proved an adequate replacement.

Sunday morning the weekend was summed up in open forum. At 12.00 noon Mass was said by Canon Abuthnott and so completed a most interesting weekend.

Although this was the Club's first attempt at a weekend of this nature, everybody agreed it had been a great success and would most certainly like Father Pearce to arrange more like it in the near future. Finally we would like to take this opportunity of thanking the Grail Members for their patients and kind hospitality shown to us all.

ooOoo

STOP PRESS Dateline -St Anne's Club – Monday, November 25th.

A group of 25 to 30 unemployed lads from the North East of England visited the Club for the evening. We thank the members for showing them our London hospitality. More thanks to the Dolphins, who provided the music, and to the two C's for providing eats. A very good time was had by all.

ooOoo

1964 Vol 1 Issue 1.

THE LEADER'S PAGE.

I should not be writing this page because by the time the magazine comes out I shall no longer be the Club leader. Unless the Bishop has moved me to another parish by that time I shall still be closely connected with the Club as its Director. But Pat Cassidy (whom you all know) and John Stanton (whom you probably all know as you read this) will then be sharing the leadership between them, or rather will be joint leaders.

Life is a series of endings and beginnings. An epoch in the Clubs history ends as the priest – Leader hands over to the running of the Club to the trained leaders who are lay people and much better qualified than he could ever hope to be. A new era starts which should see the Club become stronger more stabilised and much more effectively organised. From now on the priest in the Club will be free to serve the Club in any way that will be for the good of its members.

It is always rather sad to say good-bye to anyone with whom one has been closely associated for some years, even though that person is leaving to begin the joys of married life in the country town of Tonbridge. On Easter Sunday 1955, the Club said goodbye to George Belcher who had worked so hard as its secretary and had held it together through several difficult years. On Easter Sunday this year we shall be saying good-bye to his brother Tony. All of us have appreciated his untiring efforts for the good of the Club and I cannot pay him a better complement than to say that the Club in the early sixties owes as much to him as it owed to George in the early fifties. Make sure you are at the Club on Easter Sunday to make it a night Tony will remember.

That same evening we also hope to be celebrating the football team successes. Already the seniors have won the sea. Y. C. Premier division cup now we wait for the great day, March 22nd., when they and the Juniors play in their respective cup finals. This is an occasion which may not be repeated in a time of any of you in the Club. We shall want every member present at the NAAFI ground at Mitcham to give the team the encouragement and support they need.

This Finals day will also mark an ending in the Club's football history. Frank Burkhard will then be retiring as a weekly player. For eight years he has played for the Club and has captained his team most of that time. Any success that has been gained in those years is due to him more than anyone else. Yet it has not been just outstanding ability as a player or his gift of leadership as a captain that have marked him out; to my mind he has also been outstanding for the example he has always set both on and off the field. I think he has influenced others more than they or he have realised and as shown you can be a good Catholic as well as a good sportsman. If the first team does the double and wins the cup as well as league it will be a fitting climax to his Club career.

Before we arrive at Easter Sunday there is the rest of Lent to pass through, or, to phrase it better there is the rest of Lent to be used. It is all too easy to let the days of Lent slip by, almost unnoticed but at the same time leaving us with a vague feeling that we should be doing something. On another page you will find some suggestions as to how you can use the last three weeks of Lent try and follow them so that the great days of Maundy Thursday when the Last Supper took place, the Priesthood was instituted, the first Mass was offered, the Apostles received Holy Communion for the first time Good Friday when Our Lord suffered for you and then died for you on the cross. Use these last weeks well and then Easter Sunday when Christ proved he was God by raising from the dead, will be a day of really of true rejoicing and real happiness for you.

WELCOME TO JOHN STANTON

Nearly a year after welcoming Pat Cassidy to the Club as its first full-time Leader, we now greet John Stanton. He and Pat will be joined Club Leaders with John having a special responsibility for the boys as Pat has for the girls.

The Club was most fortunate in that the Management Committee decided to appoint another Leader just at the time John was coming to the end of his course at the National Training College for Youth Leaders at Leicester. He had previously been a leader at Hollington Boys Club for nearly 3 years. He has all the experience and qualifications needed for his position – but, perhaps even more important – the Management Committee felt that he had the right approach to youth work in addition to a most pleasing manner. No more had better be said or John will begin to feel embarrassed when he reads this.

We shall not expect miracles but just as the Club has benefited from Pat's presence it should not be many months before the Club experiences the further benefits of a fresh approach to its life as activities under John's Leadership. The Club has not been unsuccessful under its past leaders – but all have been aware of the deficiencies springing from a lack of suitable training. There should be far more successful years ahead now for the Club – and this does not mean success only in the field of competitive sport which is but a poor reason for a Club's existence.

If members give to John the cooperation and friendliness that give to Father Pearce to Pat and to Tony, he can be assured of a happy and fruitful period of leadership.

ooOoo

If a 7 mile walk through the countryside appeals to you then read on. The coach will be leaving the Club on Easter Monday morning heading for the wide open spaces. If you would like to go then make sure your name is on the list that is on the notice board. The cost will be 7/6- that's for the return coach fare. You will need to supply your own food. Here is a rough guide to the route and also a mention of that some places we will pass.

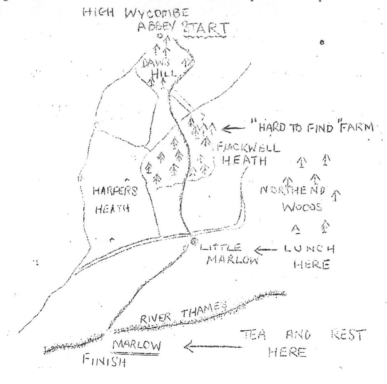

HAVE A RAMBLING GOOD EASTER.

ooOoo

[Authors note:] The photograph below is the only one photo in the Club's Photo Albums that I could not find an appropriate place for. I did not recognise any of the faces except Kenneth Wolstenholme the BBC's Football Pundit, who no doubt presented the teams with their trophy date and place unknown. But can assume that this is the presentation to the St. Anne's Football Team success in winning the Cup, circa Easter 1963- as mentioned in the Leaders Page above.

Below is Autographs of the Referee and Club Team members, who won the Cup. Taken from the Club's Autograph book.

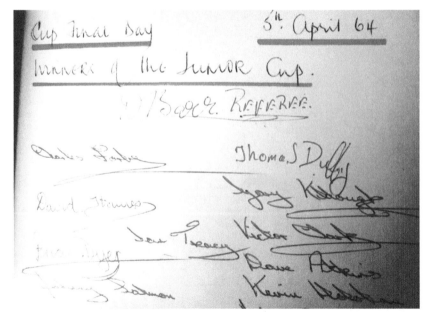

ooOoo

Having spent time, researching the only existing documents available in the Club's records. All dating back from 1935 to 1945, with a few Architects Plans detailing modifications to the Club's Premises. To piece together the passage of the Clubs History for the following years, without any records or, photographs from 1963 onwards. Provides me with no alternative, than to call a blank on how the Club survived. Yet it did for years to come. Reading through the above Magazines, although as I pointed out were more to the interest of Teenagers of that period. Yes, as times progressed through the years we all grew up, became Teenagers through the forties and fifties, when the population was recovering from austerity. But the threat of the "Atomic Age" as it was called, immediately began with the start of the Cold War. Rationing did not finish until the early fifties. The population, was coming to terms with a new lease of life, and beginning to enjoy the freedom provided by the movie industry. There were many films to be seen. The music industry provided big bands to play in dance halls. At the beginning of the fifties: The Festival of Britain provided a new outlook for the country. More cars became available, thus began to clog up the previously empty roads and streets, where we were able to play football with a tennis ball, also cricket the stumps being a lamppost that also acted as a swing. After 14 years of Rationing it finally ended in July 1954. The dress sense of Teenagers changed to the Teddy boy and the Modern style of dress and towards the latter part of the fifties, Motorbikes and Italian Scooters became the mode of transport. All in all, still very hard times. Nevertheless, those were the years we Teenagers grew up through and our outlet was. The Club. I would even go to say they were the best years of our lives.

The beginning of the sixties saw, the End of Conscription/National Service, therefore young males did not have that problem hanging around their necks. The sixties were the beginning years of Prosperity. The advent of the introduction of BBC Black and white Television, on rental terms from Radio Rentals, with only limited viewing times of programmes, became a must for home entertainment. The Queen's Coronation in 1963 saw a surge in the demand for TV's, and with the addition of a new programme provider ITV, together with the introduction of Colour TV. It grew in popularity and demand. It possibly was the beginning of the decline of many Associations and Youth Clubs over the following years. The musical media changed to that of 'POP' as illustrated by the article in the above 1963 issue, also the article on Fashion. The Club too suffered some disruption with work being carried out in the late fifties. With the aid of Government War Damage Compensation, allocated to repair / build destroyed War damaged properties. In 1950/52 Plans were drawn up to rebuild the Settlement premises of Numbers 42, 44, & 46 Harleyford Road that were demolished and deemed unfit for habitation. The work was approved and began during 1954. The foundation stone was laid by His Lordship Bishop Cowderoy. The stone was inscribed:

ON THE FAST OF ST SWITHUN IN THE YEAR OF OUR LORD 1954 THIS STONE WAS LAID BY THE SEVENTH BISHOP OF SOUTHWARK TO HONOUR THE MEMORY OF THE RIGHT REVEREND WILLIAM FRANCIS BROWN BISHOP OF PELLA AUXILLARY BISHOP OF SOUTHWARK VICAR GENERAL PROVOST OF THE CHAPTER AND PARISH PRIEST OF VAUXHALL

ooOoo

Work continued on the new building through to 1958. In the Club's files, I found a letter written by a Mr. Spaeight? That goes a long way to encapsulate the existence of the St. Anne's Settlement: The transcript is as follows:

ooOoo

LETTER OF APPEAL.

Have you ever heard of Bishop Brown? Perhaps not. That's a very ordinary name for a rather extra ordinary man. But if you have ever met Bishop Brown – or heard him speak you would realise how well the name suited him. For he spent all his life in devotion to the welfare of quite ordinary people. He had another name, an official name – The Bishop of Pella; but as that was the name of an non-– existent See, I don't fancy he set much store by it.

WILLIAM E BROWN
BISHOP OF PELLA
BORN 1862. DIED 1951

Still, he was known to the people of South London as "Old Pella", and one of the blocks of flats the Lambeth walk is called "Pella House". Now it means something when municipal authorities named blocks of flats after Bishop's. So – who, you will ask me was Bishop Brown?

Bishop Brown was assistant to the Roman Catholic Bishop of Southwark for nearly a quarter of a century and all this time he continued his work as a Parish Priest in Vauxhall. He had a remarkable wide prestige, and counted among his friends many people – like Charles Gore and Augustine Birrell – who were outside his own Communion. He had been mixed up considerably in public affairs. Read his Autobiography, "Through Windows of Memory", and you will get some idea of the contacts and causes are crowded and enriched his life.

But first and foremost Brown was a Parish Priest; and if you cross the bridge from Victoria to Vauxhall, you will see William Brown - Bishop of Pella. R.I.P.   two examples of how a good that he did lives after him. First of all, there is St Anne's Church – as fine a Parish Church as you will find in London. Nothing tawdry or tinselled or trivial; everything solid and sterling, like the Bishop who lies buried there, right down to the oak benches on which you really feel you could sit and listen to quite a long sermon. Then, just across the road, is – or rather was – St Anne's Settlement. For the Bishop didn't believe in neglecting the material needs of his parishioners, and so he built this centre where they could be properly cared for. He had got to work long before the welfare State came to our aid; such amenities were urgently needed then, and they are needed still. But when the war came St Anne's Settlement was pretty well flattened out by a bomb. So now the Bishop successor is rebuilding it and he is asking for your help.

Now what does St Anne's Settlement do? Well, it maintains a maternity and child welfare centre to look after mothers and babies, and the School Care Committee to keep in touch with children in their homes. It arranges holidays and convalescence is for those who need them; about three hundred children are sent away every year either to the country or to the seaside. It maintains an Old Age Pensioners Club, which looks after some one hundred and fifty elderly people. It holds classes in Cookery and Dressmaking for the women of the district, and provides for their recreation in the evening. It also houses a flourishing Youth Club. And it performs these services for people of any religious denomination. In fact, it does all sorts of things for all sorts of people, which they could never conceivably do for themselves. How many houses in South London could accommodate a billiard table, a ping-pong table or a stage? How many have refreshments on tap? Try giving a dance for your daughter and see how many couples you can fit into your living room. And it's not every family budget that can take the strain of the family holiday by the sea.

Now I want you to think of any Priest or Pastor or social worker that you may know who is doing a devoted job in the poorer quarters of a large industrial town. Great Britain is full, thank God, of these magnificent people. And then I want you to think that any money you send to St Anne's Settlement is, in a sense, money sent to them; because St

Anne's is doing the same kind of work. Help it to do this work as well as possible. When I motor out of London to my home in Kent, I generally pass through Vauxhall, and I've noticed lately a very handsome new building going up just the other side of the bridge. It was only the other day that I discovered this was part of the reconstructed Saint Anne's Settlement. I was taken inside and could see for myself that they had gone ahead and built worthily. Will you now help them to pray quickly? Send your donations to me,

Robert Spaeight. At St. Anne's Settlement 58 Vauxhall Grove London S.W.8.

ooOoo

Although certain renovation to the 'Youth Club' were incorporated in the overall 1952/54 plans. The majority of the work concentrated on the Settlement rebuild, and the Club's premises were left as they were! Nevertheless, I believe, some changes were made to the rear access way into the new Settlement Building. The results of its rebuild, are illustrated, by the below before and after photos.

| *The bombed Settlement. 1941* | *The new Settlement building : Photo 2014* |

However, the recommended changes to the Clubs premises remained on hold until 1982. The Centenary year of the founding of the original Mission by Fr. Brown. It was then the proposals were resurrected and some major changes were made to the existing Clubs premises. By January 1986, Cabrini's Children's Society, acquired part of the Settlement, including the old Common Room (later called Games Room), to create a storage facility for their files and archives. Therefore reducing the Clubs facility to; the Main Hall, Green Room and Leaders Office. Bearing in mind that the populace of Vauxhall had changed to that of a mixed population, also access to the Internet and media had drastically changed. Yet the Club still continued, and with the assistance of Pat Docherty a one-time Leader of the Club, who advised me that the Club continued on through to 2005 when it finished. During that period of time the St. Anne's School was demolished and rebuilt, it provided facilities for an area where Asto-turf was laid down complete with Floodlights. The Club used this facility of a Friday night when the Boys would form up teams and play games of football. Whether it finished through lack of support or not wasn't discussed.

In 2014. I contacted St. Anne's Settlement to ask if they could provide me with a contact number for the Club. I was informed by Sarah Wall, that the Club was no longer in existence and the Clinic had ceased (date unknown) The Settlement premises were then occupied by Cabrini's Children Society and the Catholic Truth Society. The Club Hall was used by St. Anne's Church for various functions. Sarah questioned me on the reason for my interest and I informed her of my research into the Club's History, Sarah informed me of the then situation of the Clubs Hall was scheduled to be demolished. I was surprised with the information but as the Hall was still in existence I suggested would it be possible to pay them a visit and take some photos for inclusion into the history. This being acceptable, arranged to visit the premises where I met Sarah Wall & Michelle Lawlor, then employees of Cabrini's, who welcomed me and showed me over the premises. By good fortune I also met Jacqui and Michelle Ginnane, representing the establishments Landlords, who were very interested in the research I was engaged in. The photo's I took in 2014 are shown within the pages of the story. Jacqui and Michelle produced old photos of the Settlement circa 1912/13 and photos of the Bomb damaged 1941. They also permitted me to access the Club's records and produced the Club's

Shield. An item I was totally unaware of. Jacqui informed me that the Club's future was then under discussion for redevelopment with the intention of demolishing the old Settlement Hall, although still on the premises, Cabrini's Children's Society were in the throes of leaving the Settlement. I asked if it was possible to gain access, to the Club Hall, after the Reunion Mass in St. Anne's on the 23rd. May. 2014. Possibly the last time the Old Members would once again tread the boards of the Dance Hall. That was agreed, and those that did attend, were more than delighted, to be once again able to reminisce about those old days, joyously spent in the Club. Before going to print once again this year I have gained access for the forthcoming Reunion.

     Although Cabrini's have vacated the premise's, the two young ladies Sarah and Michelle, have on an independent basis, continued to run the Breakfast and After school Club for two local Infant and Junior schools. Going on from that with the prospect of new plans for the development of a new Building on the existing site including a new Hall. Maybe that will be the opportunity to reform a Youth Club within its premises. Maintaining that:-

'THE SPIRIT OF ST. ANNE'S LIVETH ON.'

Sarah Wall- /
Michelle and Jacqui Ginnane
Taken at the Rear entrance

Sarah and Michelle
Taken outside the main entrance

ooOoo

IT'S LEGASY

Noted by Members

Frank O'Sullivan (Canon)

I owe much to the Club. Relationships formed there have lasted a lifetime. I'm sure that it played a part in the Lord's plan for my life as a Priest, something that I will always be grateful for.

ooOoo

Harry Spanswick:

I conclude by acknowledging the dept. owed to the Priest, teachers and people encountered at St. Anne's, both in the distant and not so recent past. I, and my family, have been blessed and we thank God for it. He surely moves in mysterious ways.

Harry Spanswick. 2010.

In addition to Harrys conclusion a fitting message is portrayed within his dialogue above, with reference to his period of unemployment and the New Enterprise undertaken by Father Bridge within St. Anne's Settlement as follows:

In 1985 the Wapping dispute put an end to that career and also an end of my time, Father of the Chapel, an official Union Office, that I had held for almost twenty years. However whilst I was unemployed I went into St. Anne's Settlement to retrieve a Missal, Josie had mislaid at a Mass held previously in honour of Father Madden. I was astonished to be asked if I had come for the job that was advertised. (of which I knew nothing).

Father Bridge (then assistant Priest at St. Anne's together with the Priest of the deanery, had set up an enterprise to counteract the large numbers of unemployed people in South London, to give them new skills and get them ready for redeployment. The imitative was based in the offices in the Settlement, and they were looking for someone to join them, who had building qualifications as well as people skills to join them. At that time it was called Cathedral Employment and was a charitable foundation within the Diocese of Southwark. Despite my reservations that I would be unsuitable because of my Union activities, during the bitter year long dispute with News International and Mr. Murdock. But, then I didn't know Father Hugh Bridge or, what a power House he was, working as he often did all through the day and night, to secure funding and premises for the range of practical craft skill courses, provided by the enterprise. He took me on.

Later came liquidation and withdrawal of funding, but the commitment and energy were there, and the Enterprise was resurrected under the new title of Myrrh Education. I retired in 2004 from a hands on role, but am pleased to say, that the Company continues to serve the local and not so local community and many thousands of students, in hairdressing, catering, carpentry, decoration, child care and computer departments. Have gone on to gain their qualifications and to find substantive work. The new offices are based in Walworth now, but the work continues and courses are provided according to changing needs and, the availability of Government funding.

Sadly Father Bridge died a few years ago, and is still missed by those who knew him. In so many ways, Father Bridge followed in Bishop Brown's footsteps, acknowledging the needs of the local community and overcoming enormous difficulties in order to address them.

ooOoo

Derek Rivers.

I don't remember anyone being out of work. By trade I was a Carpenter, as was Eddie Ford. Harry was a Plasterer and Eric with being conscripted, had decided to join the Navy. George Belcher, Eddie and I got together and started a small joinery Business. With additional discussions with Bill Bailey, he permitted us to use his ground floor Front room overlooking Harleyford Road as a workshop. Whilst doing this Eddie, decided to become a Wood Work Teacher and went to Night-school. He qualified as a teacher doing what he loved, teaching- Wood Work at Night school. His success gave me the idea. So I attended night school and eventually, after studying for three years at Night school and two years at teacher Training College, qualified to teach Metal Work at a School in Addington South Croydon. To say the least a rather rough area. My success rubbed off on Sheila and she decided also to take up teaching having qualified, taught infants as various schools? And in turn Sheila, gave inspiration to Josie Spanswick, who also eventually qualified. The success of all of us becoming teachers was all down to Eddie, with our gracious thanks. Little did Eddie realise with his ambitions to teach. It was the beginning of the making of three new Teachers. Myself, Sheila and Josie. But I might add that our Daughter and Granddaughter have a so qualified to become teachers. It must run in the Family?

ooOoo

Josie Spanswick (nee Course)

It is remarkable tribute to St. Anne's that a group of some fifty or more past members of the Youth Club continue to meet at the church for an annual Thanksgiving Mass each May, when we recall the names of past members and Priest, who are now with the good Lord and resting in Peace. Canon Frank O'Sullivan, a past member of the Club, celebrates the Mass and we find that whichever parish Priest is in place at Vauxhall, we always receive a warm welcome back to our 'roots' We all agree that we were blessed to have had our lives touched by the amazing St. Anne's experience!

Long may it continue!

ACKNOWLEDGEMENTS.

Without the assistance of Old Club members comments, photographs and written memories, this profile and tribute to St. Anne' Youth and Pella Club, would not have been possible. It was not my idea, but the idea of those Old members who met at the Annual St. Anne's Reunion. All I had to do was piece together its History. I found it was engaging, fascinating and on many occasions very funny. I must admit that my own memories come forth quite strongly, but I would add that those clinging moments, were made by all the friends I became associated with, through being a member of the Club for many years, to which I am truly grateful and thank them all.

This book is dedicated to the memory of all those members who are no longer with us.

LIST OF SUBSCRIBERS.

Anne O'Neil.

Barbara White (nee Driver)

Brian Jenkins

Canon Frank O'Sullivan.

Derek & Mary Beamish

Derek Rivers.

Eileen Healy (nee McMonagle)

Ernie Morgan

Harry & Josie Spanswick

Jacqui. & Michelle Ginnane.

Jean Lovell (nee Lyons)

Joan Mills (nee Chaddock)

Keith Ager.

Kevan Lewis.

Lily Darcy. (nee Rennie)

Margaret Brown.

Marie Martinelli (nee Coluoni)

Mary McBride (nee Macdermott)

Michelle Lawlor.

Mike & Mara MacDermott.

Mike Plant.

Nina Pinkerton. (nee Falco)

Olive Wood. (nee O'Sullivan)

Pat Doherty.

Pat Flynne.

Phil Frost.

Sarah Wall.

Teresa Wicker. (nee Clinton)

Tom Marcantonio.

Tommy Wilberham.

BIBLIOGRAPHY.

Croydon Airport Society.
Lambeth Archives.
St George's Cathedral Archivist.
St Anne's Filed Records
The Beehive.
Woodrow High House Amersham
'Through Windows of Memories.' by William F. Brown Bishop of Pella
'The Priest and the Playwright.' by M.F. Brown.

Lightning Source UK Ltd.
Milton Keynes UK
UKOW07f1524070515

251067UK00005B/41/P

9 781782 224006